Teubner (Ed.), Dilemmas of Law in the Welfare State

European University Institute

Dilemmas of Law in the Welfare State

Edited by

Gunther Teubner

1988

Walter de Gruyter · New York · Berlin

This book was originally published (clothbound) as part of the Series A (Law Vol. 3) of the European University Institute, Florence.

Library of Congress Cataloging-in-Publication Data

Main entry under title:
Dilemmas of law in the welfare state.
(Series A--Law ; 3)
Includes index.
1. Sociological jurisprudence. 2. Social legislation. 3. Law--Methodology. 4. Welfare state. I. Teubner, Gunther. II. Series.
K370.D55 1985 340'.11 85-20584
ISBN 0-89925-108-0
ISBN 0-89925-397-0 (Paperback)

Cover Design: K. Lothar Hildebrand, Berlin. — Setting: Arthur Collignon GmbH, Berlin.
Printed in the United States of America

Foreword

This book ist part of a larger research project of the European University Institute in Florence. "Alternatives to Delegalisation" is the general theme of this project which has been conducted in the last three years by my friend and colleague Terence Daintith and me. The project aims at making a contribution, from the standpoint of law, to the current debate on the capacities and limits of the Welfare State. This debate reveals an increasing disenchantment with the goals, structures and performances of the Regulatory State. The political movement of de-legalization is just one manifestation of a much broader reappraisal of the systems of law and public organization, to which we want to contribute from both the standpoints of legal theory and legal practice.

One part of the project was oriented towards questions of legal theory. In a seminar series on the theme of "The Functions of Law in the Welfare State" we asked leading legal and social theorists from different countries to discuss with us the dilemmas which result from the transformation of the law in the Welfare State. This book reflects the results of the lively and stimulating discussions we had in the "jurisprudence group" under the guidance of the Institute's President, Werner Maihofer. It represents a continuation of earlier activities at the Institute on law and welfare state, especially the work on "Access to Justice in the Welfare State" carried out by Mauro Cappelletti and Joseph Weiler.

Given the variety of languages, cultural backgrounds and intellectual traditions, the editing process for such a book is not an easy task. Constance Meldrum who was heavily engaged in the editing process, especially with the linguistic problems, was faced with the problem of attempting to strike a balance between authenticity and accessibility, especially in the cases of French structuralism and German critical theory. Iain Fraser who translated some of the texts had similar experiences. I would like to thank both of them for their dedicated work. For thorough and precise editorial assistance my thanks go to Thomas Abeltshauser, Regina Etzbach and Elizabeth Webb, as well as to Brigitte Schwab, the Institute's Publications Officer, for her professional help in the final publication process.

Firenze, January 1985
Gunther Teubner

Table of Contents

I

Introduction

The Transformation of Law in the Welfare State

GUNTHER TEUBNER
Bremen, Firenze

In the recent discussion on the crisis of the welfare state, increasing attention has been given to the "juridification" of the social world (Galanter, 1980; Voigt, 1980, 1983; Abel, 1980, 1982; Kübler, 1984). The relation between these two phenomena – welfare state and juridification – is the core theme of this book. How does the emergence of the welfare state influence the law's structures and functions? How is the juridification of social fields connected to the political instrumentalization of the law? The contributions focus in particular on the problems which the law faces when the societal guidance intentions of the welfare state seem to reach their limits, and they analyze the potential of an emerging "post-interventionist" law.

Among lawyers, juridification has been criticized predominantly as a quantitative phenomenon. The irritating growth of legal regulation has been labelled as a "legal explosion" (Barton, 1975) or as a "flood of norms" (Hillermeier, 1978; Vogel, 1979). This is perhaps not a suitable starting point since, in many respects, it limits the discussion too narrowly. "Flood of norms" stresses the quantitative aspect of the multiplication of legal material which could certainly be coped with by simplifying the law or by technical improvements in legislation. Attention should, rather, be directed towards the qualitative aspects: what substantial changes in legal structures have brought about the (alleged) crisis of juridification. The term "flood of norms" is, moreover, historically unspecific; juridification processes should instead be studied under the specific conditions of the modern welfare state (the interventionist state) and the appropriateness of legal structures in relation to different social areas. Finally, abstraction should be made from the national specificities of the "flood of norms", and a comparative approach taken so as to isolate the universal characteristics of juridification processes and the problems that result from them. It is for these reasons that, in this book, the usual approach to juridification as a problem of quantitative growth is avoided and replaced by the following guiding questions:

(1) Materialization of Formal Law: To what extent do juridification processes in different areas show a transition from classical formal law to the guidance intentions of the interventionist and compensatory welfare state and what are the consequences for the internal structures of law?

(2) Limits to Legal Instrumentalism: Can limits to the political instrumentalization of law be discerned to the extent that particular juridification processes prove inadequate to the social structures which they regulate and/or overstrain the law's capacity to control and/or disintegrate basic legal values and the unity of the legal system?

(3) Perspectives of Legal Development: Can alternatives to juridification be seen which are more adequate on the one hand to the special problems of each social area and on the other to the internal capacities of the law?

1. Materialization of Formal Law

In modern legal development different trends towards juridification can be distinguished. In his contribution to this volume, Habermas (205 infra) identifies four epochal "juridification thrusts", each involving specific features of legal functions, norm structures and dogmatic systematization. These juridification thrusts are connected to the emergence of different forms of the state: the bourgeois state, the *Rechtsstaat*, the democratic state and finally, the welfare state. Such an historical perspective avoids the fallacy of dealing with juridification processes in general as the extension and densification of law (Voigt, 1980). Instead, it allows us to concentrate on one historical type of juridification. The most pressing current problem is probably how to cope with the juridification thrust typical of the welfare state in which the law is instrumentalized as a guidance mechanism for the interventions and compensations of the welfare state. It is important here to keep to Max Weber's distinction between formal and material legal rationality, and to ask what processes in a particular area of law have replaced or superimposed a material, welfare-state orientation onto the formal rationality of the classical rule of law (Max Weber, 1968; see also Aubert, Wiethölter). Putting it another way: Does a comparative perspective in different legal areas show a trend away from "autonomous law" towards "responsive law" (Nonet and Selznick, 1978)?

The different contributions to this volume demonstrate that the application of the formal/material conceptual scheme to various sub-areas has far-reaching results. They pursue the consequences of materialization tendencies as far as questions of normative structures, methods of interpretation and application of social knowledge to legal doctrine. Our contributors agree to a great extent on the identification of new functions and structures of law in the welfare state; they differ widely, however, in assessing the causes and consequences of these developments.

Aubert provides a detailed catalogue of the new *functions* of law in the welfare state as opposed to those of the liberal state. His formula "from prevention to promotion" is paralleled by Broekman's and Ewald's concepts of "socialization of law" and by Luhmann's analysis of "social engineering as a political approach to law" and to a certain degree by Heller's reference to the "positive state". This instrumentalization of the law for welfare state purposes has a clear impact on the emergence of normative *structures* which are related to the new functions of law. Febbrajo uses the distinction "constitutive versus regulative" rules in order to analyse the change from formal framework orientation towards a network of compensatory regulation. Others describe these structural developments in terms of "individualization" and "specification" of legal norms (Habermas) and of a stronger reliance on "purposive programs" (Luhmann, Willke). Furthermore, the functional and structural changes reveal a trend toward a new legal rationality: "This rationality defines a policy of law wherein the latter appears as an element in the sociological administration of society. There is a series: conflict — balance — settlement" (Ewald 63 infra).

While Friedman's central thesis that "legal culture" has to be seen as the intervening variable between "social change" and "legal change" would probably find agreement among the various authors, disagreement arises when it comes to explaining the *causes* of the legal transformation. What are the structural social changes that "determine" recent legal change, or better, that co-variate with it? Basically, theories of economic-political crisis compete with theories of functional differentiation. On the one hand, the new functions of the interventionist law are explained by the compensatory measures on the part of the state in reaction to economic crises (Habermas, Broekman, Wiethölter, Heller, Preuß). In these approaches emphasis is put on the dilemmatic attempts of the political system to "constitutionalize" the economic system. On the other hand, the emergence of the welfare state and its legal concomitants is related to processes of functional differentiation. "Inclusion" is the main problem posed for the political system which results in unforeseen consequences for the role of law (Luhmann, 1981). A related phenomenon is "organizational differentiation"; the emergence of the organizational society which challenges the classical role of the state and the state's law. In the context of functional differentiation, social subsystems apparently develop such a high degree of autonomy that the political system is forced to experiment with new forms of legal regulation (Willke, Teubner).

Disagreement is even stronger when the social *consequences* of "legal instrumentalism" are examined. Does this imply a profound change of the relationship between law and society or is only a surface phenomenon involved that leaves the deeper structures and basic principles of society unaltered? According to Habermas, Wiethölter, and Preuß materialization of formal law leads to fundamental changes in the social structure. Luhmann, in turn, analyses far-reaching changes within the legal system. The "political" usage of law alters its internal structure, particularly its internal balance of normative closure and cognitive openness, to a degree that its autopoietic organization is overstrained. Broekman and Heller contest both these positions. They insist that the new socio-technological role of the law in the interventionist state represents nothing more than a surface phenomenon. The deep structure of law and society reveals that this modern type of law obeys the same "structural grammar" as its classical counterpart did. For Broekman, it is not only the "corpus dogmaticus" of the law but also legal subjectivity as the basic value of law that resists fundamental change. In his view, the deep structure of law and society sets effective limits to legal instrumentalism.

2. Limits to Legal Instrumentalism

There are, however, competing attempts to account for the limits of a political instrumentalization of law. The diverse explanations of the limits of legal instrumentalism (Wiethölter) represent the jurisprudential variant of the general debate on the limits of the welfare state (e. g. Lehner, 1979). Four points of criticism emerge:

(1) "Ineffectiveness": To what extent is the law unsuitable as a control mechanism (Ziegert, 1975) because it simply runs aground on the internal dynamics of the given social area? Although purposive programs are seen as political guidance instruments which are superior to the classical conditional programs, they cannot cope with the fact that complex systems behave counter-intuitively. One explanation is to relate this phenomenon to the growing tensions between the increasing guidance load and the decreasing guidance capacities of the state faced with organizational differentiation (Willke, 1983). Another is the autopoietic organization of regulated subsystems which inevitably leads instrumental law into a "regulatory trilemma" (Teubner, 1984:313 and infra).

(2) "Colonialization": Is the price of juridification the destruction of organic social structures because the law is based on quite different modes of functioning and of organization? According to Habermas, the ambivalence of guarantees of and denials of freedom has adhered to the policies and the law of the welfare state from its beginning. It is the structure of juridification itself that endangers the freedom of the beneficiary. Instrumental legal programs obey a functional logic and follow criteria of rationality and patterns of organization which are contradictory to those of the regulated spheres of life. In consequence, law as a medium of the welfare state either turns out to be ineffective or it works effectively but at the price of destroying traditional patterns of social life. Furthermore, as Peters shows, welfare state law with its symbolic representation of officialdom, bureaux, organization, and system produces a social consciousness which weakens the potential for critical opposition.

(3) "Overstrain": Does the legal system have sufficient cognitive, organizational and power resources which might enable it to respond to the

control tasks it is assigned? The result-orientation in legal practice contributes unavoidably to an overburdening of the legal system (Luhmann). The "over-socialization" of law in the welfare state necessitates such radical changes in legal structures that its very autonomous organization might be endangered (Teubner).

(4) "Systems conflict": How far does instrumental law deflect its own rationale by its interaction with other systems, especially the political and the economic system? This problem is raised by Friedman in dealing with the contradiction between the law's independence and its social responsiveness as well as by Broekman who points to the limits of "socialization of law". Aubert argues that the aims of the interventionist state clash with the rule of law as an ideal; while at the same time conflicts are continuously engendered by government policies as well as by general social and economic development. Ewald analyses the tensions between the classical "law" and the modern "norm". Peters speaks of a "bureaucratic entrapment" inherent in the welfare state's participatory mechanisms which makes autonomous thought and authentic dialogue literally impossible and which sets effective limits to "law as critical discussion". Preuß deals with the contradictions between the static structure of legal subjective rights and the economic fluctuations which limit the welfare state's capacities. For Preuß the dilemma of law in the welfare state is due to the fact that distributive rights are based on the abstraction of interests from the underlying socio-economic situation. On a more general level Febbrajo describes these system conflicts as conflicting constitutive rules of different social games which cannot be resolved by the rules of a "meta-game".

3. Perspectives of Legal Development

Depending upon how positively or negatively legal instrumentalism is evaluated and what problems are perceived as relevant, very different types of future perspective are arrived at. Three possible solutions can be distinguished: increasing effectiveness, de-legalization and legal control of self-regulation.

If in principle one holds to the overall control task of the law, the main problem of juridification will be the question of effectiveness. The point will then be to strengthen the cognitive, organizational and power resources in such a way that the law can cope in practice with its control function. In this sense, legal doctrine will have to shift its orientation from norm application to legal policy (Nonet and Selznick, 1978; Podgorecki, 1974; Wälde, 1979). The precisely opposite strategy aims at an ordered retreat of the law from the "colonialized" areas of life, either by a complete withdrawal of its regulatory function ("de-juridification" in the strict sense), or by concentrating its forces within the secured bastions of formal rationality ("re-formalization", Grimm, 1980). Finally, as alternative solutions transcending the distinction between formalization and materialization of the law, strategies are discussed that amount to more abstract, more indirect control through the law (for the recent discussion on post-interventionist law, see Brüggemeier and Joerges, 1984). The law is unburdened from direct regulation of social areas and instead given the task of dealing with self-regulatory processes (e. g. Lehner, 1979; Gotthold, 1983).

The perspectives offered in this volume fall to a greater or lesser degree within the third category. If they neither remain sceptical as to any prognosis (Friedman) nor argue for the impossibility of bridging theoretical analysis with legal practice (Heller), they refer to the necessity of "regulation of self-regulation", with, however, important nuances among them.

Probably the most cautious perspective is developed by Luhmann. He argues for a legal self-restraint in the direction of legal self-reflection. "Possibly doctrine merges with legal theory specializing in reflection. Its domain could be the self-observation and self-description of the system" (125 infra). This means moving away from the idea of direct societal guidance through a politically instrumentalized law and restricting it to cope with social self-regulation. The perspectives of "relational program" (Willke, 1983 and infra) and "reflexive law" (Teubner, 1983 and infra) build on Luhmann's theory but attempt to go further and to re-formulate the role of the law in relation to other specialized social sub-systems. They see the role of the law in structuring inter-system-linkages and institutionalizing reflection processes in other social systems. These reflection processes would internalize external negative consequences into the system's structure.

The perspectives developed by Wiethölter, Habermas and Peters are normatively more ambitious. Wiethölter offers "proceduralization" as a formula for the role of the law in promoting and controlling the setting up of "social systems with a learning capacity". He identifies two types of proceduralization. One is a system-game of guidance and control which coordinates collective actors by a "concerted action" of mutual limitation of their autonomy ("Vernetzung von Freiheiten"). The other, and that which he prefers, is to institutionalize a societal "forum" in which social transformations are reconstructively and prospectively negotiated. This comes close to Habermas' concept of an "external constitution": Although law as a "medium" of societal guidance endangers the communicative structures of the legalized spheres of social life, law as an "institution" rooted in the core morality of a given society may facilitate communicative processes by guaranteeing the "external constitution" of the communicatively structured social sphere. Law as an "external constitution" can promote "discursive processes of will-formation and consensus oriented procedures of negotiation and decision-making" (218 infra). Relying explicitly on Habermas' concept of "herrschaftsfreier Diskurs", Peters develops a model of "law as critical discussion" and relates it to theories of social modernity. He offers a series of structural components – procedure, citizenship, legal discussion, society as project, de-reification, legitimacy in depth – which support the role of law as a democratizing force in modern society.

The ambivalence of all these perspectives on legal development is perhaps best pointed out by Broekman. He contrasts changes in the legal structure with a threefold stratification of social justification structures: "firstly, a contextually sufficient justification, secondly the deep justification and lastly the justification of the basic principles of law and society" (94 infra). For Broekman, attempts to formulate new perspectives on law, especially "alternative" dogmatic figures aimed at a change in terms of deep-justification, are bound to produce only changes in terms of a contextually sufficient justification. "They do not bring about changes in the sense of the basic principles of law and society" (94 infra). This is a strong argument formulated from a structuralist position which questions the central theses of system functionalism and critical theory. If one re-formulates Broekman's assertion as an open question, it may capture the central preoccupation of many if not all authors in this book on juridification and welfare state: Are we in a position to identify the fundamental structural changes which would make possible the institutionalization of reflection processes in law and society?

References

Abel, Richard L. (1980) "Dejuridification: A Critical Review of its Ideology, Manifestations and Social Consequences," in E. Blankenburg, E. Klausa and H. Rottleuthner (eds.), *Alternative Rechtsformen und Alternativen zum Recht*. Opladen: Westdeutscher Verlag.

– (1982) *The Politics of Informal Justice*. New York: Academic Press.

Barton, John H. (1975) "Behind the Legal Explosion," 27 *Stanford Law Review* 567.

Brüggemeier, Gert and Christian Joerges (1984) *Workshop zu Konzepten des post-interventionistischen Rechts*. Bremen: ZERP-Mat 4.

Galanter, Marc (1980) "Legality and its Discontents: A Preliminary Assessment of Current Theories of Legalization and Dejuridification," in E. Blankenburg, E. Klausa and H. Rottleuthner (eds.), *Alternative Rechtsformen und Alternativen zum Recht*. Opladen: Westdeutscher Verlag.

Gotthold, Jürgen (1983) "Privatisierung oder Entbürokratisierung kommunaler Sozialpolitik," in R. Voigt (ed.), *Abschied vom Recht?* Frankfurt: Suhrkamp.

Grimm, Dieter (1980) "Reformalisierung des Rechtsstaats als Demokratiepostulat," 20 *Juristische Schulung* 704.

Hillermeier, Karl (1978) "Eindämmung der Gesetzesflut," *Bayerisches Verwaltungsblatt* 321.

Kübler, Friedrich (ed.) (1984) *Verrechtlichung von Wirtschaft, Arbeit und sozialer Solidarität. Vergleichende Analysen*. Baden-Baden: Nomos.

LEHNER, Franz (1979) *Grenzen des Regierens. Eine Studie zur Regierungsproblematik hochindustrialisierter Demokratien*. Königstein: Athenäum.

LUHMANN, Niklas (1981) *Politische Theorie im Wohlfahrtsstaat*. München: Olzog.

NONET, Philippe, and Philip SELZNICK (1978) *Law and Society in Transition*. New York: Harper & Row.

PODGORECKI, Adam (1974) *Law and Society*. London, Boston: Routledge and Kegan.

TEUBNER, Gunther (1983) "Substantive and Reflexive Elements in Modern Law," 17 *Law and Society Review* 239.

— (1984) "Verrechtlichung — Begriffe, Merkmale, Grenzen, Auswege," in F. Kübler (ed.), *Verrechtlichung von Wirtschaft, Arbeit und sozialer Solidarität. Vergleichende Analysen*. Baden-Baden: Nomos.

VOGEL, Hans-Jochen (1979) "Zur Diskussion um die Normenflut," 34 *Juristenzeitung* 321.

VOIGT, Rüdiger (1980) *Verrechtlichung. Analysen zur Funktion und Wirkung von Parlamentarisierung, Bürokratisierung und Justizialisierung sozialer, politischer und ökonomischer Prozesse*. Königstein: Athenäum.

— (1983) *Abschied vom Recht?* Frankfurt: Suhrkamp.

WÄLDE, Thomas (1979) *Juristische Folgenorientierung. "Policy Analysis" und Sozialkybernetik: Methodische und organisatorische Überlegungen zur Bewältigung der Folgenorientierung im Rechtssystem*. Königstein: Athenäum.

WEBER, Max (1968) *Economy and Society*. New York: Bedminster Press.

WILLKE, Helmut (1983) *Entzauberung des Staates. Überlegungen zu einer sozietalen Steuerungstheorie*. Königstein: Athenäum.

ZIEGERT, Klaus A. (1975) *Zur Effektivität der Rechtssoziologie. Die Rekonstruktion der Gesellschaft durch Recht*. Stuttgart: Enke.

II

The Welfare State and its Impact on Law

Legal Culture and the Welfare State

LAWRENCE M. FRIEDMAN
Stanford

Rapid social change is an obvious fact of modern life. Change affects every aspect of society, including law and government, systems which make up the very framework of organized society. Indeed, the structure of the state itself, in our times, seems new, seems dramatically different, compared to the structure of past societies, or societies outside the "developed" world.

This peculiar form of 20th century state is usually called the "welfare state," or, more broadly, the welfare-regulatory state. Basically, it is an active, interventionist state. Government is ubiquitous. It collects huge pots of tax money, and commands an enormous army of civil servants. It distributes billions in the form of welfare payments. In many countries, it runs the railroads, the postal service, the telephones; in others it has banks, steel mills and other enterprises in its portfolio. (Some of these may even make a profit.) It also controls the economy (or tries to). It has its hands on the money supply. It instructs businesses on what they can and cannot do. Its range of intervention is vast: on the one hand, it regulates mergers between giant corporations, on the other, it limits the number of people who sell candy and gum on street corners. It also tries to instil some sort of order in a crowded, busy society – it sets speed limits, controls access to television channels, makes up rules about who gets into state universities, and restricts the legal sale of aspirins and drugs.

Above all, it is sheer volume and scope that distinguishes the welfare-regulatory state from "government" in, say, medieval France, or in a New Guinea tribe: the number of rules and regulations, the size of the bureaucracy, the boldness and sweep of what the state tries to do. The state, in other words, is a giant machine for making and applying *law*. It is a giant machine of social control, but social control which is exercised through law. Hence the modern legal system evokes, quite naturally, the curiosity and interest of scholars. They worry about the state's capacity for providing justice – social justice as well as justice of the ordinary sort. They ask, what kind of legal system does a welfare-regulatory state generate? What is the role of law in this sort of society? How is it different from the role of law in other kinds of society? How can it be improved?

What is the future of law – and of justice – in the complex world of the welfare state?

These questions are not asked idly. There are important theoretical reasons for asking questions about law in the welfare state, and important practical and policy reasons too. One theoretical problem concerns the precise relationship between this form of state, and its legal system (see especially Aubert, Heller, Habermas and Wiethölter infra). One of the classic questions in legal sociology concerns the so-called autonomy (or lack of it) of the legal system. Simply put, the question is, where does one start, in trying to explain how legal systems behave? One extreme position is to look exclusively to social forces – social pressures from outside. Some scholars assume that the system is entirely controlled by these forces, whatever lawyers and others on the inside may think. Another starting point is to assume that the system is *autonomous*, that is, under its own control, and following its own logic, that it is not the creature of outside influence. Its development is explained in terms of habits of thought and concepts that operate strictly *within* the system, that is, inside the heads of lawyers and jurists. The system, in short, is "autonomous," insulated from the outside world, somewhat impervious to it, perhaps stubbornly so (for an exposition of this view see particularly Luhmann, Teubner infra).

An autonomous system is not necessarily a good one; and the same can be said for a "responsive" system, sensitive to the outside world. Indeed, both autonomy and dependency have their plusses and minuses, if we can judge by current debate (Teubner, 1983; Nonet and Selznick, 1978). The negative side of autonomy is formalism and dogged resistance to change. An autonomous system may be hide-bound, conservative, it may stick to old ways long past their time. Many people, of course, feel that law shows exactly these traits. Formalism, too, may be a mask for privilege: the rules favor the status quo, but in a disguised way; they pose as neutral norms, or as "legal science."

There is also something to be said *for* autonomy. An autonomous legal system is, or can be, one that asserts its own values, and resists the state, pressure groups, the howling mob, transient majorities, the selfishness of elites, the dogmatism and intolerance of voters – whatever. An autonomous system can preserve human values, can protects minorities and the rights of the citizen against Leviathan and Leviathan's public.

The arguments for and against a socially-responsive legal system, as one might guess, go exactly the opposite way. On the good side is sensitivity to policy, to social needs. On the bad side: helplessness against the power of the state. Obviously, the issue is central to our times (and most other times as well). The very power and scope of government throw the question of the power and scope of law into sharp relief. Scholars search for some middle ground, some reasonable posture between pure "autonomy" and the pure servant of the state. They look for some way to protect human values, without crippling government, or impairing efficiency.

To put it another way: the problem is how to balance two principles. One principle is the rule of law – needed more than ever in a dangerous, complex world. The other principle is function: government, after all, has to work. Public business must go on – efficiently, quickly, and sensibly too. The welfare and regulatory state is a state committed to *programs*. Government is a problem-solver, as well as the guardian of law (see also Aubert 35 infra).

As one can see, there is a lively debate about how legal systems *should* behave, what balance they should strike between the two basic principles. There is also a question of fact: how do systems actually behave? Are they autonomous in fact, whatever the theory?

Scholars do not agree on the answer. Nobody thinks that the legal system is totally one way or the other. My own view is that on the whole, law in the real world is far from autonomous. On the contrary, it seems quite naked, quite exposed to outside influence, and at every point in time. But this proposition, put this way, is hardly self-evident. Most social scientists and jurists, of course, assume that the outside world has *some* influence on the legal system – how could it not? But many scholars argue, rather powerfully, that the system is basically autonomous, and even that its autonomy is increasing. This means that it follows, in the main, its own logic of development (Teubner, 1983 and infra). It receives and processes material from outside, but through its own "filtering" system, which alters and converts the incoming influences (Luhmann, 1969:59 and infra).

One reason reasonable people can hold such different views of the subject is because they are basically looking at rather different animals. The key (I think) is the mental picture which the word "law" conjures up. If you think of "law" as a rather abstract network of formal doctrines, concepts that jurists play with and law students study, nice questions which scholars chew over; and if you further conceive of "legal institutions" as consisting mainly of courts (and legislatures only insofar as they enact general codes), then the legal system certainly *seems* on the whole fairly autonomous. It is in part like a windowless room, in which a little bit of light at most shines in from the outside world; in part, it behaves like Luhmann's system, carefully fitting and processing selected inputs from outside. If, on the other hand, you think of the *whole* legal order, especially today, you get a different impression. It is hard to avoid the conclusion that the "outside" played a dominant role in creating the huge apparatus of the modern welfare state, and the complex machinery for regulating business. When one considers *all* branches of law, and all institutions, including the police, that make and apply norms, not to mention the work of lawyers in shaping business transactions, one sees far less "autonomy" than if one looked only at the little corner defined as "law" by law schools and jurists.

Our assumption, then, is that the legal system, as a whole, has only limited autonomy. A second assumption is that the debate about autonomy is somewhat misguided. Some jurists seem to equate an *autonomous* legal system with an *independent* legal system; but these are quite separate and distinct. When we think about protecting minorities, or preserving human values against the power of the state, we usually have *independence* in mind. By this we mean that courts (or other institutions) carry on their work free from domination by the regime; they go their own way, pursue their own values and goals. An independent legal system *may* be autonomous, but it does not have to be.

The United States Supreme Court provides an excellent illustration. The court has thwarted the government, time and again; time and again it has defied the will of the majority (insofar as we can measure it), on behalf of racial and religious minorities, prisoners, poor people on welfare, and many others. Yet the court has not been "autonomous," whatever its pretenses, if by autonomous we mean to suggest that the court is not heavily influenced by outside events and opinions. The court discusses policy sometimes quite frankly, and there is little about its recent work that is deductive or formalistic. The court has moved markedly in the direction of "policy," of substantive rationality, and away from conceptualism and formal rationality.

An independent legal system, in other words, pursues its own brand of policy. This is usually based on current social opinion, at least as held by "enlightened" or "liberal" members of society. The modern welfare state badly needs true independence in its legal system (or at least in some parts of the system), to curb or counterbalance the power of the state. Whether "autonomy" in the sense of formal rationality is good for anything is a serious question. My own hunch is it is not. Of course, those scholars who defend the "autonomy" of the legal system in modern times do not equate autonomy with formal rationality. They insist the two are quite different. But it is hard to see what development in terms of the "inner logic" of the law would mean, if did *not* mean formal rationality in Weber's sense.

The starting point here, then, is an expansive view of law. The starting point is also a group of societies, that have, on the whole, *independent* judiciaries (although some are more independent than others). Other important segments of the legal system also have structural independence. This is notably true of a good deal of the work of the civil service. Consider for example, an administrative agency charged with deciding whether or not to allow food companies to add a certain chemical preservative to food products. In most countries, the agency will decide on technical and economic grounds, largely free from the control of the central regime.

But these "independent" parts of the legal system are not, in any sense, "autonomous." To the contrary. Western societies are relatively open societies; thus all parts of the government are (more or less) exposed to electoral influence, public opinion, interest groups, and so on. The decisions do not take place in a vacuum, even if they are not crudely subject to state coercion. "Independence" is a relative term. It means, basically, discretion to choose among a range of means and ends. It means that no boss can fire the decision-maker simply because the decision does not suit the boss' fancy. But public policy notions affect the decisions nonetheless. And all modern systems try to balance control and discretion, independence and accountability, with more or less success. (There seems to be no way to avoid the *general* problem.)

The legal system, in short, is a ship that sails the seas of social force. And the concept of *legal culture* is crucial to an understanding of legal development. By legal culture, we mean the ideas, attitudes, values, and beliefs that people hold about the legal system (Friedman, 1975:194). Not that any particular country has a single, unified legal culture. Usually there are many cultures in a country, because societies are complex, and are made up of all sorts of groups, classes and strata. One should also distinguish between *internal* legal culture (the legal culture of lawyers and judges) and *external* (the legal culture of the population at large). We can, if we wish, also speak about the legal culture of taxi drivers, or rich people, or businessmen, or black people. Presumably, no two men or women have exactly the same attitudes toward law, but there are no doubt tendencies that correlate systematically with age, sex, income, nationality, race and so on. At least this is plausible. It is also possible that the legal culture of Germany as a whole is different from the legal culture of Holland, in ways that can be intelligibly described; and even more so compared to Honduras or Chad.

Social scientists, approaching the legal system, begin with a master hypothesis: that social change will lead, inexorably, to legal change. This of course puts the matter far too simply. If one asks, *how* social change leads to legal change, the first answer is: by means of legal culture. That is, social change leads to changes in people's values and attitudes, and this sets up chains of demands (or withdrawals), which in turn push law and government in some particular direction. How the first step takes place, what the mechanism is, remains obscure. We know that social change correlates with deep, mysterious changes in ways of looking at the world. The industrial revolution went along with a massive change in consciousness. How the two were related is a question best left unexplored, at least by jurists.

In this paper, I propose to modify somewhat the usual way of explaining legal change. Ordinarily, the legal historian or social scientists goes directly (and somewhat mysteriously) from an event or series of events in the outside world (the invention of the railroad, say) to change in the behavior of the legal system (shifts in the law of accidents, for example). Here I add one step in between: change in legal culture. I look for specific changes in legal culture, which might be of use in explaining certain aspects of the welfare state — that is, how and why social change translated into specific sorts of legal change.

There is, naturally, a serious problem of method and evidence. The habit (or vice) of taking opinion surveys is pretty recent. There is no way to measure attitudes toward law in the past in any systematic way. Opinion surveys, however imperfect they are today, simply did not exist. Hence much of what is said here is basically guesswork. Still, it is worthwhile to put forward a few ideas, which might at some time be followed up by deeper explorations in the sources.

Public Law and Private People

This paper began by pointing out what is surely the most striking aspect of the modern state: its size. The state is big in every dimension. It has the money, it has the people, it has the jobs. Anywhere from a quarter to half of the gross national product flows to and through the central government. In most Western countries, a solid majority of the population either works for the government or gets some sort of money benefits — a pension, a family allowance, welfare. Thus most people, at some point in their lives, will get paychecks from public funds. Moreover, the power of the state is limitless (or seems that way). It has the police, the tanks, even the hydrogen bomb. There also seems no limit to the areas of life the government can touch. Thumb through the pages of law-books, codes and statutes: the range of activities grounded in law, and centered in government, is truly incredible. Nothing seems immune (see also Brockman infra).

What is the source of all this growth? Certainly, at one level, it must be true that the increase in scope and power has been in response to demands from society itself. The state did what people wanted it to do ("people" here meaning whoever had influence or power). To take one simple example — product safety: how did it come about the the government regulates food products, that it decides what chemicals can be added to cans of soup or vegetables? Clearly, pressure from the public — elites and ordinary people alike, in this instance, so that one does not have to assume, naively, that laws of this sort are the result of sympathy for the common man. The rich are as unwilling to trust the market to get rid of poisoned foods as anybody else.

Technological and social changes in society, of course, lie behind the rising demands. There was no canned soup in the middle ages. All societies are interdependent, but in modern industrial society there is a new, peculiar form of interdependence. *Strangers* are in charge of important parts of our lives – people we do not know, and cannot control (see also Ewald infra). We no longer always make our own soup; often we buy it. The same is true of our bread, our clothes, our furniture. The people whose hands and machines create the conditions of life we depend on are totally invisible to us. We never see in person the people who make and repair automobiles, busses, trains, and airplanes. We never see in person the people who make sure the water we drink is pure and safe. But if these people are careless in their work, their mistakes can kill us. We cannot control the processes *personally*, cannot influence the outcomes. Yet the process *can* be controlled. Hence we demand norms from the state, from the collectivity, to guarantee the work of those strangers whose work is vital to our lives, which we cannot guarantee by ourselves.

Out of this cycle of demands, the modern state builds up a body of health and safety law. The rules become denser, more formal. *Informal* norms are effective in regulating relationships, for small groups, families, people in face to face contact, in villages, in tribal life. They are not good enough for relationships among strangers, who "meet" only in the form of a product that one group makes and the other consumes; or who "meet" in an auto accident. Informal norms do not work for many problems and relationships in large, complex, mobile societies, when the villages have shattered into thousands of pieces, only to form again into the great ant-hills of our cities. For such societies, and such relationships, people demand active intervention from the generalized third party, or, in other words, the law.

I have used health and safety regulation to illustrate this point, because it is easiest there to see how the process of building up law and the state goes on. But the same forces are at work in creating the social insurance programs that are the heart of the welfare state. No doubt feelings of humanity – a sense of kinship and sympathy with the poor – explains some of the great growth of welfare laws. But one usually gets further in explaining social processes (alas) by looking for rather selfish motives, or at least for mixed motives, than in relying on pure altruism. Most of these programs benefit the strong, active middle class in some way. Old-age pensions, for example, relieve the middle class of the burden of supporting their elderly parents, in a society where family ties are strained, and in which people live longer lives.

But the main point here is a somewhat different one. It is that, in fact, the same interdependence which led to health and safety regulation created demands for forms of social insurance. There was no "unemployment" in a medieval village. Starvation and poverty, yes, but not gangs of steel workers laid off because of foreign competition, or recession, or automation. Modern unemployment is felt psychologically as a catastrophe not so very different from defective automobiles or poisoned soup. That is, mysterious strangers, who control economic process, seem to bring it about. It too evokes a demand for a social, that is, a legal solution – if not guaranteed jobs, then at least unemployment compensation.

Yet the more the state undertakes, the more it creates a *climate* that leads to still further increases in demand. This is because of a fundamental – and very natural – change in legal culture. State action creates *expectations*. It redefines what seems to be the possible limits of law; it extends the boundaries. After a while, what is possible comes to be taken for granted, and then treated as if it were part of the natural order. Taxes creep forward slowly, benefit programs are added on one at a time, programs of regulation evolve step by step. Each move redefines the scope of the system. The next generation accepts what its parents argued about, as easily as it accepts sunshine and rain. Expectations, then, have been constantly rising.

This is one reason why the welfare state is so sticky and inelastic; why movement always seems to flow in one direction: more. Patterns of expectation, like patterns of interests, are exceedingly difficult to change. This leads to a general theory of "crisis," a theory that the modern welfare state is "ungovernable" (for assessments and critique, see Lehner, 1979; Schmitter, 1981). Some scholars blame "ungovernability" on excessive expectations, or on the fact that the state makes too many promises (Brittan, 1975). Obviously, especially in hard times, the state has trouble keeping its promises; and population trends (too many old people on pensions) make things worse. All this has helped evoke conservative backlash, which such leaders as Reagan and Thatcher exploit. Conservatives want to cut back the welfare and regulatory state; more fundamentally, they are trying to change patterns of expectations. Most observers expect them to fail. Their policies have, in fact, only scratched the surface; the core of the welfare state seems remarkably solid, remarkably hard to change. There may be – and has been – some slight retrenchment; a pause in the movement, but so far nothing more.

I spoke loosely about levels of "demand." A demand is a kind of claim, which depends on a subjective feeling that there is some chance of getting what you ask for. Nobody asks the government for life after death or for good rain in the growing season. The state cannot provide these things, and everybody knows this. Demands on government in the 19th century were restrained by the feeling, in area after area, that there was nothing that could be done. People believed that the state was powerless to affect their lives in all sorts of ways, or to control the economy. This was in fact basically true. The government had about as much of a handle on the economy as it had on the weather. Nor could anybody in the early part of the 19th century do much about disease, for example. Public sanitation measures were primitive, and the causes of disease were obscure. Boards of Health came into being only in the middle of the 19th century (for the United States, see Rosenberg, 1962).

Science and technical improvement are of course a large part of the story. The germ theory, for example, helped bring about a revolution in medicine, and today doctors are actually able to cure people. The expanded role of government in health policy was unthinkable before the expansion of modern medicine. Railroads, telephone and telegraph, airplanes, automobiles, air conditioners, computers – all of these inventions had an effect on society which is simply incalculable. What they have in common is that they increae human *control* over nature – and over other human beings. Who exercises this control? In large part, the government.

This, incidentally sheds light on the notion, already noted, that the modern state is "ungovernable," or that some sort of "crisis" has gripped modern society, which lacks "capacity" to solve its problems, and therefore cannot maintain "system integration" (Habermas, 1975:11). I tend to be skeptical about the idea of such a crisis. But in any event what is meant is some sort of imbalance. The system is out of whack. *Demands* increase faster than the system's ability to meet them (for the development of a similar view see also Preuß infra). After all, the *absolute* capacity of modern government is incomparably greater than ever before; on this score, there is simply no comparison between modern and pre-modern states.

This was because so little was expected from law, state, and government. Indeed, little was expected, in some ways, from life itself. It is important to remember the gross conditions of life in past centuries, even so recently as a hundred years ago. Life was overhung by a tremendous sense of insecurity. Uncertainty was part of the human condition. Death entered the houses of rich and poor, suddenly, unexpectedly, inescapably. Its favorite victims were small children, and women in childbirth; but no one was spared the danger of sudden death from plague and disease, scourges which could not be cured or controlled (Stone, 1979).

Modern medicine, with its vaccinations, its medicines, its antibiotics, has made a tremendous difference in the quality of modern life. Medicine and technology have transformed uncertainty into a sense of (relative) security. People no longer expect their children to die off; the shadow of death does not hang over women giving birth. When people get sick, they expect the doctors to cure them. We consider death before old age the exception, not the rule.

The overwhelming, ghastly uncertainty of life was not simply a matter of health and disease. Economic uncertainty was almost as great. Whether the Industrial Revolution made daily life harder for the mass of society, whether it made daily bread more painful, is a difficult question. But whatever the answer, it is clear that in, say, the middle of the 19th century, chance, fate, and accident governed the economic condition of millions of people, almost to the same degree as they governed life itself. There was of course no such thing as unemployment insurance. There was nothing at all like the modern system of banking and currency. The government did not insure deposits in banks. When a bank failed — which happened with depressing regularity during the various crashes and panics — depositors simply lost their money. Fraud and the business cycle played havoc with investments. A merchant or storekeeper stood to lose everything if a ship sank, or creditors and customers went bankrupt, or a storm of financial distress swept over the community. Finance and commerce, like health, were completely out of control.

Of course the average person did not own ship-cargoes, or invest in stocks and bonds. The average person was a farmer, or farm laborer, a factory worker, or the wife of one of these. For all these people, there was not much security, though life was on the whole easier in some countries than in others. In the United States, economic opportunities were greater than they were in most European countries, and there was less outright hunger. But nobody had job security. In big city factories, when times got bad, the owner laid off workers or cut wages, or simply fired some men. Coal miners, railroadmen, textile workers lived from payday to payday. There were no private or public pensions to speak of. Life insurance was uncommon, and in any event few people could afford it in the 19th century (Zelizer, 1979; Keller, 1963). If the man of the house died of cholera, or lost his job, or was crushed by a machine at the factory, his wife and children might be left destitute, unless they had friends or family to support them. "Poor relief" there was, but it was poor indeed and little relief. Increasingly, after the early 19th century, "poor relief" meant the humiliation and squalor of the "poor house" or "poor farm." Nobody went willingly to these places — nobody, that is, of respectable background — except out of desperation, as a last resort.

The farmer was not much better off. There were no crop subsidies, no government programs that guaranteed him an income, or took excess butter and peanuts off his hands. If locusts ate his crop, if wind and weather destroyed it, if the price of wheat fell disastrously, the loss fell on him and his family, and on nobody else. Typically, the farmer's land was mortgaged to the hilt, to pay for farm machinery, extra land, or seeds and tools. If bad times came, the family stood to lose land and living, almost without warning (Friedman, 1973).

Life was, in short, a drama of infinite uncertainty, and this was so well known that people accepted it as the principal fact of human existence. The uncertainty of life must have had a profound effect on legal culture. People *expected* misfortune, and they expected "injustice" — not necessarily human injustice, but the injustice of an unjust world, a world so arranged as to strike out in capricious and unfair ways, or at any event, mysterious, unfathomable ways. Many people took refuge, as they always had, in religion. Some trusted to chance or luck. But they did not look to law, or the state, for salvation.

In every period, there is a kind of short-run balance between demands on state and law, and the supply of reponses — the capacity of the system, in other words. This balance is fragile and easily broken, as the riots and revolutions of the 19th century attest. There was, in particular, an acute, growing demand for change in political structure. The right to vote spread to the middle classes, then to everyone, including women. But the demands for political reform did not imply demand for what one might call *justice in general.* There was no generalized expectation of justice. Nor was there a generalized expectation that society owed everyone some social minimum, or that the state would actively protect health and safety, in some general way. One barrier that stood in the way was ideology: 19th century laissez faire, and the theory of the night-watchman state. But the power of ideology as such has been, I suspect, vastly exaggerated. What really controlled the level of demands was quite a different aspect of legal culture: ideas about what the state *could* not do, rather than what the state *should* not do (see also Aubert, Wiethölter infra).

People also had low expectations as far as *private* obligations were concerned. No doubt people expected business bargains to be carried out, though insolvency or unforeseen events could always frustate plans. For personal injury, the situation must have been quite different. In a society with sudden accidents, and very little insurance, there was no *general* expectation that somebody would pay for a lost leg, or a worn-out lung, or a life snuffed out at a railroad crossing (Friedman, 1980).

In the contemporary world, the situation has turned upside down. A great revolution in expectations has taken place, of two sorts: first, a general expectation that the state will guarantee total justice, and second (and for our purposes more important), a general expectation that the state will protect us from catastrophe. It will also make good all losses that are not our "fault." The modern state is a welfare state, which is also an insurance state — a state that knows how to spread the risks (see also Aubert, Ewald, Preuß infra).

The relationship between technology and changes in legal culture are in one sense very simple, in another sense very complicated. Let us take, for example, the problem of kidney dialysis. This is a medical technique which saves the lives of people with severe kidney failure. Not long ago, these people were doomed. Today they can be kept alive; but it is an expensive business, and nobody but the very wealthiest people could possibly afford it without a subsidy. The government, then, has to pay for kidney dialysis. This is expected and (to be sure) it is the rule, embodied in positive legislation.

Obviously, without the medical discoveries, there would be no demand on the government for these large amounts of money. But technology does not *create* demand; all it does is make demand possible. There is at least one more step in the process which has to be explained. If we had to guess, we might imagine something like this: the "cure" for a disease gives the victims hope; victims then have concrete institutions to blame if the "cure" is not made available. It is no longer luck, fate, or the finger of God, but a process under human control. And, in a society of strangers, only "the law" has the leverage to make the machinery move.

Reduction of uncertainty leads to increased demand for public action. It is, in a way, a chicken and egg proposition; but the stages in the process are apparent, at least in rough outline. Mortality is no longer the scourge it used to be. Mothers and fathers in Western countries do not expect their babies to die. Childbirth is no longer a major cause of death. Families can control much better the number of children they have. Economic life is also in some senses (of course not all) more secure. Nobody expects banks to fail. If they do, government insurance covers the depositor. This has been true for about 50 years in the United States. "Runs" on banks should no longer occur.

People, of course, still lose jobs. But they can at least collect unemployment insurance. This helps to tide them over, until they find another job. The general welfare system, whatever its faults, will keep them from sinking into complete destitution. Nobody starves. The currency is (relatively) stable. Life expectancy has increased. There are public and private pensions, and they protect most people in society. Doctors' bills, in many countries, are covered by state insurance. Even in the United States, people over 65 years have health protection (Medicare); and company or union plans protect millions of workers and their families. In some countries, medicine has been socialized outright, and disease is no longer an economic calamity at all, as it still is for many people in the United States.

The state, government, or legal system had little or nothing to do with changes that made some of these developments possible — the discovery of antibiotics, for example. The spread of life insurance and private pension plans also took place outside the formal apparatus of the state. Law had a lot to do with social insurance, of course, and with stabilizing currency and banking; the development of product liability, free public education, and subsidized medical care, also took place through law and the state.

Whether public or private, however, all these developments combined have radically transformed society — so radically in fact that we take these matters for granted. The insecure society is now the welfare society — life is still hard, still uncertain, but collective action has succeeded in cushioning the blows in important regards. Of course, people still face enormous uncertainty. In some regards, uncertainty may be *greater* than before. Think, for example, of the difference between a society of arranged marriages, and a society in which people are expected to find, and choose, and keep, all on their own, and out of the millions in the world, the single best partner for their lives. Or consider the differences between traditional society, as it was before the Industrial Revolution, with its cushion of custom and habit, and the rootless life of so many people in great cities. I am not arguing that people are better off, or should feel that they are. These are different issues.

What I am saying is that the reduction of uncertainty in some areas of life is a fact; and to an astonishing degree; and that this leads to changes in cycles of demands and responses, in short, to a changing legal culture. (I am talking of course, about the so-called advanced countries. The peasant in Bangladesh still faces certain ancient uncertainties, that the Swiss or Swedish farmer never has to think of any more.)

To repeat: What is possible always affects what the population expects and demands. People do not suppose that government, even in Switzerland, can prevent an avalanche or cure a drought. People do not blame government for auto accidents or pneumonia. But in other regards expectations have drastically altered. As uncertainty — sudden death and sudden disaster — declines, the legal culture changes accordingly. There is a general demand for still further reduction of uncertainty; payment for losses, and social insurance to soften the blows of economic ups and downs.

People also expect health and safety regulation, and indeed this is demanded, to control and prevent all kinds of calamity. The citizen also expects tall buildings to be inspected. She expects that planes will not crash, that wheels will not come off busses, that trains will stay on the track. And more: that elevators will not break their cables, food products will be free of botulism, and pure water will come out when the tap is turned on. If these expectations are *not* met, then some agency of government, or some institution, is at fault, and somebody must pay and take the blame: the manufacturer, perhaps, or the government itself. And the legal system will provide — *must* provide — machinery to make sure all this happens, whether by way of prevention, or cure, and certainly by payment of damages.

The thesis here, in other words, is about *legal culture*. This, we suggest, is a key variable in explaining the rise and life-cycle of the welfare-regulatory state. I have pointed to some specific aspects of legal culture that are, I feel, directly relevant. It will no doubt strike some readers that we have left a great deal out of the story. Nothing much has been said about tradition, politics, ideology; about capitalism itself and its variants, or about the rise of various forms of socialism, to mention only the more blatant omissions. Surely these are part of any meaningful account of the modern welfare state.

And of course, they are. Moreover, there are great differences in the experiences of the various countries. They have started off in different places, and gone about their business in very different ways. The history of the welfare state in America is, on the surface at least, strikingly different from its history in England; and both seem far removed from the experience of France or Germany, or the Scandinavian countries.

But it is all too easy to get lost in a forest of details. History is not usually written from a comparative perspective. It pretty much sticks to individual countries, and no wonder. The scholar needs all his skill to deal with (say) an account of the welfare state in England; it is too much to expect him, for comparative purposes, to cast his nets on Belgium or Italy as well, not to mention such exotic locales as Argentina or the United States. It is easy, too, to treat each country as unique. Bismarck's role in the rise of German social legislation (for example) is well known; and Bismarck of course cannot be duplicated anywhere else.

Yet it is also striking to see how individual histories do converge, in the long run. The question is: why? One way to explain this is in terms of cultural diffusion or intellectual influence. England sees social insurance in Germany and says "aha." The United States sees it in Britain. Important books get translated. Travelers bring back news, just as Marco Polo brought the noodle back from China. One country sneezes, and the others catch cold.

But cultural diffusion, as a tool of explanation, is ultimately inadequate. Societies copy what they want to copy, and what appeals to them. The question then is: why do they want to copy? It is at least as plausible (I think more so) to use similarities in *stimulus* to explain similarities in response. After all, modern medicine, the railroad, telephone, automobile and computer are common to all Western countries. Not that the welfare and regulatory state is a single, inevitable reaction to technological change. I am simply repeating the proposition I began with: social change leads to changes in legal culture, which in turn lead to legal change. A spiral of demands is characteristic of the welfare state; the spiral stems from specific changes in legal culture, which I have tried, rather briefly, to sketch out, and to relate to gross facts of social change in the modern world.

"Social change" is the first and most crucial term in the equation. New technology leads to social change. Technology does not explain everything that happens in modern society, but it is important, and must be taken into account. The countries of the West have been part of a single great adventure in social change. They have gone through the experience together, and it has had grossly similar effects on their legal cultures, hence on demands for law, hence on the system's responses. Of course, we deal here with interaction effects, not lines of cause running in a single direction. But the overall point is the same.

I used the word "equation," but this should not be taken literally. The terms are in no sense mathematical. They are statements (at best) of general correlation – *very* rough ones – and of probabilities. There is always static and noise in the data. We can explain, at most, only part of the variance. The rest *is* local history and tradition, which is important in its own right. Nor does any single theory "explain" the experience of nations. All I have tried to do, in a preliminary way, is point up one factor, too often overlooked in the biography of modern states – the distinctive legal culture of our times. I have also tried to suggest, in a rough and ready way, some specific aspects of legal culture which help explain, at least from one standpoint, how the welfare-regulatory state came about.

But not, of course, where it is going, and what will become of it. I for one do not feel able to express opinions on this subject. It is rash to predict stability or revolution, or any combination. The past does *not* (I feel) give us strong enough clues for this kind of prediction. History is not much of a science. If there are "laws" of history, nobody has found them yet. History, someone said, teaches only one thing: that there is nothing to be learned from it. This goes a bit too far. But it is hard enough to find patterns in the past; nothing we know warrants projecting the past into the future.

References

Brittan, Samuel (1975) "The Economic Contradictions of Democracy," 5 *British Journal of Political Science* 129.

Friedman, Lawrence M. (1973) "The Six Million Dollar Man: Litigation and Rights Consciousness in Modern America," 39 *Maryland Law Review* 661.

– (1973) *A History of American Law*. New York: Simon and Schuster.

– (1975) *The Legal System: A Social Science Perspective*. New York: Russel Sage Foundation.

Habermas, Jürgen (1975) *Legitimationsprobleme im Spätkapitalismus*. Frankfurt a. M.: Suhrkamp.

Keller, Morton (1963) *The Life Insurance Enterprise 1885–1910; a Study in the Limits of Corporate Power*. Cambridge: Belknap Press of Harvard University Press.

Lehner, Franz (1979) *Grenzen des Regierens, Eine Studie zur Regierungsproblematik hochindustrialisierter Demokratien*. Königstein/Ts: Athenäum.

Luhmann, Niklas (1969) *Legitimation durch Verfahren*. Darmstadt: Luchterhand.

Nonet, Philippe and Philip Selznick (1978) *Law and Society in Transition: Toward Responsive Law*. New York: Harper Torch Books.

Rosenberg, Charles E. (1962) *The Cholera Years, the United States in 1832, 1849, and 1866*. Chicago: University of Chicago Press.

Schmitter, Philippe C. (1981) "Interest Intermediation and Regime Governability in Contemporary Western Europe and North America," in S. Berger (ed.) *Organizing Interests in Western Europe: Pluralism, Corporation, and the Transformation of Politics*. Cambridge: Cambridge University Press.

Stone, Lawrence J. (1979) *The Family, Sex and Marriage in England 1500–1800*. New York: Harper and Row.

Teubner, Gunther (1983) "Substantive and Reflexive Elements in Modern Law," 17 *Law & Society Review* 239.

Zelizer, Viviana A. R. (1979) *Morals and Markets, The Development of Life Insurance in the United States*. New York: Columbia University Press.

The Rule of Law and the Promotional Function of Law in the Welfare State

Vilhelm Aubert
Oslo

Let me start by briefly indicating what I mean by law, and then present some of the various interpretations attributed to the concept of the rule of law. After then having enumerated the tasks (functions) of law, I shall consider some of the legal changes that have taken place during the last hundred years or so and which have shifted the emphasis of the law from a predominantly preventive mode to one which also includes promotion of economic growth and of welfare (Aubert, 1983:152).

What is Law?

I want to avoid an explicit definition of law. Such definitions are usually presented because of a need to distinguish normatively relevant rules and decisions from normatively irrelevant rules and decisions. Since the following presentation aims only at a description and analysis of phenomena that ought to be studied in their interrelationship with each other, no such restrictions are necessary. Illegal police activities are of interest to the sociologist of law, as are the efforts of legal counsel to propagate interpretations of customary or statutory law which may deviate from precedent and accepted legal doctrine.

Certain phenomena are by consensus and without hesitation considered legal, such as the activities of the courts and of the personnel which aid the courts in enforcing their decisions, such as the police and prison authorities. Also, the legal profession can be seen as "officers of the courts", although this does not cover all their activities or even most of them. However, legal training is another focal point for studies of legal phenomena, whereby a sociology of law may have occasion to study the possible impact of this professional training upon people who are managers of private firms or who fill non-legal posts in the civil service. Legislation is a third focal point. Here it is impossible to draw a clear line of distinction between the proper domain of the sociologist of law and that of the political scientist.

By choosing this common sense phenomenological starting point one does not avoid borderline problems. However, these borderline problems are relegated to their proper and subordinate analytical position. Whether a phenomenon is legal or not becomes, in this perspective, a matter of degree. In what follows, I do not think that the solution of borderline problems impinges upon the main thrust of the argument.

The Rule of Law

Several different meanings have been attributed to the concept of "the rule of law" (see Habermas 206, Wiethölter 222, Peters 250 infra). In the Anglo-Saxon tradition Dicey was a highly influential proponent of this principle, which he saw as intimately linked to the function of an independent judiciary. The rule of law requires that:

> no man is punishable, or can be lawfully made to suffer in body or goods except for a distinct breach of law established in the ordinary legal manner before the ordinary courts of the land (Dicey, 1968:188).

Andenæs points to a dualism in the concept of the rule of law:

> With respect to the rule of law one may have two things in mind. First, one may think of protection against interference with one's legal rights by other citizens. Secondly, there is the question of protection against the abusive and arbitrary exertion of power by the state itself (Andenæs, 1945:5).

In his second point, Andenæs concurs with Dicey and many other writers on the subject. The first point refers to "law and order" and thereby to a tension in the concept of the rule of law itself. Effective protection of established legal rights, for example property rights, is often perceived as dependent upon relatively wide discretionary powers of the agencies of enforcement, conceivably at the expense of the suspect's or defendant's procedural rights. On both points it is clear that the rule of law tends to favour those who have rights and has less to offer those who lack rights. However, certain rights are universally applicable, such as the right not to be punished except for a breach of law which is established by a court.

The International Commission of Jurists has brought the establishment of new rights, or at least of new opportunities, within the orbit of the rule of law (for an elaboration of new types of rights typical of a welfare state see Preuß infra). In their resolutions, the rule of law is given such wide scope that it covers nearly everything associated with social justice. The following quotation illustrates the point:

> The International Commission of Jurists has, since its foundation, been dedicated to the support and advancement throughout the world of those principles of justice which constitute the basis of the Rule of Law. The term "Rule of Law", as defined and

> interpreted by the various Congresses sponsored by the International Commission of Jurists, seeks to emphasize that mere legality is not enough and that broader conceptions of justice as distinct from positive legal rules are embraced by the term and, indeed, provide its more vital aspect. (International Commission of Jurists, 1965:14)

This was followed up by a reference to the Declaration of Delhi (1959), which contains this statement:

> The rule of Law is a dynamic concept for the expansion and fulfilment of which jurists are primarily responsible and which should be employed not only to safeguard and advance the civil and political rights of the individual in a free society, but also to establish social, economic, educational and cultural conditions under which his legitimate aspirations and dignity may be realized (International Commission of Jurists, 1965:15).

This heavy emphasis upon a broad conception of social justice, must be understood in the international context of these meetings. The Third World was well represented, and its problems were discussed; such discussion must highlight the relative irrelevancy of the formal application of the rule of law in countries beset by mass poverty, disease and premature death.

Later in the report, the Commission seems to retreat from the reformist or even revolutionary interpretation of the rule of law and revert to a more traditional interpretation of the principle, in line with Dicey, Andenæs and many others. The terms in which the Commission criticizes Chinese (communist) rule suggest that the more narrow procedural conception of the rule of law takes precedence over the one in terms of social, economic and cultural human rights, if and when the two clash. Such clashes are to be expected: the establishment of new rights will often take place through some infringement of established rights. Thus, the report of the International Commission of Jurists brings to the fore the tension between a human rights approach in the natural law tradition and the traditional adherence to the professional conception of the rule of law among Western and Western influenced lawyers (International Commission of Jurists, 1965:32).

In view of modern Western legislatures' eagerness to regulate social, economic and cultural affairs by law, the dilemmas posed and left unresolved in the report of the International Commission of Jurists, also serve as a focus of attention when we discuss legal changes in industrially advanced Western societies.

The Tasks of the Law

Instead of the tasks of the law, we might have spoken of the tasks of one or more legally coloured institution. Not all elements of the legal system are similarly geared to the execution of the same tasks. Instead of "tasks" we might have used terms like "functions", "purposes", "impacts" or "effects". The choice of term is determined by a wish to avoid making dubiously anthropomorphic assumptions about a system's purpose. I also wish to avoid *a priori* assumptions about the effects of a legal rule or decision. "Task" seems to be the one term which takes the least for granted with respect to unresolved empirical problems. However, even this term, which refers to what legal institutions are doing, raises many problems. The following scheme of classification aims at no more than to provide us with a way of ordering legal change in such a way as to avoid overlooking important elements in the process that has taken place. The scheme must be sufficiently abstract to make it possible to form an overview of the changes. The economy of thought calls for a limited number of categories in which to place the empirical trends. These categories should be sufficiently concrete so as to avoid the need for lengthy explanations as to what they entail, and to permit us to keep in touch with the empirical realities and common sense conceptions with which we are concerned. The following scheme has evolved as a compromise between these, partly contradictory, considerations.

Law, above all statutory law, is a means of governance through the application of sanctions. Austin defined law as commands backed by force (Austin, 1971:133). In what follows I shall not, however, concentrate exclusively upon the negative sanctions, whether of a criminal or a civil kind. We shall not assume this one-sided relationship between law and the threats of some unpleasant consequence for those who do not abide by the law or fulfill its requirements. The law may, and often does, use the promise of pecuniary advantages to those who fulfill criteria stipulated by law.

It is difficult, sometimes impossible, to separate the task of governance from the mere distribution of resources. Tax laws can be seen as elements in those distributory mechanisms which shape class distinctions, social hierarchies and interest groups. But many tax provisions aim clearly, though with varying degrees of success, at guiding people to behave in ways which further the economic goals of the government (see also Preuß infra).

Conflict resolution is sometimes presented as the one universal task of law, because it is not necessarily dependent upon the existence of a state. This is one reason why the comparative, ethnographic approach to law focuses so heavily upon instruments for handling disputes, whether by court-like institutions or through procedures which rely heavily upon negotiation. Another and perhaps more profound reason for emphasizing conflict resolution, or more accurately the handling of conflicts, is that advanced legal procedures can most fruitfully be understood as a response to the demands made upon a third party when brought into a dispute. However, the tasks of the courts are inseparably connected with the enforcement of laws and thus constitute a vital element in the machinery of governance.

Laws have been viewed as a means to secure expectations and promote predictability in commerce as well as in other areas of life. In so far as statutes are enforced with a modicum of certainty, predictability could, of course, be viewed simply as a precondition of effective governance. However, it does not seem natural always to view legal rules in this perspective, especially not in private law regulating market activities. One basic aim of the law of contracts is to lend credibility to contracts, but not to determine their contents. Law has to do with the establishment of trust in social life.

Statutes and above all, constitutions, espouse ideals and are not merely instruments with which to put ideals into practice. Not infrequently, programmatic pronouncements remain on the symbolic level. Either they are too vague to give guidance as to how they could be enforced, or they are not followed up in terms of the personnel and the finances required in order to make them operative. Although symbolism may render certain legal norms esoteric, they may serve as sources in a technique of argumentation. Interest groups may score points in a political debate if they can show that their aims correspond to programmatic statutory enactments.

Law and legal techniques are often used by governmental agencies as a shield against criticism. Laws are binding upon the government as well as upon the citizens. These bonds are often felt by government agencies to be detrimental to effective execution of the tasks allotted to them. The law protects the citizens against governmental intervention in their affairs at the expense of the achievement of more general social goals. But the reverse may also be the case. The interests of citizens might be better served if laws were more liberally interpreted or even contravened. It is the civil servant whose task is made easier by laws which restrict his discretionary powers. He sticks to rules and precedents and cannot be blamed for the unfortunate consequences of his decisions.

In what follows I shall try show how the shift of emphasis from prevention to promotion affects the execution of all these tasks.

Legal Promotion in the Welfare State

It is customary to define the welfare state by reference to certain rights of the citizen and by the state's ability to meet the claims which flow from these rights. Their aim is to secure a decent minimum of welfare in terms of health, nutrition, housing, and education. Some constitutions of what are commonly recognized as welfare states, like Sweden, are more ambitious and include the right to work, equality between the sexes and between ethnic groups, as well as the fulfilment of cultural needs.

Irrespective of nuances in the definition of welfare, however, all welfare states share the characteristic that the government disposes of a very large share of the wealth of the nation, possibly close to half of the national product. In addition to that, the state is, as a stock-holder, the single largest capitalist in the country. This amassment of wealth in government hands has put its stamp upon the law of the welfare states. The expansion in the state's command of resources creates new problems, problems which are, for understandable reasons, inadequately dealt with in traditional legal theory. Solutions are often sought on an ad hoc basis which again leads to new problems.

Governance in the Western states of the last century took place to a very large extent through the use of negative sanctions, the threat of punishment, torts, and invalidation of claims. Legal theories emphasized force and coercion and sometimes explicitly rejected the possibility of using rewards and encouragement to foster obedience to the laws. Bentham did both (Bentham, 1948:415), as Blackstone had done before, the latter basing his argument in part on considerations of economy (Blackstone, 1847:47). The economy of sanctions was introduced as a theme by Macchiavelli (1952:97) but can be found even in the writings of contemporary sociologists of law. (Schwartz and Orleans, 1973:69—70).

Although Blackstone and others offered economic limitations as an argument for their emphasis upon negative sanctions and penalties, we must not jump to the conclusion that, to any great extent, the wealth of modern states is used to reward. We are on safer ground when we claim that the government is distributing much more wealth, in absolute as well as in relative terms, than it did in the period of the Rechtsstaat. Some of this power to distribute is used to reward, and the withholding of resources from people who feel that they have a claim may be subjectively experienced as a punishment. It may sometimes be so intended on the part of a public agency. The distribution of money and of resources which cost money is the major means of governance. In this situation it is well nigh impossible to distinguish between law as governance through the use of sanctions and law as a mechanism for the distribution of resources with other aims (see also Preuß infra).

Within the welfare sector in the narrow sense, it is relatively clear that the resources offered to the needy citizens are not construed as positive sanctions. Pensions and medical aid are not intended as rewards for behavior which creates a need for assistance, since most of these circumstances, like illness or old age, are not the result of purposive behavior. Borderline cases exist, of course. Pension systems for the aged are often so construed as to entail an inducement to seek regular employment and remain in the labour market until the age of retirement. Rules on disability pensions may punish alcoholics.

Punishment follows upon the act, by whatever means it is executed. If we assume a symmetry between penalties and rewards (a common assumption in much psychological and sociological writing) rewards should also follow upon preceding meritorious acts. Social life is full of rewards which correspond to this assumption of symmetry. Prizes, honours, grades in schools, smiles and tokens of gratitude have this character. However, if we move on to areas regulated by law, it becomes harder to find unambiguous examples of rewards, of positive sanctions administered directly by public agencies. Indirectly, the law has always had as its aim the promotion of good behavior, and this not merely at the minimum level of preventing crime.

Let us return to the observation that to a large extent the government distributes resources under and by the means of some legal regulation. This forces upon the government a promotional function whatever its ideology is, Marxist, Keynesian or Friedmannian. It must create something with all the money; it cannot use it simply to control, as was a dominant task of the law state. It is this necessity to promote, both inside and outside the public sector, which constitutes one of the greatest challenges to the traditional procedural conceptions of the rule of law.

The problems can only be illustrated here by a few examples where it would seem that we are faced with a typical use of positive sanctions or rewards which are aimed at the promotion of production goals. I am referring to the numerous statutory enactments which offer tax reductions or exemptions, as well as direct government subsidies in the form of cash, loans or guarantees of loans. The conditions stipulated guide the effort and investments in certain directions, often, but not always, in accordance with government policy; for example to aid the development of trade and industry in economically backward, and often geographically peripheral, districts.

Are these advantages to be considered as rewards, and if so, do they constitute a symmetrical, positive counterpart to the penalties upon which legal theory has been so heavily focused? It is reasonable to maintain that some people or corporate actors are rewarded for behaving in a certain way. The carrot functions as the stick might have functioned under other social circumstances, in the sense that activities are in some way influenced and directed. That tax exemptions are construed as a relief from general burdens instead of as a direct hand-out is technically important and makes for a certain shield against envy. Rewards as well as penalties raise the question of the relationship to an assumed baseline. There is a parallel between relative deprivation and relative satisfaction. However, both tax exemption and subsidies differ from prizes, honors and grades in that the reward is not retroactively oriented and is offered almost simultaneously with the decision of the investor. It is very much like a contractual deal in that two decisions are linked together. And this is closely related to another characteristic of these economic rewards which distinguish them from penalties.

Penalties are usually extraneous to the acts which produce them. There is no organic link between theft and imprisonment or between speeding and a fine. Due to the promotional aim of tax rewards and subsidies, it is the offered advantage which makes the investment of one's own resources worthwhile. Nay, more than that, the subsidy is often a necessary condition for the achievement of the production goal. The private investor and the government become, as it were, partners in a joint entrepreneurship. The reward becomes a part of the activity which is being rewarded; and this is a process, not a single act.

This points to a technical difference between the tax exemption and the subsidy. Anyone who spends his money in a certain way, by a decision at a certain point in time, is entitled to the exemption. This constitutes no problem in relation to the rule of law. Formal equality can be observed, notwithstanding the glaring social injustice in some of these statutory enactments. Procedurally most of these exemptions are fairly easy to handle in accordance with the rule of law. And those which are technically difficult to handle, because they raise questions of how "deals" are followed up, will often be handled without intervention of the judiciary. We shall shortly return to methods of conflict resolution which sidestep the challenge of the rule of law.

Unlike most tax exemptions, direct subsidies, when they are administered under legal regulation, are appropriated through competition. Discretionary decisions on whom to support and with what, are inevitable. They are based upon assumptions about the probable success of the enterprise, which again depends upon an interplay of numerous factors, some of which are relatively inaccessible to rational calculation. What about the rule of law in the case of complaints?

A detailed study of the functioning of the Norwegian law concerning district development shows the enormous problems which arise if one tries to apply the traditional concept of the rule of law to the enforcement of this law (Boe, 1979). One reason is that government subsidies are made contingent upon additional support from municipalities and local banks. An intricate tangle of contractual arrangements emerges. The government agency becomes one of several players in the market rather than a superordinate controlling authority (for a development of this see Ewald infra).

This is also the case when the government is the owner of a company. The legal construction may be modelled on the limited liability company, with a board of directors who are appointed by the government but who are not *of* the government. The board of directors, as well as the manager, function in very much the same way as does the leadership in private industry. In Norway, the minister functions as the stockholders' committee. Its function is to control, not to direct. To some extent, this arrangement protects the government against blame for failures, deficits, or inefficiency. The company is a player in the market, and the market is exempt from the rule of law.

As a general thesis it may be claimed that the rule of law is inapplicable to a creative process, although a legal framework based upon the rule of law may be a necessary precondition for this initiation of creative processes. However, people increasingly demand a creatively interfering government at the same time as they demand procedural protection of their interests (see Habermas 209 infra). This is one of the basic dilemmas of modern (Western) governments.

The dilemma is brought clearly to the fore when a formal law, such as the one on district development, clearly stipulates a responsibility of the government, albeit in a very general and programmatic form. In the case of publicly owned companies the dilemma is hidden under the cloak of private law, regulating market operations. The integrity of the legal system is preserved through abdication and "delegation" to the market or to other arenas where the application of the rule of law was traditionally considered unnecessary or inappropriate. Such views are increasingly being challenged, in part because public opinion often expands the rule of law to cover also the broader issue of human rights, as the quotation from the International Commission of Jurists indicated.

The health service operates within a legal framework but most decisions are made by medical personnel under conditions which, by and large, preclude interference by legal personnel. This is again based upon assumptions about the importance of law in creative processes, as well as upon assumptions about a harmony of interests between personnel and patients or clients. Such assumptions have increasingly been applied outside the traditional medical sphere, through a "medicalization of society". Problems which could have been formulated under the heading of the right to work, have instead been "solved" by medical personnel awarding disability pensions. In Norway the ensuing complaints are handled by specialized tribunals, thus protecting the ordinary judiciary from a heavy case load as well as the possible blame for dubious discretionary decisions.

In other areas also the professions are left with tasks which they deal with without the government taking direct responsibility through legislation or public administration. The educational system is a case in point. Just like health, the acquisition of knowledge is considered to be a human right, and one which requires the administering of a creative process. However, this right is conceived of mostly in terms of time spent in schools. Although curriculae may be established in the form of legally backed instructions, results in terms of achievement of knowledge cannot be established by law. Nevertheless, since level of achievement, as measured by grades, is so important for future job opportunities and for standard of living, the demand for legal protection of the pupil and student is increasing. Conflicts result between the legislator's wish to regulate and instruct and the teacher's demand for professional autonomy (compare Habermas 218 infra).

The function of the professions and, more generally, the experts is related to the securing of expectations and the basis of trust in society. Above, this was presented as a task of law. The law of property and of contracts provides a basis for predictability and trust which are necessary conditions for the functioning of a market. This was essential in the Rechtsstaat and still is in the welfare state. However, in the modern state, science and technological perfection constitute an additional, sometimes more important, basis of trust.

It is important that the doctor or the captain of the plane have a duty towards the patient or the passenger. But it is at least equally important that they possess the necessary expertise and technological equipment. Where people in the older society worried about the moral or legal failure of others to comply, we worry as much, or more, about the failure of experts and equipment. The remedies against the latter are, however, different from the remedies against the former. The rule of law is of little use when science or technology fail, although it may be of great value when they are unscrupulously applied (see also Friedman supra).

From the government's point of view the principle of professional autonomy is a double-edged sword. It may obstruct government policy at the same time as it may relieve the government of responsibility. A paradoxical example of the latter is the use of legal experts, often judges and professors of law, to sit on legislative committees. We have registered in Norway several instances where the government has appointed such experts to prepare legislation in politically sensitive areas, apparently on a purely professional basis. The result is a proposal based upon improved legal quality, but ignoring political programs. The experts seek legal perfection under the aegis of the rule of law at the expense of substantive reform. Adherence to the rule of law, as conceived of by legal experts, becomes an excuse for putting reforms on ice in an ambiguous political situation.

To sum up, the government's reluctance to act may be aided through the rule of law, and it may get protection for active interference by choosing means which seem to render the rule of law irrelevant. The latter strategy is executed in part by the legislature's use of the budget and its authority to appropriate money, in part through collective or individual contractual arrangements, in some cases by a combination of both.

Subsidies of agriculture is a case in point. In Norway, the farmers operate under a vast number of arrangements intended to preserve or to increase the level of food production and to insure a fair standard of living for the farm population. Most of this, however, is not directly regulated by law or other ordinances. The principles are implicit in the state budget, and general levels of direct subsidies are arrived at through yearly negotiations between the government and the farm organizations. Although cries of social injustice are a permanent feature of the political scene, the form of the subsidies, as well as the intricacy of the system, makes it hard to claim that the rule of law is violated.

An important instrument of economic steering is the government's role as a purchaser of commodities and services from private or publicly owned companies. It is a politically sensitive issue whether the state-owned oil company, Statoil, should buy rigs and other equipment from national or from foreign firms. A politically unpopular choice of a foreign company will be explained in market terms, in which the state takes on the role of purchaser seeking advantage by encouraging competitive bidding and giving the contract to the best and cheapest bidder.

The rule of law is closely linked to the task of conflict-resolution and, more specifically, to the courts. Although the aims of the welfare and interventionist state clash in some respects with the rule of law as an ideal, conflicts are continuously engendered by government policies, as well as by general social and economic development (cf. in this respect the views of Luhmann and Willke infra). This is probably one, but not the only, reason for the emergence of a large number of extra-judicial means of handling conflicts.

We have already mentioned the pension tribunal which deals with problems related to the work of the medical profession. In order to protect their autonomy, many professions and semi-professions (such as journalists) have devised their own tribunals to handle complaints from clients as well as internal professional disputes. The government has set up bodies to handle disputes arising from administrative decisions, e. g. to settle complaints from tax-payers. A contractual and discretionary element is present in these decisions.

Institutions of mediation and boards of arbitration abound, again with more of a contractual character than a court decision. To some extent the growth of such instruments is related to the growth in the economy as well as to the intervention of the government. But they are also devised to meet a demand from the parties involved and their wish to avoid some of the disadvantages of litigation, disadvantages which represent the dark side of the rule of law. Whatever the causes, all these conflict-resolving bodies relieve the regular courts in practical terms and lessen their ideological burden as protectors of the rule of law.

The promotional goals of law may appear most clearly in the increasing tendency to include ambitious programmatic statements, either in the enactment or in the form of a preamble (for changes in the norm structure cf. Friedman supra, Luhmann, Willke, Teubner infra). Important instances of this tendency are to be found in laws aimed at equality between the sexes as well as in legislation concerning protection of work environment, workers' participation and industrial democracy. Parts of such legislation correspond to the formalities required to meet the demand if litigation ensues. Relatively precise rules establish minimum rights of women in relation to employment and of workers in relation to environmental standards, admissible level of noise is an example.

But such statutes aim beyond the minimum and point to a maximum, or at least to an optimum. Such clauses are not applicable in adjudication. They may, however, be accompanied by prescription for procedures on the administrative level, avenues for the channeling of grass root initiatives (on modern proceduralization as a major trend in legal development see Wiethölter infra). Albeit not justiciable, such clauses are more than empty words. They provide legitimation in a fight for reform, but without offering any guarantee of the achievement of desired goals. They are not tailored to fulfill the traditional requirements of the rule of law. On the other hand, they show that law is more than a guardian of the ethical minimum in social life.

References

ANDENÆS, Johs (1945) *Grunnlov og rettssikkerhet.* (The Constitution and the Rule of Law). Bergen: Chr. Michelsens Institutt

AUBERT, Vilhelm (1983) *In Search of Law.* Oxford: Martin Robertson.

AUSTIN, John (1971) *The Province of Jurisprudence Determined.* London: Weidenfeld & Nicolson.

BENTHAM, Jeremy (1948) *A Fragment of Government and an Introduction to the Principles of Morals and Legislation.* Oxford: Basil Blackwell.

BLACKSTONE, William (1847) *Commentaries on the Laws of England.* 2nd edn. London: John Murray.

BOE, Erik (1979) *Distriktenes Utbyggingsfond.* (The District Development Fund). Oslo: Tanum-Norli.

DICEY, Albert Venn (1968) *Introduction to the Study of the Law of the Constitution.* London: Macmillan.

INTERNATIONAL COMMISSION OF JURISTS (1965) *The Dynamic Aspects of the Rule of Law in the Modern Age.* Geneva.

MACCHIAVELLI, Niccolò (1952) *The Prince.* New York: Mentor Books.

SCHWARTZ, Richard D. and Sonya ORLEANS (1973) "On Legal Sanctions," in Michael BARKUN (ed.) *Law and the Social System.* New York: Lieber-Atherton.

A Concept of Social Law*

François Ewald
Paris

What is the crisis of the Welfare State?[1]

The fact that, because of the economic crisis, the growth in social security expenditure has been accelerating while revenue has been declining? Not just that; but more deeply, the awareness that we members of the developed societies are now living within a new type of State. The very name given to it — "Welfare State" — suffices to show that as yet it has scarcely been considered in its positive aspects[2]. It denotes a State that, while no longer analysable in terms of the liberal model, is not seen as being in transition to a future socialist State either.

This hypothesis suggests a thorough reconsideration of the perspective from which both the institutions and the practices that characterise this new positive entity should be looked at. They ought no longer to be analysed as a mere set of measures aimed at correcting the harshness and injustices of a liberal State, but as the coordinates of a new type of political space with an internal logic of its own.

This is the case for *social law*, which is the term for the legal practices that typify the Welfare State. It ought not to be analysed as a series of particular provisions in the two areas of labour and social security, but as the formation of a new legal system from the viewpoint of sources as well as logic and modes of application. What makes social law is much more than the legalisation of objects or situations too long excluded from law. It is rather a process of transformation, able to move through the whole set of legal disciplines, from civil law to international law via administrative law; and this is a process of socialisation. This process amounts to the transformation of the political and governmental rationality linked up with the sociological conception of society that characterises the Welfare State. What changes the old legal system into the new one is the way of

* Translated from the French by Iain Fraser.

[1] The analysis below concerns the French example.

[2] The term "Etat-providence [Welfare State]" was the one used by liberals in the nineteenth century to deride the social reformers' projects.

thinking about the relationships of the whole to its parts, about the mutual relationships of individuals, about the whole they set up thereby; in brief, the way in which the social contract is conceived. Whereas the classical contract is analysed as an immediate relationship between sovereign, autonomous individuals, from which there emerges a State with powers limited to guaranteeing contracts arrived at more or less without it, in the social law concept ot the contract the whole has an existence of its own independently of the parties — it is no longer the State, but Society — and the parties can never undertake obligations directly, without passing through the mediation of the whole. "Socialisation" designates this way of conceiving of obligations, where the link between one individual and another is always mediated through the society they form, with the latter playing a regulatory, mediatory and redistributive role (cf. Broekman's argument regarding the unalterable character of the legal subject infra).

If social law is thought of both as a process of transforming the law, bound up with specific governmental practice, and as the development of a new type of law with a structure no longer the same as the old one, it takes on quite a different sense from that given to it by its reduction to labour and social security law alone. Firstly, because clearly the structure of social law does not necessarily belong to labour or social security law, for these types of law may well be conceived of as existing without obeying the rules of social law. Secondly, because the process of socialisation of law is not limited to this or that field of law, so that the two classical types of social law should be regarded as only two examples, no doubt noteworthy albeit special, of a law with a more universal application. For instance, it is clear that, as regards liability, the development of a *law on accidents* belongs directly to social law (Tunc, 1981). It will be seen as has been noted, that, as regards contract, the appearance of *consumer law* points to a general trend in contract law to move toward social law[3]. In public law, *environmental law* i.e. protection against nuisances and other pollution, has a structure typical of social law (Caballero, 1981). The same is true of international law, for everything connected with the new international economic order and *development law*. As we see, the process of socialisation of law is no respecter of the distinctions between legal disciplines. Furthermore, the foregoing enumeration does not bring out the importance of the area covered by these new practices from either the quantitative or the strategic viewpoint.

Social law has taken on a sufficiently wide range for one to cease regarding it as a *solution* brought in to fill the lacunae or shortcomings of classical law. It is time to approach it in its own positive being, having

[3] Cf., for France, the Law of 10 January 1978 on *protection of consumers against improper clauses*.

regard to the specific problems that its structure poses for the law itself. What is social law if thought of in its own positive being? What is its own logic? What are its limits?

I. Settlement

The fundamental law that set up labour law, and social law in general, is certainly the law of 9 April 1898 on the "liability for accidents to workers in the course of their work". It not only organised a system for compensating industrial accidents according to a principle of spreading burdens that opened the road to social insurance and the future social security provisions, but in doing this it was to go beyond the classical notion of a contract for the hire of services (Civil Code Art. 1780) and think of the wage relationship as a *labour contract*. An understanding of how this law was at all possible may be essential to an appreciation of the inherent structure of labour law and social law.

The law of 9 April 1898 first of all organises a system for compensating industrial accidents on the basis of more or less *a priori* employer liability. The head of the undertaking is declared liable for accidents that his workers may be subject to within the work relationship. This was not possible as long as the wage relationship was conceived of on the basis of the classical contract of hire – which involves only the exchange of work for a wage – and as long as accidents were analysed in the terms of Civil Code Art. 1382 ff., whose articulation of the concept of fault implied a principle of selection in compensating for damage. How then was the head of the undertaking to be made liable *a priori* for accidents at work? The legislator's fundamental idea in 1898 was to be, not the counterposition (i.e. to compensation based on fault) of compensation based on *risk*, as perhaps too often maintained by a particular legal tradition, but the conception of the solution to the problem as a *settlement* between conflicting rights: the worker would always be entitled to compensation, but this would no longer be in full but only according to a scale. The law of 9 April 1898 on work accidents is not so much a law laying down who is liable for accidents (whence its most singular status in liability law), as a law laying down a legal settlement. It is indubitably here that its profound novelty lies, which changes the very structure of the law. The legislator can in fact be seen as abandoning the consideration of an action or a piece of behaviour in itself, so as to sanction it in terms of what it ought to be. He does not say what should or should not be done. He thinks of the *relationship* between two activities, the one as essential as the other. Or rather, he defines the terms of their relationship.

This completely new way of thinking about the law is characteristic of social law. It in turn refers back to a transformation in political rationality without which this legal transformation is not itself comprehensible. This was the transition from the liberal political rationality that dominated the nineteenth century until the advent of the Third Republic to a rationality of the solidaristic type — though this term is not to be understood in the restricted sense given to it in the doctrine of Léon Bourgeois (1896). This transition from one political rationality to another was accompanied by a transformation in political doctrine itself — from a doctrine based on philosophy and morals to a sociology — and in the very notion of the *social contract*: the Rousseauist contract (for instance), articulated round the notion of exchange (and by the same token presupposing the principle of property, for all had to have something to bring into the initial contract) was succeeded by the practice of what may be called *solidarity contracts*, founded on ideas of fair distribution or equitable allocation of social burdens and profits (for the development of a similar view see Preuß infra). Specifically, the settlement was to define the general form of these "solidarity contracts", of which the labour contract was but one example.

The term settlement is defined in Article 2044 of the Civil Code: "a contract whereby the parties end a conflict that has arisen, or provide against one that may arise". There follow three propositions: a settlement is a *contract*; it presupposes a *dispute* or conflict; and finally, *mutual sacrifice*[4]. Does this correspond to the practice in social law?

1. The settlement as contract. Specifically, social law is a fundamentally contractual law, a law which to the extent that it presupposes relationships of interdependence and solidarity among all and each is brought to thinking that beyond or before any declared intent there is a contractual relationship of all with each. Everyone lives by others, profits by their activity and their labour and would be nothing without them; it is up to society to ensure that the burdens and profits produced by all these interdependent activities, which all need each other, are equitably distributed (see also Friedmann supra). This can be articulated only on the basis of solidarity contracts, the clauses of which are, at least in part, for 'society' to determine[5]. In labour law, this is precisely the way the labour contract is conceived of. The contributions of workers and of employers are not only equally necessary, but could not exist without each other. They are interdependent, and it is appropriate for the law that is to regulate this labour relationship to correspond accordingly to the relationship of solidarity that sets it up.

2. Second idea: settlement presupposes a conflict or dispute. To speak of social law as a law of settlements assumes that it is supported by a

[4] Cf. Planiol and Ripert (1954: 1011); Mazeaud and Mazeaud (1980: 1082); Boyer (1976); Giroud (1901); Rabinovics (1936); Boulan (1971).

[5] This is the doctrine developed by Bourgeois (1896), with his theory of "social quasi-contract".

philosophy or a sociology that makes objective the whole set of social relationships as a conflictual order. That was certainly the positivist conviction most widely shared at the end of the nineteenth century; it may be summed up in a term borrowed from G. Clemenceau: "The social fray"[6].

[6] Clemenceau (1895). Here are some extracts from the preface:

Is it not truly remarkable that humanity needed centuries of thought, observation, research, the thinking effort of the greatest minds, to arrive, with surprise after so many ages, at the discovery of the *struggle for existence?* ... (i).

The struggle for existence! The fight for life! As soon as the word was uttered, generalisations abounded, and the law of each and all appeared. What are bodies but a more or less stable balance of forces? The same law for living beings: with the difference that, in proportion to its sensitivity, each organism, big or small, oscillates, in joy or pain, between the forces of conservation and evolution that are in conflict. To maintain the resultant, which is life everything strives, everything toils, whether plant or animal or near-divine man. The one's law of development clashes with the other's. Conflict. Battle. There must be a victor and a vanquished. (ii-iii).

Death, everywhere death. The continents and the oceans groan with the frightening sacrifice of the massacre. It is the arena, the immense Colosseum of the Earth, where everything that could not live except by death bedecks itself with light and life in order to die. From the grass to the elephant, there is no law but the law of the strongest. In the name of the same law, the last-born of living evolution throws everything alive together into a monstrous hecatomb offered to the supremacy of his race. There is no pity. The flea comes back, and deals out death. The ungrateful soul repudiates the ancient solidarity of beings interlinked in the chain of transformed generations. The hardened heart is closed. Everything that escapes the premeditated, desired carnage kills its fellows for the delectation of the great barbarian. The glory of life's flowering is extinguished in blood, is reborn from it, founders therin anew. The arena, continually emptied, is continually refilled ... (vii).

Patience. Here comes the avenger. The law has said, "The strongest kills." And man has killed. Through him, everything that lives succumbs, and is born again only to expire at his hand ... (vii).

He does not cease. He killed the weakest of the animals. He kills the beaten man. He kills him to live too, to appease the inexorable hunger that cannot wait. Nothing is sacred but the need to live at any price. and so the dumb victim has bequeathed his vengeance to the executioner. Against the man that tortured the beast arises man torturer of man. He wields the sword, he rends, he racks, in the anticipated joy of the feast or in the intoxication of slaughter he kills, he eats ... (viii).

Since the first murder, symbolised by Cain, man has remained the murderer of man throughout the earth ... (ix).

And Clemenceau goes on:

"Slavery, serfdom, 'free labour' of the wage-earner, all these stages of progress rest on the common foundation of the defeat of the weaker and his exploitation by the stronger. Evolution has changed the terms of the fight, but under the changing appearances, the mortal combat remains. Taking over others' lives to aid one's own is, from the cannibal to the slaveowner or serfmaster, to the feudal baron, to the big or small employer of our own days, the whole effort of the most active. Man has barely ceased being an object of commerce when his labour becomes a commodity, and a one-sided contract still binds him with a solid chain ... (xv)

Such is the law of evolution.

The motor of history, the principle of evolution, lies in war: race war (A. Thierry), class struggle (Marx—Engels) and, more generally, struggle for existence (Malthus, Darwin)[7]. To be sure, the natural-law theorists too had seen the origin of society in war, the struggle of all against all (Derathe, 1970: 125). But there are two differences: 1. This war was not seen as a positive historical fact; it was, as Rousseau stressed, a rational construction aimed at realising what ought to be — in a certain sense retroactively — the nature of the State which was to put an end to it. 2. For the natural-law theorists, the state of society puts an end to the state of war. The passage from the state of nature to the civil state sets up a radical break in history, a before and after, not recognised by the theoreticians of social law, for whom war, struggle and confrontation are, no doubt for ever, constitutive of social life — as both the savage play of economic competition and the violence of social movements were to graphically illustrate in the nineteenth century[8].

The solidarist programme is based on the idea of conflictual interdependence of the various elements making up society[9]. Solidarist solidarity is qualified solidarity: solidarity in suffering , exploitation of the weak by the strong, solidarity included within relationship of hostility which solidarist policies aim at regularising and pacifying; the institution of a legal order does not constitute the act giving birth to society. On the contrary, the state based on the rule of law is, as it were, still to come. It is a guiding idea, an "idea with force" in the expression used by A. Fouillée, towards which one should seek to move, and which is no doubt progressively being realised, but the definitive arrival of which is infinitely postponed (Fouillée, 1920; Clemenceau 1895: XXII).

In connection with this conflictual, divided vision of the nature of society, social law arrives at the abandonment of the idea that the law ought to be the same for everyone; firstly, because this type of law could

[7] This positivist idea that social reality consists of conflict, that life is first and foremost struggle for life, was the most widespread one at the end of the nineteenth century. Cf. for instance Fouillée (1920); Prins (1910: 37); Tanon (1900: 94); Chamont (1927: 119). The story of this history of society, from antagonism to association, is expressed by the followers of Saint-Simon (1924). For a summary, one may consult Nicolet (1982).

[8] As was brought out very well in Emile Zola's work, especially *Germinal*, "The struggle for life is, then, the major principle of society;" comment by de Lattré (1975: 159).

[9] Cf. for instance Buisson (1908: 211). The realist positivism of L. Duguit, who sees in the State nothing but the relationship of forces "between rulers and ruled", proposes a similar "polemical" model of the political functioning of society. Cf. e.g. Duguit (1901: 265; 1928: 22) "Within the nation, a differentiation is effected between weak and strong, and it is this very fact that constitutes the State". Also Jèze, (1927: 165); Hauriou (1896: 84) has one paragraph headed "The universal contradiction"; "Social material is formed and lives in the midst of contradictions".

not be the expression of any kind of social compact, but solely of the interests of some class or group; and secondly, because in its abstract universality it can only be an instrument of oppression of the weak by the strong[10]. (cf. Aubert supra). The 1789 Declaration of Rights, with its ideas of liberty, equality and property could thus become, if not the statement of the bourgeoisie's rights of domination, at any rate an inadequate text needing completion through a list of economic and social rights[11]. The idea of social law is at the opposite pole from the idea of law put forward by Kant, namely a set of rational statements which, detached from desires, interests, and passions — even moral ones — might be the foundation for an order of coexistence of liberties. Social law, it is important to note, does not define an order on which, despite differences, agreement might be reached. On the contrary, it arrives at the dissolution of this idea: social law seeks to be an instrument of intervention which is to serve to compensate and correct inequalities, to restore threatened equilibria[12]. Social law is a law of preferences, a law of nonreciprocity, a law of positive discriminations[13]. If social rights can through abstractness of statement — right to life, to health, to housing, to development, etc. — look as if they may constitute common rights, it would be contradictory if in practice they gave the same rights to all.

Social law is seen as an political instrument, as an instrument of government. In defiance of the classical opposition between legality and appropriateness, governing becomes something for the sake of the law; rights are refused any autonomy. Special rights are distributed as so many counterweights. The right is no longer the general framework, the abstract rule within which special forces can be picked out and can enter freely into confrontation with each other in open interplay; it is instead now seen as a weapon, a strength, an advantage one should seek to have[14], and as being for government to distribute differentially to each in line with policy needs (for a parallel discussion on the transformation of 'rights' see Preuß infra). *The issue is no longer so much being in the right, as having rights.* By becoming objectified, the right becomes a force comparable with other forces: for

10 Cf. Thaller (1904: 478); Tessier (1904: 73); Gaudemet (1904: 975). Also Glasson (1880).

11 Karl Marx's criticism, (Marx, 1919) of the notion of equality of rights is familiar. A list of social rights can be found in Gurvitch (1944). This list cannot, be it noted, be exhaustive in principle, for social rights are unlimited. Cf. note 16 below.

12 Lacordaire's saying goes: "Between the strong and the weak, it is liberty that oppresses and the law that liberates".

13 This is the principle of thresholds and transfers in internal social law. It is what governs the measures taken in favour of the developing countries in international economic law. Cf. Carreau et al. (1980: 343).

14 The point is to secure the ability to make the coercive power of government act in one's favour, for one's own advantage. Cf. e.g. Ripert (1949: 27).

instance, the worker's *right* is balanced against the employer's power[15]. To the idea of the identity of right, social law opposes a multiplicity of differentiated rights. This is why one speaks of social rights in the plural[16].

[15] This is the principle of labour law, which, let us note, has no meaning as long as the conflict is kept on an individual level.

[16] Here are some extracts from the declaration of social rights, as formulated by Gurvitch (1944). These are not rights of man and citizen, but of producer and consumer:
The preamble to the Declaration should indicate that the French people: Convinced that the absence of guarantees of the rights of *producer* and *consumer* may compromise the effectiveness of the rights of man and citizen, has resolved solemnly to proclaim a *Declaration of Social Rights*, to complement and strengthen the Declaration of political and human rights, the validity of which is thereby reaffirmed. (91).
Art. IV – The social rights of producers consist in: the *right to work*, guaranteed to every healthy man or woman in accordance with their ability and training, and providing renumeration to assure them of the dignity of their condition; the *right of labour* to participate on an equal footing in the control and administration and in the profits of the firm, the occupation, the industry and the entire economy, in functional, regional, national and international aspects; the *right to leisure and to retirement*; the *right of trade-union freedom* and the *right to strike*.
Art. V – The social rights of consumers consist in: the *right to subsistence* in conditions worthy of man, freeing them from oppression through poverty; the *right to share in the distribution of the products of the national economy*; the *right to economic security, guaranteed by an independent insurance scheme, freeing them from threats and fear*; the *right of user associations to participate on an equal footing with producers in running services, firms and industries, and in the direction of the regional, national and international economy*; the *right of consumer cooperatives to participate on an equal footing with user associations in such direction*; the *right to freedom of cooperatives, user associations and their federations*.
Art. VI – All the wealth of the country, whoever be the owner, is subordinate to the Right of the Nation. Ownership confers obligations; it should in all its forms be considered as a social function. Any form of property contrary to the interest of the Nation, the interest of the National Economy (for instance ownership by trusts, cartels, banks and private insurance companies), and the rights of producer, consumer, man and citizen, is forbidden. Any ownership privilege contrary to the rights of labour and the dignity of man as such, as producer and as consumer or user, is abolished.
Art. VII – The social rights of man consist in: the *right to life* (rights of the mother, rights of childhood, rights of large families), *right to equality of the sexes*; *right to an education worthy of man*; *right of immigration and emigration*; *right fo free choice in joining or leaving at will the various economic, political and cultural associations*.
Art. VIII – All, producers and consumers, men and citizens, as individuals and as groups, shall have the capacity to defend their social right by appeal to the various types of court, and to ask the protection of groups and assemblages acting as counterweight to other groups and assemblages where they may also be members.
Failing these different means of protection, individuals and groups whose social rights have not been safeguarded shall have the ultimate recourse of the right of resistance to oppression.
Art. IX – The individual and collective liberty guaranteed by the social rights is limited only by the equal liberty of all other individuals and groups, by their fraternity and by the general political, economic and cultural interests of the Nation.
Art. X – Any abuse of individual and collective freedom that brings it into conflict

Social law does not complement the old civil law; it is not that it fills up lacunae in it. Its programme is no longer the same; social law introduces and organises the conflict of rights. Its novelty lies not so much in the content of the rights that it grants[17] as in *its way of bringing the conflict under the law*[18]. The law is no longer a factor external to the conflict whereby it may be resolved. The revolution introduced by social law is to make law, if not the sole issue, at least one of the principal one in disputes. It is this kind of inversion of the relationship between conflict and law which explains why social law can have no other form than that of settlements.

3. The final characteristic of the settlement is that it presupposes sacrifices and mutual concessions. This characteristic too is constitutive of the contract in social law and inseparable from the idea of solidarity. Since each exists only in relationship to all, no-one can claim to exist independently of others and demand the enjoyment and the exercise of absoute rights. Social law necessitates at least the limitation of individual sovereignties in line with the respect for mutuality. Social law asks each to compromise on what he might consider as his absolute right[19]. Social law is a great promotor of mutual concessions, between rich and poor, between individual interests and social groups, which relate precisely to these rights: civil rights (in particular that of ownership) and social rights[20]. Social law may

with the principles of equality and fraternity or with the various aspects of the general interest founded on the balance of contrary interests shall be suppressed. This suppression shall be the responsibility of each organisation, to the extent that it represents an aspect of the general interest. Should the separate action of one of these organisations be insufficient, their joint action shall be provided for. In the event of conflicts among these organisations, abuses shall be suppressed by the joint tribunals of various categories, and in the last instance by a Joint Supreme Court acting in the name of the National Community (94).

The sequel contains: — the *social rights of producers* (9 printed pages); the *social rights of consumers and users* (4 pages); the *social rights and duties bound up with ownership* (4 pages); the *social rights of man* (5 pages); to a total of 58 articles.

17 Which, from the viewpoint of content, are in the main nothing but the development of those represented by the object of charity of the past. However, the technique is different.

18 Perhaps it was the German jurist R. von Jhering who most radically erected conflict into the principle of law. Cf. von Jhering (1878; 1881; 1916).
This idea that the conflict is within the law (and not that the law serves to resolve conflicts) haunts whole edifice of social law. It was, no doubt, G. Ripert, who made it the basis of his legal philosophy, that gave it the most radical formulation. Cf. in particular Ripert (1918; 1955). More recently, cf. Javillier (1973: 157 a). Supiot (1979) has shown in masterly fashion how the conflict ran through labour law. His demonstration might be extended to many other areas.
As far as international law is concerned, cf. Bettati (1983: 124).

19 Cf. e.g. Fouillée, (1896: 261). Also, below, the study on the issues of abuse of law.

20 The model of such a settlement is supplied by the law of 9 April 1898 on accidents at work.

thus be seen as a great teacher of mutual tolerance. We must understand that what has to be tolerated is not only the difference, the otherness, the equal value of the other, but even, for our benefit, the restriction of our right. Social law is symbolic of a mass society in which, because space is running short, each must learn to put up with the other and his unavoidable encroachments. Putting up with each other because we rub shoulders with each other: that is the new meaning of tolerance.

Paradoxically, while the solidarity-based societies refuse to locate their birth in a primitive contract, the ideology of the contract dominates them much more than the old liberal society, about which, nevertheless, it has frequently been said that the contract constituted the basis of the political and legal system[21]. Henceforth there is to be a simultaneous realism and idealism on contract. The factor of solidarity has replaced the contract as the primitive form of the social bond. At the outset, there is no law, but instead war. And the history of humanity is one of advancing awareness of solidarity, of the need to substitute "arrangements" (Bourgeois, 1896), and therefore law, for the non-law of the struggle for existence[22]. Specifically, it is through the notion of contract that the fact of solidarity is held to become progressively aware of itself, and law to be substituted for force. The ideal, with one of its first formulations no doubt being that of Proudhon, continues, as we all know, to inspire our politicians[23]; it is that every social relation should take on the form of a contract. The contract becomes the bearer of all virtues. Thanks to its reign, justice will be achieved: "He who says contractual, says just"[24]. More, it is to be the instrument which allows one to contemplate the disappearance of the State and its constitutional oppressiveness: thanks to it, society could become

[21] From reading Portalis (1827), which contains (vol. II) a whole criticism of the idea of a primitive social contract, one may judge as rather excessive the retrospective theses of Gounot (1912: chap. 1), "La doctrine de l'autonomie de la volonté", concerning the imperialism of the contract at the beginning of the nineteenth century. The civil-law contract, which is a practical tool, has no need of a primitive social contract for it to render the services expected of it.

[22] The development of social law is steeped in a whole eschatology of the contract and of law. "The future form of societies will be contractual; their original form was not", Worms (1896); Durkheim (1950: 198), "Le droit contractuel"; this contractual progressivism has certainly been best developed by A. Fouillée (1896: 42) with the notion of "contractual organism". "Mechanism at the beginning, contract at the end, that is the whole history of society", (1896: 124); Leroy (1908: 202). There is a distant echo of this contractual dream in the speech by E. Maire (1983) for the CFDT: "We need a state power that lets the contractual outweigh the legislative".

[23] Mr J. Delor's contractual policy is after all nothing but the latest manifestation of this government programme. That it could seem new at the time proves nothing but our amazing powers of amnesia.

[24] Fouillée (1896: 410). It will be seen in the conclusion why this political rationality implied the equation justice = contract, and with what logical inconsistency.

self-managing, and social obligations could be the norms of liberty[25]. In brief, the generalised conversion of social relations into contractual ones would finally enable society to coincide with itself[26]. The contract would thus become the bottom line of politics, the privileged tool of a new social "management": beside planning contracts, solidarity contracts or economic contracts (Laubadère, 1979: 433), the civil code contract can certainly no longer lay claim to primacy, "take-off of the contractual concept", some say, with pompous certainty (Josserand, 1935: 333); in any case, an expansion of contract, which comes under very different legal provisions when the only "contractual" thing about it is the name[27]. But this is a magic word, the mere invocation of which might well give birth to the real thing, with all the virtues that surround it. Specifically, social-law contracts would not be able to be embraced by the too-rigid framework of the civil-law contract. They should, as it were, be variable-geometry, to be able to adjust to the diversity of social needs, to the constant state of flux of solidarity relationships. Strictly, one ought not any longer to speak of the social contract in the singular, but of flexible social contracts, manifold and amendable: in a word, the term "contract" no longer refers to a well-defined legal category, but to an order, the *contractual order*.

25 The theme of self-management, i.e. of the opposition of civil society to the State, dates back to Saint-Simon. It was taken up again by Proudhon (and Marx) and has become the political dream of the most rigorous theoreticians of social law, and even the objective assigned to the new type of law. This is, for instance, what is meant by by Duguit (1928: 58) with the notion of *public service*: "The State is not, as has been made out and as was for some time believed, a power that commands, a sovereignty; it is a cooperation of public services organised and controlled by governments". Cf. also the commentary by Pisier-Kouchner (1972: 141) and Leroy (1909: 202).
"Thus, the authoritarian State will be succeeded by the cooperative State, with officials instead of leaders. The notion of law will disappear; there will no longer be democracy in development, authority that expands and spreads; it will be occupational unionism that there will be, with the federalist rules that Proudhon was the first to observe. No more laws; in their place, contracts. And even if general rules seem needful to the freely associated, they can only be, as contemporary trade-unionists say, 'indicative decisions', no longer orders, but a sort of teaching, and in any case of a nature to accord with the Saint-Simonian theory."

26 This coinciding now constitutes the moral ideal that each should seek to attain. It is the principle of every social and moral obligation. It will be noted that it is a purely formal ideal, indifferent to the content of the will: one ought to will "evil" if it were thereby that society could coincide with itself. For then evil would be good, and there can be nothing better than the good. This is a curious formulation of the problem of ends, of the moral problem that characterises its *sociological* position. In a word, evil is transcendence.

27 Have we not heard the President of the Republic, Mr. Mitterand, launching the idea of a "contract of trust" between the State and managers? "L'enjeu" magazine, TF 1, 15/9/83.
On these "wildcat" usages of contract, cf. Boy (1979: 400).

Besides law of settlements and law of groups in conflict, social law may also be characterised as law of *interests*. It would assuredly be in no way false to see its birth in the chapter of the *Geist des römischen Rechts* where R. von Jhering, abandoning the definition of law in terms of will, declared, "rights are legally protected interests" (v. Jhering, 1888). This formulation contained the critique of the whole classical construction of law: critique of natural law, critique of subjective rights as absolute rights, in favour of a teleological vision of law where the individual will is made subordinate to a social purpose of the laws. This reversal is found explicitly in a disciple of Jhering's, L. Michoud:

> What the law seeks to protect when it sanctions will is not the act of volition in itself, but its content. One cannot will without willing *something*; it is that something which is the object of legal protection, not solely because it has been willed, but because it is in conformity with the ideal, whatever that be, that the legislator has formed of order and justice. The law protects not the will, but the interest represented by that will (Michoud, 1932: 105).

For the law, to objectify its subject as *will* is to enable it to will everything it can will, to offer it a sphere of autonomy and of impunity, and thus to refrain from controlling it from within, from the viewpoint of motives or of goals pursued; to objectify it as *interest* is, on the contrary, to make the laws, the State, the body that will have the power to determine what interests are worthy of protection, into the master of the law and of rights: it is to socialise the law[28].

Jhering's formula was put forward not only as a positivist recognition of a hitherto unrecognised truth. It had a programmatic value. Firstly, it implied a positive policy on the part of the legislator: to organise the protection of those interests judged by society as useful to protect. The task of the law was now to recognise socially legitimate interests and give them the means to fulfil their social function[29]. (See also Friedman supra). Inversely, in this new economy of the law no one could any longer hope for a social existence except by having the social legitimacy of the interest he might represent recognised. In other words, grouping, association, organisation or unionisation round identical interests became a necessity for all; and all the more so because interests, as we know, naturally exist in conflict. If in theory a sociological conception of society led to conceiving

[28] Does this socialisation of law through interests imply the disappearance of the "rights of the human person" in favour of "limitless power conferred on the State to determine what interests it deems worthy of protection"?, asks Michoud (1932: 110). No, he replies, opposing – (1932: 112) an "*objective* law" existing "outside the State, at least as power idea" to *positive* law. "The State," he says, "does not create nor concede the law; it recognises it and takes up its defence". But, he clarifies, in a concluding formula that states the problem in all its acuteness, "The whole difficulty is knowing what rights it *must* recognise".

[29] Thereby aiming to resolve the legal theory of corporate personality.

it as made up of simultaneously solidary and antagonistic groups, in practice the idea that rights were nothing but protected interests led each to identify his personal interest with some collective interest, and therefore to group and to unionise[30]. A law of interests is unavoidably a law of groups; and for these groups the law becomes a fundamental stake, to the extent that it will decide on their existence and on the share of the general interest that will go to the interests that they represent.

To be sure, "interest" already had a legal existence; there was the familiar opposition and articulation between general interest and particular interest[31]. But the new interest approach overthrew that old allocation. The interests that now had to be recognised were of a different type; they were "collective" interests.

> Man is a social being. His destiny can be fulfilled only if he associates his efforts with those of his fellows. Isolated in the face of nature, he can achieve nothing through his own individual strength alone. For humanity to reach the degree of civilisation we have seen him attain, what was needed was the collective, continued work of successive generations. If the law is to meet humanity's needs, to find the formula that most exactly expresses the relationships that exist in human society, it must not only protect the individual's interest, but also guarantee and elevate to the dignity of subjective rights the *collective and permanent interests of human groupings*. (Michoud, 1932: 115).

On the one hand, the collective interest tends to absorb an individual interest which itself no longer has social existence except as the individualisation of a collective interest[32]. (For an opposing view cf. Broekman infra). On the other, the collective interests obey a logic which leads to the dissolution of the notion of the general interest understood as the common interest of a group[33]. The collective interest cannot be reduced to the idea of particular interest; the principle of recognising it socially

30 The programme can be found formulated by Duguit (1908: 121): trade-unionism is the organisation of this amorphous mass of individuals; it is the formation within society of strong, coherent groups with a clear legal structure, made up of men already united by community of social task and occupational interest — let it not be said that it is the absorption, the annihilation of the individual by the trade-union group. By no means. Man is a social animal, as was said long ago; the individual, then, is all the more man for being more socialised, I mean for being part of more social groups. I am tempted to say that it is only then that he is a superman. The superman is not at all, as Nietzsche made out, he who can impose his individual all-powerfulness; it is he who is strongly tied in to social groups, for then his life as social man becomes more intense."

31 Cf. e.g. Rousseau (1762: book II, Chap. I) "That sovereignty is inalienable". Commentary in Derathé (1970: chap. I), "Theory of sovereignty" (248), Appendix III: "the notion of legal personality" (397).

32 When indeed the individual interest and the collective interest remain legally separate.

33 "It must be understood from that that what makes the will general is not so much the number of votes as the common interest that unites them." See Rousseau (1762: book II, chap. IV).

presupposes that it is the bearer of the general interest, that it "represents" it, and that therefore the general interest is reached through the recognition of collective interests, the solidarity and conflictual interplay of which will enable it to be arrived at. Once society is conceived of as divided into groups and the possibility of an identity of interest between particular interests has faded into the fact of polemical solidarity, the general interest takes the form of collective interests. The general interest cannot then any longer exist as a totalising principle, but only as a compounding of particular interests with respect to each other, bearers though they all equally be of the general interest. The general interest can no longer be defined by a content alleged to be special to it; it is a form, a goal, namely the maintenance of the interplay of solidarities. And the general interest, understood as the interest of the State, is itself no more than a particular interest vis-à-vis the collective interests. So much so that the proposition according to which the particular interest must yield to the general interest loses its meaning. We arrive at a logic of interests which is no longer that of the subsumption or subordination of the particular in or to the general, but of balance, of equilibrium, and therefore of arbitration[34]. This transformation of the notion of general interest has been pithily put by G. Vedel, who explains that

> the public (or general, since it amounts to the same thing) interest is not the sum of the particular interests. That would be absurd, for the public interest would then be the sum of the interest of alcohol producers and that of victims of alcoholism ... The public interest is not different in essence from the interest of persons or of groups; it is an *arbitration* among the various particular interests (Vedel, 1980: 414).

The societies based on solidarity are, in theory and practice, organised so as to be able continually to compromise with themselves. This is on the one hand a sociological objectification of society, segmenting it into groups, classes and orders endowed with genuine social existence — individuals never being anything but an individualisation of the group from which they draw the essence of their being[35]. On the other hand, it is a legal recognition of groups as legal subjects. Social law, as is well known, is a law of groups, of associations, of bodies corporate; in particular, a law of occupational groupings[36]. Though one might maintain that the series of

[34] Which is why we speak of "general interests" in the plural, without asking whether the very notion of general interest does not imply the singular. The general interests are themselves in conflict and need to be arranged in a hierarchy, cf. Linotte (1975).

[35] "Society is not composed directly of individuals. It is composed of groups of which the individuals are members." See Worms (1903: 63). On the idea of "group democracy" cf. Vedel (1947).

[36] Cf. Gurvitch (1932: 11) which precisely defines social law as that law which is autonomously secreted by social groups: "social law is the autonomous law of communion whereby every active, concrete, real totality that embodies a positive value is objectively integrated". Also Leroy (1913); Paul-Boncour (1901); Morin

public freedoms that were to be recognised at the end of the nineteenth century — trade-union freedom, freedom of the press, freedom of assembly and association — owes its existence less to the ineluctable advance of liberty alleged to be the essence of the Republic than to a need of a political and constitutional nature; the setting up of the new political rationality known by the name of "democratic government"[37] would not have been possible otherwise. How, indeed, can one imagine the introduction of a law of groups without collective freedoms, that is, without giving them the means to act?[38]

This dream of a truly sociological administration of society, of a political economy that is social, decentralised, associative (Brice, 1892), federalist (Paul-Boncour, 1901) and syndicalist[39], in which contractual order would take the place of State sovereignty, brought with it a whole series of legal problems that are characteristic for social law. Among these are the problem of the *legal personality* of groups, of their capacity to act legally, of the definition of the interests they are fitted to defend, the problem of their *representativity*, of their capacity to express the group's interests, and finally the problem of their normative power both over their members and over those they are held to represent[40]. This means the pursuit of a whole range of legal issues, about which one cannot but say that they are at the opposite pole from any revolutionary conceptions or assumptions[41]. These issues,

(1920). See also the two great masters of public law, Hauriou and Duguit. "The starting point is that, more than other branches of law,social law is close to the practical reality it is built on; a reality constituted by the existence of *social groups* in situations of conflict over questions affecting their conditions of existence." Fournier and Questiaux (1982: 699).

37 The term "democratic government" was currently employed at the end of the nineteenth century to denote this type of government, held to constitute an alternative to liberal government. Cf. Nicolet (1982: part 1).

38 One might perhaps say that, as the individualism of the Revolution went via the recognition of individual liberties, so the sociologism of the late nineteenth century implied that of collective liberties.

39 It is in fact the trade union that represents the political form in which, at the time, the achievement of the organisation of civil society by itself was imagined. Cf. Paul-Boncour (1901),subtitle "Study on compulsory trade-unionism"; Gurvitch (1937); Morin (1920), pleaded for compulsory trade-unionism; "The growth of associations and foundations is the most characteristic phenomenon of our age, and shows to what extent the genuine right of social solidarity is penetrating the minds of all. The social and political future is there", Duguit (1901).

40 The basic work here is that of Michoud (1932).

41 Such as may have been expressed through the *Le Chapelier* law. This phenomenon of the reconstitution of "class law" could not fail to arouse legal thought. Views differed widely: see Dabin (1938: 66), is more than favourable. Josserand (1937: 1), fears that by binding a man to his occupation one may be loosening the bond linking him to his country (4); he is further afraid that its development may be a seed of civil war (4).

as one can see in connection with consumer, environment or compensation problems, have lost nothing of their topicality[42]. Nor is this surprising, since the political imagination has hardly changed since the turn of the century.

The new contractual order could not be satisfied with mere recognition of these new legal subjects, the groups. It further implied development of those practices by which "society" was continually able to compromise with itself. In principle, settlement excludes the trial, i.e. a mode of conflict resolution where the law says that one party is in the right and the other in the wrong. The policy of settlements or compromises must be accompanied by forms of conflict resolution outside the courts, more in line with the solidarist idea that conflicts structure the social order, that conflict does not mean contradiction (rather interdependence), that the rights of the one are just as worthy of respect as those of the other and that therefore recognition of one set of rights need not exclude others', and that what has to be reached through a settlement is not the crushing of one by the other, but the affirmation ot their solidarity.

This gives rise to the fundamental practice of *collective bargaining and agreements*, initially encouraged and regulated in the area of labour, but with much more general application[43]. This is a major practice of social law,

[42] A most recent example is furnished by the law of 22 June 1982, known as the Quillot law.

[43] Collective bargaining, like the collective agreement that concludes it, indubitably constitutes the major politico-legal innovation of the century. It encapsulates the issues referred to by the term democratic government.
Its prehistory would take us back, no doubt, to the demand for a "tariff" by the silk-weavers of Lyons in 1830-31. That scale was to be declared illegal by the administration of Louis-Philippe. Cf. Levasseur (1867).
The first official experiment with a collective agreement was presumably the wage agreements in the mines in Nord and Pas de Calais, known as the "Arras agreements", concluded in 1891 between the miners' union and the Nord and Pas de Calais Collieries Committee. On the origins of that agreement cf. Gillet (1973: 161). The practice, born in the area of work, continues to dominate our political imagination, as shown, in particular, by the recent Auroux laws, esp. the law of 13 November 1982. Cf. Auroux (1982: 30): "The contractual policy must become the favoured practice of social progress ... negotiation [must] be made the normal mode of operation in social relations" (31); "In the parliamentary debates, the Labour Minister again stressed the philosophical foundations of the reforms, which represented 'two ideas that can bring freedom, solidarity and responsibility; bargaining and the contractual policy'," cited by Javillier (1984: 351). Also Supiot (1983: 63).
These ideas of the Minister's were echoed by the trade-unionist Murcier (1982: 532): *Negotiation, the regulator of change.*
For the CFDT change constitutes a dynamic that must be regulated by negotiation. It is the best way of adapting change to the diversity of situations it has to be applied to and the levels on which it has to be achieved. Negotiation also enables all who will be concerned by the decisions being taken to be consulted. There is no better

but not the only one it has sought to promote: apart from settlements in the civil sense of the term[44], there are the practices of *conciliation, arbitration and mediation*[45]. From collective bargaining to mediation, there is a whole

way of starting from solid reality, and also of arousing intelligence, imagination and creativity, in an ever more complex society. At a more general level, negotiation is essential for any society that wants to avoid despotism, whether political or economic. It is necessary to the development of social life, to the overcoming of economic challenges, to changing the content of work; in short, to the participation of men and women in the construction of a new society.
Working men and women have their role to play in change. They must become its movers.
This vision of affairs means that, for change, it is not solely the law that is to be relied on. The temptation is great when there is a left majority in Parliament; it seems to make everything go faster and farther than through collective negotiation.
Certainly the law's role in the institution of new individual and collective freedoms is irreplaceable; certainly it is for the law to define the social minimum of protection guaranteed to every worker, whatever firm he works in. But workers and unions must be allowed to intervene themselves to change the situation they find themselves in. The law must guarantee the necessary free space for their interventions."
The question has for more than a century been the object of a considerable literature. An important bibliography will be found in Despax (1966).
Note should be taken of an important issue of the journal Pouvoirs, 1980/15, devoted to *negotiation*, in particular the articles by Merle (1980) and Raynaud (1980), which show that negotiation sets up a legal order of its own, since the object of a piece of bargaining is at least as much the (formal) law that will govern it as the content of the decisions taken. It will thus be understood how the contractual policy and collective bargaining can be put forward as an *alternative* form of social regulation to the classic democratic representative rule. But there is the difficulty — or advantage — that whereas in classical democracy the rule is laid down once and for all (it is the constitution), in the case of an order of negotiation the rule is itself perpetually negotiated and is the object of negotiation.

44 The economic importance of which seems considerable, in both civil and administrative law; in 1962, out of 12 000 tax offences, 11 790 were settled; in customs matters, 95% of disputes are settled. (Cf. Boulan, 1971: 5).
Compensation for traffic injury to the person is mainly through settlements; cf. Commaille (1956: 214). As far as compensation for material damage arising out of the same accidents is concerned, it is by settlement all through, because of the knock-for-knock agreements among insurance companies.
On the law of administrative settlements see Delvolvé (1969: 103).

45 These practices were an integral part of the social programme of the Second Republic. Cf. Pic (1919: 1041). On the law of 27 December 1892 on optional conciliation and arbitration, (1084). On the Millerand project for a system of contractual if not compulsory arbitration (1098). On the historical background to these practices see Perrot (1974: 193).
The Popular Front declared arbitration compulsory in matters of collective labour dispute (law of 31 December 1936 and 4 March 1938). Cf. Laroque (1938: 365); Savatier (1938: 9). Laroque (1953: 468) stressed the interdependence of the practices of collective bargaining and compulsory arbitration, while emphasising that compulsory arbitration had certainly become unconstitutional with the Constitution of 27 October

range of practices aimed at allowing "society" continually to reach a compromise with itself, to bring forth its own law, its own normativity (see Willke's "relational programmes" infra). These practices, made compulsory in a law of settlements, bring along the dream of a self-managing society. And as we know, in the main the "new" rights of workers adopted after May 1981 are aimed directly at strengthening them[46].

The policy of settlement has not solely had the effect of creating new forms of conflict resolution; it was also to transform the old ones. It will be seen how, with the increased use of the equity approach in judgments — characteristic of the logic of social law — the procedural forms themselves have tended to align themselves on the model of the settlement[47]. But in a system of social law, the practice of settlements and the establishment of the contractual order remain fundamentally within the powers of parliament: if the law is tending to take on the form of a settlement, the settlements must take on the formal garb of the law[48]. The decisive reason for this is that, since social law is no longer referred to a rule of abstract, external and intangible justice — in a word, to a primitive

1946, which states: "The right to strike shall be exercised within the framework of the laws regulating it".
The *Auroux Report* (1981) stresses the organic need for recourse to mediation if collective bargaining is itself to succeed (61). It is well known that the Minister of Labour did not hesitate to call on the mediation of M. Dupeyroux in two major labour disputes (Citroën, Talbot). *Le Monde* for 22 March 1983 also states that M. Dupeyroux had been given a sort of mediation mission in a dispute between UNEDIC and the staff of ASSEDIC. This new appeal to mediation was incorporated in the law of 13 November 1982.
These practices are obviously not tied down to the work situation. But they are to one type of law. There is every chance of their invading other areas; let us recall in this connection the institution of *medical conciliators* following the MacAleese report. And the report sent by P. Bellet, Honorary President of the Court of Appeal, in 1982 to the Keeper of the Seals on reform of traffic accident compensation proposes the institution of a conciliation body (34).

46 For the programme, see J. Auroux, *Les droits des travailleurs*, Paris, 1982. For the achievements, cf. in particular the law of 28 October 1982 on the development of staff representative institutions; law of 15 November 1982 on collective bargaining and the settlement of collective labour disputes.
This legislative series has been the object of numerous commentaries, in particular in the journal *Droit Social*, No. 4, April 1982 and No. 5, May 1982.
A colloquium was held on the evaluation of the "newness" of these reforms.

47 See, below. It may further be noted that the Conciliation Boards (set up by Napoleon in 1806) for settling individual differences between employers and workers had from the outset a settlement set up. Cf. Pic (1919: 1063); Supiot (1983: 342).

48 Which is why the hypothesis that the development of civil society could go only against the State is at least disputable. It may equally well be maintained, and the history of the last century would tend to testify, that social or sociological administration of society instead implies ever more State. G. Ripert in particular has sought to show this.

social contract — but to "society", to division, to conflict and the ever-present clash of interests therein, it is only a constitutional body like parliament, where "society" is held to be represented as a whole, that can decide which "collective" interests ought from time to time to be given legal personality, can render the necessary arbitration in terms of the general interest, and at the same time decide which settlements are legitimate, and which necessary and therefore to be made compulsory — even if that affects certain particular interests[49]. While the social partners can, no doubt, thanks to collective bargaining, determine the terms of contract as far as they are concerned, only parliament is in a position to define general social obligations concerning the population in relation to itself. This is the case, for instance, with the right to health: what should the amount of that right be? Who is to pay for whom? According to what rule of justice? Only parliament is in a position to decide. Some people have been able to entertain the dream of a system of generalised settlements enabling the development of a continually negotiated legal order that would allow one to create the economy of the law[50]. They forgot that the segmentation of society into groups, and indeed the very principle of collective bargaining, impose as their necessary correlative a body that, if not central, is at least federal, and represents the interests of society as such.

Correlatively, the fact that the law is no longer so much the expression of the general will as the form taken on by the endlessly renewed settlements of society with itself profoundly changes its economy. The law no longer conceals that it is at once the effect and the prize of particular interests in conflict. Its value is no longer related so much to its constitutional status as to its technical advantages as an instrument for the sociological administration of society[51]. That legislation is class legislation is no longer a characteristic that condemns it; instead, it defines the new legislative

[49] It has several times been noted that the law was tending, in the most diverse areas, to take on the explicit form of settlements; to be sure, one thing always to be mentioned is the law of 9 April 1898 on work accidents; but more recently, laws tending to make settlement compulsory: compulsory arbitration, 1936-38; compulsory collective bargaining in the Auroux laws in the work area; law of 1976 on protection of the environment. In quite another context, the law of 10 July 1975 on divorce. Cf. Carbonnier (1979: 151); Commaille (1982: 47); Commaille and Marmier-Champexois (1978:205). More recently, cf. the above-mentioned law of 22 June 1982, known as the Quillot law.

[50] Let uns mention among these dreamers Gurvitch (1931; 1932); Morin (1920); Paul-Boncour (1901).

[51] Leroy (1908: 330) noted this already for legislative practice at the beginning of the century. He explained that this shift in the characteristics of the law ought to be thought of in relation to the shifts in the conception of law in the exact sciences. The law would become "experimental".

arrangement[52]. There is no longer anything but group interests jockeying to assert themselves as being the general interest[53]. The law thus becomes particular in source, as well as in its object (see also Heller infra). The positive law will depend on the relative strength of the groups attacking or asserting it. "The law," in G. Ripert's expression, "becomes the law of the strongest"[54]. We are in a system of *compromises*[55]. This amounts to saying that the enactments of social law must not be expected to obey over-rigorous plans or too rational programmes; the fine edifice with a planning rationality that had seduced its advocates is liable to become rapidly transformed, in terms of the interests present, into a composite structure. The history of social security from social insurance to the abandonment of the single fund in favour of a multiplicity of occupational schemes and special arrangements supplies a good example of this[56].

In terms of this new programme where the law can no longer be conceived of as an immutable and intangible legal principle but as an arrangement, an ever-revisable compromise among groups and interests in conflict, the problem ought to be posed of parliament's capacity to do the job it now has to perform. Should the law of numbers (one man one vote) not be replaced with more adequate representation of the true social actors: groups, unions and associations with their own interests? These problems, of *proportional representation* in the broad sense, have been haunting the organisation of democracy for a century, in France for example, giving rise in 1925 to the institution of the National Economic Council, which has since become the Economic and Social Council[57].

52 "Have we entered the age of merciless struggle for existence, where those most in favour with the legislator abuse this to shift the game in their favour, thanks to the guilty compliance of the laws?" Waline (1969).

53 Cf. e.g. Ehrlich (1971); he shows how the interplay of interest groups intensified with the Welfare State (174).

54 Ripert (1949: 28) also Ripert (1948) "Modern France is a democracy which universal suffrage makes force of numbers rule" (2) ... "The laws have become special and temporary; many are only improvised solutions to difficulties of ever-changing aspect" (24) ... "The law is no longer anything but the momentary representation of the success of a part of a man" (35); Ripert, (1955: 92).

55 Leroy (1908: 329); "The laws are peace treaties between various forces", Ripert (1946: 6); "The law is almost always the result of a compromise between opposing forces," Ripert (1955: 83). A remarkable example of the *constitutional* character of the compromise in the contemporary legal system is supplied by the preamble to the constitution of 13 October 1946. Cf. Rivero and Vedel (1947).

56 On Social Insurance, i.e. the amendment of the 1928 law by the 1930 one under pressure form the internalist and mutualist farmers, cf. Durand (1953: 79). On Social Security and the attack on the principle of the single fund, cf. Galant (1955: 105), and Laroque's preface to that work (xv—xvi).

57 This problem, as old as the institution of universal suffrage, has given rise to a considerable literature; cf. e.g. Benoist, (1899); Duguit (1924: 667); Cruet (1907: 321).

If the notion of the settlement provides a description of the practices of social law, the general form of the obligations of the new legal order, it does not suffice for its characterisation. One might, indeed, very well maintain that the law is by nature a matter of compromise[58]. This idea was given expression by the authors of the Civil Code at the conclusion of their work: not only should the practice of settlement be encouraged, as a far superior means of conflict resolution to the trial[59], but that the signal merit of this new code is that it constitutes the great settlement thanks to which the French people, hitherto legally and socially divided, would be able to find the peace of coinciding with itself: "How can one pronounce this word [settlement]," says the Albisson Tribunal, "without one's mind going back with lively satisfaction to the proximate achievement of our Civil Code, which is itself the greatest, most useful and most solemn settlement that any nation has ever shown the world?" (Fenet, 1827: 120).

If then social law can be described as the law of settlement, that does not suffice to characterise it. It will be noted that, for its authors, the reason why the code can have this function of settlement is that it formulates a *law* (Fenet, 1827: 114). An order of settlements does not, as might seem, exclude the law; on the contrary, it calls for it (see also Luhmann infra). Let us, indeed, imagine an order of settlements not regulated by law: instead of making possible the desired social pacification, it would immedediately produce the opposite effect. It would be merely so many opportunities for the strong to abuse strength and exploit the weakness of the weak. An

A good presentation of all these problems will be found in de Laubadère (1979: 136). On the Economic and Social Council cf. Rivero (1947: 35).

Let us recall finally that the 1969 referendum, the "no" at which brought about General de Gaulle's departure, related to a reform of the Senate to merge it with the Economic and Social Council.

58 Let us think of the judgment(s) of Solomon. Carbonnier (1979: 278).

59 Bigot-Préameneu speaks of it as the "most desirable of all the means of putting an end to disputes. Each party then abandons all prejudice, and in good faith and with the desire for conciliation balances the advantage that would result from a favourable verdict with the loss that a condemnation would bring; it sacrifices part of the advantage it might hope for, so as not to suffer all the loss it might fear ... which one cannot in coming to terms, for whatever sacrifice that imposes, the gain in return is the greatest of all goods, namely tranquillity ... Better a bad settlement than a bad trial", cited by Giroud (1901: 7).

And the Albisson tribunal declares that "settlements deserve the favour of the law, whose final end must be to maintain the peace among the citizenry", and continues, "the usual effect of settlements is to stifle the spirit of contention, fatal to the repose of society; to reunite long-divided families, to renew old friendships; and the more this touching sight might be repeated, the more its influence might be felt on the agreeableness and smoothness of society", Fenet (1827: 113).

Accordingly, the law's function is not to permit trials, but to avoid them. Perhaps this is also what is meant by J. Carbonnier (1979: 18) in speaking of case-law and courts as pathological law.

order of settlements, if it is not immediately to cancel itself out in injustice, needs to be regulated by a system of law. And it may be said that social law found its first historical bases in the recognised need to legalise "wild", improper, inconscionable or burdensome settlements[60]. Even in an order of settlements, not all settlements can be either possible or permissible. How then is the choice to be made between good and bad settlements? How, on what principle, is one to select, to distinguish? All these questions are raised by the problem ot the settlement logic of social law, i.e. the problem of its very identity. At bottom, it is nothing else but a recasting in other terms of the old problem, unavoidable in study of law, of tracing the *boundary* between what is proper and what cannot be: the problem of the demarcation line between the just and the unjust.

II. Balance

As for social law's logic of settlements, the answer is in no doubt. This whole enquiry has never stopped coming up against the key notion of the new law, the one whereby lawyers themselves apprehend and plan the transformations of legal practice: the notion of *balance*. What principle does the new law of liability obey, if not the concern for a balance to be restored between the victims of damage and those responsible?[61] What governs the discriminatory provisions of labour law, or social security policy, if not again the idea of balance?[62]. What is the key notion of environment law? (Caballero, 1981: 93) What is the concern dominating consumer law? (Ghestin, 1980: 138) In penal law, what concern does victim compensation policy pursue?[63] In each and every case, the idea of a balance, to be maintained, arranged or restored.

Let us be clear that when, from the late nineteenth century on, lawyers use the term "balance", it is obviously not to designate the vague idea, tautologically contained within that of justice and claimable by any legal system, that being just means keeping an equal balance between two parties[64]. The term is instead used diacritically, to draw a distinction. There are two major usages. Firstly, a philosophical one, in connection with the

[60] This is obviously the case with work accidents and the law of 9 April 1898. More generally, the practice of settlements, bound materially to increase with the growth in accidents, called for regulation by legislative intervention. Cf. e.g. the note by T. Bouzat, under cass. 14 March 1934, S. 1935, 1, 377.

[61] Cf. Savatier (1951: 1); Stark (1972: 34). The theory of the "guarantee" developed by that author rests entirely on the idea of equilibrium. For a more general viewpoint cf. Husson (1947: 127, 335).

[62] As is implied by the notions of transfer of distribution.

[63] Cf. the *Law improving protection for victims of offences*, National Assembly, 6 April 1983.

[64] Still less the idea that a "just" judgment must be balanced, weighed, without excess, and be a just mean.

foundations of law, which are now set side by side with a sociology: the notion of balance designates both what the social logic is and what it ought to be. It is used in this first sense both by Proudhon, and by M. Hauriou, R. Saleilles or G. Gurvitch, to name but a few[65].

But it is mainly found used in a second, more legal and more polemical, sense: to designate what constitutes the logic of a law that has finally arrived at a social self-awareness. It is, then, the concern which is held to govern, and rightly so, the practices of social law. This could make the new law of obligations "just" where classical civil law proves "unjust".

We shall give two examples.

This principle, which might be called the principle of the *balance of interests arising*, ought to guide the jurisconsult in his interpretation of the law just as it guides the legislator or the customary bodies whenever, lacking an adequate and legitimate private arrangement, it is necessary to enact with authority the rules of conduct that constitute the positive legal organisation. The latter's object is, in fact, none other than to give the most adequate satisfaction to diverse rival aspirations, whose just conciliation seems needful in order ro realise the social objective of humanity. The general means for securing this result consists in recognising the interests arising, evaluating their relative strength, weighing them, as it were, in the scales of justice with a view to ensuring the preponderance of those more important in accordance with some social criterion, and finally, establishing among them the supremely desirable balance[66].

The concept of subjective right has benefitted from this profound renewal, the practical reality of which it attests; of old, such rights as ownership, *patria potestas* or marital authority were thus considered as powers conferring on their holders absolute prerogatives, with no effective reciprocation. They were seen as unilateral relationships putting all the benefits on one side and all the duties on the other. Then that simplistic, worn conception grew old; if it gained a new lease of life under the impetus of the French Revolution and through the intermediary of the Declaration of the Rights of

[65] Cf. Proudhon (1930: 298): "How the idea of the principle of balance is given us by the opposition of interests"; (vol. II, chap. VI, 74): "economic balances". G. Guygrand, in his introduction to the work, writes, "If equality is the moral name for justice, its scientific name, as an objective reality, is *balance*. Balance, symbolised by the pans of the scales, is a constant concern for Proudhon. His whole philosophy is a system of economic, political, national and international balances ... Balance is order, is peace. All social disorders come from breaches of that fundamental law", On Proudhon as founder of social law cf. Gurvitch (1932: 327). Hauriou (1896: 27, 187, 257; 1929: 34) "The social order"; "The viewpoint of order and balance", cf. Hauriou (1909). for an overall view see Sfez (1966: 7) "The theme of balance or movement, the fundamental theme of the entire work". Saleilles: "Social reality is in the mystery of *counterbalancing antinomies*", quoted by Gurvitch (1932: 633).

[66] Cf. Gény, (1919: 167). Also Gény (1922: 50):
"At bottom, the law finds its own, specific content only in the notion of the just, a primary, irreducible and indefinable notion, implying essentially, it would seem, not only the elementary precepts of not wronging anyone (*neminem laedere*) and assigning to each his own (*suum cuique tribuere*), but the profounder idea of a balance to be established between interests in conflict, with a view to assuring the order essential to the maintenance and progress of human society."

Man and Citizen, which bears the stamp of an extreme individualism, it has for years now fallen into ever more perceptible discredit. Henceforth, rights are considered as synallagmatic relationships, imposing on their holders, in compensation for the prerogatives they assure them, more or less numerous and far-reaching obligations; as relative, social values, to be used in accordance with the spirit of the institution. *The idea of the balance of rights has supplanted the dogma of sovereignty* (Josserand, 1936: 160).

These are two examples, from among many others[67], which testify that the notion of balance designates very precisely what seems to us capable of characterising a system of law: its *rule of judgment*, that is, the type of rationality whence law and jurisprudence proceed, and whereby, at a given moment, the justice of a judgment is identified[68]. It is through the notion of balance that the endeavour has been made (and is still being made) to understand the difference between the rule of judgment of social law and the old rule of civil law, still aligned on liberal political rationality, on notions of fault, will, freedom; in a word, of responsibility.

The notion of balance functions on two levels. First, a political level: balance describes the political rationality that corresponds to the practice of settlements. This rationality defines a policy of law wherein the latter appears as an element in the sociological administration of society. There is a series: *conflict — balance — settlement*. On the basis of a society conceived of as naturally conflictual, where the protagonists of conflicts are considered as equally deserving of respect because all contribute to the common effort, settlement and balance become two commutative notions, referring back to each other (Prins, 1895: 33). But over and above this political logic, the notion of balance also describes the structure of a type of law, a legal logic, or rationality: social law's logic of judgment. That is, that whereby one may distinguish what may or may not be proper — the criterion of *juridicity* — and also the content and system of the rights to be accorded. This is why, after a certain point, it was to be "discovered" that there were gaps

[67] The idea had been expressed with great force by von Jhering (1916): "The idea of justice represents the balance imposed by society's interest between an act and its consequences for the person doing it ... legal dealings bring about this balance in the most perfect way. Thanks to them, each contracting party receives back the equivalent of what he has given ... ".
It can be used just as well to express the rule of judgment of criminal liability; cf. in addition to R. Saleilles and L. Josserand, already cited, Teisseire (1901), which on p. 170 gives this formula for the liability: "All damage must be allocated between perpetrator and victim according as each has caused it by his act"; also Ripert, (1902: 330); for the demand for a new contractual justice, cf. esp. Maury (1920); Pérot-Morel (1961).
The idea of balance was to be put forward explicitly by the Standard school as what ought to supply the rule of legal judgment: Al Sanhoury (1925: 7); Stati (1927: 159). From a more general viewpoint, cf. Husson (1947: 335); Henriot (1960: 32).

[68] Cf. Sfez (1966: 104), gives a good example: M. Hauriou's analysis of the Council of State ruling of 17 July 1925, "Bank of France staff association".

in the civil code and that there was a need to set up a whole series of social rights. The traditional idea that social law is never anything but the historical product of workers' struggles leads one to overlook the fact that, for these struggles to have an effect on the law, a transformation of legal rationality itself was called for. It must be repeated: what characterises social law is not so much the proliferation of legislative and regulatory measures that go more or less beyond the common law, as the fact that such measures have been taken and have been deemed necessary. It is the rationality of social law that explains the content of social-law legislation[69]. (Cf. Heller infra).

It will have been understood that the point is not to claim that one had to await the end of the nineteenth century for issues of balance to appear in policy. Everyone knows that the notion is an old one, used by the Greeks in both philosophy and medicine (Svagelski, 1981), that it has a whole political presence among the moderns both in international politics, with the issues of the "European balance" (Livet, 1976), and in internal matters with the problem of the separation of powers (Montesquieu, 1948), and that it constitutes one of the fundamental concepts of political economy (Granger, 1955; Stewart, 1967). Nor is it the point to say that the notion is entering the law for the first time; M. Villey has adequately shown that it forms part of the categories of law in antiquity (Villey, 1975: 36; 1978: 77).

The problem is by no means to establish in what time and what field the notion of balance was used in for the first time. Such an endeavour would have little sense, given that this notion, in contrast to a Platonic idea, does not designate an essence for ever condemned to remain identical with itself. When lawyers, philosophers or sociologists use the notion, in the circumstances of the end of the nineteenth century, it is not in application of a preconstituted essence, but as a polemical and pragmatic notion. It was the notion that seemed to them best suited for understanding the transformations of law of which they were both the actors and the commentators[70]. That is to say that while since the end of the nineteenth century the term "balance" does not cease to turn up in legal literature as an instrument for identifying and describing the new logic of the law, there are no legal texts where the notion was pondered in itself. On the other hand, by comparing judicial and legislative practice with the doctrinal commentaries, it is possible to construct the concept there was of it.

[69] Which clearly does not mean that social struggles have no importance in the production of law. Since the contrary is true, one must endeavour to evaluate the kind of positive effect they have been able to have on the structure of the legal system.

[70] It should moreover be noted that the lawyers of that time were not only well aware of their difference, but were so of the need the time they lived in created to differentiate themselves. Cf. Bonnecase (1933).

One may give four main characteristics of the rule of judgment articulated round the notion of balance.

1. The notion of balance serves first of all to designate a type of judgment where weight is given to the *relationship* between two (or more) terms, rather than to the intrinsic quality of each of them. In connection with contracts, for instance, the point is no longer so much to know whether the consent given is valid, but rather to evaluate the appropriateness of the terms of the exchange. A problematic of 'causa' and of the equivalence of 'causae' doubles the problematic of 'consent'[71]. In connection with liability, the point is no longer so much to compare the conduct of an individual with an abstract model of impeccable conduct (the good husband and father), as to determine, given that one or the other culprit or victim, must bear the burden of damage, albeit resulting from two activities of equal usefulness, why one rather than the other ought *fairly* to bear that burden. This may be answered using the idea of fault, but also by taking account of a social inequality to be compensated[72]. A judgment of balance will necessarily be much more social than moral[73]. The axis of judgment is brought down from reference to abstractly defined good or evil to an axis of social relationships[74]. This is the *principle of socialisation of judgment*.

71 As shown by the process of increasingly wide recognition of amendment of contracts for *burdensomeness*. Consumer law can only be a law of burdensomeness, for it there seems that protection of consent is no longer capable of ensuring contractual justice. Durkheim (1950: 232) had already sought to reduce the causes of nullity of contracts to burdensomeness.

72 It is true that the preparations for the Civil Code contain this awareness for balance. Thus, Bertrand de Greuille, in his report to the Tribunate on the future articles 1283 ff, declares: "Each individual is guarantor of his act; that is one of the first maxims of society. Thence it follows that if such act cause some damage to another, he by whose fault it occurred must be bound to make reparation. This principle admits of no exception ... it leads even to the consequence of reparation of wrong resulting only from negligence or rashness. One might at first sight wonder whether this consequence be not too exaggerated, and whether there not be some injustice in punishing a man for an action that partakes solely of weakness or misfortune ... the reply to this objection is to be found in the great principle of public order, that the law may not hesitate between him who errs and him who suffers." Cf. Fenet (1827: 474). But as the continuation of the text shows — "Wherever the law finds that a citizen has undergone a loss, it considers whether it was possible for the person that caused that loss not to have done so" — the idea of balance here supplies less the principle of judgment of liability than the principle that should delimit the extension of the notion of fault. It is also true, as the history of case-law on work accidents shows, that the natural derivative of such a definition of the notion of fault was its own elimination in favour of considerations of the legal balance between the parties.

73 In fact there is only inversion of the relationship between the two terms, not elimination of one of them in favour of the other.

74 The proof of this was given in masterly fashion by Ripert (1902: 332 and 408); Appert,

2. The judgment of balance must be a flexible judgment; it must always be able to adapt to history, to development, to social change[75]. It must not get hung up on *a priori* respect for principles. The judgment of balance seeks its justice as a judgment of adaption of society to itself. The value of things, or of actions, cannot be derived from their nature. A thing may very well at the same time be itself and its opposite: good, an evil; evil, a good. One can no longer say of an action that it is good *or* bad. It depends: in some cases yes, in others no; up to a certain threshold still, beyond no longer. Only the background, the circumstances, the relationship of this activity to others, and to the common good, can allow this to be decided, and then only for the moment[76]. This is the *principle of the generalised relativity of all values*.

3. Judging in terms of balance presupposes the focussing of all attention on *distribution*, on *allocation*. The whole goes before its parts; any attribute of the parts is first of all an attribute of the whole. Where classical law reasoned in terms of individual appropriation (contract) or accident (offence), one acts as if nothing ever happens to anyone which is not first of all a happening to all. Wealth is counted twice; as individual property, and as part of a common good individually distributed. The misfortune that happens to you may leave you alone in your suffering, but it is never anything but the statistical distribution of a common sum of ill. To be just is to restore the equality in individual distribution of social goods and evils. Liberal "justice" was aligned on the principle of "truth", that one should not (by regulation) contradict the natural play of distributions effected by the economy. Likewise, what was just according to society ought to follow what was just in nature; they were confused, with no way of distinguishing between them. Now the social order of distribution (or of justice) is split off from the economic order of production[77] (for a similar view see Preuß infra). So much so that the question of *who* produces the wealth, on what terms and at what prices tends no longer to be relevant when it comes to the social question of its distribution. The natural

note on Bordeaux, 5 March 1903, S. 1905, II, p. 41; more recently, Linotte (1975: 210) has shown how the Council of State ruling "Ville nouvelle Est" was articulated round such a transformation of the rule of judgment: before, he says, "the judge confined himself to verifying that the project considered was among those that might legally be carried on by way of expropiation" henceforth the judge would evaluate the operation *in concreto*, in relative terms, from the viewpoint of consequences, balancing the drawbacks and advantages (Linotte, 1975: 305, 413).

75 Cf. Ripert (1902) and especially, below, the theory of abuse of law.

76 Which as will be seen cannot fail to upset the problem of the sources of the law. It immediately becomes apparent that such a logic of judgment is contrary to the principle that it should only be application of a law.

77 It is this principle of reduplication of everything that permits the existence, if not of the social, at least of an autonomy of the social.

allocation of wealth can no longer be just because justice has deserted nature in favour of society. There then arises the anguished question, with all the force of vertigo in the face of the sudden vanishing of a goal, of the "measure" in the new relationships of justice – which till then had seemed obviously solved. Justice is no longer linked to relationships of causality; it is read in the social relationships of *equality and inequality*. And there opens the chasm of knowing what ought to be the just combination of the two. This is the *principle* (and problem) *of social justice*.

4. The idea of balance goes back to that of the *scales*, and that in turn to the *counterweight*. Specifically the image of a pair of scales is a good expression of the idea of conflictual solidarity. Equilibrium is maintained only because one pan balances the other. The point is neither to sacrifice one pan or privilege the other; the whole art of judgment must be to maintain the balance between them. *The judgment of balance presupposes a whole art of compensation* (Svagelski, 1981). It may also call for a principle of comparison that allows a fair evaluation of the relative value of everything. The operation is already difficult where there exists an equivalent, such as a price[78]. One may wonder how it can be at all possible where, as with the environment, the point is to balance incommensurables[79]. Judging in terms of balance presupposes a generalised principle of equivalence, a possibility of determining the value of all values; that the whole can have an adequate knowledge of itself. This amounts to the possession of absolute knowledge[80]. If truth is defined by the appropriateness of a discourse to its object, it would seem that truth is debarred from a judgment of balance, which implies that a judgment is just only as a continually updated judgment of society about itself. There is no longer any referent. The subject vanishes into the object, the content into its expression, and vice versa. That is, unless "society" finds a way to split itself in two, to stand aside from itself, to oppose itself to itself as subject and object. Socialisation of judgment implies sociologisation of judgment – sociology being taken to be that branch of knowledge which enables social judgment to find the conditions of objectivity that it needs.

78 This problem of the "common measure" is admirably formulated by Aristotle (1955: para. 1133). Also von Jhering (1916).

79 This is the problem posed by the Council of State ruling "Ville Nouvelle Est", already cited, and similar ones. "It is not conceivable to bring fundamentally different interests to balance. How can one compare the interest of traffic with that of public health?" B. Odent, on C.E. 20 October 1972 "Société civile Sainte-Marie de l'Assomption", quoted by Linotte (1975: 381).

80 Which involves a completely totalitarian virtuality. Knowledge is a fundamental stake for the "social": finding a generalised equivalent, a general principle of evaluation, which would, by the way, be nothing else but the social itself. We know that sociology is the knowledge that should fulfil this function.

One term sums up the whole set of characteristics of this logic of legal judgment: the term *norm*. A judgment of balance, in the social law sense, is a *normative* judgment[81]. Judging in terms of balance means judging the value of an action or a practice in its relationship to social normality, in terms of the customs and habits which at a certain moment are those of a given group. In therefore means judging relatively: the same act may at one place be punished, at another not[82]. What furnishes the principle of the sanction is not the instrinsic quality of the act, but its relationship to others: it is the abnormal, the abuse, the excess – what goes beyond a certain limit, a certain theshold, which in themselves are not natural but social, and therefore variable with time and place. Not that the abnormal is amoral or wrong. Quite the contrary; it may be useful and necessary, like industrial development with its accompanying nuisances. But it introduces a social imbalance which it seems just to compensate for, in terms of a certain idea of equality in the collective distribution of burdens[83].

[81] The term should be understood in its proper sense, and not the vague sense – coming no doubt from Germany – of a generic word to designate any type of obligations whatever. Rule, law, obligation, provision and norm are not synonyms. A rule is not a norm, if the term is to have a meaning, except when it obeys a specific regime of formation, the one that might be called "sociological". G. Canguilhem, in the fundamental work on the meaning of the concept of norm (1966: 182) indicates that the term "normal" dates from 1759, and "normality" from 1834. It is clear that the authors of the Civil Code could not conceive of drawing up "norms" in the sense we understand thereby today. Otherwise the Civil Code would have had to begin, instead of with the (deleted) preliminary section stating that "there exists a universal and immutable law, which is the source of all the positive laws: this is none other than natural reason, as it governs men" (art. 1), with a treatise on sociology.
One may hypothesise that the inflation of the notion of norm in law dates from the late nineteeth century, from sociologisation, from the time when, specifically, the rule of law was mixed up along with social norms. Cf. e.g. Duguit (1928: 65). Gény (1919: 146), says:
"The interpreter of positive law must put at the basis of his evaluation the notion of normality, as dominating all overall judgment", and refers in a note to Durkheim. When below we use the term "norm", it is in this precise sense, and not to denote any type of constraint whatever.

[82] This type of judgment certainly found one of its privileged areas of expression with the question of troubles between neighbours. Cf. esp. Ripert (1902: 408).

[83] Cf. Saleilles (1905:336):
"We have recognised that there are in our social world bodies functioning in a quite regular and legal way, indubitable manifestations of genuine law, which however can only achieve their end by sowing around themselves risks and damage. The most lawful acts, those included in the material content of law, may become generators of damage, and will be so without ceasing to be lawful acts, that is, acts performed in full conformity with the law whose expression they are.
Take a factory, a large manufacture, using dangerous machines: it cannot work towards the social goal it must fulfil save by making victims and causing individual damage. Not only damage to the workers, who are, it is only too true, but cogs; but also

One might of course fear the arbitrariness of such judgments. It will be asked who sets the thresholds of abnormality. It will be wondered at that one may be condemned while not only exercising one's rights but per-

damage to third parties living in the neighbourhood and to properties in the immediate vicinity. Certainly, the factory manager will be obliged to take all precaution appropriate to his process; and if he does not, the damage resulting from that professional error will come under the sanction and under the formula of Article 1382, in the sense that the act will have acquired the character of a wrongful act, or if you wish a quasi-crime. But we must go further. Whatever be the precautions taken, there will always come a time when one comes up against the irreducible, the unforeseeable, the unpreventable – except by closing the factory. Will it be said that the acts and accidents whence such damage, which I shall call occupational, arises are still wrongful acts? One does have to, with the archaic terminolgy and still more archaic conception of Article 1382. At bottom there is the fact of risk. There is neither fault, nor crime, nor quasi-crime. There is a perfectly lawful act performed in pursuance of a right; but it is an act which, while being lawful, is performed at the risk and peril of those involved.
It is lawful; for if it were not, justice could require removal of the cause, and that cause is the factory. Is one to require closure of the factory because it is an inevitable cause of damage? One will content oneself with charging to the industry the risks that are its necessary concomitant. There are rights which can be exercised only on condition of paying for the risks involved. To eliminate the right on grounds of the dangers inherent in its exercise would be to strike a mortal blow at individual activity in its most productive aspect, to dry up one of the wellsprings of the national life. To exempt the exercise of the right from the risks which are its inevitable concomitant would be to disregard individual interests and rights, and to put all the benefits on one side, without the burdens they imply. There would be a violation of social justice. This has finally been understood as far as industrial risks go ...
The idea is bound to grow and develop incrasingly. Do we not see every day how human activity, even by private individuals, takes on forms that are assuredly lawful in themselves, but all imply risks that constitute the price to pay? Does not the mere fact of driving along a road in a motor car, event a moderate speed, in all justice imply that he who benefits from a sophisticated but dangerous means of transport should assume all the risks, however unforeseeable, that may arise? The car is proceeding at a normal pace – what could be more lawful? But suddenly a tyre blows out and a passer-by is injured. There is no fault on the part of the driver, but purely and simply the act of the machine, the risks of which must be imputable to him who, in his own assuredly legitimate but exclusive interest, uses a means of transport that in itself constitutes a permanent danger. There is no reason for treating the owner of the machine any differently from a railway company in a similar situation. The area of fault is becoming ever narrower, and the area of risk gaining all the territory lost; and one might wonder whether the most appropriate way for our modern social State might not be to reword Article 1382 as follows: "Any act whatsoever of man, performed in circumstances such as to imply, according to received usages and social conventions, that it is done at the risk and peril of the doer, shall oblige the latter to make reparation for damage caused.
Be that as it may, there is a trend here that cannot be impeded, and a case law that will go on growing stronger, for case law perforce follows the drift of mores and of opinion. There will increasingly be facts of ownership considered lawful in themselves

forming an activity that is useful and ultimately beneficial to all. There will be fears of a certain woolliness about obligations such that one may, for the same act, be at one place condemned and at another absolved. There will be denunciations of the attacks on the principle of equality that such judgments might involve[84]. But this would be to fail to understand that what is being disputed in this new legal logic is not a fault, but very exactly the effect sought. The norm is mobile, changing, variable; it changes like society and with it. Or better, the norm designates both a fact and a value[85]. The norm is found; it has the objectivity of a statistical average. At the same time, it supplies a principle of obligations that are immediately in line with what the social order requires at a given moment. The wonder of the norm is that it allows the passage from is to ought, from *Sein* to *Sollen*, from the descriptive to the prescriptive, that some had thought to see as the ultimate stumbling-block to the project of defining moral and social obligations on the basis of the sole consideration of social positivities. Thanks to the norm, "society" will be able to judge itself in continual adjustment to itself, which is what the social lawyers have been claiming as the ideal to aim at.

Since the end of the nineteenth century, concern for the norm has not ceased to penetrate (and to transform) the law of obligations[86]. It is what explains the systems of liability for risk, the principle of which can, as we have seen be found in the need for equitable distribution of social benefits and burdens. The norm is here set up as a principle of justice. Again, it is the foundation for the system of redress for troubles between neighbours, which was the occasion for the construction of the theory of *"dommage*

but exercised only at the risk and peril of the owner. And this will be true of most facts of freedom; the more human activity multiplies its initiatives, the wider open it will find the field of freedom. But in exchange and as a compensation, it will run the risk only on condition of accepting, whether there be fault or no, the costs."

[84] It would doubtless be fairer to speak not so much of attack on the principle of equalitiy as of a specific legal practice of equality, with negative and positive aspects. Thus, the principle amounts to favouring equality of situations or conditions over equality of right considered *in abstracto*. In Vedel's happy phrase (1980: 375): "The point is not so much equality as non-discrimination". Two individuals in identical situations should have the same treatment, and different treatment in different situations. But this may also lead to justifying some rather shocking inequalities: it will, for instance, be judged that a given pollution from a factory in a working-class suburb is "normal", whereas the same pollution in a middle-class residential area would entail liability and compensation. Cf. G. Appert, note on Bordeaux, 5 March 1903, cit. Ripert (1902:409). The liability, he says, depends on the "usages", on "customs", on the "commonly accepted" (425).

[85] Cf. Lalande (1962), article on "norme"; Canguilhem (1966: 81); "The concept 'normal'," explains Canguilhem elsewhere (178), "is itself normative."

[86] But not only there; one could certainly say as much of family law. Cf. Commaille (1982).

anormal" as a ground of liability, apart from any consideration of fault (Girod, 1901: 47; Caballero, 1981: 193). It is again what we find at the basis of government liability, where it is expressed in the form of the principle of equality vis-à-vis public office (Michoud, 1932: 276; Delvolve, 1969: 260, 272, 371, 378, 415; Henriot, 1960: 32). In contractual matters, the demands for "fair wages" and for "fair remuneration" (in salary matters) or a "fair price" (in consumer matters) are not to be understood in the sense of what their true value would be if objectively calculated, but by reference to an average. A fair price is a price which, in relation to the average of prices charged, is not excessive; a fair wage is a "normal" wage, both socially and in the occupation, in relation to needs and to what at a given time is considered the subsistence minimum.

Thus, social law should be conceived of in relation to the notion of *norm*. Of course, this term designates, not certain legal expressions, but a system for formulating certain expressions, and a specific way of judging. In classical law, the Law – we give it a capital to distinguish it from the individual laws promulgated by the legislator – designated such a system for formulating expressions. In order to belong to the legal order, these had to take the form of (or derive from) the Law, a general expression intended to have perpetuity. For social law, the norm corresponds to what the Law could be for classical law.

The passage from classical law to social law should, then, be analysed as the passage "from the Law to the norm" (Foucault, 1976: 189). The notion of norm would thus allow the putting forward of a concept of social law, and the identification of what in any given legal system has to do with social law: it is where judgment becomes of the normative type. At the same time, however, it is on the basis of the notion of norm that the limits and problems of social law ought to be thought about.

References

Al Sanhhoury, AA. (1925) "Les restricitions contractuelles à la liberté individuelle du travail dans la jurisprudence anglaise". Thesis, University of Paris: Giard.

Aristotle (1955) *The Nicomachean Ethics*, book V. (translated by J.A.K. Thomson). Harmondsworth, Penguin Books.

Auroux, Jean (1982) *Les droits des travailleurs*. Paris: La documentation française.

Benoist, Charles (1899) *La crise de l'Etat moderne*. Paris: Firmin-Didot.

Bettati, Mario (1983) *Le nouvel ordre économique international*. Paris: Presses Universitaires de France.

Bonnecase, Jean (1933) *La pensée juridique française de 1884 à l'heure présente*. Bordeaux: Delmas.

Boulan, Fernand (1971) "La transaction en droit positif". Thesis, Department of Law, University of Aix.

BOURGEOIS, Léon (1896) *Solidarité*. Paris: Colin.
BOY, Lawrence (1979) "L'intérêt collectif en droit français". Thesis, University of Nice.
BOYER, Louis (1976) "Transaction", in Dalloz (ed.), *Répertoire de droit civil*. Paris: Dalloz.
BUISSON, Ferdinand (1908) *La politique radicale*. Paris: Alcan.
BRICE, Hubert (1892) *Le droit d'association et l'Etat*. Paris: Rousseau.
CABALLERO, Francis (1981) *Essai sur la notion juridique de nuisance*. Paris: Librairie Générale de Droit et de Jurisprudence.
CANGUILHEM, Georges (1966) *Le normal et le pathologique*. Paris: Presses Universitaires de France.
CARBONNIER, Jean (1979) *Essai sur les lois*. Paris: Répertoire Dufresnois.
— (1979) *Flexible droit*. Paris: Librairie Générale de Droit et de Jurisprudence.
CARREAU, Dominique, Patrick JUILLARD and Thiebaut FLORY (1980) *Droit international économique*. Paris: Librairie Générale de Droit et de Jurisprudence.
CHAMONT, Jean (1927) *La renaissance du droit naturel*. Paris: Librairie de Jurisprudence Ancienne et Moderne.
CLEMENCEAU, Georges (1895) *La mêlée sociale*. Paris: G. Charpentier et Fasquelle.
COMMAILLE, Jacques (1956) "Contribution à un approche sociologique de la pratique judiciaire: les accidents de la circulation". 27 *Année sociologique* 214.
— (1982) *Familles sans justice?* Paris: Le Centurion.
COMMAILLE, Jacques and Marie-Pierre MARMIER-CHAMPEXOIS (1978) "Sociologie de la création de la norme, l'example de changements legislatifs intervenus en droit de la famille", in CNRS (ed.) *2nd Franco-Soviet Legal Sociology Colloquium*. Paris.
CORNIL, Georges (1924) *Le droit privé, essai de sociologie juridique simplifiée*. Paris: Giard.
CRUET, Jean (1907) *La vie du droit et l'impuissance des lois*. Paris: Flammarion.
DABIN, Jean (1938) "Droit de classe et droit commun", in: *Introduction à l'étude du droit comparé, Recueil d'etudes en l'honneur d' E. Lambert*, Vol. III. Paris: Sirey.
DELVOLVE, Pierre (1969) *Le principe d'égalité devant les charges publiques*. Paris: Librairie Générale de Droit et de Jurisprudence.
DERATHÉ, Robert (1970) *J.-J. Rousseau et la science politique de son temps*. 2nd ed. Paris: Vrin.
Despax, Michel (1966) *Coventions collectives*. Paris: Dalloz.
DUGUIT, Léon (1901) *L'Etat, le droit et la loi positive*. Paris: Fontemoing.
— (1908) *Le droit social, le droit individuel et la transformation de l'État*. Paris: Alcan.
— (1924) *Traité de droit constitutionnel*. Paris: de Boccard.
— (1928) *Traité de droit constitutionnel*. Vol. II. Paris: de Boccard.
DURAND, Paul (1953) *La politique contemporaine de la sécurité sociale*. Paris: Dalloz.
DURKHEIM, Emile (1950) *Leçons de sociologie*. 2nd ed. Paris: Presses Universitaires de France.
EHRLICH, Stanislaw (1971) *Le pouvoir et les groupes de pression*. Paris: Monton.
FENET, P.-Antoine (1827) *Recueil complet des Travaux préparatoires au Code Civil*, Vol. XI. Paris, 51, rue St. André des Arts.
FOUCAULT, Michel (1976) *La volonté de savoir*. Paris: Gallimard.
FOUILLÉE, Alfred (1896) *La science sociale contemporaire*. Paris: Hachette.
— (1920) *L'idée moderne du droit*. Paris: Hachette.
FOURNIER, Pierre and Nicole QUESTIAUX (1982) *Traité du social*. Paris: Dalloz.
GALANT, Henry C. (1955) *Historie politique de la sécurité sociale française 1945—1952*. Paris: A. Colin.
GAUDEMET, Eugène (1904) "Les codifications récentes et révision du Code Civil", in: *Livre du Centenaire 1804—1904*, Vol. I. Paris: A. Rousseau.
GENY, François (1919) *Methode d'Interprétation et Sources en droit privé positif*. Vol. II. Paris: Librairie Générale de Droit et de Jurisprudence.

– (1922) *Science et Technique*. Vol. I. Paris: Sirey.
GHESTIN, Jean (1980) *Le contrat*. Paris: Librairie Générale de Droit et de Jurisprudence.
GILLET, Marcel (1973) *Les Charbonnages du Nord de la France au XIXe siècle*. Paris, The Hague: Mouton.
GIROUD, Jean (1901) "Etudes sur la transaction". Thesis, Bourg.
GLASSON, Ernest (1886) *Le Code civil et la question ouvrière*. Paris: Pichon.
GOUNOT, Emmanuel (1912) *Le principe de l'autonomie de la volonté*. Paris: Rousseau.
GRANGER, Gilles (1955) "Concept, structure et loi en science économique". Thesis, Paris.
GURVITCH, Georges (1931) *Le temps présent et l'idée du droit social*. Paris: Vrin.
– (1932) *L'idée du droit social*. Paris: Sirey.
– (1937) *Le temps présent et l'idée de droit social*. Paris: Vrin.
– (1944) *La déclaration des droits sociaux*. Paris: Vrin.
HAURIOU, Maurice (1896) *La science sociale traditionelle*. Paris: Lanose.
– (1909) *Recueil de législation de Toulouse*. Vol. V. Toulouse: Prirat.
– (1929) *Précis de droit constitutionnel*. Paris: Sirey.
HENRIOT, Georges C. (1960) *Le dommage anormal*. Paris: Cujas.
HUSSON, Leon (1947) *Les transformations de la responsabilité*. Paris: Presses Universitaires de France.
JEZE, Gaston (1927) "Le dogme de la volonté nationale et la technique politique", *Revenue de droit public* 165.
JAVILLIER, Jean C. (1973) "Recherche sur les conflits du travail", Vol. I. Thesis, University of Paris I.
– (1984) *Les réformes du droit au travail depuis le 10 mai 1981*. Paris: Librairie Générale de Droit et de Jurisprudence.
JHERING, Rudolph von (1878) *Der Zweck im Recht*. Leipzig: Breitkopf und Härtel.
– (1881) *Der Kampf um's Recht*, 6th ed. Vienna: Manz.
– (1888) *Geist des römischen Rechts auf den verschiedenen Stufen seiner Entwicklung* (5th ed.) Leipzig: Breitkopf und Härtel.
– (1916) *Der Zweck im Recht* (5th ed.) Leipzig: Breitkopf und Härtel.
JOSSERAND, Louis (1935) *Recueil d'études sur les sources du droit offert a F. Gény*, Vol. II. Paris: Sirey.
– (1936) *Evolutions et actualités*. Paris: Sirey.
– (1937) "Sur la reconstitution d'un droit de classe", in Dalloz (ed.), *Dalloz Hebdomadaire*. Paris: Dalloz.
LALANDE, André (1962) *Vocabulaire de la philosophie*. Paris: Presses Universitaires de France.
LATTRE, Alain de (1975) *Le réalisme selon Zola*. Paris: Presses Universitaires de France.
LAROQUE, Pierre (1938) *Les rapports entre patrons et ouvriers*. Paris.
– (1953) "Les chances de l'arbitrage obligatoire", 8 *Droit social* 468.
LAUBADERE, André de (1979) *Droit public économique*. Paris: Dalloz.
LEROY, Maxime (1908) *La loi*. Paris: Giard et Brière.
– (1913) *La coûtume ouvrière*. Paris: Giard et Brière.
LEVASSEUR, Emile (1867) *Histoire des classes ouvrières depuis 1789*, Vol. II. Paris: Hachette.
LINOTTE, Daniel (1975) "Recherches sur la notion d'intérêt général en droit administratif français." Thesis, University of Bordeaux.
LIVET, Georges (1976) *L'equilibre européen*. Paris: Presses Universitaires de France.
MAIRE, Edmond (1983) "Vive l'initiative", in *Liberation*.
MARX, Karl (1919) *Zur Judenfrage*. Berlin: Rowohlt.
MAZEAUD, Henri, and Louis MAZEAUD (1980) *Leçons de droit civil*. Vol. III. Paris: Montchrestien.
MAURY, Jacques (1920) *Essai sur la notion d'équivalence en droit civil français*. Paris: Jouve.
MERLE, Marcel (1980) "On negotiation", 15 *Pouvoirs*.

MICHOUD, Léon (1932) *La théorie de la personnalité morale.* 3rd ed. Paris: Librairie Générale de Droit et de Jurisprudence.

MONTESQUIEU, Charles L. (1964) *The Spirit of the Laws.* Kaniel Oster (ed) Paris: Seuil.

MORIN, Gaston (1920) *La Révolte des faits contre le Code.* Paris: Grasset.

MURCIER, Jean P. (1982) "La CFDT et les droits nouveaux des travailleurs", 78 *Droit social* 532.

NICOLET, Claude (1982) *L'idée républicaine en France.* Paris: Gallimard.

PAUL-BONCOUR, Joseph (1901) *Le fédéralisme économique.* 2nd ed. Paris: Alcan.

PERROT, Michelle (1974) *Les ouvriers en grève.* Paris, The Hague: Mouton.

PEROT-MOREL, Marie-Angèle (1961) "De l'équilibre des prestations dans la conclusion du contrat". Thesis, University of Grenoble.

PIC, Paul (1919) *Traité élémentaire de legislation industrielle.* Paris: Rousseau.

PISIER-KOUCHNER, Evelyne (1972) *Le service public dans la théorie de l'Etat de L. Duguit.* Paris: Librairie Générale de Droit et de Jurisprudence.

PLANIOL, Marcel and Georges RIPERT (1954) *Traité pratique de droit civil français.* Vol. XI. Paris: Librairie Générale de Droit et de Jurisprudence.

PORTALIS, Jean-E. (1827) *De l'usage et de l'abus de l'esprit philosophique durant le XVIIIe siècle.* Paris: Moutardier.

PRINS, Adolphe (1910) *La défense sociale.* Bruxelles: Misch et Thron.

- (1895) *L'Organisation de la liberté et le devoir social.* Brussels: Falk.

PROUDHON, Pierre-Joseph (1930) *De la justice dans la révolution et dans l'église*, Vol. I. Paris: Rivière.

RABINOVICS, Jean (1936) *La transaction dans le règlement des sinistes.* Paris: Librairie Technique.

RAYNAUD, Jean D. (1980) "Negotiation and Rules", 15 *Pouvoirs.*

RIPERT, Georges (1902) *De l'exercice du droit de propriété dans ses rapport avec les propriétés voisines.* Paris: Rousseau.

— (1918) "Droit naturel et positivisme juridique", 1 *Annales de la Faculté de droit d'Aix.*

— (1946) *Aspects juridiques du capitalisme moderne.* Paris: Librairie Générale de Droit et de Jurisprudence.

— (1948) *Le régime démocratique et le droit civil moderne.* 2nd ed. Paris: Librairie Générale de Droit et de Jurisprudence.

— (1949) *Le déclin du droit.* Paris: Pichon et Durand—Auziers.

— (1955) *Les forces créatrices du droit.* Paris: Librairie Générale de Droit et de Jurisprudence.

RIVERO, Jean (1947) "Les institutions économiques et sociales de la constitution: le conseil economique", XXXI *Collection Droit Social*35.

RIVERO, Jean, and Georges VEDEL (1947) "Les principes économiques et sociaux de la constitution préambule", XXXI *Collection Droit Social.*

Rousseau, Jean-Jacques (1762) *Du Contrat Social.* Paris: Garnier Frères.

SAINT-SIMON, Cte. Claude-Henri (1924) *Doctrine de Saint-Simon, Esposition.* Paris: Bouglé—Halevy.

SALEILLES, Raymond (1905) "Rapport à la société d'études législatives", *Bulletin de la Société* 336.

SAVATIER, René (1938) "Les rayons et les ombres d'une expérience sociale: l'arbitrage obligatoire des conflits collectifs du travail", in Dalloz (ed.) *Dalloz Hebdomadaire.* Paris: Dalloz.

— (1951) *Traité de la responsabilité civile.* Vol. I. Paris: Librairie Générale de Droit et de Jurisprudence.

SFEZ, Lucien (1966) *Essai sur la contribution du doyen Hauriou au droit administratif français.* Paris: Librairie Générale de Droit et de Jurisprudence.

STARK Boris (1972) *Droit Civil, Obligations.* Paris: Librairie Technique.
STATI, Mario (1927) *Le standard juridique.* Paris: Duchemin.
STEWART, Michael (1967) *Keynes.* Paris: Seuil.
SUPIOT, Alain (1979) "Le juge et le droit du travail". Thesis, University of Bordeaux.
– (1983) "Les syndicats et la négociation collectives", *Droit Social* 63.
SVAGELSKI, Jean (1981) *L'idée de compensation en France 1750–1850.* Lyon: Hermès.
TANON, Louis (1900) *L'évolution du droit et la conscience sociale.* Paris: Alcan.
TEISSEIRE, Maurice (1901) *Essai d'une théorie générale sur le fondement de la responsabilité.* Paris: Rousseau.
TESSIER, Albert (1904) "Le Code Civil et les Classes Ouvrières", in: *Livre du Centenaire 1804–1904.* Vol. 1. Paris: Rousseau.
THALLER, Edmond (1904) "Rapport présenté sur la question de la révision du Code Civil", 3 *Bulletin de la Société d'Etudes Législatives* 478.
TUNC, André (1981) *La responsabilité civile.* Paris: Economica.
VEDEL, Georges (1980) *Droit administratif.* Paris: Presses Universitaires de France.
– (1947) "Conceptions sociales et organisations politiques", in XXXI *Collection Droit Social.*
VILLEY, Michel (1975) *La formation de la pensée juridique moderne.* Paris: Montchrestien.
– (1978) *Philosophie du droit.* Vol. I. Paris: Dalloz.
WALINE, Marcel (1969) "Paradoxe sur l'égalité devant la loi" in Recueill. Paris: Dalloz.
WORMS, René (1896) *Organisme et société.* Paris: Giard et Brière.
– (1903) *Philosophie des sciences sociales.* Vol. I. Paris: Giard et Brière.
ZOLA, Emile (1978) *Germinal.* Paris: Gallimard.

Legal Subjectivity as a Precondition for the Intertwinement of Law and the Welfare State

JAN M. BROEKMAN
Leuven

Introduction

Discussions on the language of general jurisprudence and the function of law in the welfare state focus on the problem of the materialization of law. Should this materialization follow the formalistic principle without restrictions, or be based upon new models of legal thinking and application of the law? This general theme leads to a multitude of theoretical points of view concerning both legal science and legal theory. Such views include, for instance, the claim to fill the gap between legal theory and legal practice. The method adopted here is the use of materialized and rational argumentation in the law (Summers, 1982a; 1982b; Mackie 1982). Besides this there is the claim that legal science is relevant to sociology. This claim concerns particularly the decision-making process in the law. (Luhmann, 1970; Hirsch and Rehbinder, 1967; Mauss, 1980; Mishra, 1977; Unger, 1976). It has also been suggested that there is the need for responsive law (Nonet and Selznick, 1978) and the conceptualization of a reflexive law (Teubner, 1983). The same train of thought is behind the characterization of law as a process of social engineering (Pound, 1922; Jenkins, 1980; ch. XIII) as well as behind the quest for a more defined material rationality and the development of new levels of formal rationality in law (Eder, 1978). Lastly, the same point of view can be seen in the claim regarding the interdisciplinarity of legal science and legal theory.

These differing points of view also constitute many theoretical reflections on a much more complex social problem. In the first place it must be taken into consideration, notwithstanding Keynes and all the consequences of similar theories, that law has only recently been forced to play an omnicompetent role in our society. Jenkins describes this development as one of the most important background elements in the demand for law as social engineering:

> Law is now intervening in areas that it has hitherto steered clear of; it is imposing its opinions and principles upon other social bodies; it is settling questions that were

formerly thought of as being political economic, or moral, rather than legal, in nature; and it is issuing detailed directives about the ordering of various aspects of society and social life. From being ultimate but relatively unobstrusive, law has become pervasive (Jenkins, 1980: 215, see also Friedman supra, Habermas infra).

Another observation can be made here, namely that law must be considered as a particular articulation of a comprehensive process of social life. The power of the legal apparatus in our society is not only limited by the nature of law as an institution, but it is also totally dependent on the fact that law itself must express and maintain certain images of man, cultural ideals and ideologies (Broekman, 1979; 1982a; 1983).

Economic factors, economic structures and systems currently dominate legal strategies as well as the way in which law is conceptualized. This can also be considered as a process of articulation of the basic values within a certain society. The quest for a responsive law; a reflexive law; law as social engineering; the quest for a just application of law, which takes into consideration all the economic and social factors of a given situation and carefully balances all components of the conflicting interests in a particular case, are expressive of the theoretical reflections in the process of articulation. The result of this process is that the concept of law becomes burdened with sociological content (a socialized concept of law) and it is also formulated in rather general terms. An important reflection in this connection is that the generalization and sozialization of legal concepts is always accompanied by a legalistic residue. The latter cannot be eliminated by whatever functionalist theory of law. The central theoretical question here is to determine the extent to which the legalistic residue is important in the formulation of the concept of law.

A first consideration concerning this question is that the relation between law and a given social situation is neither immediate nor direct. It is always mediated and at the same time also censored. It is impossible to move directly and immediately (without mediation) from the economic to the psychological aspects of society, from the monetary to the political aspects, or more generally from the material to the ideological aspects.

The situation of law within society, however, is different. On the one hand, social development itself is the most important cause of this difference; on the other, epistemological problems play a decisive role. With regard to the first point of difference, Luhmann (1970: 200 and infra) has explained that a political society never supports or tolerates a general omnicompetence of law. This omnicompetence of law is in the final analysis a process of the positivization of law. But, states Luhmann, a comprehensive positivization can take place only in a social structure in which the primacy of law has disappeared and has been superseded by economics. In a society with complex economic and social functions, with an economic system that has been developed in both the industrial and the monetary subsystems, there is much less risk that legal and political systems will determine the whole society.

But even if both the legal and the political systems were to gain more power, as they clearly have in our times, the political control over the juridification of the above-mentioned problems is not in the hands of lawyers. This is considered by Luhmann to be a rather complicated socialization of law. Political, legal, and administrative decisions no longer depend on fixed rules, but have become dependent on socially relevant problems and purposes (for this question see Luhmann 118, 122, Wiethölter 225 infra). In our view, however, the question is how far this socialization can penetrate into the legal decision. Although it has been said that this socialization can never lead to the disappearance of all legal conditions and characteristics, this has been constantly underestimated or ignored in sociological jurisprudence and in theories concerning law as "social engineering" or the development of a "reflexive law".

This remark already bears on the second point, i. e. the epistemological problem. It must not be forgotten that legal science is a dogmatic science, in the sense of the German notion of *Rechtsdogmatik*. Each moment of legal practice is determined by legal dogmatics and not by legal theory or legal science in the broadest sense of the word. This observation is valid for the common law system as well as for the codified legal system of European countries. In both cases, the realization of law depends not only on a given situation, but also on the given dogmatic structures within the national legal system. In this respect, precedents and norms regulate the legal construction of social reality to the same degree. The epistemological structure of law is thus dominated by the corpus dogmaticus (Broekman, 1983: ch 1; 1982b: 81). It is exactly this corpus dogmaticus that distinguishes legal science from other social sciences. It also determines legal practice in our society. In general, it can be said that scientific and everyday observations of life are strongly determined by, and dependent on, the construction of theories. Legal thinking, particularly legal practice is no exception to this. But for the most part the meaning of "theory" in legal practice is entirely determined by legal dogmatics. Through legal dogmatics "theory" takes on a different color from that which it has in the scientific sense of the word. From the point of view of the theory of science, a practising jurist conceives of legal theory as a closed technique of application of norms and rules to reality. It is precisely this interweaving of theory and technique which results in the fact that legal dogmatics invariably permeates all aspects of the application of law in practice.

This notwithstanding it is clear that legal dogmatics is a restricted and specific perspective on reality and it deviates in many ways from the everyday-life interpretation of reality (for a development of this thesis see Teubner 300 infra). Despite this, legal dogmatics persists and adheres to every generalization and socialization of the notion of "law". Thus the jurist's interpretation of the everyday-life reality is always dogmaticist precisely because of its inextricable bond with legal dogmatics.

I. The Intertwinement of Law and the Welfare State

The welfare state is generally understood as the integration of economic facts and general ideas about justice. It also includes the pervasive presence and functioning of law in various aspects of social life. It is thus evident that law is intertwined with the welfare state. Such intertwinement has often been understood as a direct and open relation between law and the welfare state (see Aubert 32 supra). Accordingly, there is an important process of interaction between law and the welfare state. As already stated, specific legal and social problems arise from the intertwinement of law and the welfare state. The problems usually relate to the social economic conditions, social options or alternatives regarding administrative and institutional structures. These also include the ideological components relative to the various problem areas. The idea of a welfare state has a rather inchoate beginning at the initial integration of economic and political facts with the general idea of law and justice. As previously suggested, the general idea of law is inextricably interconnected with legal dogmatics. Only when this and its consequences are not taken into consideration can it be said with Luhmann that the total positivization of law in the welfare state, as contrasted with political forms of society, is necessary and can be accepted without objection. Luhmann indicates that the degree of complexity, freedom of choice, and possibility for adaptation which characterizes the economy is at the same time the main reason for according social primacy to economics. Therefore, states Luhmann, society achieves a level of possibilities for experience and action, hitherto unknown, and this enables politics to gain more power, the family more love, and science more truth than ever before. The structure of our society must adapt itself to this complexity. In the area of normative expectations with regard to conduct this happens through the positivization of law (Luhmann, 1980: 202). The basis of this optimistic view is the idea that law is able to influence social relation in a direct way. This implies that there is no need for the legal systems to transform reality in order to make this reality conform to the categories of the law. It also means that it can stimulate the complexity of social life in a direct way and that this results in the realization of ideas like freedom, love and social efficiency. The same presupposition holds regarding demands for a "responsive law".

These considerations necessarily lead to the more fundamental question concerning the legalist components of the relation between law and the welfare state. Should they be neglected? Do they determine the structure of social life? This arises clearly with regard to the problems of the welfare state where it is necessary to incorporate some economic facts and regularities in a less determined and more general notion of law. The basic idea is that some legal decision which should be taken in a given situation suggest at the same time an analogy between the basic structures of legal decision-making and those of the economic sector. Thus it can be understood that an immediate identity between both structures is suggested when economic-legal points of view prevail over formal legal viewpoints. This factor has often been considered to be one of the most essential elements of modern legal development. It is an old suggestion which again expresses the idea that the adequacy of law and the possibility of its socialization must be dependent upon a process by which the formal aspects of law will be abolished. But this suggestion would hold only if legal-economic decisions were to replace formal decisions in such a way that the formality of law could be retained while the law which arose therefrom would be formally acceptable. This would effectively demonstrate the existence of an immediate identity between the structures of legal decision-making and those of the economic sector. It is conceivable that novel economic conditions could arise and in turn require specific legal decisions. If the latter were to be based on previously unknown legal principles an analysis of the legal reasoning involved in such a situation would reveal the ineluctable necessity for a minimum of formalization and especially dogmatization. This minimum of dogmatization must remain because law cannot accept legal measures which endanger the unity of law; a unity which has always been and always will be determined dogmatically and autoreferentially. This is a general thesis which can be proved by a careful analysis of decisions and legal measures dictated by economic relations. One can neither fatally preclude nor forestall the result of such an analysis by mounting the argument that after all legal decisions must always be subject to parliamentary control which control is generally predicated on the assumption that parliament is the legislative or law-making body. In this sense legal decisions are confronted by the law even before they are made. Yet the crucial question in this connection is whether or not such control as well as the ensuing legal measures are indeed reproductions of rules and principles which have already been formulated by economic concerns (Mauss, 1980: 11; Kohler, 1967). The quest for an immediate identity between the structures of legal decision-making and those of the economic sector could hardly be wholly satisfied by the development of a perfect social technique, that is, a type of law that functions perfectly in a purely technical framework, whereby both structures could be rendered immediately identical. In order to achieve complete satisfaction of this quest it is necessary to recognize that such attainment ultimately depends upon the fact that the dogmatic conditions of law would accept and allow for the development of such social techniques. Thus legal dogmatics remains an almost unassailable part of the whole legal structure.

In the light of the preceding considerations, it is pertinent to enquire whether or not the existing structures of society are the sources of law within the context of the actual development of economics. Mauss observes that this question (however useful on a technical level), demonstrates that a highly developed industrial society presents a certain tendency to one-dimensionality with regard to its need for law. In the opinion of Marcuse, this one-dimensionality could be derived from the identification of law and its social substrate. On the other hand, the social technological version of contemporary legal theory wants to make formal rational legal structures enter at the levels of social economic facts and regularities. Therefore a major convergence has arisen between a positivistic and a sociological conception of law. Mauss concludes from this:

> The fundamental question considered this far, as to whether law should primarily serve a social or a technical function, would appear to have been practically answered already in those modern industrial states whose social reform policies are always oriented according to the data of economic processes. (Mauss, 1980: 16).

Notwithstanding this rather pessimistic conclusion concerning the fundamental identity between legal structure and social structure in the welfare state system, it must be said that two models, nearly incompatible with each other, are to be found in the intertwinement of law and the welfare state. The central idea concerning the two different models with regard to the relation between law and the welfare state is reducible to the fact that the problem of formality plays a dominant role in both Continental European and common law legal systems. We have already considered this aspect when we dealt with the legalistic residue in every concept of law. Formality, in the opinion of Max Weber, implies a legal system that always tends to need certain basic features such as totality, autonomy, publicity, and positivity. These four characteristics of the legal system are, at the same time, characteristics of a system of rules according to which the legal system maintains itself. Seen as a whole, they constitute the form or face of systemic self-maintenance. The lack or absence of one ingredient, though not wholly destructive, nevertheless distorts the physiognomy of the form. Indeed, one of the main problems of legal theory is the fact that nearly all concepts developed in it are still measured according to this one concept of formality. This applies to Anglo-Saxon legal thinking on the function of standards as well as to the discussions in codified law on the relation between "principles" and "norms", or on the "modalities" of legal application-thinking. The criterion of formality is to a large extent auto-referential and it has a tendency to embody other arguments, such as usefulness, sociability, utility, and even "fairness". No wonder then that it seems impossible to make formality totally disappear from the legal system and legal practice. It is, however, exactly this that a total social-technocratic conception of law and a complete functioning of law in the welfare state ultimately suggests (Unger, 1976: 204).

With this conception the tendency to neglect the activity that brings about the specific dogmatic-formalistic nucleus of law arises: the shifting of semantic fields through which an identity is suggested. But great differences continue to exist in the deep-structure of the unities of meaning with which the law and the idea of a welfare state work. In other words, the fundamental structures of meaning and value orientation relative to both law and the welfare state remain unaltered while a new value orientation is generated at the surface (for an opposite opinion see Peters infra). As a result tension and discord ensue between the deep and surface structures of meaning and value orientation. The problem here boils down to this: should the deep-structure of meaning undergo radical transformation itself or may it remain unaltered but modify and incorporate the emergent value orientation at the surface level into its meaning structure and value orientation?

Jenkins once described this phenomenon as a translation of the purposes of law towards its own meanings

> (T)he legal apparatus transforms ... goals into conditions that it can effectively promote. It does this by translating 'similarities' as '*equality*' and 'differentiations' as '*freedom*'. The shift that this brings about in interpretation and intention is quite radical. The similarities and differentiations that cultivation aims at are conceived in terms of human character and conduct. The equalities and freedoms that law aims at are couched in terms of social conditions and treatment. Law envisages an outcome in which equals will be treated equally and personal freedom will be protected (Jenkins, 1977: vol. 1, 120, see also Habermas re: role of law as medium, infra).

On this basis, it must be said that the two models always continue to act as reference points for each other. Jenkins described the relation between the two models as follows:

> The legal apparatus should take advantage of scientific knowledge and technological efficiency to effect desired social reforms, or scientific and technical experts should employ law as an instrument to realize their blue-print of a good society (1980: 216).

This characterization brings out the fact that the two models can never become completely identical. This is so even if one concedes that law and legal regulations may be employed as an instrument to realize specific social objectives.

This leads us to reflect that the intertwinement of the legal system and the welfare state can be consistent only because of the two functioning models. The first model is the *legalistic* conception. In this model the attempt is made to include, optimally, all social and economic developments into the legal system. But these developments are transformed into determining factors in a legal system which is in itself more or less autonomous. As a consequence, ***welfare in the welfare state remains dependent on the possibilities of a legal articulation of social reality***. Legal dogmatism functions within this circumference as does the activity of articulation. The second model is the *functionalist* model. This model argues that social developments can on the whole be considered as sources of law. They must articulate themselves within the legal system in such a way that the legal system itself develops in a way favorable to the desired articulations. In this way of thinking, *the welfare of the welfare state is dependent on the decisive strength of social complexity*. This strength must take the legal discourse change and make it contribute to the functionalization and instrumentalization of law (see Friedman, Aubert supra and Peters infra).

It is obvious that the first mentioned legalistic perspective can be considered as a *pessimistic* vision concerning the basic idea of a total identity of law and welfare structure. The second vision is a more *optimistic* one concerning the possibilities of identity between legal structure and the idea of a welfare state. Those who advocate for a functional perspective basically plead in favor of an identity between legal system and welfare state. In doing so, they underestimate the transformational conditions imposed by the legal system, as an automatic system, on functional thinking. In particular this is true of the claims made by legal dogmatism within the scope of legal science and the practice of law. Legal dogmatism neglects, at the epistemological level, the claim to the specificity of legal science in relation to both the social sciences and social reality. This neglect imposes by implication a false identity between legal science and the social sciences as well as social reality. Thus legal science purports to swallow or embrace every aspect of social life precisely because of the instrumentality of law in the welfare state. But the optimism arising from the conception of the instrumentality of law in the welfare state is clearly indefensible.

Indeed what emerges with regard to this line of thinking is the idea that for its preservation the welfare state is at least dependent upon the effectiveness of legal discourse as a function in the organization of society. In order to realize an effective functioning legal discourse, it must fulfill the required conditions for the juridification of social problems. The conditions for such juridification are not factors belonging to a system-theoretical or sociological method of considering law, but they are the object of theoretical legal studies. They concern the specificity of legal knowledge of reality. They focus upon the specific cognitive character of the structure and content of social reality defined from the standpoint of legal science. As has already been suggested, the basic dogmatic structure of legal science is a decisive factor in the construction of characteristically specific legal knowledge. It must also be said that these problematic aspects of legal science are important not only for the intertwining of the legal system and the welfare state as such, but also for the question of whether *alternative dogmatic figures* can be developed and what their social impact would be. There is a tendency in this respect to neglect the important epistemological difference between sociology of law and legal theory (for a critical account of such tendencies see Teubner 300 infra). There is apparently a great need to temporarily forget the above-mentioned conditions or to ignore them totally. As Unger formulates it

> (T)he immediate courses of the post-liberal moves toward purposive legal reasoning and procedural or substantive justice are directly connected with the inner dynamic of the welfare state. These moves appear as ways to deal with concentrated power in the private order or to correct the effects of a system of formal rules (1976: 196).

According to this conception, the idea of a welfare state is still struggling with the problem of the positivist and formalist character of law.

II. Political Theory and Theory of Law

The above-mentioned conditionality regarding the function of law in the welfare state can be found in the sphere of politics and economics. We will begin with a consideration of politics, i. e. with the sphere of political theory. Theories of the welfare state often suggest that individual welfare and the development of individual qualities form the ultimate goal of the function of law in the welfare state. The underlying assumption here is that law is the instrument whereby human character may be formed. This includes the idea that latent human capabilities could also be tapped and developed through the law. However, it is interesting to note that an author like Jenkins discounts, with some qualification, the idea that in welfare state the ultimate goal of law must be the formation of human character and the development of the individual's potentialities.

> Law is simply not an effective instrument for the formation of human character or the development of human potentialities. There is, however, a great deal that law can do indirectly to promote these goals. Stated generally, it can keep a watchful eye on the entire institutional structure of society to see that its several elements properly discharge their responsibilities (1979: 119).

There is a certain discrepancy in the political theory. If the latter is concerned with macro-structures and institutional facts it is difficult to see how it can simultaneously sustain the claim that it is also concerned with the welfare of the individual in a direct and immediate manner. The point here is that the welfare state — the repository of the individual's welfare — is a microcosm which stands in sharp contrast to the macrocosmic world of institutional facts.

In political theories concerning the welfare state, three elements have been noted. Firstly, in this area attention is always paid to *distributive* connections. The main question of social policy concerns distributive mechanisms in society, their functioning, and especially their harmony or disharmony within that society. Moreover, no attention is paid to the legal composition when conflicts arise concerning disharmony or when legal regulations must be made in order to accomplish the distribution successfully. This apparent neglect of the legal composition might have beneficial effects for the smooth functioning of the mechanisms of distribution. But the most important aspect of this neglect is the fact that it serves to conceal the true character and role of the legal composition in the sphere of distributive connections. In its nature and character the legal composition is that *legal subjectivity is a condition because legal imputation can only exist when legal subjectivity is accepted.* In this respect parallels can be drawn between theory-building in the social, political and legal spheres. Socio-political theory-building deals with macro-structures and yet suggests that individuals make up its ultimate subject matter. What is certain, but also lost sight of, is that this individual is no other than the individual of these macrostructures (for a different viewpoint see Ewald supra). The transformation is not elaborated theoretically, nor is any practical importance accorded to it. Nevertheless, from an epistemological point of view this must be regarded as important. To a greater extent the observations just made apply similarly to law. Distributive mechanisms are realized by law in the welfare state with the aid of the dogmatic concept of imputation. But this concept cannot come into existence without the concept of the legal subject. Here the gap between legal subjectivity (a legal-dogmatic construction of the first order) and life-factual subjectivity is still greater than that between the individual of the macro-structures and the life factual individual in political theory-building.

The second-main accent within political theory-building concerns the rational relations in society. It must be said that, depending on the theoretical model in operation, a different emphasis is given to the question of individualism, a notion which plays an essential role in the theory of actual society. In the field of political theory-building with regard to the welfare state, individualism is often interpreted as atomism and hedonism. This interpretation always has an ambiguous character, since individualism plays a role in determining the structure of society itself. In fact, this structure is always considered as a structure of elements which are none other than individuals. The other side of this theoretical viewpoint is the desire to abolish the worst consequences of atomization (i. e. of strict individualism).

It has become clear in many theories that the idea of the welfare state cannot be fully realized because of the extreme individualism prevalent in legal thinking. We then arrive at theories that construct a society with reciprocal social structures. This reciprocity should lead to a more universal type of social structure. Different values are then attached to this movement of universality depending on the theoretical starting point. Provided it is assumed that individuality is the condition for the possibility of constructing any social or political theory and that as such a conditionality stands outside the pale of criticism, it is nevertheless pertinent to observe that as an aspect of social-political theory individualism can be and has often been criticised. But here it must also be said that individualism in political theory can be criticized without questioning its conditionality for every social and political theory. In fact, even critics of individualism are themselves affected by it and it is even present in the critical need for a reciprocal societal structure. Reciprocity itself can be thought of on the basis of an individualized vision of society. It is the individuals in society who are held to construct mutuality and reciprocity. It is also individuals who ought to adopt a universal attitude in order to improve the cohesion within the welfare state. In law the element of individuality also plays a major role. But the dogmatic conditionality of that individuality is of greater import.

This dogmatic conditionality appears sharply in the construction of legal subjectivity. Theory of law can criticize exaggerated individualism, but it cannot avoid the dogmatic conditionality that declares individuals to be legal subjects (i. e. bearers of rights and duties). Thus, the generality and universality of legal subjectivity makes autonomy, publicity, logicity, and the internal cohesion of law effective. Therefore, when law attempts to exercise its task in the welfare state the realization of the legal subject becomes a condition for law and politics. In both cases legal subjectivity has to be considered to be of the greatest importance.

A third element which is stressed in political theory-building is the dimension of *information* and *knowledge*. Besides the distribution of existing goods and services and besides the promotion of relational competition, the production of *information* and *knowledge* arises as an independent factor in the welfare state. Information has become one of the most important instruments of social control and system-regulation. As a consequence, knowing as such, has become an important element of the welfare state. Every instrument of control and system regulation carries with itself the danger that in the welfare state an omnipresent power is constructed. Nevertheless, one can scarcely imagine how a welfare state can function without a high degree of information and regulation. No social laws or social provisions function without a highly differentiated system of information. The giving and providing of information are also an issue in Karl Mannheim's idea that the fundamental democratization of society cannot be realized without a far-reaching distribution of information to individuals, and especially to groups. It is essential that groups have information which provides them with specific knowledge of the logistics of the decision-making process and its background. Discussions on norms and prescriptions must be made *compulsory*. Against this background, some problems on the border-line between law and politics can play a role, as in the case of data-banks. From the perspective of the welfare state and political decision-making, there arises the need for a high degree of accessibility; while from a legal point of view the protection of the individual from the consequences of general accessibility plays an important role. But what has been said on the two preceding aspects also applies here: the legal composition clearly indicates that law contains the conditions for successful politics in a welfare state. For example, the dispersal of information and knowledge, in so far as it concerns groups, is settled through the legal theory of representation. It is precisely this representation which reveals that law can regulate social problems only through individuals. The individuals here are no longer considered as everyday-life individuals, but as inserted into the context of law and policy through the dogmatic image of legal subjectivity.

These three facets of the distributive connection, the relational connection and information have a legal relevance in political theory. Political theory shares here with law a vision of society as well as a particular basic structure of theory-building. Both attempt to develop a high degree of equilibrium in society. The notion of equilibrium can be found in the ideas of justice which comprise the background to the concept of a welfare state. In addition, political and legal theory share the pre-supposition of rationality. Individuals who are the objects of the promotion of just distributive connections, just relational connections and an inflow of sufficient information, are considered as rational beings in both political and legal theory. This rationality is already legal rationality, concerned as it is with the rationality attributed to a person as bearer of rights and obligations in society, i. e. to a legal subjectivity.

These two conditions, rationality and equilibrium, are the goals of political and legal theory. That is an ideological articulation. In ideological forms of thinking conditions are generally represented as goals. This happens in a very subtle manner in this argumentation. Rationality and equilibrium, as conditions, are presented as goals in the shared context of political and legal theory. They are thought of as elements which could reduce the formality of law in order to achieve a more socialized and useful law. Thus, it appears that both political theory-building and legal theory, stress "equity" and "solidarity" as necessary backgrounds for political and legal decision-making in the welfare state (for an exposition of this analysis see Ewald supra). These are also the two factors which contribute to the demolition of strict and dogmatically conditioned legal structures. In many cases it has been suggested that the dogmatic character of law could even disappear through the promotion of "equity" and "solidarity". This reduction of the impact of dogmatics is described by Unger as a process of decline of the rule of law (1976: 192; Benn and Peters, 1959, Mahnschke, 1982). Unger even speaks of a dis-integration of the rule of law in a post-liberal society, which directs its attention more to welfare than to the formal structures of society. This decline in the influence of the rule of law is closely related to the suggestion that the dogmatic character of law could be rejected in favor of solidarity. In the first place, this has dogmatic consequences. Unger remarks that in Anglo-Saxon legal thinking an expansion of "open ended standards" and "general" clauses in legislation, in the administration and in general legal thinking itself has taken place. An increasing number of open-ended prescriptions which ought to be filled according to time, place and circumstances, are incorporated in the law.

This could result in the disappearance of a legalistic model in favor of the predominance of the functional model of law described in the previous section. It could lead to a legalistic reasoning on policy in which the purposes of law are of paramount importance and their ideological structures have no chance of being taken into consideration. "Equity" and "solidarity" could make the formal character of law disappear. A general system for applying the law through general rules could consequently be established, and law would no longer be held to be the key-stone of justice. The deductive process of decision-making in law is no longer socially adequate in the theory of the welfare state; decision-making must be understood in a functionalist sense. It must be obvious that a rule, in a particular legal judgment, can be used effectively to achieve socially acceptable goals. In this way, law becomes an instrument in the hands of welfare ideas and ideals.

New conditions arise concerning the legitimacy of the processes by which social advantages are exchanged or (re)divided. The legitimacy of law is consequently made dependent on the ideals of the welfare state. Ultimately, a development originates making theory of law part of political theory. Curiously enough, closer consideration must lead to exactly the opposite conclusion.

The basic values and theoretical presuppositions of political theory are approximately identical to those of the legal system. The dogmatically concealed presuppositions of the law are not a subject of research within political theory. The intertwinement of law and the welfare state is persistently dominated by the same set of dogmatic rules. If such intertwinement were to become an issue in political science, the latter would ineluctably be shaped and colored by the main principles of legal dogmatics. For this reason concepts like "equity" or "solidarity" always function within the framework of a dogmatic view of politics and the law. The determination of social and political goals is co-determined by the main constitutive forces of the legal discourse, its teleology, its rationality, its conceptualization of causality.

The legal construction of social reality needs the general idea of the rule of law and the basic structure of the legal model, which is the *application* of norms to facts. This can be gathered from the fact that the lawyer invariably construes the political situation in terms of a case because he is always guided by the idea of legal composition to which we have already referred. Accordingly, for the lawyer any given political situation is seen in terms of a sequence of ad hoc situations.

These situations are deemed to be autonomous entities, elements that are to be judged individually by the law. What is striking in this is that the legal apparatus always constructs or reconstructs the cohesion of the political apparatus a posteriori. The justification of this cohesion and of the expedience of an enacted legal decision is constructed afterwards. In this a posteriori legitimation law remains true to itself, since this justification belongs to one of the basic structures of legal thought. The decision to be made is in most cases projected intuitively and is legalized afterwards by means of dogmatic rules. Intuition and rationality are brought together by the dogmatic legal figure (image) in an unbroken unity of legal judgment.

III. Legal Theory and Economic Theory

The theses formulated up to now remain on a rather abstract and general level. This also applies to the intertwining of law and economy, one of the most important aspects of the welfare state (Brüggemeier, 1982: 60). It is also important to realize that the influence of politics can increase without destroying the influence of the economy. Repoliticization of societal structures and the juridification connected with it go along with the deprivatization of the economy. These processes of repoliticization, juridification and deprivatization are highly complex. They become even more complex due the fact that their continuity is interrupted and even destroyed by hidden measures of a crisis policy and the influence of change within the theory of crisis.

Both are directed towards the problems concerning the rationality of the interrelations of societal segments and especially with regard to the crisis in the distributive segments of the welfare state. The intertwining of economy, politics, and administration leads to a concept of the state that increasingly loses its character as the classical concept of the legal state. It is this nascent concept of the state which is of great importance for the intertwining of economics and the welfare state. The legal state is supplemented by the administration and the work of parliament within a more liberal pattern of a thought, while at the same time it is also interpreted as a constitutional state. All this happens because unlike the legal state, the idea of a complementary social state originates as an expression of co-operative federalism. Through the ideas of solidarity and equity, this cooperative federalism tries to enter into legal dogmatics.

It seems moreover, as if the postulates of an individualistic and atomistic natural law are disappearing as far as the connection of individual and society is concerned. The state becomes more of a societal unit and the societal unit becomes more of an economic structure. Thus it is apparent that the relation between law and economics is such that the idea of the welfare state is shaped by those arising from and based upon theories of civil law. Here the interconnection between economic liberty and private property assumes particular significance against the background of liberty as the basic model of civil law. This implies that the individual as *legal subjectivity* has the capacity to acquire rights and assume obligations freely. Seen from this perspective, it may well be suggested that contractuality adheres, as it were, like a quality to the individual. Contractuality in the form of liberty is translated into political freedom which is guaranteed by parliamentary democracy on the one hand and the rule of law on the other. When this translation occurs the citizen becomes no longer tied to the idea of contractuality which was previously a main element of the relation between the individual and the state. In other words, this could imply a transition from contractuality to organization (see also Wiethölter 246 infra). The contractual relations between citizens in a state are based, according to this theory, on the belief that the intentions of individuals are always the intentions of individuals in society and that these individuals together form a structure based on free will and autonomy. The organizational context, on the contrary, takes such individualistic starting-points less into account. Instead it insists on the necessities arising from the super-structures and which have a bearing upon individuals. The individualized elements which play a role in the relationship between economic thinking and ideas of private property can be legitimated and guaranteed only by a more abstract dependence on the rule of law and on representation through parliamentary democracy. The question is whether such a transition from contract to organization is really effective.

The problem already raised emerges here clearly in all its aspects. Contractual thinking on society simply cannot get lost in an organizational thinking about this society because organization is also treated as a structure built from autonomous elements. These elements are the individuals as interpreted in individualistic and hedonistic natural law.

This generates the thinking and actually imbues the individual with the attitude that at all times he must experience himself as autonomous and contractualistic. No wonder then that the individual wishes himself to be interpreted as such by legal and economic institutions. The result is a remarkable ambiguity in the interpretation on the notions of "freedom" and "individuality". On the one hand, in a welfare state there are social structures which have a more political character and are directed to the organizational aspect. On the other hand, the experience of the individual continues to be bound to the problem of individualism and the relation between economy and private property. The emotional world of the individual, which is entangled in the welfare state is determined by a private legal conception of state, society, and welfare. But that same individual is forced to realize his feelings in structures which are more oriented to organization. This involves collisions which often require legal solutions. The requisite solutions can only be found when the conditions of transformation from everyday-life subjectivity into legal subjectivity have been fulfilled. This legal subjectivity is itself linked with the traditional, individualistic natural law concept regarding the individual in state and society (see also Habermas).

This situation continues to exist even in the welfare state where the state must clearly intervene, e. g. in periods of economic crisis and unemployment. Economics in the welfare state is then forced to try to absorb these destabilizing cumulative effects in order to build up a new quasi-equilibrium. Such interventions can be seen in law.

The transition from a private law model to a legal model of the welfare state could be seen as a crisis in autonomy. The private contract loses its importance in the transition from private to collective autonomy and is replaced by a collective contract. This is the case in collective wage-agreements in labor law. In this manner a distinct departiculization of the contractual element emerges and thus individual contractuality gives way to collective contract. In addition, expressions of behavior emerge, clearly moving farther and farther away from the basic model of private autonomy. Obligatory rights of protection are formulated for larger groups in society. These exclude the operation of a general model of private law. However, it must be said that one cannot characterize this crisis in private autonomy as a real and fundamental transition (for a different viewpoint see Ewald supra). This is so because the individual contract is transferred into a collective contract. Individuality and collectivity are in the given case interpreted in terms of individualistic natural law and so they join the dominant concept of the self relative to the individual in the welfare state. From this point of view, there is evidently no far reaching transition from contractuality to the organizational type of legal, economic, and welfare state. The thesis that the development of the welfare state with regard to law, not only guides a *means* in law but also a *condition* to attain welfare can be maintained. It now becomes clear how in the *deep structure of legal composition in relation to social reality, the concept of welfare is already totally politicized and legalized* (see also Heller infra). The individual, who wants to claim his right to welfare, possess his welfare, interprets himself as an owner in terms of private law. This is also the case when the issue concerns collective contracts, such as wage-agreements or protective legal regulations that have a general character and surface structure which is more organizational then contractual.

In the light of the foregoing, the problem arises as to whether or not the development from the depositivization of law towards its socialization can be seen in the same light. The crucial point to remember in this connection is that the process of the socialization of law increasingly leaves a dim imprint upon the previously bright formalistic character of law. The functionalist model, which has been described as the opposite of the legalistic model in the theory of the welfare state, often strives to develop general legal programs based upon general clauses. It even attempts to develop a law which can be called "judge's law", to use Marcic's term. In "judge's law" many relativizations of the dominancy of the private-law model occur because of the influence of the goals of the welfare state. This can be seen in penal and economic law. The need for materialization of private law leads to forms of organization which are less dominated by contractuality. Institutional forms of representation are developed in welfare state thinking and not those forms of organizations which are based on *contracts concluded by citizens*. An exemple of this development is the construction of legal and social structures relating to general participation in factories. Another example is that of autonomous decision-makers (understood in the sense of the traditional meaning of European private law) in contemporary economic law. These decision-makers lose their autonomy and become constituent elements in more comprehensive finance-planning activities. The function of decision-making does itself get lost in the wider context of organisms that govern the economic situation as a whole.

The thesis of Brüggemeier becomes interesting in the assertion that law in the welfare state is no longer defined by the notion of freedom but by the variable forms of increased state activity. We cannot here go into the newly constructed legal solutions which emphasize the non-contractual element of organization (Brüggemeier, 1982: 63). Consideration of the implications these developments in political and economic theory have on the law, generates the idea that it is doubtful whether it is still possible to put forward the thesis that legal subjectivity, for exemple, is the decisive dogmatic factor for the functioning of the law in the welfare state. Many developments easily show how far the influence of legal dogmatics is relativized. They also indicate the types of changes in law which lead to the dimunuition of the influence of legal subjectivity. It is thus conceivable that in the final analysis the persistence of the idea of the welfare state and the correlative changes in law could become so important that the dogmatic conditionality of law would disappear totally (Broekman, 1984: 136).

Here the deep structure of the argumentation is reached. Peczenick made a distinction between "contextually sufficient justification" and "deep justification" in theory of law (Peczenik, 1982a: 137; 1982b: Vol. II, 103). Referring to this distinction, it could be said that the development outlined above seems to be true in the contextual justification and argumentation structure. It is also interesting to observe that political theory as well as the sociological theory of law harmonize with this contextually sufficient justification. This brings about the idea that concepts like elasticity, reflexivity and responsivity of law are formulated within a *contextual* justification of law. It is thus not the task of politics, economics or sociology to go beyond these elements of contextual justification, since they are located on the level of legal dogmatics. The latter is satisfied with contextually sufficient justification. As far as the *deep* justification is concerned, we refer to the remarks made in the previous section, where it was argued that reference is still made to legal subjectivity as a condition for the cohesion of law and the welfare state in spite of the surface structure which appears to be different. In this deep justification-structure the cohesion with the values of society, which are the basic values of law itself, is dealt with. At the same time the possibility of justification as such is considered. In the deep structure of our reflections, however, the transition from a legalistic to a functional model cannot be completely realized. The loss of every formalistic-legalistic element in law would not bring about a change in the legal interpretation of the welfare state, because it remains within the same legal paradigm. A change of that paradigm would result in a completely different legal system, that, as far as Marx is concerned, could only be the result of a changing society.

Legal dogmatism remains intact because the basic values of the law can be found in the welfare state. These are connected with individuality, causality and equilibrium. The decisive power of law in the welfare state remains established on these three basic values and is therefore chained onto legalistic and formalistic principles. Transitions from contractual to non-contractual forms of organization or from a private law model to other political and social forms of organization are extremely interesting from a sociological point of view. However, they do not seem to lead to a neutralization of the individualistic-contractual values.

This general idea can only be verified through legal theory by way of causal analysis in the positivistic sense. It will be clear therefore that the cases most suitable for analysis are found in economic law, tax-law, social and criminal law. These are the legal spheres in which legal subjectivity as a fixed point of reference for the definition of the concept of law is on the decline. At the same time changes in dogmatics can be pointed out. However, it is our thesis that even these changes remain on the level of contextually sufficient justification and do not affect the deep structure of law. These dogmatic figures are appropriate for articulating unchanged basic values in a changing structure of cohesion between law and welfare state. Such an articulation can be extremely efficient from a social point of view and can serve the purpose of the welfare state. But the same articulation does, however, conceal the question whether or not the changing structure of cohesion between law and the welfare state constitutes a real change of law with regard to its basic values and conditions. This line of questioning transcends the perspective of the problem in that it leads to an insight of a much more general nature and the insight itself is related to the increasing attempts to develop alternative dogmatic figures.

The need for the construction of alternative dogmatic figures of law such as alternative sentences, judgments and legal commentaries coincides with the transition from a legalistic to a functional model. It is often suggested that only on the basis of the possibility of alternativity can a fundamental change of law take place. The hope for this possibility is undoubtedly part of the complex problem of the cohesion between law and welfare state. It is possible to develop a legal theoretical hypothesis with regard to this. *Attempts to construct alternative dogmatic figures of law carry with them the articulated and unelaborated need for change in the sense of deep-justification. But they manifest themselves as real factual changes in the sense of a contextually sufficient justification.* Deep-justification here does not relate to the problems of change and justification of the basic principles of law and society, as is the case in anarchistic theories. Consequently we could adopt a threefold stratification: firstly, a contextually sufficient justification, secondly the deep-justification and lastly the justification of the basic principles of law and society. Attempts to formulate alternative dogmatic figures which aim at a change in the sense of deep-justification, bring about changes in the sense of a contextually sufficient justification. They do not bring about changes in the sense of the basic principles of law and society. On the basis of this reasoning, a general theory of alternative commentaries, sentences and judgments can be developed.

IV. Legal Subjectivity

Legal subjectivity is one of the strongest dogmatic concepts of law. However, this concept is not completely umambiguous especially when one considers the relation between legal subjectivity and the concept of law. In legal terminology the word 'law' has at least two meanings: it refers to objective law, i.e. the positive law which is ultimately the result of a sovereign power. It also refers to the claims of a concrete legal subject with regard to that positive law. Philosophically speaking, the concept of law implies both the negation of the autonomy of the individual as well as the confirmation of that autonomy. From Hobbes to Kelsen theoretical attempts have been made to legally overcome this ambiguity. Until now neither legal theory nor legal philosophy has been successful in this attempt. It is interesting, however, that this ambiguity implies an antinomy between sovereignity and law. Two dimensions, namely the *political* and *rational*, seem to exclude one another here. Law is, in a political sense, always an element of power. It is a measure of sovereign authority which scarcely questions the content of its law in a differentiating and subtle manner. Thus the genesis of the concept of law is both derived from and based upon the view that law is always — in a political sense — a moment and a measure of sovereign authority. In this sense law is the expression of the will of sovereign authority. The sovereign's decision is thus always embodied in every legal measure or enactment. Accordingly, there is always a decisionistic basis of law. So it is that decisionism is the specific type that emerges in the modelling of the law. But there is also a rational concept of law that is characterized not so much by its formal origin as by its content. Here norm and rationality are closely interwoven. The correlated ethical postulate is mostly expressed in the form of the postulate of equality of the legal subjects. In that case, law is ratio and not necessarily will. That type of legal thinking can no longer be called decisionistic, it shows clear resemblances to classical natural law.

In both cases the foremost problem is legal subjectivity. The legal subject is the form in which objective law or subjective rights emerge within the framework of legal dogmatics. In both cases, however, these conceptions of legal subjectivity express a dogmatic articulation of the image and nature of man and their function in law. In law, human rationality and the concept of a free and autonomous will are the basic repositories of the nature of man. In both cases an anthropology is implicitly present. This anthropology is not an innocent speculation concerning an indeterminable "nature" of man, but it is an enforced scheme that is shaped according to a legal dogmatic concept. This process also determines the intertwinement of law and welfare state. Marxist critisism on the concept of legal subjectivity asserts that through the concept of the legal subject other items, like private property, are reified and interpreted a-historically. The aura of eternity which is granted to the legal subject, is closely connected with the suggestion of eternity as far as private property is concerned. However, we cannot overlook the fact that this reification and eternalization of reality seems to be abolished at the level of politics and economy in the welfare state.

But this is only the mask of the surface-structures of everyday-reality. The legal subject and its philosophical implications remain, in the strongest sense of the word, a condition for the functioning of law in a welfare state. All elements of the legal discourse find their point of convergence in this concept of subjectivity. The individualizing effect of subjectivity in legal practice needs to be emphasized (Broekman, 1979: ch VII). This is not a coincidence which can be put aside by alternative legal measures or by changes of the surface-structure of the corpus of legal dogmatics.

We meet here a necessity which is anchored in the basic structures of the law. These exist in the first place in order to *articulate* the basic values of civil culture. Without this individualization legal practice is consequently out of the question. This is also the case when, on the level of the contextually sufficient justification, the principle of contractuality and its legal concretization is passed on to more general forms of organization. This process of individualization is in itself always a process of *abstraction*: from the definition of the legal subject as a bearer of rights and duties now it appears that the individual is present as an abstract and mathematical entity, that is: a product of reduction. Legal subjectivity is an abstract expression of the human being as it exists, or is supposed to exist within the framework of legal dogmatics. The specifically individuated form of consciousness and subjectivity in bourgeois philosophy finds its counterpart in the same form of legal subjectivity which ultimately expresses congruent bourgeois values. It is our thesis here that for the law, there exists an absolute identity between the nature of man and this legal form of individualization. Consequently this form is used as an ontological argument in legal philosophy and legal theory; and also on a less reflexive level, in legal practice.

This ontological way of thinking has practical consequences in the law. Unborn children and mental defectives are treated as legal subjects in everyday-legal practice. This construction brings out the autonomy, omnipresence and omnipotence of law. The legal subject is a construction of the law. Every human being is, within our legal system, a legal subject without consideration of his individual qualities, mental capacities, will or intelligence. Partly for this reason, legal dogmatics make a difference between legal capacity in general and the legal capacity to exercise civil rights in particular. A formal universality is awarded to legal subjectivity. Marxist criticism assumes as a consequence that law is not concerned with the subject as a living individual, but with the abstraction of it, namely the bearer of subjectivity. Legal dogmatics constructs such a bearer — it is the legal subject. It is important to consider in this context that although legal subjectivity is detached from the behavior of the individual it exercises rule over it. The behavior of the individual, through his belonging to the society in which legal discourse functions, is always thought of as a pattern of behavior, governed by legal subjectivity. Legal subjectivity and the ideological forms of society are thus closely related. This might be the reason for the fact that freedom, or autonomy of will are the main characteristics ascribed to legal subjectivity. Freedom is understood primarily as the freedom to conclude contracts, i. e. to enter into the area of exchange of goods. This freedom has become a general phenomenon in the welfare state. It is ideologically considered to be the most important aspect of human "nature". Therefore, it is important to keep in mind that freedom, thought of as legal subjectivity, contains above all a form of self-determination which is nothing other than a matter of property relations. This is the basic principle of the idea of contractual capacity. The counterpart of this idea is to be found in another form for freedom; the freedom to participate in exchange (see also Ewald 43 supra). These forms of freedom necessarily imply equality of legal subjects as participation in market exchange and freedom to conclude contracts both presuppose a general pattern of exchange relations among subjects. Equality is, in the terminology of the legal discourse, not considered to be a *concrete* equality, but an equality *in the service of exchange*. It is a *pro forma* equality in which subjects become mutually interchangeable. They can take each other's place not only because of their abstract character but also because they are anonymous in the sense that the fullness of their concrete humanity is not required for legal purposes. This anonimity and abstraction find shape in political ideas concerning the equality of man. Even in politics this equality serves generality. This equality is not concerned with the individual qualities of the every-day life subjectivity. Here we notice how political theory is based on the presuppositions of legal theory. The concept of legal subjectivity and the legal interpretation of equality are points of reference for the objective legal order, which ultimately coincides with the political order.

From this consideration concerning legal subjectivity we can conclude *that the technocratic illusion of the identity between constitutional and welfare state is the reflection of the legal illusion with regard to collective property.* To live in the welfare state is to live on the borderline of private and collective property. These are the problems that a planned economy has to face. For this reason such an economy is sometimes based on the idea of collective property. However, in most cases it is based on decrees issued by experts. Therefore a planned economy is a reflection of contractual thinking.

In connection with this principle, *industrial rationality finds its companion in legal rationality.* Even here, the figure of legal subjectivity remains a *conditio sine qua non* for the development of the welfare state and a planned economy. In this framework, an apparent contradiction evolves between legal property (still based on the private law model) and property relations which are situated on the level of industry. The concept of the welfare state develops in favor of the latter. Economic property increasingly becomes a possession of separate companies. This goes hand in hand with a segmented economic vision of society. Companies are acting more and more as separate corporate bodies, as legal subjects. They all try to achieve their own aims, through their contractual relations in society. Companies strive for a key position in the welfare state through the dogmatic figure of the legal subject. As so-called corporate legal subjects they would be conferred with the status of bearers of rights and duties. This is a position they can only hold when the contractual relations form a compensating counterbalance to the central plan (for a parallel view see also Ewald supra). The economic coordination in the welfare state becomes, in this way, a striving for economic equilibrium between contractuality and the centrally directed plan.

It is in this triangular relation within the welfare state, between law, economics and politics, that it becomes clear that the legal subject does not really succeed in controlling the world of objects, but is rather a projection of this world. The legal subject is a necessary condition for the goods in society. In this way, we can see the market as the incarnation of the anthropological claim of the law to realize a right to natural freedom and equality which is in fact no more than a compulsory system of laws of exchange. In this connection, the remark of Pashukanis is still valid: there is a mutual implication of exchange, private-property and legal subjectivity. These mutual implications remain operative in spite of attempts towards socialization and generalization of the law, which favor a system of encompassing legal regulations in the welfare state. From this point of view, one often hears the remark that legal subjectivity implies necessary alienation, which has to be taken for granted in a welfare state. Legal subjectivity is reified because it is chained to the goods in a welfare society and to the ideological compensations for this reification. These attempts are heavily inclined towards a system of encompassing legal regulations in the welfare state. In these circumstances, a form of alienation emerges in which the sovereignty of the will is dominated by the idea of private property in the welfare state. The formula according to which the legal subject is the carrier of rights and duties, is at the same time an adumbration of the law that awards to the already formulated and defined legal subject the "jus untendi et abutendi". Only in this context can we speak of the freedom of the legal subject. One must bear in mind that the freedom of that subject cannot be described as an illusion, as some Marxist authors would have it; but as a specific speech act within the legal discourse. It is consequently a speech act, which does not function at the level of everyday-life speech acts. The freedom of the legal subject is only a freedom in as far as this concept of freedom can be interpreted dogmatically. Hence it has the real content of legal subjectivity as its counterpart: legal subjectivity provides the dynamics of law in the welfare state. But this process reveals itself as a dogmatic figure of law: a precondition that cannot be abolished by any legal development or legal change in the welfare state.

V. The Formalization of Legal Subjectivity in Legal Reasoning

As previously stated, the proposition that subjectivity is the condition for the possibility of positive law remains apparent and even highly significant changes in theory and jurisprudence. This observation applies not only to civil law but also to disciplines such as tax- or commercial law. So it is that social contract thinking is anchored in the image of man upheld by collective law. It is also apparent in various dogmatic forms concerning individualization and more especially in the problem of the representation of collective interests. The enquiry here relates to the question of representation through class, conditions relating to such representation as well as the power of law in general. The connection between capacity to litigate and legal subjectivity, a special theme of civil law, already assumes recognizable parallel forms in other legal disciplines. In such cases the jurist is confronted with a differentiated reflection with, as it were, unconsciously predetermined structures of individuality including the tendency to individualize. This does not happen willy-nilly. On the contrary, it reveals the basic structure of a collective of juridical discourses which separately lead to dogmatics. These are also relevant to the modern problem of access to the legal process (access to justice). Are the traditional, dogmatically determined possibility conditions really changing as far as their normative structures are concerned (deep-justification), or are the new forms of theory and jurisprudence to be understood optimally as variations upon structures which remain the same (contextually sufficient justification)?

Cappelletti and Garth consider this question to be the determining criterion for the protection of diffuse and fragmented interests (Cappelletti, 1981: 1). H. Kötz formulates it as follows

> We are interested in to what extent and in which way traditional standing requirements have been liberalized in the past years in order to broaden the role played by private litigation as a means of vindicating the public interest. (Kötz, 1981: 101).

More importantly, it is here matter of situations in which:

> (T)he traditional standing rules would prevent the plaintiff from submitting an issue to the court because the basis of his argument is not that there has been an injury or a threat to a particular right of his own, but that he is seeking to guard the public or a segment of it against allegedly illegal conduct of private persons or governmental agencies (Kötz, 1981: 101).

The present-day technique on the traditional requirements to have access to justice is the perspective to moderate the capacity to litigate and to promote the defence of collective interests. Thus the only good is that which articulates litigation in terms of class interests. This happens either through legislative enactment or the finding of the law (Kötz, 1981: 104). In Belgium, there is an interesting ongoing discussion with regard to this question. The discussion centers on the interpretation of the concept of 'interest' which, as an appropriate pre-requisite, will still acquire the capacity to litigate (Lemmens, 1984). Belgium's "Cour de Cassation" has a different view with regard to these problems from that of the "Conseil d'Etat". With regard to legal verdict and jurisprudence, there is a common catalogue of concepts between these two organs and through such concepts concern or interest may be defined juridically. Both organs define "interest", for instance, as personal, direct, real, secured and in accordance with the law, as of material or moral nature (Lemmens, 1984: 2001). Interestingly, the discussion does not touch upon the qualities of this catalogue, but on the question of how an interest can be understood as being personal and direct, that is, as something that belongs specifically to one as one's own. As such this requires an identification with one's interest. The standpoint of the Conseil d'Etat is the formal investigation of issues. Here the only concern is to identify a certain collective purpose determined by statue. Accordingly, the argumentation remains within the boundaries of the legal discourse. On the other hand, the Cour de Cassation takes material investigation as its major standpoint. It argues that, with regard to the natural or the legal person, a fact is that which will defend interest on the basis of statutory stipulation. It does not, as a consequence, create a peculiarly individual interest. Therefore, the presumption of the Cour de Cassation is fixed upon other criteria (Charlier, 1982: 199). Individual interest is now defined in terms of the existence of a particular person, his material or moral good, his capabilities, occupation and reputation (Lemmens, 1984: 2032). Thus material investigation does not focus upon the formal definition of individual interest. Rather it focusses on the non-formal definition which is heavily influenced by the existential foundations of the natural person. This creates the impression that the frontiers of the legalistic-dogmatic discourse are being transcended (see Peters 260 infra).

In both cases, so the argument goes, the concern is with the ownership forms of interest. These are beyond the pale of discussion. Somehow it is required that ownership interest must be identified with individualization. Even when the requirement for evidence of legal subjectivity no longer plays an important role, formal subjectivity is nevertheless retained in legal dogmatics. What does this mean within the wider context of legal philosophy?

One may even venture to suggest that the view of the Belgian Conseil d'Etat will become generally accepted in the near future. Similar assumptions will appear in other European countries. This is already concretely apparent in H. Achterberg's comparison of the characteristics of law. What stands out remarkably in this connection is the norm structure of law, the availability of subjects as final points and the conceivably differentiated number of such subjects. These subjects cover not only the state and its citizens but also a large number of organizations conceived as juristic persons. Consonant with his own viewpoint, Achterberg reserves the term "organization" for the definition of the anthropologically loaded concepts of "natural" and "legal" person. He redefines them as parts of an organizational whole with and without inner differentiation. These are to be understood as the terminal points of excogitation. Legal relations can exist between such points. (Achterberg, 1982: 33).

This important contribution to legal theory cannot be fully discussed here. Apparently, the view already described also plays a role in the debate between the Belgian Cour de Cassation and the Conseil d'Etat. It is important to keep in mind here that Achterberg's idea, according to which "the tradition of anthropomorphising terminology" should be abolished, must be taken seriously. (Achterberg, 1982: 37). From which scientific-theoretical or dogmatic assumptions does this attitude arise? What is the role of each abstraction and novel formulation in both dogmatics and legal theory? What is the perspective that is given by the constitutive idea already described? What other things become restored by this attitude? Much more important here is the fact that an element of abstraction is required for legal subjectivity so that the ordering of subjects in their relations may be explained as insignificant.

The concretization of the concept of the legal subject is based upon legal norms which determine legal relations. The question concerning which legal relations may abstractly exist between subject is determined normatively. On its own the subject cannot bring about (concrete) legal relations except through co-operation with others. (Achterberg, 1982: 59).

The binary character of legal subjectivity is consequently transformed by a perspective with a strong element of abstraction in legal anthropology. At the same time, it consists of a concretizing element. Thus this theory claims that through this new understanding of the legal perspectives reality is then grasped in a more concrete way than it was previously. This assumption does of necessity imply concretization as well.

It is also to be expected that through this wider concept of differentiation and the distancing of anthropomorphisms in dogmatics and legal theory, the ontological basis of law remains unquestioned. Every thought on legal relations ultimately assumes the form of legalistic thinking. Thus it would appear that facts — in the legal sense — are deemed to be dependent upon a special concept of causality. The beginning and the end of legal relations must be presumed to be rational only when they function as elements of a causal thought-pattern. Traditional theory finds its legitimacy in the argument that the concept of the freedom of the will is anchored in causality. The anthropologically founded idea of freedom of the will becomes socially effective in legal acts that are supported by legal dogmatics. Does this state of affairs become altered by wider abstraction in the specifically individual form of legal relations? It may well be that the desire to dislodge anthropomorphic concepts from law could be fulfilled. But the point of discussion is always the question whether or not legal dogmatics could abandon its own image of man.

Philosophy and anthropology found themselves upon legal theory with greater self-understanding in the official theories of science. This refers to the dominant attitude in the thirties, namely, logical empiricism. This "received view" is a formulation of known claims or assumptions which are valid for every science. It is a reflection of the basic structure of legal dogmatics. In turn, legal dogmatics itself is a reflection of the "received view". It is therefore hardly surprising that the tendency towards subjectivization of legal discourse is intimately connected with the assumptions just referred to. Indeed, it is rooted in them. This becomes abundantly clear with regard to the relation between speech and context. Legal dogmatics regards itself as the speech-act of the legislator. Tradition, notwithstanding its bond to the scientific attitude, regards itself as the speech-act of the researcher. In both cases, the outlook on the speech-acts of a given subject invariably assumes the form of social contractarian thinking which always tends towards individualization. Here we recognize the presence of an underlying value. This may be expressed thus: it is denied that the infinite variety of the social situation (dogmatics) and the extremely complex meaning of phenomena (science) are the starting-point and the high-point of both law and science. Rather, what is asserted is that beneath the surface of legal discourse and science lie the speech-acts of the jurist. This kind of application is regarded as progress in the realm of values. It is deemed to be social and cultural normativization. Application with regard to speech-acts and context is realized in this way that accent is placed upon all forms of scientific and social speech-acts including the law. Thus accent is not placed upon context. On this basis it is suggested that it is self-evident that as far as the binary structures are concerned, law proceeds along the path of truth or falsity, right or obligation. The same holds with regard to morals where the same human beings are to be understood in terms of good or evil. But this is not the natural path. It touches upon a certain application which is an expression of known preferences; a form of social valuation. A thoroughgoing investigation of law should not be confined to the motivations on law. It must also focus upon this constitutive path in order to bring about knowledge about the path. The bases of law are firmly anchored upon the already-mentioned preferences. In the first place, these bases determine the forms of dogmatic stipulations on social reality. The legal image of man facilitates and legitimizes such stipulations in the most direct manner. This is so even when the legal practitioner no longer stands as the cautious mediator between dogmatic structures and the (legal) image of man. Thus it may well be inferred that from this kind of not-knowing, law is descriptive of a complex speech-act constantly ontologizing itself. In this way law conceals the fact that the external distinction between right and obligation has its place in the discontinuity between truth and falsity.

The bases of law are also concealed in human rationality. One may well inquire as to whether *ratio* and *logos* are the appropriate instruments through which such concealment is realized. In this connection reference is made to the tensile relationship that obtains between normative postulates and reality. This tension consists of two poles. On the one hand, it is found at the level of legal dogmatics and facticity as well as in internal legal discourse. On a much wider plane, it is also discernible at the level of law and society including their corresponding external discourses. The question that arises is whether or not a change in the dogmatic evaluation of facts as well as in the dogmatic judgment of the externally changing social situation could in turn lead to a change in the relation between speech-act and context. It is possible to determine that any reaction upon changes with regard to the relationship between normative postulates and reality has a bearing on the fixed ordering of speech-act and context. Legal anthropology must bring this particular ordering to light. It must raise the question whether or not a wide-ranging and fundamental ordering can bring about change in such a way that an adequate reaction of law with regard to the changing social situation is thereby called for.

VI. State and Law

A few remarks of a general nature about the relationship between law and state are, in this context, important. They can serve as a means to clarify the above-mentioned problems concerning the conditions of legal subjectivity. From early days the theme of the relation between state and law has been considered of great importance in philosophy. Philosophical rationalism has been pervaded with the idea that the ideas of philosophical discourse can be realized in political concretization, especially in the governance of the state. The autonomous and individual will of the individuals which played an important role in rationalist natural law, was understood as the will that controls human relations. Man can recognize himself in the universality of law as a human being who possesses a similar universality. This will, located at the crossroads of politics and law, is the externalization of the philosophical concept of human subjectivity. Legal subjectivity is its dogmatic form. The free will obeys its own dictates, which means that it functions as an auto-referential concept. This auto-referentiality is at the same time to be understood as autonomy, which means philosophically that the object is its own externalization. Only on this condition, is reciprocity possible: a reciprocity which is thought of as sociability. The basic idea of the welfare state is based on this transition from autonomy to sociability. The welfare state is one of the results of this transition from autonomy through reciprocity to sociability.

This is a way of thinking which is found in many variations in European thought concerning law and state (Ladrière, 1982; Grimmer, 1976; 1978; Hartmann, 1981: 144, 200). Two remarks can be made. Firstly, it is representative of all variations of contractual thinking on law and state from Hobbes to Nozick. Secondly, according to these theories, the *legitimacy* of the modern state (and especially the welfare state) can only be found in its rationalty. One must specify: that does not focus upon every form of rationality but only legal rationality. Or, as Luhmann puts it, "Human nature lies in freely-moving reason, giving itself the right to autonomy, and the need for constraint is conceived of within the concept of law" (Lumann, 1981: 139).

It is interesting to conclude that this legal rationality (characterized by legitimation through legality) includes the formal as well as the material elements of law. It includes a legitimation through competence and procedure and through consensus. Neither system can be reduced to each other's immediate opposite nor it is possible to think of a structure of legitimation based exclusively on either of them. Competence and procedure will never be satisfactory, not even in an exclusively formalistic legal system. Consensus will also be inadequate and unsatisfactory even in an exclusively funtionalistic system. This twofold function of the concept of law can be found in what has already been said on objective and subjective law. As a result, Maihofer argues that law functions: "in its function as guarantor of the freedom and guarantee of the security of existence of the people as both grounds and limits for a legitimization of the state." (Maihofer 1981: 22). The anthropological motive seems to function here as a central category with regard to the basic principles of law and state: "The legitimization of the state has its grounds and justification in the function of the law, and this in its turn has its grounds and measure in the existence of the people." (Maihofer, 1981: 22). This reflection *seems* to be congruent with the hedonistic, individualistic natural law philosophy which is at the basis of the contract theory of law and society. It even looks as if we are moving, on the basis of such considerations, towards a society of solidarity, coexistence, mutual need or a caring for others. But this would, according to the same reasoning, involve other forms of state and law. To avoid this fundamental change which concerns not just the deep but even the basic structure of the law, a reversal takes place, in general terms, towards a Hegelian form of contractual thinking. The uncertainty of the individual, his caring for others and for sociability, his dependence on other people, must be allayed in the social contract, and finally in law and state. This is related to the definitions of freedom and equality which form, in accordance with the definition of individuality, the basic definitions of legal thought. Only when individuality, freedom and equality can be thought of as belonging together, may a pattern evolve that reproduces social contract thinking. It is here that state and law find their legitimation. As Hegel said

> The principle of the modern state has this terrific power and measure of determination in that the principle of subjectivity permits itself towards the independent extreme of personal need fulfilment and at the same time drives itself back into the substantial unity in a way that it will itself contain this unity (Hegel, 1955: 200).

The consequence is quite clear. The constitutional democratic state, with its ideas regarding representation, separation of powers and the role of political parties, offers guarantees to actualize this process. Hartmann paraphrases Hegel as describing

> a legitimate constitution is the determination of the freedoms of others and the state purpose to limit these freedoms together with stipulations on free political organization with elements of representation; it is a constitutional dispensation (as against naked categorial affirmativity) and operationality. (Hartmann, 1981: 215; see also Maihofer, 1981; Haverkate, 1977; Gysin, 1969: 126).

VII. Legal Subjectitity, Social Contract and Welfare State

Legal subjectivity is an epistemological condition for the interference of law in the welfare state. In dealing with the intertwinement of law and the welfare state, however, this condition is usually left out of consideration.

It is taken for granted just as it is accepted that law is a dogmatic science. Yet, this conditionality determines not only the more abstract social structures, but also deals with man in concrete terms: the man of law and society (which calls itself a welfare state). There remains the question whether man really is as he is legally held to be. This is a central question of hedonistic individuals, as well as of the model of solidarity and legal functionalism. Clearly this question reaches the foundations of law and state and it is thus worth emphasizing that in considering these foundations of state and law reference is always made to anthropological structures. This accounts, as explained above, for the defence of a model of parliamentary democracy, for a liberal model, for a welfare state model and models that are not yet in concrete terms politically organized though they are more ideal models of society.

Social changes in the structure of society are the articulation of these anthropological motives. This is something Maihofer has clarified extremely well in the above quotation. But he has left out of consideration that the concept of man to which he refers applies because of a definable and permanently hidden anthropological element *within* the legal discourse. This anthropological element turns the operative legal discourse into a discourse of power. State and law, as they have been thought of in social contract philosophy from Hobbes until now, are, for this reason, connected to a hidden discourse of power. This anthropological element goes back to Cartesian philosophy. The essence of its dualism, interpreted in a Cartesian way, is to be found in the sphere of subjectivity. Since Cartesian reflections, the *ego cogito* has been taken to be the center of will, action, language and thought. It leads to a "*self*", that is thought of as independent of other regions of subjectivity. In this egological structure lies the basis for a rationalistic voluntarism, which still dominates ideas on state and law. Thus we can understand how strongly legal subjectivity is brought into the grip of reification. The increasing independence of legal subjectivity is the source of the dynamism of all reification. It hardly needs to be demonstrated that this process fits into a mechanistic concept of the world. When the subject projects his activity into the external world, activity should be interpreted in terms of mechanisms and automatisms. This mechanistic interpretation of reality of one of the most important elements of anthropological discourse. The state, understood as a mechanistic and coercive organization, reflects this discourse. The state too, acts in the same reificative and reductionistic way with regard to the individual.

Legal subjectivity can be described according to its autorepresentative and especially its auto-referential basic structure. In connection with this basic structure, state and law can be considered as two aspects of the same anthropological motive. Both are, in Luhmann's systems theory, two poles of a closed auto-referential system:

Auto-referential systems are closed systems if they have to refer each operation back to themselves, and if "auto" is taken here to be "overall operation control". We can take the brain as a model and see at once that a closed auto-referential system is in no way the opposite of a system open to the outside world, but is much rather precisely a condition for enabling a system to behave towards the outside world in a self-controlled way (Luhmann, 1981: 69; see also Willke, Teubner infra).

On the basis of studies concerning Canon law, the French jurist and psycho-analyst, Pierre Legendre, has defined the role of law in terms of an *instaurateur idéalisé*. He claims that the legal system is directed at one purpose: to maintain the love of power. In this view, he considers the task of the lawyer to be the art of inventing the love-object of power and this would be the political element of law (Legendre, 1974: 38).

All this deals with the anthropological and legal structure of the legal subject. When power is spoken about in this context it is not suggested that law can be understood only in terms of power in the sense of repression. Rather, we are here concerned with the intertwinement of power, state and law. In state and law, power lies in the characteristics which law ascribes to itself and claims to be necessary for the state. We have already met these characteristics: invariableness; permanency; abstraction; generality. (Lenoble and Ost, 1980: 264).

In fact, we can say that the structure of power which can be unveiled by analyses of legal subjectivity refers to a power which is an element of the generally presupposed rationality of law and the welfare state. This remark should make it clear that our central thesis — *legal subjectivity as a fundamental condition for the functioning of law in a welfare state* — is not limited to a technical legal problem, or to a sociological problem. It concerns the foundation of law and therefore problems of power. These problems are always linked to the inquiry into the nature of man. This concerns both man as he actually functions in the law as well as man of future legal structures within a constantly changing society.

References

Achterberg, Norbert (1982) *Die Rechtsordnung als Rechtsverhältnisordnung.* Berlin: Duncker & Humblot.

Benn, Stanley I., and Richard S. Peters (1959) *Social Principles and Democratic State.* London: Allen & Unwin.

Broekman, Jan M. (1979) *Recht und Anthropologie.* Freiburg i. Br.: Alber.

— (1982a) *Recht en Antropologie.* Antwerpen: S.W.U.

— (1982b) "La forma interna del pensiemento legal", in *Communicationes Primer Congreso Internacional de Filosofia del Derecho.* Vol. 2. La Plata.

— (1983) *Mens en mensbeeld van ons recht.* Leuven/Zwolle: Acco/Tjeenk Willink.

— (1984) "Changes of Paradigm in the Law", in A. Peczenik et al. (eds.) *Theory of Legal Science.* Dordrecht: Reidel.

BRÜGGEMEIER, Gerd (1982) "Wirtschaftsordnung und Staatsverfassung", 8 *Jahrbuch für Rechtssoziologie und Rechtstheorie* 60.

CAPPELLETTI, Mauro (ed.) (1981) *Access to Justice and the Welfare State*. Alphen a. d. Rijn et al.: Sijthoff, et al.

CHARLIER, Paul (1982) "De la qualité pour recourir devant le conseil d'Etat", *Revue Reg. Droit*, 199.

GRIMMER, Klaus (1976) "Zur Dialektik von Staatsverfassung und Gesellschaftsordnung", 62 *Archiv für Rechts- und Sozialphilosophie* 1.

– (1978) "Die Funktion der Staatsidee und die Bedingungen ihrer Wirklichkeit" 64 *Archiv für Rechts- und Sozialphilosophie* 63.

GYSIN, Arnold (1969) *Rechtsphilosophie und Grundlagen des Privatrechts*. Frankfurt a. M.: Klostermann.

HARTMANN, Klaus (1981) *Politische Philosophie*. Freiburg/München: Alber.

HAVERKATE, Görg (1977) *Gewissheitsverluste im juristischen Denken: zur politischen Funktion der juristischen Methode*. Berlin: Duncker & Humblot.

HEGEL, Georg F. W. (1955) *Grundlinien der Philosophie des Rechts*. Hamburg: F. Meiner.

HIRSCH, Ernst E., and Manfred REHBINDER (ed.) (1967) *Studien und Materialien zur Rechtssoziologie*. Kölner Zeitschrift für Soziologie und Sozialpsychologie, (Sonderheft 11).

JENKINS, Iredell (1977) "The Human Person and the Legal Person", in Gray Dorsey (ed.), *Equality and Freedom*, Vol. I. New York/Leiden: Oceana Publications Inc./ Sijthoff.

– (1980) *Social Order and the Limits of Law*. Princeton: Princeton University Press.

KOHLER, Klaus (1967) *Die moderne Praxis des Schiedsgerichtswesens in der Wirtschaft*. Berlin: Duncker und Humblot.

KÖTZ, Hein (1981) "Public Interest Litigation, A Comparative Survey", in M. Cappelletti (ed.), *Access to Justice and the Welfare State*. Alphen aan den Rijn et al.: Sijthoff, et al.

LADRIÈRE, Jean (1982) "Philosophie et politique", in *Hommage à Alphonse De Waelhens*. Bruxelles: Publ. Fac. Univ. St. Louis.

LEGENDRE, Pierre (1974) *L'amour du censeur: Essai sur l'ordre dogmatique*. Paris: Seuil.

LEMMENS, Paul (1984) "Het optreden van verenigingen in rechte ter verdediging van collectieve belagen". *Rechtskundig Weekblad* 2026.

LENOBLE, Jacques, and François OST (1980) *Droit, mythe et raison*. Bruxelles: Publ. Fa. Univ. St. Louis.

LUHMANN, Niklas (1970) "Positivität des Rechts als Voraussetzung einer modernen Gesellschaft", 1 *Jahrbuch für Rechtssoziologie und Rechtstheorie* 175.

– (1981) "Selbstlegitimation des Staates und Legitimation des modernen Staates", (Beiheft 15) *Archiv für Rechts- und Socialphilosophie* 69.

MACKIE. John. L (1982) "Rules and Reason", 1 *Law and Philosophy* 291.

MAHNSCHKE, Gunther (1982) *Philosophische Grundlagen des demokratischen Verfassungsstaates*. Freiburg i.Br.: Alber.

MAIHOFER, Werner (1981) "Die Legitimation des Staates aus der Funktion des Rechts," (Beiheft 15) *Archiv für Rechts- und Sozialphilosophie* 20.

MAUSS, Ingeborg (1976) *Bürgerliche Rechtstheorie und Faschismus*. München: Fink.

MISHRA, Ramesh (1977) *Society and Social Policy*. London: McMillan.

NONET, Phillip, and Phillip SELZNICK (1978) *Law and Society in Transition: Toward Responsive Law*. New York: Harper & Row.

PECZENICK, Aleksander (1982a) "Rationality of Legal Justification," 68 *Archiv für Rechts- und Sozialphilosophie* 137.

– (1982b) "Legal errata," in Antonio A. Martino (ed.), *Deontic Logic, Computational Linguistics and Legal Information Systems*, Vol. II. Amsterdam: North-Holland Publishing Co.

POUND, Roscoe (1922) *An Introduction to the Philosophy of Law*. New Haven: Yale University Press.

SUMMERS, Robert S. (1978) "Two Types of Substantive Reasons: the Core of a Theory of Common Law Justification," 63 *Cornell Law Review* 707.

– (1982a) "Working Conceptions of 'the Law'," 1 *Law and Philosophy* 263.

– (1982b) "Reply to Mr. Mackie," 1 *Law and Philosophy* 303.

TEUBNER, Gunther (1983) "Substantive and Reflexive Elements in Modern Law" 17 *Law and Society Review* 239.

UNGER, Roberto M. (1976) *Law in Modern Society*. New York: Free Press.

III

Dilemmas of Law in the Welfare State

The Self-Reproduction of Law and its Limits

NIKLAS LUHMANN
Bielefeld

I.

The predominant conception of the legal system refers to its organized and/or professional activities. People who do not work in the system appear as "clients" and thus, the main question becomes how the system serves its clients. Critique of the system is incited by the demand for better service. Apparently, this demand does not have much success, since the system seems to resist and to repel all attempts to improve the service. The bureaucratic and professional ways of handling issues have to be taken as facts and given these facts, the critique changes its goals and proposes delegalization, deformalization, deprofessionalization[1]. Again, the results are not very convincing: they tend to make things easier and more difficult at the same time, probably for a different set of persons. Left-wing and right-wing critics, having lost their ideologies, vacillate between apocalypse and intrigue. The next step may well be more desperate and more radical claims combined with pre-adaptive resignation.

In such a situation a reasonable strategy may be to reconsider the theoretical foundations. Theoretical choices can be characterized by the kind of difference which they propose as the core problem. To select the difference between professionals and lay-men or bureaucrats and public for defining the legal system is a highly questionable decision — understandable in terms of everyday life but not in terms of theoretical refinement. For to be clients of the legal system, people have to operate within the system. They have to be aware of a legal problem; have to define their situation accordingly and have to commit themselves to advance legal claims or at least to communicate about them. They participate in the legal system using its system-reference to give meaning to their activities. And even the decision not to use the legal framework for handling affairs of everyday life is a decision *within the system*. The legal system is responsible also for thresholds and discouraging effects (Luhmann, 1981: 234).

[1] This is again under critical review today. See Abel (1980: 27).

The difference between professionals and clients, seen as difference of roles, or motives, or activities, or expectations, is an *internal* structure of the legal system. The legal system includes all acts or failures to act which are selected by reference to its mode of operation. Strategies of "delegalization" are at best proposals to restructure the legal system. They may, for better or worse, change the way in which law is taken into account. They may discourage people from using the law because of costs, congestions, delays, or because appealing to legal remedies is no longer fashionable. But they will probably (and hopefully) not bring about a state of affairs in which the law is no longer acknowledged as relevant, giving legal and illegal behavior the same chance.

As theory, and in its practical results as well, the paid-work paradigm of professionals and bureaucrats leaves much to be desired. Above all, it lacks any clear understanding of the specific function of the law. Using the general framework of the theory of society as a functionally-differentiated social system, we can conceive of the legal system as one of its functional subsystems (Luhmann, 1982a: 122). Such a system constitutes itself in view of its function. The function is a problem which has to be solved at the level of the societal system. A one-function/one-system arrangement requires complete autonomy of the system because no other system can replace it with respect to its function. Hence, *autonomy is not a desired goal but a fateful necessity*. Given the functional differentiation of society no subsystem can avoid autonomy. Notwithstanding all kinds of dependencies and independencies in relation to its social and its natural environments that system alone can reproduce the operations which fulfil its function. Whatever serves as unit in the system, including the unity of the system itself, has to be constituted by the system itself. All elementary units (e.g. legal acts) and the unity of the system as well are achieved by the reduction of complexity. They are performances of the system itself and are never given to it by nature or by other environmental conditions. Therefore, given the general regime of a functionally differentiated society, all law becomes positive law which, of course, is not necessarily statute law but can also be created by the courts and by contract.

In this sense, functional subsystems of society are always self-referential systems: They presuppose and reproduce themselves. They constitute their components by the arrangement of their components and this "autopoietic" closure *is their unity* . This mode of existence implies self-organization and self-regulation, but it has to be realized not only at the level of the structure but also, and above all, at the level of the elements of the system[2].

[2] In fact, the most important paradigm change in general systems theory, brought about during the last decade, consists in extending the concept of self-reference from the level of the structure to the level of the elements of the system. This requires a redefinition of the conceptual apparatus of systems theory and shifts its focus from

II.

This general theoretical conception can be applied to the legal system. If such a system evolves within the context of functional differentiation all regulation must be self-regulation. There may be political control of legislation, but only the law can change the law. Only within the legal system can the change of legal norms be perceived as change of the law. This is not a question of power or influence, and this not to deny that the environment and particularly the political system has an impact on the legal system. But the legal system reproduces itself by legal events and only by legal events. Political events (e.g. elections) may be legal events at the same time, but with different connections, linkages and exclusions for each system. Only legal events (e.g. legal decisions but also events like elections in so far as they are communicated as legal events) warrant the continuity of the law and only deviant reproduction, merging continuity and discontinuity, can change the law.

A simple fact never bestows the quality of being legal or illegal upon acts or conditions. It is always a norm which decides whether facts have legal relevance or not. After many centuries of doubts and discussions we are today used to admit that neither natural nor religious nor moral conditions have this law-making potential but only legal norms. The legal system is a *normatively closed system.*

It is at the same time a *cognitively open system.* Following recent developments in systems theory we see closure and openness no longer as contradictions but as reciprocal conditions. The openness of a system bases itself upon self-referential closure, and closed "autopoietic" reproduction refers to the environment. To paraphrase the famous definition of cybernetics by Ashby: the legal system is open to cognitive information but closed to normative control[3].

Normative closure does not exclude cognitive openness. On the contrary, it requires the exchange of information between system and environment. The normative component of legal meanings provides for *concurring* self-reference[4]. Concurring self-reference *is not a rule* as we are used to thinking as successors of Kant. Therefore the normative quality of legal operations

design and control to autonomy, from planning to evolution, from the distinction of statics and dynamics to problems of dynamic stability etc. See Maturana and Varela (1980) and Varela (1979, for a biological version of this approach.

3 Ashby defines cybernetic systems as "open to energy but closed to information and control". See Ashby (1956: 4). Another source of this recent interest in combinations of closure and openness is Lettvin, Maturana, McCulloch, Pitts (1959: 1940).

4 It may be helpful to remember the theological ancestors of "concomitans", implying the co-presence of God in everything that happens on earth. Seen against this background the idea of concurring self-reference reveals itself as a figure of secularization.

cannot be reduced to the enactment or the application of a rule. Rather, it is the necessary and continuous reformulation of the unity of the system. Having its reality *in actu* it binds the following operations to confirm and to reproduce the system. It needs for this very purpose limitation and guidance — but not determination! — of choice. In this sense, concurring self-reference uses the difference of system and environment to create information. This would never work if the system were a system of norms only and its environment the realm of cognitions. The legal system is not a normative system if that means a system the elements of which are norms. It is a system of legal operations using normative self-reference to reproduce itself and to select information. The legal system, basing itself on its normative self-reference, is an information-processing system, and it is able to adapt itself to changing environments if its cognitive structure is sufficiently generalized.

Normative closure requires *symmetrical* relations between the components of the system where one element supports the other and vice versa. *Cognitive openness*, on the other hand , requires *asymmetrical* relations between the system and its environment. The operations of the system are contingent on those of the environment and adapt to changing conditions. The impact of the system on its environment, for example compliance with rules, is again an asymmetrical relation in which the environment adapts to the system. Both contingencies have to remain separate to avoid circularity.

For this reason normative structures are highly vulnerable. They are sensitive to open defiance and unenforceability because doubts have a spill-over effect and spread over the system. Cognitive structures, on the other hand, may be specified and remain relatively isolated. The concurring involvement of normative closure and cognitive openness in legal events and operations combines symmetrical and asymmetrical, general and specific commitments. The emergence of a normatively differentiated system does not lead to a state in which cognitive orientations are less important. They become more important — for that system!

Other systems use other ways and other semantic forms to distinguish and recombine openness and closure. The economic system, for example, operates openly with respect to needs, products, services etc. and it is closed with respect to payments, using payments only to reproduce the possibility of further payments. Linking payments to the exchange of "real" goods interconnects closure and openness, self-reference and environmental references. General purpose money provides for closure and remains the same in all hands. Specifiable needs open the system toward its environment. Therefore, the operations of the system depend upon a continuous checking of one in terms of the other. This linkage is a prerequisite for the differentiation and self-regulation of the economic system (Luhmann, 1983: 153). The same holds true for the legal system, of course with different mechanisms to provide for self-regulation by closing off self-referential procedures. In this case, the reference to the normative framework of the law serves to establish circularity within the system: decisions are legally valid only on the basis of normative rules because[5] normative rules are valid only when implemented by decisions.

The validity of law cannot be founded on authority or will, as the legal positivism of the 19th century did. Nor does the "fait social" of human society grant validity. It is not the "existence" of the legal order which is the source of itself[6], and it is not the hypothesis of a basic norm that constitutes (or simply postulates) the object of legal cognition[7]. Austin, Durkheim, and Kelsen offer competing attempts to avoid circularity and to found the validity of law on something else. However, *validity is circularity* – circularity, of course, in need of logical unfoldment.

Finally, the legal system, for its own reproduction of legal events by lega events, needs a binary structure in terms of which all events can be described as not being their counterpart. The system uses the code of right and wrong to duplicate all meanings – the right events being not wrong, the wrong events being not right. By this very description, whatever happens and whatever can be done becomes contingent. It remains possible to select the right or to select the wrong but not without committing oneself to negate the opposite value. The right path, then, may become a bit too righteous and the wrong may be overburdened with consequences stemming from the fact that it was not right.

Such a binary schematization is neither a fact of nature nor a law given by divine logic. It is an achievement of evolution, an evolutionary universal. At the time of the Greek tragedies it could not be taken for granted (Wolf, 1950; 1952). On the other hand, it is not simply an analytic device, structuring the recognition of the law by discerning right and wrong. It links the reproduction of the law with the reproduction of the contingency of the law and it serves as *prerequisite of conditionality*[8]. Based on this prerequisite, the legal system can be erected as a network of conditions pre-programming events (and particularly actions) to be either right or wrong.

III.

This outline of a theory of self-referential legal systems uses the distinction of normative and cognitive orientations to distinguish and recombine

[5] "Because" in this phrase is no mistake but intention. It corroborates a point made by Eckhoff and Sundby (1975: 123). Also see Eckhoff (1978: 41).

[6] See Virally (1966: 5) specifying a Durkheimian position for "l'ordre juridique" as such. Similar opinions use the notion of (social) institution. See McCormick (1974: 102).

[7] Further reading will lead to many variants of late transcendental or idealistic positions looking for validity in the realm of spiritual beings. See Henkel (1977: 550).

[8] See Section IV.

closure and openness. Any further development of this line of thought depends upon the way in which we conceive of norms and cognitions.

It will not be very helpful to define norms by self-implication – referring to the meaning of "should" or to the justification of sanctions[9]. This would give us a self-referential concept but not a theory of self-referential objects. To avoid all kinds of conceptual circles we start with defining the difference between cognitive and normative orientations as the difference between learning and not learning[10]. The problem of choice between learning or not learning arises in face of inconsistent experiences[11]. If an experience contradicts our expectation we can either accept the fact and change our expectation; or we can try to maintain our expectation and to treat the experience as deviant, as unusual exception or as wrong choice. Since this problem of changing or not changing expectations comes up regularly in everyday life and particularly with respect to human behaviour it may be required that one commits oneself before the event and declares one's intention to change or not to change the expectation in case of contradicting experiences. The symbolism of cognition and of norms, of "being" and of "should", of "existence" and of "axistence"[12] provides general semantic forms and recognizable patterns for such commitments before the event. Using these forms, we may bind ourselves to expect either cognitively or normatively and, accordingly, to change or not to change our expectations in the case of disappointing experiences. And if this is possible we may build expectations of expectations; we may normatively expect normative expectations or may be normatively expected to apply cognitive expectations and vice versa.

Expectations of expectations can be called *reflexive* expectations. Normal expectations never become reflexive. I do not expect to expect to be able to start my car or to get a response at the reception desk of the hotel asking whether accommodation is available or not. Only if the car does not start do I feel that it would be inappropriate to stick at the expectation

9 "Norm here means, obviously, what people ought to do", writes Bohannan (1963: 284). Also for Robert Nisbet is "the most vital character of social norms – the sense of *oughtness* they inspire in human conduct"; see Nisbet (1970: 226). Such formulations may rely on others which state that " 'Ought to be' is a primary, irreducible content of consciousness"; see Timasheff (1939: 68).

10 We follow a suggestion of Galtung (1959: 213), who tries to link normative and factual expectations within a behaviouristic framework. For further elaboration see Luhmann (1972: 40).

11 Inconsistency, of course, is always a culturally defined fact, and it is well known, that advanced societies perceive as inconsistent what primitive societies would treat as regular irregularity. See Winch (1972: 8). This increasing awareness of inconsistencies can be explained as a result of an increasing differentiation of cognitive and normative orientation.

12 This neologism has been invented, it seems, by Le Moigne (1977: 58).

that it should start. And only if I get the answer "no rooms available" and discover later that it was false do I feel I have a right to get at least an honest and true answer. Reflexive expectations are evoked only if there is a point in making a choice between cognitive and normative expectations, i.e. reflexivity depends on forced choice, so to speak, on the level of primary expectations.

Looking more closely at the research about reflexive expectations would lead to significant refinements[13]. For legal theory it is more important to connect this field of research with systems theory and particularly with the theory of self-referential systems. Social systems in general use expectations as structures which control the process of reproduction of communications by communications[14]. Therefore, differentiation of social systems requires the specification of expectations which maintain the autopoietic process of reproduction. The legal system becomes differentiated by distinct standards of self-reference in everyday operations. It uses the normative quality of expectations, i.e. resistance against learning, to include operations in the system and to refer to further operations (e.g. execution) of the system. It can associate further meanings as additional conditions of legal validity and it may try to warrant some kind of conditional predictability. But these normative meanings work as concurring self-reference only, assuring the reproduction of legal events out of legal events. There is no need and not even the possibility of complete self-determination. The legal system does not determine the content of legal decisions – neither logically nor by some kind of crafty procedures of hermeneutic interpretation. It operates as a closed and at the same time as an open system, normatively referring to the maintenance of its own self-reproduction and cognitively referring to adaptive requirements with respect to its environment.

If all legal events are normatively bound to push on the process of autopoietic regeneration and are nevertheless cognitively prepared to learn from the environment the system will have to face up to problems of compatibility of these divergent and perhaps even contradictory attitudes. Such combinatorial constraints may bring about limits to the growth and the complexity of the system . Since closure and openness can be combined this is not a hopeless contradiction and not a real impossibility. But we have to specify what kind of mechanisms extend the realm of feasible combinations. And our presumption is that the actual symptoms of overstrain in the legal system are generated by these mechanisms as a kind of immune response against environmental (and particularly political) pressures and are not primarily problems of enforcement or problems of insufficient legitimacy or justice.

[13] See Blumer (1953: 185); Glaser and Strauss (1964: 669); Laing *et al.* (1966); Maisonneuve, (1966: 322); Scheff (1967: 32); Lefèbvre(1972: 181).

[14] See Luhmann (1984). See also Luhmann (1982b: 366).

IV.

Mechanisms which differentiate and recombine normative and cognitive orientations work on two different levels: the one general, the other specific. At the general level the system uses the fundamental technique of conditioning[15]. Special events (actions, decisions) within the system are activated if, and only if, certain other events are realized and thus are conditioned on pre-programmed information. Conditionality gives the chance to differentiate and recombine norms and cognitions. The conditioning programme itself can be stated as a norm which foresees deviant behaviour and does not become invalidated by it. Applying the programme, on the other hand, requires cognitive operations. It relies on the capacity to handle information and to learn whether certain facts are given or not. With this kind of "iffish" attitude long chains of events can be built, each step depending on previous others and all depending on the legal validity of themselves and of others[16].

In this sense, conditional programmes are the hard core of the legal system (for a rather different account cf. Willke infra). All legal norms are conditional programmes and if they are not formulated that way they can be translated into if-then relations. This makes it difficult to confer to future states the status of a condition of legal validity[17]. Legal rules may mention future states. The prospects of the child's welfare should guide the decision about which of the divorced parents should take care of the child. But this does not mean that the decision and all acts based on it will lose their legal validity if the future falsifies the prediction. The decision depends on present informed guesses about the future, and legal validity is used (or misused?) to absorb risks and uncertainties. Law is not specialized in fortune telling, and the legal validity of gambling has always been a subject of suspicion[18].

15 In a very general sense conditionality is a prerequisite of any complex system which cannot activate all variables at once but has to condition the state on the actualization of others. See Ashby (1968: 108).

16 In more "philosophical" terms the reality of law is a process (in Whitehead's sense) consisting of events which combine for themselves and for the others' self-identity and self-diversity. See Whitehead (1929). It may be necessary to say that this holds true not only for legal procedures in the narrow sense but for all events which are communicated (and thereby given unity) with reference to the legal system: for contracts, offences, bith, re-marriage, divorce, death etc.

17 Unger also hesitates: "Modern jurisprudence ... increasingly accepted the notion that the meaning of a rule, and hence the scope of a right, must be determined by a decision about how best to achieve the purposes attributed to the rule. But all such purposive judgements are inherently particularistic and unstable: the most effective means to any given end varies from situation to situation, and the purposes themselves are likely to be complete and shifting". See Unger (1976: 86 and 194).

18 Within the context of the German discussion about the predictive capacity and responsibility of legal decisions my own position is rather extreme — if not on the

This, however, is only half of the truth and only one way to relate normative and cognitive components of the legal system. Conditionality is the general and indispensable device, but there are also more subtle, subcutaneous ways to infuse cognitive controls into normative structures. Judges are supposed to have particular skills and contextual sensitivities in handling cases. They apply norms according to circumstances, and if necessary, generate exceptions to confirm the rule. They try to do justice — and postpone the perishing of the world from case to case. Other learning processes take place at the dogmatic level of legal concepts[19] (Broekmann and Heller supra argue against the possibility of change at this level). The conceptual framework of legal doctrine adapts to changing conditions and changing plausibilities and it may reflect and control its own change because concepts are not yet normatively binding decisions[20].

The actual problems within this area are more or less problems of time and of speed. The unity of the legal system requires an integration of changes on both levels: court decisions and legal dogmatics. New conceptual developments or new dogmatic rules have to wait for stimulating cases and cases can be aggregated into types of problems only if the conceptual development is sufficiently advanced. All this takes time — and under modern conditions apparently too much time. Sufficient speed can be achieved only by legislation and legislation will change the law again and again without leaving time for court traditions and for dogmatic refinements to settle down. Within the legal system the priority passes onto the legislature. This means, to some extent, a new primacy of cognitive over normative considerations. The law has to fit the society around it and we are lucky if it nevertheless remains able to fulfil its own societal function (see also Teubner infra).

V.

From ancient times we are familiar with a critique of law which assumes several forms (Nörr, 1974; Muratori, 1958). Law is unjust or at least not quite in conformity with the idea of justice. This seems to be inevitable as

right side then on the side of "taking rights seriously". For more balanced views seeTeubner (1975: 179); Wälde (1979); Rottleuthner (1979: 97); Lübbe-Wolff (1981). Hopefully authors who see good chances for the legal control of consequences are not the same as those who increasingly begin to complain about "Verrechtlichung" and overstrain of law.

19 The distinction of a juridical and a dogmatical level applies to the Parsonian distinction of technical and institutional levels in formal organizations. See Parsons (1960: 59). There is also a place for managerial levels in between, materialized for example, in the form of court-policy decisions, organizational policies, inter-court relations etc.

20 See Luhmann (1974: 49), on the societal adequacy of legal concepts and see Teubner (1983: 239) on "responsive law" (I would prefer "responsive dogmatics"); stimulating also Esser (1970).

long as we need property. Moreover, legal norms are never completely enforced. We know of hidden and even open deviance. Lack of justice and lack of compliance and enforcement have to be taken as normal in this world. In both respects, ideal and material, the legal system lacks perfection. We may add the famous *ius vigilantibus scriptum* or its modern equivalent: the differential access to law. And last though not least we are aware of many ways in which sophisticated legal forms are misused to bring about effects which were not intended by the legislator[21] – one of the most famous examples of tricky misuse being the emancipation[22]. All this remains on the agenda. In addition, however, we have invented a new kind of discontent. We feel that the legal system suffers from overstrain: that we have too much legal regulation, too much of the good.

What does this mean? I know of no legal theory which explains how the good turns into the bad and at what point. Sociologists could, once more, call up Max Weber. His analysis of bureaucracy shows how rationality can become a nuisance. But this "paradigma" is a rather impressionistic kind of theory. If we try to transfer this insight from bureaucracy to the law in general (i.e. from organization to a societal subsystem) the conceptual construction will break down. It is not strong enough for transmission.

Undeniable symptoms of overstrain have suggested that alternatives to the law or at least new ways of delegalization (including deformalization, deprofessionalization etc., etc.) should be looked for (Abel, 1980: 27). This may suggest practical innovations, but it is wrong as a principle. A functionally differentiated society cannot provide for alternatives to its functional subsystems. All functional equivalents are part of the functional subsystems because these are organized in view of their functions. It is not possible to inaugurate functional equivalents outside of the system because being an equivalent includes them in the system. Moreover there is no way to speak of "alternatives" except in terms of functional equivalents. Otherwise, an alternative would simply be something else which may or may not have an impact on the system. The political system cannot replace the economic system, the economic system cannot replace the educational system, the educational system cannot replace the legal system, the legal system cannot replace the political system, *because no functional subsystem is able to solve the core problems of another system*. Functions are points of view for comparison and substitution and, therefore, society which bases its differentiation on function builds self-substituting *and not other-substituting* subsystems. Hence, each proposal of an alternative has to specify the function-in-view. If it is the function *of* the law it cannot stimulate an

21 Holy law in particular needs this kind of treatment in view of secondary intentions. See Schacht (1926: 211).

22 Based of the prescription of the XII Tables "Si pater filium ter venumduit, a patre filius liber esto".

alternative *to* the law. If the proposal relates to secondary functions — say, slowness of procedures, insensitivity to personal feelings, overcentralization — there may be remedies available ***within the system***. There may be also remedies *outside of the system*, but using them implies either using the means of other systems (e.g. using money to establish more courts to speed up procedures; using political power to suppress conflicts which otherwise would come before the courts) or reducing the domain of law, or both.

In general, the extensive dicussion of overstrain and similar problems lacks clear statements about problems, functions and system-references. The present German debates about "Verrechtlichung" have more or less political overtones. They are part of the unanimous critique of the welfare state (whether this be the last resort of capitalists and technocrats or an attempt to ruin the economy by socialism) (Voigt, 1980; 1981: 3; Ellscheid, 1979: 37). The main suggestion is to look for self-healing forces of the society, to engage the life world of small communities, the self-organization of discussion groups and the reasoned elaboration of everyday activities[23]. However, this communal approach has nothing to do with the law and its function. The recommendation reads: be nice to your neighbour, fellow-man and co-worker and avoid conflict. But the law becomes relevant only in view of conflicts. The point is: who can afford to push his point and how far this can be made independent of local reputation, merit and exchange of gifts and good will. In fact, the only great delegalizer with a minimum of rules and a maximum of effects that has been invented in legal history is the institution of property because of its clear and simple way of pre-deciding conflicts. Judged against this background, the present problems of overstrain in the legal system are to a large extent consequences of the deterioration of property.

A different theory of the legal system — not only calling it a system but in fact using systems theory as a framework for theoretical developments — will lead to different results. A precise definition of the function of law is essential[24], otherwise it would be impossible to limit the consideration of functional equivalents or alternatives to the law. Moreover, systems theory requires and offers a conceptualization of structural strain and its sources. Structural strain is a quite normal affair, resulting from the fact that no structure can absorb all problems which emerge in the relation between

[23] With slight modifications this small group approach can be extended to the small head group of the "New Corporatism". Here, conflict repression by the "holy watching" of well-disposed neighbours and the immobilization by partners can be avoided. But the mechanism of delegalization will be power rather than peace.

[24] My own proposal would be: *using the possibility of conflict for a generalization of expectations in temporal, social and substantive aspects* — a slight variation of the definition given in Luhmann (1972). It is certainly not sufficient to use very general definitions — say contribution to the order of society, because this would confer on anything the status of being a functional equivalent of the law.

system and environment. Overstrain simply means the probability of structural change[25] stimulated by too many unsolved problems and overburdened activities.

The theory of open systems that are based on concurring self-reference (or: autopoietic closure) proposes a way of reformulating this problem. All autopoietic systems have to live with an inherent improbability: that of combining closure and openness[26]. Legal systems present a special version of this problem. They have to solve it by combining normative and cognitive, not-learning and learning dispositions. On the screen of the analytic framework of scientific description this requirement may appear as contradiction. In fact however, a social system can live up to opposed necessities. In the course of its evolution the system hits upon exceptional conditions which permit such combinations if they become incorporated as structural constraints. The system uses incidental chances and makes them work, thus developing by accident. In this way the improbable becomes probable (Morin, 1977: 294; Luhmann, 1981b: 122).

From this point of view strain can be conceived of as *residual improbability* and overstrain as too much of it. Given a certain institutional framework routinizing the improbable there may be a non plus ultra. In other words, although we shall feel unable to outline last limits, the institutions show signs of suffering. They show signs of overload and of more or less unsuccessful attempts to solve fundamental problems by insufficient means. "Involution" becomes the predominant reaction to evolution — involution in the sense of progressive complication, variety within uniformity, virtuosity within monotony[27].

VI.

If increasing improbabilities are the problem, neither technological nor communal devices will satisfy. The social engineering approach to the law is a political approach — and, of course, completely legitimate as a perspective of the political system. In fact, increasing differentiation and autonomy of the legal system must entail a relative loss of control over other systems, and the increasingly instrumentalistic view of legal institutions and norms

25 Or of "collective behaviour"! See Smelser (1963: 67).

26 I have to admit that the authors of the theory of autopoietic systems, Maturana and Varela (1980), probably would not subscribe to this formulation. They underline the necessity of closure and assert that the distinction of system and environment presupposes an observer. Taking this into account we have to postulate that self-observation is an essential characteristic of autopoietic systems. See also Pask (1981: 265).

27 See Goldenweiser (1936: 99) and Geertz (1963: 80), describing involution as increasing tenacity of basic patterns, internal elaboration and ornateness, technical hairsplitting, and unending virtuosity.

can be understood as an attempt to compensate for this loss of control[28]. The communal approach appears as a counter-movement, shifting the power base of the law from central to local pressures and from written instructions to face-to-face interaction. Both converge in negating a proper function of the law as such. Both solve the problem of high improbabilities by transferring it to another system — be it the political system or the countless systems of face-to-face interactions. However, these systems cannot solve it by legal or illegal means; they can only act *extra legem*.

Moreover, the law has to offer protection against reasonable designs and against moral pressures because in an open, post-Gödelian society reason and morality are partisan values[29]. At least, the law has to make sure at which points and how far resistance against demands propagated in terms of a reasonable or moralistic "discourse" might be successful. To maintain this possibility of conflict with reason and morality is one aspect of the differentiation and the improbability of the law[30].

Given the proper function, the normative closure and the autonomy of the law as constraints, how can the legal system "factorize"[31] its inherent improbabilities? Pursuing this question we have to revisit the mechanisms which combine closure and openness (sect. IV). The central device is conditionality. In this respect residual improbability and hence overstrain comes about by using conditional programmes for the attainment of ends which are not within the reach of immediate causal operations. (see also Willke infra). Task-setting and technology always imply control over some of the causes and lack of control over others (Mathew, 1975: 103). The controlled sector (instruments) may be more or less decisive in relation to the uncontrolled sector. The combination may be more or less arbitrary and contingent. The constellation of causes may be more or less complex. In general, the task is less representative for the unity of the system (i.e. its autopoiesis) if the combination of causes needs a higher degree of contingency and complexity[32].

[28] See Ziegert (1975), insisting on instrumental and expressive functions of the law. I would prefer to distinguish between political and legal uses of the law.

[29] With this (not strictly post-Gödelian but post-French-Revolution) evidence in view, authors of the 19th century maintained that the function of the law is to create and to warrant freedom. See Puchta (1856: 4), putting this function explicitly in contrast to the exigencies of reason and morality, i.e. in contrast to Kant. "Freedom", in other words, is the normative counterpart of the fact that a functionally differentiated society cannot base its integration upon the traditional semantics of nature, reason, and morality.

[30] By the way, the legal system is not the only one pretending to independence from the supremacy of reason and morality. For politics, read Machiavelli. For love, see the Dialogue de l'Amour et de la Raison, see Joyeux (1667: 1). Value-free science is but another version of the same issue.

[31] This term is taken in the sense of March and Simon (1958: 191).

[32] One of the hermeneutic laws of Schleiermacher reads: "Der Zweck entfernt sich um

There is no apodictic objection against using conditional programmes as sub-routines in goal programmes. The law can very well organize patterns of higher security within result-oriented projects. But including, the desired result, in spite of all risks, in the normative framework of the law contributes unavoidably to overstrain, depending on the degree of complexity and contingency of the goal programme. To localize and factorize overstrain, a careful task analysis will be helpful. It will reveal many cases in which the law is misused to convey the impression of security where in fact only reasonable guesses can be obtained. Result-oriented legal practice endows opinion with authority. This is a useful device to implement politics by collectively binding decisions. From the point of view of the legal system we have to think of those who lose in litigation and of those who want to invest in legal security. Both will not be served by a legal system which spoils the self-reproduction of normative meanings by conjectural justice.

The way of handling conditionality has an important impact on the sources and patterns of complexity. Until the end of the 18th century common opinion attributed the complexity of the legal system to the quarrels of lawyers and to never-ending disputes over the interpretation of law and over problems of legal doctrine. On the other hand, legislation was hailed as the source of simplification, clarification and transparence of the law. From time to time the formal prohibition of any citing of legal opinions before the court has been considered (and even enacted)[33]. Today, the reverse fits the facts: legislation is seen as the main source of complexity and the quest for order-in-variety is, with less and less hope to be sure, addressed to the general principles of legal doctrine.

This reversal correlates with the increasing differentiation of the legal system and with the increasing stress on learning and non-learning dispositions within the system. It has become irreversible by evolution. However, this is not to say that we have to accept the status quo. Legislation creates complexity because it is at the same time the implementation of policy and result-oriented legal practice. Obviously, result-oriented practice is the most important single source of complexity within the system (in older times, it was litigation and diversity of interests *as such*). Result-orientation will, to a large extent, not achieve its ends and will produce unintended side-effects. If no-fault divorce increases the rate of divorce or if it changes the bargaining position of husband and wives, was this intended? And if not, what can be done to cope with such results? Such disappointments are fed back into the system and legislation is again its main learning mechanism. Thus, legislation incites legislation. Ecclesia

so weiter von der Idee (=internal unity of the work), je mehr Willkuer in der Produktion ist". See Schleiermacher, (1977: 175).

[33] For a discussion of this topic see Muratori (1958: 111).

reformata semper est reformanda. Observation of the results of the law means change of the law: the change of conditions conditions the change.

It is difficult to see how legal doctrine can develop in face of such a state of turbulence. Any attempt to compete with legislation on the same level producing an own set of principles or decision rules will be a futile exercise. Possibly, doctrine merges with legal theory specializing in reflexion. Its domain could be the self-observation and self-description of the system (for different developments of the idea of "reflexivity" see Wiethölter, Willke, Teubner, Peters infra). It may produce sober, detached and "experienced" statements like: no-fault liability means shifting the costs of insurance. This will not immediately slow down the process of change and certainly not contribute to delegalization. It may speed up the process of exhaustion of good intentions, pointing to the fact that the stock of better states is indeed limited. This does not interfere with political responsibility but it may prevent innovation by comment. But will the legal system and society support a representation of the law which specializes in balanced judgments and lacks commitment to "essential" norms? If this comes out as an unavoidable adaption to overstrain we shall find ourselves no longer motivated to fight for the law or, as Socrates thought to be his duty, to die for the badly-applied law.

References

ABEL, Richard L. (1980) "Delegalization. A Critical Review of its Ideology, Manifestations, and Social Consequences," 6 *Jahrbuch für Rechtssoziologie und Rechtstheorie* 27.

ASHBY, Ross (1968) "Principles of the Self-Organizing System," in W. Buckley (ed.), *Modern System Research for the Behavioral Scientist*. Chicago: Aldine Pub. Co.

BLANKENBURG, Erhard, Ekkehard KLAUSA and Hubert ROTTLEUTHNER (eds.) (1980) *Alternative Rechtsformen und Alternativen zum Recht*, Jahrbuch für Rechtssoziologie und Rechtstheorie vol. 6. Opladen: Westdeutscher Verlag.

BLUMER, Herbert (1953) "The Psychological Import of the Human Group," in M. Sherif and M. O. Wilson (eds.), *GroupRelations at the Crossroads*. New York: Harper.

BOHANNAN, Paul (1963) *Social Anthropology*. New York: Holt, Rinehart and Winston.

ECKHOFF, Torstein (1978) "Feedback in Legal Reasoning and Rule Systems," *Scandinavian Studies in Law* 41.

ECKHOFF, Torstein, and Nils K. SUNDBY (1975) "The Notion of Basic Norm(s) in Jurisprudence", *Scandinavian Studies in Law* 123.

ELLSCHEID, Günther (1979) "Verrechtlichung sozialer Beziehungen als Problem der praktischen Philosophie," 17 *Neue Hefte für Philosophie* 37.

ESSER, Josef (1970) *Vorverständnis und Methodenwahl in der Rechtsfindung: Rationalitätsgarantien der richterlichen Entscheidungspraxis*. Frankfurt a. M.: Athenäum.

GALTUNG, Johan (1959) "Expectations and Interaction Processes," 2 *Inquiry* 213.

GEERTZ, Clifford (1963) *Agricultural Involution: The Process of Ecological Change in Indonesia*. Berkeley: University of California Press.

GLASER, Barney, and Anselm STRAUSS (1964) "Awareness Contexts and Social Interaction," 29 *American Sociological Review* 669.

GOLDENWEISER, Alexander (1936) "Loose Ends of a Theory on the Individual, Pattern and Involution in Primitive Society," in Robert H. Lowie (ed.), *Essays in Anthropology, Presented to A. L. Kroeber.* Berkeley: Berkeley University Press.

HENKEL, Heinrich (1977) *Einführung in die Rechtsphilosophie.* München: Beck.

JOYEUX, François (1972) *Traité des combats que l'amour a eu contre la raison et la jalousie.* Paris: Hautville.

LAING, Ronald D., Herbert PHILLIPSON, A. RUSSELL, and A. R. LEE (1966) *Interpersonal Perception: A Theory and a Method of Research.* London: Tavistock Publ.

LEFEBVRE, Vladimir A. (1972) "Formal Method of Investigating Reflective Processes," 17 *General Systems* 181.

LE MOIGNE, Jean-Louis (1977) *La théorie du système général: théorie de la modèlisation.* Paris: Presses Universitaires de France.

LETTVIN, J. Y., Humberto R. MATURANA, W. S. MCCULLOCK, and W. H. Pitts (1959) "What the Frog's Eye Tells the Frog's Brain", 47/11 *Proceedings of the Institute of Radio Engineers* 1940.

LÜBBE-WOLFF, Gertrud (1981) *Rechtsfolgen und Realfolgen.* Berlin: Duncker und Humblot.

LUHMANN, Niklas (1972) *Rechtssoziologie*, vol. 1. Reinbek: Rowohlt.

— (1974) *Rechtssystem und Rechtsdogmatik.* Stuttgart: Kohlhammer.

— (1981a) "Communication about Law in Interaction Systems", in K. Knorr-Cetina and A. V. Cicoural (eds.), *Advances in Social Theory and Methodology: Toward an Integration of Micro- and Macro-Sociologies.* Boston: Routledge and Kegan Paul.

— (1981b) "The Improbability of Communication," 33 *International Social Science Journal* 122.

— (1982a) *The Differentiation of Society.* New York: Columbia University Press.

— (1982b) "Autopoiesis, Handlung und kommunikative Verständigung," 11 *Zeitschrift für Soziologie* 366.

— (1983) "Das sind Preise", 34 *Soziale Welt* 153.

— (1984) *Sotiale Systeme. Grundriß einer allgemeinen Theorie.* Frankfurt: Suhrkamp.

MARCH, James G., and Herbert A. SIMON (1958) *Organizations.* New York: Wiley.

MATHEW, D. J. (1975) "The Logic of Task Analysis", in Peter Abel (ed.), *Organizations as Bargaining and Influence Systems.* New York, London: Heinemann.

MATURANA, Humberto R., and Francisco J. VARELA (1980) *Autopoiesis and Cognition: The Realization of the Living.* Dordrecht: Reidel.

MCCORMICK, Neil (1974) "Law as Institutional Fact," 90 *The Law Quarterly Review* 102.

MORIN, Edgar (1977) *La méthode*, vol. I. Paris: Seuil.

MURATORI, Lodovico (1958) *Dei difetti della giurisprudenza.* (1. ed. Venice 1742). Milan: Rizzoli.

NISBET, Robert (1970) *The Social Bond: An Introduction to the Study of Society.* New York: Knopf.

NÖRR, Dieter (1974) *Rechtskritik in der römischen Antike.* München: Beck.

PARSONS, Talcott (1960) "A General Theory of Formal Organization," in T. Parsons, *Structure and Process in Modern Societies.* Glencoe, Illinois: Free Press.

PASK, Gordon (1981) "Organizational Closure of Potentially Conscious Systems," in M. Zeleny (ed.) *Autopoiesis: A Theory of Living Organization.* New York: Elsevier.

PUCHTA, Georg F. (1856) *Cursus der Institutionen*, 5 ed. Leipzig: Breitkopf und Härtel.

ROTTLEUTHNER, Hubert (1979) "Zur Methode einer folgenorientierten Rechtsanwendung," in (Beiheft 13) *Archiv für Rechts- und Sozialphilosophie, Wissenschaften und Philosophie als Basis der Jurisprudenz*, 97.

SCHACHT, Joseph (1926) "Die arabische hijal-Literatur," 15 *Der Islam* 211.

SCHEFF, Thomas I. (1967) "Toward a Sociological Theory of Consensus," 32 *American Sociological Review* 32.

SCHLEIERMACHER, Friedrich E. D. (1977) *Hermeneutik und Kritik*. Frankfurt a. M.: Suhrkamp.
SMELSER, Neil J. (1963) *Theory of Collective Behaviour*. London: Routledge and Kegan Paul.
TEUBNER, Gunther (1975) "Folgenkontrolle und responsive Dogmatik," 6 *Rechtstheorie* 179.
– (1983) "Substantive and Reflexive Elements in Modern Law," 17 *Law and Society Review* 239.
TIMASHEFF, Nicholas S. (1939) *An Introduction to the Sociology of Law*. Cambridge Mass: Harvard University Committee.
UNGER, Roberto M. (1976) *Law in Modern Society: Toward a Criticism of Social Theory*. New York: Free Press.
VARELA, Francisco J. (1979) *Principles of Biological Autonomy*. New York: Elsevier.
VIRALLY, Michel (1966) "Le phénomène juridique," 82 *Revue du droit public et de la science politique* 5.
VOIGT, Rüdiger (ed.) (1980) *Verrechtlichung: Analysen zu Funktion und Wirkung von Parlamentarisierung, Bürokratisierung und Justizialisierung sozialer, politischer und ökonomischer Prozesse*. Königstein/Ts: Athenäum.
– (1981) "Mehr Gerechtigkeit durch mehr Gesetz? Ein Beitrag zur Verrechtlichungsdiskussion", 21 *Aus Politik und Zeitgeschichte* 13.
WÄLDE, Thomas W. (1979) *Juristische Folgenorientierung*. Frankfurt a. M.: Athenäum.
WHITEHEAD, Alfred N. (1929) *Process and Reality: An Essay in Cosmology*. Cambridge: Cambridge University Press.
WINCH, Peter (1972) *Ethics and Action*. London: Routledge and Kegan Paul.
WOLF, Erik (1950) *Griechisches Rechtsdenken*, vol. 1. Frankfurt a. M.: Klostermann.
– (1952) *Griechisches Rechtsdenken*, vol. 2. Frankfurt a. M.: Klostermann.
ZIEGERT, Klaus A. (1975) *Zur Effektivität der Rechtssoziologie: Die Rekonstruktion der Gesellschaft durch Recht*. Stuttgart: Enke.

The Rules of the Game in the Welfare State

ALBERTO FEBBRAJO
Macerata

I. Introduction: Ideologies and the Welfare State

Welfare State is much more than a slogan for intellectuals; it is a sort of skyscraper from which sociologists and political scientists can enjoy a rare view of our society; much wider than is allowed from the lower windows of the respective disciplines and, moreover, with the possibility of choosing glass windows as colored as their ideological attitudes. This high ideological risk of a topic like welfare state is, in particular, connected with the usual antithesis "welfare state – constitutional state". There are good reasons for this.

We can say firstly that the conceptual reconstruction of the welfare state is based more on its differences from the constitutional state than on its specific characteristics. Therefore, as the same constitutional state is usually presented in a stylized way, the image one gets of the welfare state runs the risk of appearing to be the result of a *double distortion*. Secondly, the welfare state, unlike the constitutional state, stems from the pressure of events and is without a precise ideological-political design. It is therefore easy to transform an eventual theorization ex-post of the welfare state not only into an instrument of explanation, but also into an instrument of ideological justification – which is still lacking. Thirdly, the welfare state, seen as a corrector of injustice, is more intuitively connected with widespread eudomonistic ideologies than is the constitutional state which is seen as an impartial controller of coercion. In fact, independently from the form it assumes (ex-post compensation or preventive restriction for economic or social asymmetries of power; reduction of heterogeneity or production of homogeneity of chances; "first aid" for exceptional needs or assistance and care for normal needs), the welfare state presupposes not a static defence of the actual society but the "evaluation" of actual needs, with a view to the evolution of a "better" society. Finally, among intellectuals today, preaching the crisis of the welfare state, seen as the late product of a previous crisis of the constitutional state, has become a sort of self-fulfilling ritual which is ideological in so far as it aims not only at hiding a theoretical ignorance about the very object of the crisis but also at contributing directly to the realization of the relative prophecy.

In this paper, by associating the usual socio-political consideration of the phenomenon with a legal theoretical one, I am going to try to avoid ideological implications as much as possible. In my opinion, legal theory, despite (or better because of) the typical limitations of its horizon, could enrich a socio-political analysis of the welfare state. In order to provide evidence for the plausibility of this opinion I will touch upon two main issues. The first shows some limitations of the general systems theory approach which, at first sight, seems to be one of the most powerful and un-ideological means we have for studying the welfare state. The other suggests some parallels between a systems approach and a game approach in order to undertake a sort of constructive criticism with which to attempt enlightenment of some dilemmas of the welfare state, conceived not only as a system but also as a game.

II. The General Systems Approach

One of the approaches most clearly directed towards overcoming the lack of theory and the strong ideological risks that the subject matter "welfare state" presents is certainly that of the general systems theory. In spite of its title, expressed in the singular form, such a "theory" is, as we shall see, hardly monolithic or univocal. For heuristic purposes only, it is possible to start from a general definition of "system" which cumulatively collects various elements of the general systems theory. A system, for this very general definition, is a set of elements that, being linked by structural interrelationships, can be regarded as a unit which entails a certain distribution of resources and of information, and which is fundamentally directed to the actual conservation and/or reproduction of the system itself.

Such a system can be, (and has been) at least partially, studied from several points of view: from the external point of view of the onlooker, typically concentrated on the problem of (a) *identification* and delimitation of the system; and from internal points of view which typically concentrate on such problems as (b) the *selection* of possibilities for action and decision in the given system, (c) the *change* of, and the related problem of the conservation of the identity of a developing system, and finally, (d) the communication of *information* filtered through structures which elaborate the inputs of the system. On the basis of such a general distinction of perspectives, it is possible to distinguish corresponding variants of the general systems approach:

(a) an *epistemological* variant, which focuses above all on the instances of the delimitation and interpretation of a certain system (Stachowiak, 1965);

(b) a *personalistic* variant, which stresses the role of the social actors inside the system, and tries to weld together the needs of the individuals, seen as possible consumers, and the needs of the system (Crozier and Friedberg, 1977);
(c) an *organistic* variant, which underlines the method of production and of resource management with respect to the survival of the system (Buckley, 1967; Gallino, 1980).
(d) a *structuralist* variant, which concentrates on the compatibility of the different structures for receiving and re-elaborating outside data in internal decision processes (Luhmann 1981c and supra).

Given this framework, the approach of Luhmann can be seen as specifically "structuralistic" in as much as he does not emphasize the observer's, the consumer's or the producer's point of view but concentrates, more impersonally, on the structural distribution of the burden of decision within the system. The general systems approach adopted by Luhmann would then seem well suited to overcoming the theoretical deficit and ideological risks of the welfare state. However, the almost universal explicative ambitions of his approach inevitably create many theoretical difficulties. In particular, the above mentioned problems (the external problem of identification and the internal problems of selection, change and information) remain, within his perspective, without satisfying answers. Focusing especially on Luhmann's contribution to the theory of the welfare state (1981c; 1983), I will try to summarize some corresponding criticisms.

a) Firstly, one can observe that the problem of the identification of the welfare state is confronted by Luhmann in a functionalistic perspective. This perspective leads him to establish a fundamental functional antithesis between welfare state and constitutional state. According to Luhmann, the characteristic function of the constitutional state is based on a "negative feedback" i. e. on elimination of deviation from a given expected position, which means that deviations are prevented, or else removed, by law. On the other hand, the welfare state is presented as being based on the opposite function of "positive feedback", i. e. on the "amplification of deviations", on "growth values" aiming not at a restoration of the status quo but at producing increasingly differentiated situations.

This antithesis, based upon a monofunctionalistic logic, appears suggestive at first but, looked at closely, also reductive and unilateral. It is reductive in that it presupposes a dichotomy of the functions of law that does not seem much more elaborated than the Durkheimian distinction between "repressive" and "restitutive" law and ignores or makes meaningless other important functions of law, such as the "promotional" ones (Bobbio, 1977; Maihofer, 1970 and Aubert supra). It is unilateral, in that it presupposes a restrictive concept of equilibrium which seems incompatible, at least in the constitutional state with any change of the status quo, with any attempt to reach a more stable position — in this sense a "better" equilibrium.

b) Correspondingly, the problem of change in the welfare state is confronted by Luhmann in his latest works in terms of the "solipsistic" concepts of autopoiesis and self-reference. He suggests that politics today has overwhelmingly to do with difficulties that it itself is involved in creating (Luhmann 1981c: 10). This would mean: (a) in practical terms, that every decision of the state is considered as the presupposition of the following decision in a self-reproducing continuum (of decision, decision on previous decision, and so on) with which the system defends its own identity; (b) theoretically, that according to the growing exigencies of the historical situation, reflexion can be integrated by a self-reproducing process of "reflexion on reflexion", and so on. In both cases, the change is not conceived as coming "from" but as oriented "on" the system: towards higher and higher levels of practical complexity and theoretical abstraction — with the possibility, for instance, in the case of the welfare state, that the practical level grows faster than the theoretical one — or vice versa (see also Luhmann supra).

c) The problem of the selection within the welfare state of different strategies available for political reactions is confronted and (apparently) resolved by Luhmann mainly by means of a re-interpretation of the Weberian category of "sense". This re-interpretation, however, seems to be ambiguous. In fact, while on the one hand "sense" is connected with a process of de-subjectivation according to which the individual subject belongs in terms of the political system to the environment; on the other hand, it cannot avoid an "anthropomorphization" of the system's rationality which clearly emerges when Luhmann speaks of "reduction of risks", "canalization of disappointments", "security of expectations". These recurring themes suggest mainly adaptive strategies for the system and make it strictly connected with, if not inspired by, an external model of "conformist man" obsessed by the fear of the unexpected and by the need for security; a model which is not adequate to grasp other individual needs that play, at the level of the welfare state system, an equally (if not more) important role for the understanding of its social environment.

d) The consequent problem for the political system is how to obtain the elaborate information coming from the outside. In fact, political systems must constantly involve communication over environmental situations (Luhmann, 1981c: 62). This problem is faced by Luhmann by means of a combination of the principles stated above: the function characteristic for the system is a criterion for accepting, the (subjective) "sense" for rejecting information because the individuals as such are not part of the system but of its environment. However, by this means the problem is only apparently resolved. Surprisingly enough, Luhmann ignores the promising possibility of fundamentally redesigning a "geography" of the social systems and of their communicative interrelations that is separated from traditional classifications (family, economy, religion etc.). Furthermore, he does not give due consideration to important "para-systematic" institutions which filter the flow of information and therefore influence substantially the political system without being included in it.

All in all, Luhmann's conception of the welfare state seems not able to solve the various problems which it implicitly or explicitly confronts (identification, change, selection and information in political systems) because of (a) the one-sideness of the functionalistic approach, (b) the tautology of the concept of autopoiesis, (c) the ambiguity of the concept of "sense", (d) the reductionism of the dichotomy system/environment. These shortcomings do not on the whole seem to allow a satisfactory awareness of the complexity of political equilibrium, historical perspective, social needs and external intermediaries which are relevant for the analysis of a modern welfare state.

III. A Dilemma of the Welfare State

The difficulties pointed out do not take by surprise such a theory as Luhmann's — which studies how a system (and science is also a system) can survive in a difficult world. Therefore, considering the same conceptions of Luhmann as a system, it is possible to say that it can face these difficulties by choosing essentially between two strategies: (a) it can receive new theoretical contributions and so enlarge its syncretistic character, perhaps at the expense of coherence — for example by accepting a more articulated theory of human needs (one can define this strategy in Luhmann's terminology as "increase of the internal complexity") or (b) it can eliminate the above-mentioned difficulties from the praxis of the political system and normatively advise the political system to concentrate its interventions within very limited areas (one can define this strategy as "reduction of external complexity"). As is clearly seen in the fundamental dilemma of the welfare state which he himself points out, Luhmann chooses the latter path.

In the welfare state, more and more demands are directed to the state by so many differentiated social sectors that it becomes impossible for the state to control the effects of its interventions. Politics, then, is faced with two alternatives: either to provoke an immediate disappointment (refusal to intervene), or to accept inevitable disappointment when intervention is perceived as ineffective and/or accompanied by unpredictable adverse effects (dysfunctions). But this is not all. Even admitting that in at least some cases the state intervention will have short term foreseeable effects it needs to be taken into account that this tends in any case to widen the distance between the new and the previous situations (conception of "positive feedback") and even in these cases it will end in the long run with provoking politically uncontrollable effects. The phenomenon shows that politics today is very much involved with practical difficulties. To overcome these, Luhmann correctly emphasizes that there is no adequate political theory or, in somewhat paradoxical terms, he "theorizes the lack of a theory".

Following this approach, the practical solution to this dilemma is a non-solution. In the face of a growing request by part of society for "generally binding decisions", the political system, which should have the institutional function of providing them, can only react by lessening the interventions and, at the same time, by increasing the awareness of its limits and of its incompetence. The recipe for a working welfare state is then, according to Luhmann, a sort of self-reduction of politics. But then, who is to determine the content of this reduction? Who has to decide how far the function, sense, and structures of information of the political system can really change in a welfare state? Who can say "Stop!" to the continual enlargement of the set of elements we usually call 'state'? Luhmann's somewhat tautological answer is that this is the function of the same theory with which we try to interpret the welfare state.

This mixture of theoretical realism and practical conservatism has roused the suspicion that here we are not confronting a theory but an ideology in disguise. This is only partially true. Even in such a sophisticated interpretation as that of Luhmann, the general systems theory reveals itself as something less ambitious than a theory in the proper sense of the word. Rather it seems to be a way of thinking – a sort of general "model" which can be elaborated more or less deeply and applied more or less coherently but cannot be substantially revised or corrected except by integrating it with other "theories" or "models". The general systems approach is thus more likely to be seen as an example of an explicative procedure with heuristic, not assertive, functions and with metaphorical characteristics (cf. also Teubner 1982).

One finds a confirmation of this theoretical weakness in considering Luhmann's treatment of the constitutional state. This important part does not seem directly inspired by the general systems theory but rather by pre-existent legal theory which Luhmann rediscovers and (critically) translates into his own sociological terminology. For instance, he can transform the principle of the division of power into a non-hierarchical but organizational differentiation of the legal-political system in sub-systems characterized by different types of decision programs (e. g. the legislative sub-system by a formal, conditional program and the administrative sub-system by a mixture of both)(Luhmann, 1981c: 19).

It is also true that the explicitly anti-ideological approach of Luhmann, because of its emphasis on actual impotence of theory and practice, can easily be misused as an ideological alibi for anyone who wants to do little or nothing politically and/or theoretically. It must be remembered, however, that a discourse on the welfare state rarely escapes the danger of ideological instrumentalization (which is different from saying that it is itself ideological). Further, even admitting that Luhmann's approach is ideological, it is so for very special reasons; not for an excess of explanation, as so often happens, but for a lack of explanation; not for having undervalued or oversimplified, but for having overrated practical and theoretical constraints.

Therefore, in spite of all the previous criticisms, it must be admitted that, given today's theoretical situation, Luhmann's construction seems to be realistic and unideological enough in its *pars destruens* since he speaks of the Welfare State's structural constraints, rather than of its purposes and values. A wholesale refusal of Luhmann's construction as maintained by some critics, would thus really mean throwing away the baby with the bath-water; and moreover it would ignore the strong internal dynamics of his proposal which today is still in its intellectual infancy. Rather, it is possible to say that the criticism that has so far been directed against the "instruments" used by Luhmann does not lessen but, on the contrary, exalts the merits of their author. It is, in a sense, like admiring a violinist who succeeds in producing many varied sounds from a violin deprived of some strings (in the case of Luhmann, perhaps it would be more accurate to say one which has only one string).

IV. From Law as a System to Law as a Game

So far, we have underlined some limitations of a general systems approach to the welfare state. The final point of our discussion — that even an extremely sophisticated application of the general systems theory does not reach the level of internal coherence and explicative power of a "real" theory — must now be used as the starting point for a new series of considerations in which we search for integrations or alternatives to the general systems theory approach. In this context it is almost too obvious to refer to another analogy that, in the same area of the sociological and empirical reflections on law, has known its heyday — although it is now mostly overshadowed by the system analogy: that between law and game. Our hypothesis is that in comparison to the system analogy, a game analogy provides a more satisfying distinction between model and reality and also succeeds in overcoming some barriers that the system analogy approach of Luhmann cannot overcome because of its indifference to the normative dimension of its object. This point will be discussed later; here it is only possible to try to legitimate our efforts to substitute a system analogy with a game analogy by making some few observations on Luhmann's position.

Luhmann affirms that the welfare state needs to rely on an intact constitutional state in order to avoid, as a consequence of its shortcomings, a civil war to which all that is still lacking is the weapons (Luhmann, 1983:

15). In so doing, he presupposes the existence of two possibilities: either a legally regulated social reality or an explosive conflict which is incompatible with the survival of the society. But he does not recognize a third possibility: the canalization of conflicts in institutions which, although legally accepted or tolerated, are not necessarily themselves legal institutions, whose structures, strategies and legitimations are founded on a bargaining basis and therefore are highly uncertain from the point of view of the constitutional state.

On this level, however, as we shall see, lies an important sector of the reality of the welfare state, which is developing through the creation of new institutions with new players, new strategies and new games for the re-distribution of money and power. In this context, the game analogy, unlike the system analogy, seems to provide: a) a multifunctionalistic approach, and a concept of law more compatible with the concept of a centerless society as adopted by Luhmann himself (concerning the problem of identification); b) a perspective directed not towards the legitimation of past decisions but towards the calculation of possible future chances (concerning the problem of change): c) a better framework for introducing a pluralistic perspective which is not a limited rigid dichotomy "state vs. citizen" (concerning the problem of information); d) a wider and deeper sensibility for conflicting role-strategies which are nearer to the real decision processes of the actors than the logical purity of a particular system rationality (concerning the problem of selection).

In what follows, the demonstration of these general statements will be articulated in three steps which demonstrate the superiority of the game analogy in grasping the normative character of legal structures (Section 5); the distinction between constitutional state and welfare state (Section 6); some crucial dilemmas of the welfare state (Section 7).

V. Some Preliminary Definitions

It is useful to define explicitly, even if schematically, the meaning of 'game', as we have already done for 'system'. Starting with a negative definition; we can exclude one of its more obvious variants: a game understood simply as a competition of two or more actors aiming, under the supervision of an umpire, at a result which establishes univocally who is the winner and who the loser. A frequent application of such an analogy to the law has concentrated on trials, the essential features of which seem to perfectly fit this definition (Huizinga, 1938). The intuitive character of this analogy, however, transforms itself into a disadvantage as it is unable to reach a level of abstraction which can be applied to the legal order as a whole. Therefore the concept of game adopted here is on the one hand much wider because:

(a) it is not necessarily competitive;
(b) it does not necessarily include the particular figure of the umpire;
(c) it does not necessarily define a winner and a loser.

But, on the other hand, it is not so wide as has been suggested by some representatives of game theory. It cumulatively takes into account two components that are often used singly:

(a) the personalistic component which underlines the presence of two or more interacting players ("the key idea of a game in that the players make decisions that affect each other") (Hamburger, 1979);
(b) the structural component, which underlines the presence of a normative structure of reference; a code based on messages which have to be exchanged between the participants. This component too has often been considered as the only essential one ("The game is simply the totality of the rules which describe it") (Neumann and Morgenstern, 1944).

On the basis of this two-element definition, one can attempt to outline a parallel between the game concept which has just been defined and Luhmann's concept of the system (although our concept of game seems to take into account both the structural element and the personal perspective of the law consumers). As has been seen, in the functional-structural conception of Luhmann, the system schematically contains the following elements (some essential to every systems theory, others peculiar to Luhmann's):

(a) a plurality of components;
(b) their delimitation with respect to an environment;
(c) their reciprocal correlation to this basic nucleus; Luhmann has also added other elements (see particularly Luhmann, 1972);
(d) the "sense" with which such correlations are provided;
(e) the capacity of the various components to elaborate strategies of reaction to external pressures;
(f) the aiming of such strategies at simultaneously reducing the complexity of the environment and increasing the complexity of the system;
(g) the perpetuity of such a process as every increase in the level of complexity of the system is correlatively accompanied by an increase in the level of complexity of the environment; and finally,
(h) the presence of "points of no return" in the course of this process.

In general, if one confronts this sophisticated concept of system with the concept of game defined earlier, one realizes that the latter can easily comprehend elements in a similar way to the former. To develop point by point a parallel between the two concepts one can see that:

(a) the game's structure is also composed of plurality of components (for instance, the different players);

(b) the game is also delimited in relation to an environment (i. e. to circumstances irrelevant for the game);
(c) the game also requires a reciprocal correlation between its various components (if for no other reason than because the players direct their actions reciprocally);

and further:

(d) in the game such a correlation is also provided with a sense (i. e. the sense of the game itself);
(e) in the game the various components also elaborate strategies of reaction to external pressures (i. e. the moves of the counterparts);
(f) in the game one also finds the double intent, on the one hand, to reduce the external complexity (understood as the chances of reactions of the other players), and on the other hand, to increase the internal complexity (understood as the actor's chances of action);
(g) in the game such a process is also endless (as otherwise it would exclude the contingencies, and the reason for existing, of the game);
(h) in the game the history of each play also contains "points of no return" (the single move cannot be cancelled out but is rather a precondition of future developments).

One can even add that the field of relationships between system and environment can be interpreted at a higher level of abstraction in terms of a game in which the system (somewhat like a child who plays with a ball against the wall) tries not to be taken by surprise by the environment. But if this is true, it is also possible to invert the relationship which is sometimes established between "system" and "game" and to consider, with a change of perspective characteristic of Luhmann, not the game analogy as a particular case of the system analogy, but the system analogy as a particular case of the game analogy. From the "analogy of analogies" arises the further question of why the different applications of the game analogy and of the system analogy have not up to now overlapped in an adequate way with possible advantages for both — and for the sociology of law itself. To understand this, it is necessary to bear in mind two fundamental differences between the two analyses:

a) While in identifying a system one concentrates on its constant function because its structures are variable; in identifying a game one concentrates on its constant, normatively fixed, structures because its function is variable (as will be seen better later, one can play not only to win or to lose, but also to change the game).

b) While the system analogy has been directed principally towards establishing a framework for organizing symmetrical or asymmetrical interrelations between the various components of the system and between this and its environment; the game analogy has been principally directed towards establishing a point of reference for the recognition of the normativity of certain regularities of behavior. In short, one can say that the first analogy has been used, above all, as an input-output model; the second as a model of qualification. To verify this assumption one only needs to glance at a few classical examples of the application of the game analogy in the field of law.

VI. Three Examples

In general, the authors mentioned below use a law game analogy which assumes the epistemological point of view of the onlooker who tries to recognize, on a purely empirical basis, the existence of a normative order like that of a law game.

a) The sociology of Max Weber is notoriously based, at least in his methodological writings, on an interactionistic approach in which attention is concentrated not only on the intention of the actor but also on the orientation of his behavior towards other players of the social game (Weber, 1966: 2.) While it is possible to find an implicit game analogy in many Weberian analyses of social life, I prefer to concentrate on one of his most important methodological essays in which the analogy between law and game is explicitly developed (Weber, 1977).

Starting from the critique of a "refutation" of the materialist conception of history suggested by a contemporary social philosopher, Rudolf Stammler, Weber tries to work out a game analogy which is more sophisticated than that of Stammler. Before entering the domain of law in the usual sense of the word, Weber considers a typical German card game: the game of skat. In this introductory example, he distinguishes carefully between an empirical and a normative consideration of the "law of skat", and tries to develop a further conceptual differentiation within both types of consideration. On this basis Weber tries to articulate a comparison with law, which not only focuses on the judicial process but also includes the legal system as a whole. The following passage is of central importance in the Weberian argument.

> As a matter of fact, the judicial process is perfectly analogous to the "game of skat", and presumably no further discussion is necessary in order to establish this. In the judicial process, the empirical legal order is a "presupposition" of the empirical process: the "maxims" employed by the judges who decide the case and the "means" employed by the parties to the dispute. Knowledge of the conceptual "import" of the law — in other words, knowledge of its meaning as established by dogmatics or jurisprudence — is also an essential heuristic technique for the empirical-causal "explanation" of the actual proceedings of a concrete judicial process. The legal order, therefore, has the same status occupied by the rules of skat in an "historical" analysis of a skat game. Moreover the legal order is also constitutive for the definition of the "historical entity". Suppose we attempt to provide a causal explanation of a concrete judicial process as a judicial process. In such an "explanation", it is the legally relevant aspects of the process which are of interest. Therefore the analogy between the legal order and the rules of skat is complete.

The empirical concept of the concrete "case of law" — exactly like the empirical concept of a concrete game of skat — is exhaustively defined by reference to those aspects of reality which are relevant from the standpoint of the "rule of law" — or, in the case of skat, those aspects of reality which are relevant from the standpoint of the "rules of skat" (Weber, 1977: 133).

The "rules of skat", he says, can have three functions as "presuppositions" of an empirical enquiry. From a logical point of view these three functions are completely different. The rules of the game can be employed for taxonomic and conceptual-constitutive purposes in order to define the object of the investigation. They can be employed heuristically in order to establish causal knowledge of this object. And finally, they can function as causal determinants of the object of knowledge itself.

From a normative standpoint, Weber further distinguishes:

(1) An "ideal" question concerning "the politics and jurisprudence of skat" ("Consider for example, the 'skat congresses' which were formerly held. In view of the ('eudemonistic') 'values' which the game skat serves, would it not be fitting to introduce certain new rules which would govern all future games?")

(2) A "dogmatic" question concerning the general theory of the law of skat. ("For example 'must' a certain kind of incentive 'consistently' produce a certain ordered sequence of games as its consequence?"). And:

(3) A question concerning the "ethical norms of skat" (for example, the partner "will solemnly reprimand the careless player who has allowed the common opponent to win the game") (Weber, 1977: 123).

b) Although Weber's reflections on this subject matter are much more complex than appear in this short resume, for our purposes it is only necessary to add that in the history of legal theory the game analogy has been frequently employed to focus on the same aspects as have been stressed here: law parallels the game because both are seen as cultural phenomena, the interpretation of which requires a clear distinction between factual regularities and norm-oriented regularities (Weber, 1977: 71).

For the Danish legal theorist, Alf Ross, the main question is: is it possible to reconstruct a legal order, at least in its effective norms, which starts from an empirical observation of individual moves or is it necessary to have an a priori idea of what game the actors are playing? This question is clearly relevant for an empirical sociology of law and the game analogy determines once again the terms of the problem.

Let us imagine — (says Ross) — that two persons are playing chess while a third person looks on. If the onlooker knows nothing about chess he will not understand what is going on. From his knowledge of other games he will probably conclude that it is some sort of game, but he will not be able to understand the individual moves or to see any connection between them. On the contrary, if the onlooker knows the rules of chess, but beyond that not much about the theory of the game, his experience of the others' play changes character ... Thus the norms of chess are the abstract idea content (of a directive nature) which make it possible, as a scheme of interpretation, to understand the phenomena of chess (the actions of the moves and the experienced patterns of action) as a coherent whole of meaning and motivation, a game of chess; and, along with other factors, within certain limits to predict the course of the game. (Ross, 1958: 11, 16).

On this basis, it becomes finally possible to widen the focus of the comparison and also include the law.

The law too may be regarded as consisting partly of legal phenomena and partly of legal norms in mutual correlation. Observing the law as it functions in society, we find that a large number of human actions are interpreted as a coherent whole of meaning and motivation by means of legal norms as the scheme of interpretation (Ross, 1958: 17).

A similar of view, even if with different substantial implications, can be found in the works of the English legal scholar H. L. A. Hart, who notoriously concentrates his consideration of law as a game on the distinction between an "external" and "internal" point of view. With the combination of these he is able to correct the realistic approach of Ross. The starting point is, as usual, the game of chess.

Whatever the rules are, whether they are those of games, like chess or cricket, or moral or legal rules, we can, if we choose, occupy the position of an observer who does not even refer in this way to the internal point of view of the group. However, the observer really keeps austerely to this extreme external point of view and does not give any account of the manner in which members of the group who accept the rules view their own regular behaviour, his description of their life cannot be in terms of rules at all, and so not in the terms of the rule-dependent notions of obligation or duty (Hart, 1961: 87).

For this reason, Hart suggests that, without leaving an empirical basis, we also have to take into account "internal" factors to be able to recognize a norm-oriented game like law.

The most important of these factors which show that in acting we have applied a rule is that if our behaviour is challenged we are disposed to justify it by reference to the rule: and the genuineness of our acceptance of the rule may be manifested not only in our past and subsequent general acknowledgements of it and conformity to it, but in our criticism of our own and others' deviation from it. ... It is thus that we would distinguish, as a compliance with an accepted rule, the adult chess-player's move from the action of the baby who merely pushed the piece into the right place. (Hart, 1961: 136).

We cannot follow up these single interpretations in all their details. We can only emphasize that, reduced to bare essentials and put together, these theoretical nuclei are sufficient to produce relevant shifts in a concept of law based upon the traditional model of a constitutional state. They extend the horizon of the theory of law to make visible the fact that in the welfare state there is a deeper structural homogeneity between legal structures and social structures since the legal structures are neither a) only coercive nor

b) only statual. (see also Febbrajo, 1983 a; Aubert, 1977). In fact, they stress the presence in the legal institutions of the welfare state, of a "rewarding law" understood as a law typically characterized by positive "prizes" rather than by negative sanctions and suggest the possibility of building up juridically relevant, even if not statual, games within a pluralistic vision of the law.

VII. A Further Step: From Regulative Rules to Constitutive Rules

Another element needs to be underlined which draws attention to the distinction between "regulative rules" and "constitutive rules". This distinction, widely discussed in the philosophy of language but still not sufficiently in the sociology of law, stresses that rules which consist in prescribing some behavior (regulative rules) do not exhaust the normative content of social and legal institutions. In his book *Speech Acts*, John Searle draws the distinction between "constitutive" and "regulative" rules which he believes philosophers have commonly overlooked or disregarded with serious consequences. He writes: "we might say that regulative rules regulate antecedently or independently existing forms of behaviour" while "constitutive rules do not merely regulate, they create or define new forms of behaviour". So for instance: "many rules of etiquette regulate interpersonal relationships which exist independently of the rules" while "the rules of football or chess ... do not merely regulate playing football or chess but ... create the very possibility of playing such games. In short, the activities of playing football or chess are constituted by acting in accordance with (at least a large subset of) the appropriate rules" (Searle, 1969: 33).

Searle extracts two formulae for characterizing constitutive rules. The first is that the creation of constitutive rules, creates the possibility of new forms of behavior. The second is that "Constitutive rules have the form: X counts Y in context C", and so far are "alchemical devices for the transformation of brute facts into institutional facts" (Searle, 1969: 64). The combination of these two formulae show that the distinction between regulative rules and constitutive rules suggests not only a) a heterogeneity of the so-called "facts" ("Some operative facts are purely factual — for example, birth, death, fire, collision at sea; others are legally conditioned, which means that they are defined relative to law"), and consequently, b) the institutional character of the legal order ("institutions are a system of constitutive rules which constitute the basis for activities, the existence of which is logically dependent upon the underlying rules") (Searle, 1969: 83; cf. Luhmann infra). Looked at more closely, it also shows c) the homogeneity (neither material nor functional, but structural) of legal and social games. This homogeneity, often neglected by a too zealous acceptance of traditional dichotomies (fusis and nomos, Sein and Sollen), is based on the fact that both legal and social games are not only regulated but "constituted" by virtue of norms.

Obviously, this does not exclude the concrete possibility of having mixed forms of regulative *and* constitutive rules. On the basis of the prevalence of particular kinds of regulative or constitutive rules in the legal system, we can even try to outline the building up of the welfare state which appears rational to the extent that each of its phases represents a step in a trial and error process. We can say, for instance, that in less complex societies legal control can be exercised mainly by "regulative rules" formulated ad hoc which explicitly require the fulfillment or avoidance of certain behavior in given circumstances. In the relatively advanced stage of legal evolution characterized by the predominance of the so called "liberal state", legal control is exercised mainly through "constitutive rules" (i. e. not by *ad hoc* directives but by *ad hoc* games for the distribution of power and money) in which, at least formally, the ultimate result is not determined at the outset. Besides its constitutive rules, each game also requires regulative rules to establish the necessary internal prescriptions. Because these prescriptive rules refer to, and presuppose the existence of a certain game, they can be called "constitutive-regulative" rules to distinguish them from the "regulative" rules which, strictly speaking, refer only to non-institutional facts. The evolution from the liberal state to the welfare state can be connected to the growing consciousness of the limits of the economic and legal games constituted by the liberal state. This consciousness suggests a corresponding differentiation of the norms depending on the increased use, in a legal system dominated by constitutive rules, of regulative rules which no longer have only prescriptive functions inside a game, but have "corrective" functions with regard to already constituted games ("regulative-constitutive" rules).

In all these possible variants, however, the constitutive rules have a constant feature which seems to be crucial for a better understanding of the welfare state: their nonviolability (see Broekman supra). The welfare state is characterized by an overwhelming presence of norms which can be used or not used. Law becomes, therefore, something to consume, not to observe: something not only to restrict the realm of possible actions but to create many areas for the action of the law clients in which it is always possible for them not to enter. As Searle observes in referring explicitly to the game analogy: "It is easy to see how one could even violate the rule as to what constitutes checkmate in chess, or touchdown in football". (Searle, 1969: 41). It is clear that "Whoever behaves in a wrong way (for example whoever moves a knight as if it were a pawn) does not violate a rule of the game in strict sense, but is simply playing another game" (Margolis, 1965: 301). Therefore, in the law game the sanction of nullity sui generis is legally foreseen, for a deviation from the inviolable constitutive rules, which "cannot ... be assimilated to a punishment attached to a rule as an inducement to abstain from the activites which the rule forbids" (Hart, 1961: 34).

The general statement that the single legal institution of the welfare state can be better analysed by reference to constitutive rules will now be articulated on the basis of the four fundamental problems mentioned above. In particular: a) the constitutive rules could contribute in throwing new light on the problem of the "identification" of the game. In this context they supply a criterion of recognition and delimitation, not (apparently) descriptive as with the functional criterion adopted by Luhmann, but explicitly normative.

As Searle puts it, "the institutional facts can only be explained in terms of the constitutive rules which underlie them" (Searle, 1969: 52). Moreover, as Weber, Ross, and Hart have already suggested, the observer who ignores the constitutive rules of the game could never discern the institutional behavior from other acts accidentally committed by the players (see in particular Weber, 1977: 120).

b) The constitutive rules establish a new basis for the discussion of the problem of "change". For their ability to conventionally modify their object, they normally undertake a "performative function that has been discussed in the field of the game theory in general ("The rules of chess are constitutive since, in a sense, chess could not exist without them") (Allwood, 1976: 29) as well as in the field of the theory of those games established by the legal order, where it has been expressed somewhat imaginatively, as the "magic" dimension of law (Olivecrona, 1971).

c) The constitutive rules also highlight the problem of the "selection" of behavior alternatives by defining what is possible for the law consumer. In fact, the establishment of those moves which are possible in a certain situation are the constitutive rules of the game, not an abstract "sense" of the system. The game theory distinguishes between three levels of selection. While "the game" is simply the totality of the rules which describe it", the play is "every particular instance at which the game is played — in a particular way — from beginning to end" and the move "is the occasion of a choice between various alternatives, to be made either by one of the players, or by some device subject to chance, under conditions precisely prescribed by the rules of the game" (Neumann and Morgenstern, 1944: 49).

On the basis of this distinction it is, moreover, possible to integrate normatively the "double selection" which, according to Luhmann, is provided by the structures of every system and in particular those of the legal system, and which closely recalls the distinction proposed by Saussure as regards the linguistic systems between *langue* and *parole* (Luhmann, 1983: 40).

d) Finally, the constitutive rules allow the problem of "information" particularly relevant for the distribution of norms, to be better illuminated. Every game, through its constitutive rules, creates and transforms the perception of the environment by imposing a code to receive, interpret and transmit the incoming information and explain to others what is being done. In other words, since the constitutive rules establish conventionally the *Sein* of the object of institutional activities, especially those defined by law (*quod non est in regula non est in mundo*), it is clear that only by referring explicitly or implicitly to them can one speak of this object and describe it (Hart, 1961: 99; Lewis, 1969: 104).

VIII. New Dilemmas of the Welfare State

The adoption of a game analogy also allows one to throw light on some important dilemmas of the welfare state which ensue, not from theoretical deficit or material failures but from structural predicaments. The dilemmas of the welfare state we want to identify here by means of the game analogy and the bargaining dimensions it involves, are reciprocally interrelated. We can try to order them as in a series of Chinese boxes i. e. in such a way that the possible answer to the preceding dilemma discloses a new dilemma the answer to which makes the process start again. In the last box will be discovered a fundamental dilemma of the welfare state which remains without a definite answer.

First dilemma. Since the welfare state wants to authoritatively correct the consequences of the economic game, the game theory can reveal in it the co-existence of two distinct games (the market game and the state game) which are interrelated in such a way that whoever loses at the board of the first game can become a winner at the board of the second game. This "double game", and the consequent double constitutivity, is not in itself contradictory (the correlations of more games are a normal situation in social life and among different constitutive rules, each one belonging to a different game, there cannot be logical antinomy) (Conte, 1983). The definition of the welfare state in terms of an uncontrollable "positive feedback" becomes instead a correlation between two games reciprocally controlled, because the input of the one is the output of the other and vice-versa.

A relevant dilemma arises then at the level of the individual decision-maker since it is clear that it is the anticipated knowledge of the existence of the second game that usually tends to be institutionalized and which can substantially modify the strategies in the first game. As a matter of fact, the subject can either try to win the first game or take into account both games and measure the possible advantages in an overall manner. In this case, the already institutionalized intervention of the state in the second game becomes a factor of decision in the first game, so that the first game is played rationally not only to win but also to lose (at least, either not to win everything possible or to deliberately lose something, in the hope that it will be possible to gain more in the long run).

Second dilemma. The preceding dilemma can be overcome by making the theoretical frame of reference a little more complex and inserting between the two players (as suggested by the game theory itself) a third figure: that of a "mediator". In such a way it is not the singular individual who has to decide his strategy autonomously; rather, it is the mediator who filters the interests, translates them in a politically relevant language and decides on the strategies which will fulfill them in the best possible way. This arrangement would seem ideal as everybody has something to win: the state, because it will have clearly set out needs; the subjects, because they will increase their political relevance; and naturally the mediator, because of the central role he attains in the so-called "political exchange".

But this is exactly where the problem lies. In fact, the mediators are faced by the following alternatives: either to restrict themselves by playing a purely intermediary role, or to begin playing a game of their own which aims at increasing their own political influence. Needless to say, the mediators frequently choose this second path and, in order to keep their own central role in the political exchange, play in such a way that they can prevent the other two players from definitively winning. They normally obtain, from a state increasingly preoccupied with taming them, a more or less open recognition which institutionalizes them and, at the same time, they entertain with the state a complex relationship as regards the distribution of political legitimacy. On the one hand, they oblige the state — with an inversion of the traditional political coercion that no longer comes from the state but is turned against it — to concede certain benefits; but on the other hand, they absorb the advantages in terms of political legitimation that the state would expect by such a concession.

The result of this process is an emptying of the traditional concept of sovereignty; the state is left with the financial burden of the politics of welfare while the political advantages are devolved to non-statual institutions (such as trade unions) which can then present themselves as those who have forced a reluctant state to make certain concessions. So a self-reproductive process begins because a progressively weakened state will always be less able to resist new pressures and therefore will always be more exposed to a subsequent loss of legitimacy (cf. Willke infra).

Third dilemma. The state can get out of this situation in various ways by playing in order to "change the game" of welfare. In the area of the politically practicable, two groups of alternatives then confront the state:

a) it can entrust the selection of the interests, not to intermediary groups without its control or even opposed to it, but to local organizations controlled directly or indirectly by the state (decentralization), or else – and this is a variant of the previous alternative – the state can remain open to the influence of more or less hidden pressure groups or even of individuals, on a pure "*do ut des*" basis (clientelism). In both cases, the advantage will be that the state, which concedes the benefits, can receive in return political legitimation directly or through its own organs.

b) The state can, on the other hand, assume the most impartial role possible in the concession of benefits in such a way that if it does not achieve substantial advantages in terms of political legitimacy by favored groups, it is also not exposed to losing legitimacy through unfavored groups. This low profile of the state can also be accompanied by a process of limitation of the social interest considered worth protecting, which can even arrive at political intervention by the state geared more towards imposing "sacrifices" than towards conceding benefits. This last trend is not, as it might seem, incompatible with the welfare state but can be brought back to the internal logic of the welfare state and in particular to the exigency of recharging the financial as well as the political reserves of the welfare state in a situation of a (real or apparent) political and economic emergency.

Fourth dilemma. From the previous dilemmas a complex picture emerges in which the elements of consumption (first dilemma), distribution (second dilemma), and production (third dilemma), of norms tend to build up different games, guides by different strategies. Therefore, from an external point of view a further dilemma arises which confronts the onlooker: one can hypothesize either that these different games combine in a "meta-game" governed by a still invisible rationality or that there are no general rules behind the behavior of all the players involved. This, evidently enough, implies a corresponding alternative on which future empirical research depends: either to try to decipher the meta-rationality of this meta-game as well as its non-written rules, or to limit the analysis to an interpretation of each game performed by the different players.

Whatever the chosen alternative is, the previous arguments certainly tend to show that the game analogy, because of its higher degree of abstraction and greater capacity to analyze the normative dimensions inherent in the welfare state, can be, with respect to the system analogy elaborated by Luhmann, a more useful point of reference not only for theoretical but also for empirical research. To be aware of that, it is only necessary to confront the system related concept of "inclusion", introduced by Luhmann in his consideration of the welfare state (to point out the progressive entrance into the political system of the different groups of population) (Luhmann, 1981: 25; Marshall, 1964), with the more flexible concept of "access" which leaves ample space for the possibility of ascertaining "if", "to what extent", and "by whom" the chances of effective participation in the judicial games of the welfare state are taken advantages of (Cappelletti, 1981).

IX. Conclusions

The route taken up to this point has led us to substitute the system paradigm with a game paradigm which seems to make for not only fewer ideological dangers, but also greater flexibility and a deeper insight into the possible dilemmas of the welfare state. The usefulness of the substitution of the system paradigm with that of the game can be confirmed by an analysis of the work of Luhmann. Under the dominating system analogy, we can easily find many examples of a fruitful use of the law-game analogy; as, for instance, in the definition of the concept of legitimacy.

In several places, but above all in the book *Legitimation durch Verfahren* (1969), Luhmann proposes a conception of procedure presented explicitly as a system, but implicitly as a game which compels the participants to accept its results because of the simple fact of their participation. This participation a) includes a promise to accept the uncertain outcome of the game and b) prevents the loser from transforming his disillusionment into a political issue, leaving him only the possibility of blaming himself for having played his cards badly (see also Luhmann, 1965).

On the basis of such an analogy, Luhmann succeeds in overcoming the conception of legitimacy considered as the outcome of an exchange between *legitimans* and *legitimandum*. The legitimation is no longer seen as the result of a process in which the *legitimans* concede something to the *legitimandum* (consensus, recognition, obedience) in exchange for something that the *legitimandum* guarantees the *legitimans* (realization of certain values, respect of certain interests, concessions of certain benefits). It is seen instead as an impersonal process, the result of which is the exclusion of any possibility of dissent. In this context, the legitimation is seen not positively but negatively: as delegitimation of the refusal to legitimize. It thus has the structure of the "negation of a negation".

This interpretation of the concept of legitimation represents one of the most controversial points of Luhmann's work, but is also one of those points where the author clearly refers, even if critically, to a model of constitutional state. Still remaining in the field of games-theory, however, Luhmann's position can be further developed. Taking into account the reality of the welfare state, three integrative questions can and must be put forward: In the first place, how can "passive" participation, directed towards accepting the result of the game, be substituted by an "active" participation directed not only towards influencing the development procedure of the game but eventually also towards modifying its own rules? In the second place, to what extent, if at all, is it possible to decentralize the given structure of distribution of money and power in order to bring the area of the decisions closer to that of their relevant consequences, and so to multiply the elements of factual responsibility and self-control for the decision-makers? (For a parallel development in this direction see Willke infra). In the third place, are self legitimating games part of another game which must be substantially legitimized?

It seems to me that all these questions emerge in the composite and widely discussed concept of "responsive law" (Nonet and Selznick, 1978; Teubner, 1983). This concept appears to me as a way of taking into account the reality of the welfare state by making reference not to a system but to a process of regulation which is no longer exercised through prescriptive norms but through self-regulating institutions based on autonomous bargaining strategies: in our terminology, on the meta-game stemming from the combination of legal and political "games". Moreover, it is possible to observe here that even Luhmann's own construction can be considered as a theoretical game, the constitutive rules of which cannot be violated, thus leaving open to the interpreter only two possibilities: of either staying inside this linguistic game with the risk of forgetting that the system is a non-descriptive, purely heuristic, instrument; or else trying to change the game as well as its constitutive rules. Here we have tried to do the latter, playing, so to speak, the "game-analogy game".

References

Allwood, Jens (1976) *Linguistic Communication as Action and Cooperation.* Göteborg: University of Göteborg.

Aubert, Vilhelm (1977) "On Sanctions", in B. M. Blegvad, C: M. Campbell and C. J. Schuyt (eds.), *European Yearbook in Law and Sociology* The Hague: Nijhoff.

Bobbio, Norberto (1977) *Dalla struttura alla funzione. Nuovi studi di teoria del diritto*, Milano: Comunità.

Buckley, Walter (1967) *Sociology and Modern Systems Theory.* Englewood Cliffs, N. J.: Prentice-Hall.

Cappelletti, Mauro (ed.) (1981) *Access to Justice and the Welfare State.* Alphen aan den Rhijn et al.: Sijthoff et al.

Carcaterra, Gaetano (1979) *La forza costitutiva delle norme.* Roma: Bulzoni.

Cherry, Christopher (1973), "Regulative Rules and Constitutive Rules". 23 *The Philosophical Quarterly* 301.

Conte, Amedeo Giovanni (1981) "Konstitutive Regeln und Deontik" in E. Morscher and R. Stranzinger (eds.), *Ethik. Grundlagen, Probleme und Anwendungen. Akten der 5. Internationalen Wittgenstein-Symposiums.* Wien: Hölder—Pichler—Tempsky.

— (1981) "Variationen über Wittgensteins Regelbegriff" in R. Haller (ed.) *Sprache und Erkenntnis als soziale Tatsache*, Wien: Hölder—Pichler—Tempsky.

— (1983) "Regola costitutiva, condizione, antinomia", in U. Scarpelli (ed.), *La teoria generale del diritto. Problemi e tendenze attuali. Studi dedicati a Norberto Bobbio, Milano*, Milano: Comunità.

CROZIER, Michel, and Erhard FRIEDBERG (1977) *Les contraintes de l'action collective*. Paris: Seuil.
EMERY, F. E. (ed.), (1969) *Systems Thinking*. Harmondsworth: Penguin Books Inc.
FEBBRAJO, Alberto (1975) *Funzionalismo strutturale e sociologia del diritto nell'opera di Niklas Luhmann*. Milano: Giuffrè.
— (1983a) "Pene e ricompense come problemi di politica legislativa", in *Diritto premiale e sistema penale*. Milano: Giuffrè.
— (1983b) "Teoria del diritto e legittimazione del welfare state", in *Transformazioni e crisi del welfare state*. Bari: De Donato.
GALLINO, Luciano (1980) *La società. Perché cambia, come funziona*. Torino: Paravia.
GENOVA, A. C. (1970–71) "Institutional Facts and Brute Values", 81 *Ethics* 36.
HÄNDLE, Frank and Stefan JENSEN (eds.), (1974) *Systemtheorie und Systemtechnik*. München: Nymphenburger Verlagshandlung.
HAMBURGER, Henry (1979) *Games as Models of Social Phenomena*. San Francisco: Freeman and Co.
HART, Herbert, L. A. (1961) *The Concept of Law*. Oxford: Clarendon Press.
HUIZINGA, Johan (1938) *Homo Ludens*. Haarlem: Tieenk Willink.
KLAUS, Georg (1968) *Spieltheorie in philosophischer Sicht*. Berlin (DDR): Deutscher Verlag der Wissenschaften.
KRAWIETZ, Werner (1984) *Recht als Regelsystem*. Wiesbaden: Steiner.
KRYSMANSKI, Hans Jürgen, and Peter MARWEDEL (eds.), (1975) *Die Krise in der Soziologie*. Köln: Pahl-Rugenstein.
LEONI, Bruno (1961) *Freedom and the Law*. Princeton, N. J.: Van Nostrand Co.
LEWIS, David K. (1969) *Convention. A philosophical Study*. Cambridge: Harvard University Press.
LUHMANN, Niklas (1965) *Grundrechte als Institution. Ein Beitrag zur politischen Soziologie*. Berlin: Duncker & Humblot.
— (1969) *Legitimation durch Verfahren*. Neuwied a. R., Berlin: Luchterhand.
— (1970) *Soziologische Aufklärung. Aufsätze zur Theorie sozialer Systeme* 1. Köln, Opladen: Westdeutscher Verlag.
— (1971) *Politische Planung. Aufsätze zur Soziologie von Politik und Verwaltung*. Opladen: Westdeutscher Verlag.
— (1979) *Trust and Power*. London: Wiley.
— (1981a) *Gesellschaftsstruktur und Semantik. Studien zur Wissenssoziologie der modernen Gesellschaft*. Vol. 2, Frankfurt a. M.: Suhrkamp.
— (1981b) *Ausdifferenzierung des Rechts. Beiträge zur Rechtssoziologie und Rechtstheorie*. Frankfurt a. M.: Suhrkamp.
— (1981c) *Politische Theorie im Wohlfahrtsstaat*. München: Olzog.
— (1982) *The Differentiation of Society*. New York: Columbia University Press.
— (1983²) *Rechtssoziologie*. Opladen: Westdeutscher Verlag.
MAC CORMICK, David Neil (1974) "Law as Institutional Fact", 90 *The Law Quarterly Review* 102.
MAIHOFER, Werner (1970) "Die gesellschaftliche Funktion des Rechts", in R. Lautmann, W. Maihofer and H. Schelsky (eds.), *Jahrbuch für Rechtssoziologie und Rechtstheorie*. Bielefeld: Bertelsmann.
MARGOLIS, Joseph (1963) "Chess and Possibility", 8 *Logique et Analyse* 301.
MARSHALL, T. H. (1964) *Class, Citizenship and Social Development* New York: Doubleday Anchor.
MATURANA, Humberto R., Francesco E. VARELA and R. URIBE (1974) "Autopoiesis: The Organization of Living Systems," 5 *Bio Systems* 187.
MULLIGAN, Glenn, and Bobbie LEDERMANN (1977) "Social Facts and Rules of Practice", 83 *American Journal of Sociology* 539.

NARR, Wolf-Dieter (1969) *Theoriebegriffe und Systemtheorie*. Stuttgart: Kohlhammer.
NEUMANN, John von, and Oskar MORGENSTERN (1944) *Theory of Games and Economic Behaviour*. Princeton: Princeton University Press.
NONET, Philippe, and Philip SELZNICK (1978) *Law and Society in Transition*. London: Harper and Row.
O'CONNOR, James (1973) *The Fiscal Crisis of the State*. New York: St. Martin's Press.
OLIVECRONA, Karl (1971) *Law as fact*. London: Stevens and Sons.
PARSONS, Talcott (1977) *The Evolution of Societies*. Englewood Cliffs: Prentice Hall.
POGGI, Gianfranco (1979) "Niklas Luhmann's Neo-Functionalist Approach. An Elementary Presentation", Introduction to Luhmann, *Trust and Power*, London: Wiley.
RAWLS, John (1955) "Two Concepts of Rules", 64 *The Philosophical Review* 3.
ROOM, Graham (1979) *Th Sociology of Welfare. Social Policy, Stratification and Political Order.* Oxford: Blackwell.
ROSS, Alf (1958) *On Law and Justice*. London: Stevens & Sons.
SAUSSURE, Ferdinand de (1922) *Cours de linguistique générale*. Paris: Payot.
SEARLE, John R. (1969) *Speech Acts. An Essay in the Philosophy of Language*. London: Cambridge University Press.
STACHOWIAK, Herbert (1965) *Denken und Erkennen im kybernetischen Modell*. Wien, New York: Springer Verlag.
TAYLOR-GOOBY, Peter, and Jennifer DALE (1981) *Social Theory and Social Welfare*. London: Arnold.
TEUBNER, Gunther (1982) "Substantive and Reflexive Elements in Modern Law", 17 *Law and Society Review* 239.
— (1978) *Organisationsdemokratie und Verbandsverfassung. Rechtsmodelle für politisch relevante Verbände*. Tübingen: Mohr (Paul Siebeck).
WEBER, Max (1966) *On Law in Economy and Society*. Cambridge: Harvard University Press.
— (1977) *Critique of Stammler*. London, New York: The Free Press.
WITTGENSTEIN, Ludwig J. J. (1964) *Philosophische Bemerkungen*, Frankfurt a. M.: Suhrkamp.
WRIGHT, Georg H. von (1963) *Norm and Action*. London: Routledge and Kegan Paul.

The Concept of Rights and the Welfare State

ULRICH K. PREUSS
Bremen

Introduction

The world-wide economic crisis has considerably worsened the living-standards of the masses in the industrial societies of West Europe and the United States; the simultaneous phenomena of mass unemployment, the reduction of spending power and cut-backs in governmental welfare programs prove that market failures are not compensated for but rather paralleled, even if not reinforced, by the institutional devices and financial mechanisms of the welfare state. Certainly this means a serious crisis of the welfare state.

But there is a more profound interpretation of this crisis which refers to structural limits of the welfare state not simply attributable to scarcity of material goods and financial means of governments but rather to the overstraining of the political and administrative — and subsequently of the economic — capacities of a society to steer its integration and development — the more so if this development has to be subsumed under the goal of 'social justice'. One aspect of this 'structural' critique of the welfare state is the hypothesis of the crisis of regulatory law. The political catchwords are well known: inflation of legal claims; over-regulation; over-bureaucratization; over-equalization, all of which tend to suffocate the incentive and initiative of free market activities. The serious scholarly discussion about 'deregulation' (Reich, 1983/84) shows that this problem does not belong entirely to the field of political polemics. At a theoretical level, Teubner has tried to show that 'reflexive law' might be a way out of the dilemma of the goal-oriented regulatory law which often produces more negative side-effects than positive solutions to the problems at which it had been aimed (Teubner, 1983: 239 and infra).

This essay deals with this latter aspect of the — real or alleged — crisis of the welfare state. The analyses of the legal structure have mainly stressed the law's role as a steering device of the politico-administrative system and its capacity to make the functioning of different societal sub-systems compatible. But as Habermas suggests (Habermas, 1981: 536 and infra) we have to discriminate between the law as a normatively neutral organization medium and the law as an institution; the latter being based on moral or other normative principles of a 'good social order'. To fully understand the structural features of the legal order this distinction seems to me indispensable. For the malfunctioning of legal regulations might well be on account of either a too good technical quality or a too bad one. In the first case many problems arise from a legalization of normatively ordered institutions of the 'life world' by adjusting them to the functional requirements of economic and administrative planning and control, which Habermas calls the 'colonialization of the life world' by system imperatives. Only in the latter case – if the law cannot cope with the complex problems of coordinating and compatibilizing most of the functional requirements of many societal sub-systems – should we speak of 'over-regulation'; although the term 'under-regulation' might be equally or even more adequate.

I shall not discuss this hypothesis but rather will deal with one segment of the legal order which deserves specific attention: the role of (subjective) rights within the legal order of the welfare state. At the outset I give a short account of the welfare state (as opposed to the German '*Sozialstaat*') (I); I then analyze the features of (subjective) rights as opposed to mere interests (II) and subsequently their 'irresponsible' character (III). The following section deals with those rights which are typical of the welfare state and which I call distributive rights (IV); they are based on some underlying assumptions, the cessation of which contributes to the dilemmas of the welfare state (V). Finally, I make some very brief remarks on strategies to overcome these difficulties (VI).

I. A Concept of the Welfare State

The notion of the welfare state is far from clear; in German political and scholarly discussion it is less familiar than the term '*Sozialstaat*' and often both are used synonymously. But there is more at stake than a mere difference in terminology. The two words represent different concepts of coping with the economic and political problems of capitalism under conditions of mass democracy (see also Habermas infra). The concept of the '*Sozialstaat*' or '*Sozialer Rechtsstaat*' dates back to the conservative German theorist Lorenz v. Stein and is rooted in the 'social question' which dominated political discourse in the 19th century: how could the industrial proletariat be integrated into bourgeois society and its institutional frame of political power? How could capitalism and the incidental hegemony of the bourgeois class be made compatible with a fully extended democracy for the industrial masses? The constitution of 1871 abolished census suffrage and established universal suffrage for the male population in the '*Reich*'. Moreover, Bismarck transformed the traditional poor relief into a social policy which aimed at the protection of the working classes against their very specific risks as wage workers. This development in favor of the working class was supplemented by the Weimar Constitution which explicitly protected the labor force; established a system of collective bargaining; announced a comprehensive labor law and restricted economic liberty for the sake of social justice. When in 1929 Hermann Heller postulated the '*Sozialen Rechtsstaat*' as an alternative to the bourgeois economic (and finally political) dictatorship of liberal capitalism as well as to Leninist theory and the Soviet practice of the dictatorship of the proletariat, he regarded it as an institutional means of fettering the dynamics of capitalist market society by extending the political principles, not only of the rule of law but also of democratic self-determination, to the sphere of the production and distribution of goods. This pathetic idea of the '*Sozialer Rechtsstaat*' aimed at the "subordination of the means of life to the ends of life" which Heller regarded as a precondition for the revival of European culture (Heller, 1971: 443, 451, 461; Voigt, 1983).

It is important to remember the close connection between the idea of the '*Sozialstaat*' and the goal of economic and political emancipation of the working class in order to understand the core of its difference from the concept of the welfare state. This has close links with the economic theory of John Meynard Keynes which – roughly speaking – explained the crisis of the capitalist economy in the late twenties and early thirties as being based not on a lack of supply but of demand, i. e. of spending power of the masses. In contrast to the assumptions of classical economic theory, he asserted that flexibility of the price of the labor force (i. e. of wages) would not solve the unemployment problem by adapting the supply of and demand for this commodity. The starting point for the abolition of market failures was consumer demand, which in times of economic depression meant increase of mass incomes. Keynes observed that workers resisted a reduction in their nominal wages (but to a certain extent were ready to accept a decrease in their spending power through inflation) because their relative position on the labor market was important for them and he stated the "psychological law" that the increase of income would increase consumption (if not to the same degree) (Bombach *et al.*, 1976). After World War II all advanced capitalist industrial societies established some sort of welfare state on the basis of Keynes' economic theory and thus institutionalized the dynamics of increasing mass spending power and consumption. The differences in the theoretical fundaments of Heller's concept of the '*Sozialer Rechtsstaat*' and of the 'Keynesian Welfare State' are clear. Heller's idea is based on a socio-political theory with strong ethical motives to overcome capitalism and to emancipate the proletariat, whereas the Keynesian Welfare State is the application of an economic theory for the sake of unfettering the potential of capitalism under critical conditions – and fortunately this entailed the protection and permanent increase of mass income.

In the Constitution (*Grundgesetz*) of West Germany the '*Sozialer Rechtsstaat*' has become a leading constitutional principle, but the concept has remained controversial. Very few theorists referred to Hermann Heller's theory of the twenties or postulated the constitutional integration of democracy, rule of law and 'social state', i. e. the extension of the democratic principles of equality and self-determination to the economic order (Abendroth, 1967: 109). Main stream jurisprudence in constitutional law restricted the normative principle of the '*Sozialstaat*' to a rather general principle of social justice within the institutional framework of capitalist order[1]. The problem of institutional relations between capital and labor was reduced to the question of how to best distribute the national gross product and this necessarily entailed its being redefined as a question of providing economic growth and spending power of the masses and of increasing life chances by increasing consumption. It was a conservative theorist, Carl Schmitt, who stated that it was typically liberal to solve the 'social question' by increasing production and consumption, thus reconciling economic freedom with the material needs of the masses (Schmitt, 1958: 489). There are reasons to assume that the dynamics of an indefinite and permanent increase of mass consumption and the absence of any sociocultural goal have contributed to the present difficulties of the welfare state. For its institutional functioning has become more and more dependent upon economic conditions which can no longer be ensured.

So the structural differences between '*Sozialstaat*' and welfare state in its Keynesian version have vanished. And it must be admitted that the latter fitted the institutional pattern of mass democracy rather well. Claus Offe has shown very clearly that the social conflict between labor and capital has been successfully transformed into different institutional mechanisms of distribution of the national gross product. One of these is the competitive party system which translates the social energies of the class struggle into the choice between different abstract political programs which tend to level the different social interests and life worlds in terms of the common denominator of individual income (Offe, 1983: 225). Certainly this reconciliation of capitalism and democracy is the main reason for the outstanding performance of the welfare state in the first decades after World War II.

II. Subjective Rights and Mere Interests

So far I have spoken about the intimate connections between the welfare state, Keynesian economic theory and the competitive party system which

[1] Meanwhile constitutional scholars have discovered "growth provision" as an important element of the "Sozialstaat". See Maunz et al. (1983: Rdn. 14 zu Art. 20).

have caused an unprecedented innate incentive for the permanent increase of mass income and consumption of the gross national product. Critics of this type of welfare state have reproached it for its consumerism and its tendency to destroy traditional social, cultural and political values and the sense of collective identity as a source of individual life satisfaction (Lane, 1978: 799). This seems to be a paradoxical judgement since the welfare state is regarded and legitimized as the institutional means of bringing about social justice which is a normative rather than a purely economic goal. Moreover, the welfare state is characterized by a great number of individual rights and legal regulations which are destined to order the economic process in favor of a just and good society. We should therefore expect the legal order to be something like a counterweight against the unfettered dynamics of industrial growth and its incitement by increasing mass spending power. Indeed, if we read liberal and conservative critiques of the welfare state, we get the impression that it is the specific shape of the legal order which — by over-regulation and over-legalization — has caused the troubles of the present situation by suffocating too many free-market initiatives. Although this latter argument may be true I shall not scrutinize it here. What is important for this discussion is that there are reasons to assume that the legal order of the welfare state has contributed to the dynamics of the growth-oriented economic process.

Two main characteristics of modern law have contributed to a great extent to the differentiation, change and social integration of capitalist industrial societies. Firstly, Kantian separation of morality from legality, that is, the institutionalization of obedience without any reference to the moral grounds on which this compliance is based. This allows for the dissolution of particularistic societal units and their very specific regional, local, traditional, and conventional rules. Their moral justifications are substituted by general rules which can be established by a centralized legislator. The law now encompasses and is binding for all members of society irrespective of their moral, religious, or political convictions and this makes possible the contact between strangers who do not have shared values or common traditions. Closely connected with this quality of modern law is its positivity: legal rules are established by a sovereign legislator and it is this rather than tradition or reason which constitutes the binding character of the law. It has become a function of power and will and its capacity to separate obedience from moral (or any other) justification has made it a steering resource of political power. More importantly, the positivity of modern law allows for the establishment and change of law on mere grounds of expediency, and since circumstances change very quickly we can say, as Luhmann does (Luhmann 1972: 209 and infra), that positivity implies the institutionalization of legal changes and, by virtue of this, the abstraction from social relations which are integrated by commonly shared values. As Polanyi stated for the market, we can speak of a high degree of "disembeddedness" of modern law in relation to other institutions of society (Polanyi, 1957: 68; Hopkins, 1971: 271, 294).

Reference to these two characteristics of modern law does not yet explain if or to what extent the legal order has contributed to the development of the dynamics of the modern welfare state. The law of the European absolutist states of the 18th century had already been greatly emancipated from traditional moral values and was mostly positive. Moreover, the absolutist states were "welfare states" in that they regulated the economic and social (and of course the religious and cultural) life very intensely, but here of course we do not find the self-executive dynamics of the modern welfare state. I think the key difference between these two legal structures is the absence of rights in the absolutist and their institutionalization in the modern welfare state (cf. Habermas 205 infra).

Of course, we must not separate legal analysis, especially the analysis of rights, from overall social relations. Feudal entitlements, which at times are associated with modern rights, were founded in duly acquired claims and justified by holy traditions; thus they were obstacles to positive legislation and from the modern legal point of view they were privileges and immunities rather than rights. In the liberal capitalist societies of the 19th century, rights were not regarded as obstacles to legislation nor to public welfare but rather as inseparable elements of them. The history of bourgeois society proves that the institutionalization of private as well as of civil rights was the pivotal element of bourgeois claims to emancipation.

Generally speaking, rights are interests whose satisfaction is secured by corresponding duties of other persons (or institutions), while the fulfillment of these duties — with some negligible exceptions — is guaranteed by the state's executive power. I leave out further qualifications[2]; at this point I am interested in the question about the criteria on which interests are transformed into rights. It should be clear that not every interest receives the guarantee to be satisfied by corresponding duties, and that the holder of a right gets power over the obligated person (or institution). The distribution of rights has a very specific pattern which reflects the distribution of "privileged" chances of life satisfaction. It is well known that the bourgeoisie asserted the existence of "natural" and inalienable rights which every individual inherently possesses by birth, namely — as stated the Virginia Bill of Rights — the enjoyment of life and liberty, the means of acquiring and possessing property and pursuing and obtaining happiness and safety. The equal liberty of all men would be transformed into equal rights by the duty of everybody not to interfere with liberty, life, and property of any other individual — but this is hardly possible since social relations necessarily imply continual intervention in the sphere of the

[2] See especially the differentiations between rights, powers, privileges and immunities in Hohfeld (1923: 23).

individual's material and immaterial interests. If A pollutes the air and B suffers asthma from this — has A to compensate for the immaterial and material damages to B, have we to assume a joint liability, or has B to bear the burden all by himself? If X and Y compere for a favourable contract and Y gets it — has he to compensate for the disadvantages of X? What I want to say by this is that even if we assume the equal liberty of all men we must not ignore the social relations of individuals and their consequence that rights have a different distributional pattern from that of equal liberty, or, to put it in a more simplistic way, that not all interests are taken into account when rights are shaped.

One of the key distinctions of the bourgeois legal order from the 19th century until recent times was that between private and public law: the former had to organize the relations of private individuals, the latter had to restrict and control the political power of the state, i.e., to prohibit the state from interfering with the private, and especially the economic sphere of the individual. This distrinction was, as Morton J. Horwitz has pointed out, paralleled by and related to the economic distinction between allocation and distribution (Horwitz, 1980: 5). Allocation was the inherent, apolitical and neutral principle of the market and its efficiency, whereas distribution was a political principle of justice. It was therefore a plausible idea to shape rights according to the allocational requirements of the market, i.e. to facilitate market transactions for the sake of economic efficiency and the increase of the gross national product. In contrast to this, in the American agrarian economy of the 18th century the property right protected the claim to absolute dominion over land, except for any restriction to the neigbor's enjoyment of the property. The legal doctrine of the 19th century, the age of the beginning industrialization, explicitly favored those who made efficient use of land and water, "profitable of the owner, and beneficial to the public" and restricted the power of obstruction of any owner who resisted the most efficient allocation of resources (Horwitz, 1977: 31). The influential utilitarian doctrine rationalized this "allocative" criterion for the conception of rights by judging that in the case of competing private interests the right is attributed according to the principle of maximization of the total net social utility, i.e. according to economic efficiency. In this doctrine's view it was an objective, neutral and apolitical criterion, and public rights had the function of shielding the quasi-autonomous working of the allocative rules of the market against any political or distributional (that is, distorting) intervention by state authority.

I should add that originally the legal doctrine of the European continent was not rooted in utilitarianism but rather in the ethical doctrines of economic liberalism and their concept of the autonomous person. But in Germany, the industrialization process in the second half of the 19th century also entailed a change in the justification of rights according to the new requirements of industrial take-off. The right lost its ethical foundation in the moral qualification of the person and became rather a mere technical means of attributing economic goods and powers to (natural or corporate) individuals. According to Jhering's influential concept of 'interest jurisprudence', it was an instrument of interest enforcement (Wieacker, 1967: 450, 474; Preuß, 1979: 21). Against the background of the pervading German absolutist tradition, competing interests were balanced and decided by the law, but the result was not very different from that in the U. S. A. As the German Code of Civil Law (Bürgerliches Gesetzbuch 1896/1900) shows, private rights were biased by the underlying assumption of the neutrality and objectivity of the market allocation which was reflected by the dominant legal doctrine of positivism as an inherently logical system of rules and rights which was immune from any "material" (i.e. distributional) and political impulse. Consequently, public rights were purely negative rights, obligating the public authority to forbear any intervention into the apolitical private sphere of the individual save but a law stated an explicit permission.

To summarize briefly: the concept of rights, private as well as public, is inherently connected with the establishment of market society; liberating every man but transforming only those interests into rights which satisfied the allocative goals of the market and protecting — by public rights — efficient market transactions against distorting authoritative state interventions. Of course, even such private law as the German BGB contained so-called general clauses (such as sect. 138, 242, 826 BGB) which left a certain degree of judicial discretion for the invasion of distributional (i.e. subjective), political aspects, but their function was restricted to correcting evidently "unjust" results. Apart from this qualification, which was to become more important after the First and especially after the Second World War, rights were incidental elements in the unfettering of the dynamics of the market and their distributional effects.

III. The 'Irresponsibility' of Subjective Rights

But this does not tell the whole story. To avoid misunderstandings, I do not mean to say that the intimate connections between the capitalist market and rights entail a logical or sociological incompatibility of rights with distributive as opposed to allocative social institutions. We shall see that it is the concept of 'distributional rights' itself which is characteristic of the modern welfare state and which has also caused considerable problems. Second, we have to be aware that what I said about the allocative character of rights applies only to private property rights, i.e. rights which serve economic goals. There are many private rights — especially in the law of domestic relations — which serve non-economic goals and are therefore not subject to the rules of economic efficiency. And there are many civil rights, e.g. the rights to exercise freedom of speech and of religion, which do not protect a sphere of undisturbed and efficient market allocation but rather a moral sphere of personhood or of public communication as opposed to the realm of strategic action.

Despite these differences between the various categories of rights, we must not conceive of them as contradictory. They are commonly rooted in the basic structures of bourgeois society which has liberated the individual from any responsibility for society at large. Two main elements characterize any right; first, rights protect a person's sphere of self-interest or, to put it in a utilitarian manner, they guarantee personal preferences as opposed to external preferences, i.e. the interest or desire to assign some goods or opportunities to another, my interest being that the other person has not this or that good (Dworkin, 1978: 234, 275; Flathman, 1976: 41). I may have the right to utter communist opinions and I may have the interest that others, too, hold these convictions — but it is incompatible with the concept of rights to have a right that others have and utter communist attitudes. External preferences are taken into account only in the political process and institutionalized by legal duties: a law can stipulate everybody's duty not to utter communist opinions, but there is no corresponding right.

Second, rights are not balanced by counter-rights, i.e. rights are non-reciprocal (Luhmann, 1970: 322, 325, see also supra). They stipulate duties on the part of others irrespective of any distinct justification for the specific act (or forbearance) which is the object of the duty. Having a right is in itself a justification for the claimed duty, regardless of how beneficial for the holder of the right or damaging for the obligated person it may be and regardless of its moral justification. This non-symmetric character of the right reflects the Kantian separation of legality from morality which I mentioned above and which relieves legally ordered social relations of moral reasoning. And it dispenses with individual responsibility for the functioning of society at large.

To fully understand these two main traits of rights and their significance for the welfare state, I want to refer to Polanyi's typology of different kinds of economic and social exchange (Polanyi, 1957: 244, 250). He distinguishes reciprocal, redistributive, and market exchange. Reciprocity means a more or less symmetric division of social functions and an exchange of goods and benefits within a social group which is institutionalized on the basis of a pattern of division of labor, religious creeds and cultural traditions. Reciprocity does not merely mean reciprocal behavior but rather the existence of institutions — such as kinship — the functioning of which is based on reciprocity and which encompass not only and not even primarily economic exchange but organize all social relations within a group, including the supply of material goods. Thus the material survival of the individual is inseparably interwined with his cultural and social existence as well as with the survival of the whole group of which he is a member. Reciprocal exchange is typical of particularistic collectivities in which persons give and receive "just by virtue of their status relationship" (Barber, 1977: 15, 24).

Redistributive exchange designates a hierarchical order in which a center collects the material goods necessary for the survival of the group and redistributes them to the original donors in different proportions. This type presupposes a sufficiently dinstinct supra-individual public welfare, but the centralized allocation and distribution is embedded in a comprehensive set of institutions which submerge the individual into the communal life and connect his fate to that of society at large. Finally, market exchange is based on the rational and self-interested behavior of the utility maximizing person, who does not treat, as is ideally the case in redistributive exchange societies, strangers as brothers, but rather brothers as strangers, i.e. impersonally. It should come as no surprise that rights in this sense of protecting self-interest (personal rather than external preferences) and of non-reciprocity are inherently connected to market exchange. By this I do not suggest that there is no self-interest in reciprocal or redistributive exchange societies, but rather that the interests are shaped by the institutions which devise the social behavior of the individuals. In pre-bourgeois societies which inseparably encompassed religious, cultural, social, and economic motives it is not possible to conceive of a distinct economic interest of the individual. "The outstanding discovery of recent historical and anthropological research is that man's economy, as a rule, is submerged in his social relationship. He does not act so as to safeguard his individual interest in the possession of material goods; he acts so as to safeguard his social standing, his social claims, his social assets. He values material goods only in so far as they serve this end" (Polanyi, 1957: 46). This applies not only to economic interests, but to the whole concept of individual interests which underlies the concept of rights. I suggest calling this a concept of de-institutionalization: it designates the dissolution of comprehensive social institutions and the distinct institutionalization of economic, cultural, religious, familial etc. motives, interests and interactions, the societal integration of which is provided by the main "compatibilizers", law and money.

The precondition of this societal differentiation and integration is a certain degree of rationalization of the individual's aspirations. And indeed the notion of interest which is the fundament of the rights concept is a very specific one. As Hirschman has pointed out, the conception of interests arises in the 17th century as a 'new paradigm' which overcomes the traditional opposites of passion and reason (Hirschman, 1977). Sociological theory understands institutions as social devices for taming man's passions but since the 17th century it is interests which have become more and more the "tamers of the passions" (Hirschman, 1977: 31). More specifically, it is the self-interest of the rational man which is regarded as a calculable guide to a person's actions and social behavior and which entails predictability and constancy in a social order in which the dissolution of traditional social institutions has destroyed the old and highly predictable social patterns of economic, social, religious and cultural life. Thus to a certain extent interests have become functional equivalents to the taming power of comprehensive institutions. On the other hand, self-interest has no innate end, but forces the individual to an everlasting and restless striving for the satisfaction of his aspirations because competition with other self-interested individuals produces permanent insecurity. The endlessness of interest and the finiteness of the world and its resources transform life into a rational calculation of strategic actions under conditions of scarcity. This is the dynamic element of interests which would become self-destructive if there were not some elements which are exempt from the overall conditions of insecurity.

This is why, despite the Hobbesian *bellum omnium contra omnes* which, by the way, clearly refers to the competition for scarce resources (Hobbes, 1978), the individual's interests in the enjoyment of life, liberty and property have become rights; they are an indispensable means of acquiring safety, safe preconditions of an overall lack of safety. From the point of view of limiting the range of insecurity, the Lockean concept of assigning rights to individuals is the most important alternative to the Hobbesian theory of absolutist state power. Thus from the very beginning, rights have had an ambivalent character: they are based on the dynamic principle of self-interest competition and its inherent tendency towards insecurity. On the other hand, they safeguard islands of interests from being overruled by the mere fact that there are stronger or more urgent interests of others or of society at large. Therefore we also must observe an inherent tendency of rights towards restricting the competition of interests. Trusts are a prominent example of this structural element: to keep them compatible with the requirements of an efficient resource allocation by the capitalist market either their scope has to be restricted so as not to immobilize economic resources, or they themselves must be amenable to market transactions. Both things happen: the former by, e.g., the already mentioned anti-trust laws which prohibit the stipulation of rights not to be exposed to competition; the latter by property rights which can be bought and sold on the market-place. Property rights reconcile the individual's interest in safety and, by virtue of this, in exempting productive resources from the risks of market competition and the capitalist principle of efficient resource allocation by mobilization of all productive forces. Their exchangeability lures the owner of resources into the market place by incentives which are valuable enough to motivate him to bargain his resources for money, so that at the end of this transaction both buyer and seller are better off.

Finally, the nontradeable rights, especially, but not exclusively civil rights, e.g. the rights to vote, to equal justice, or to hold and to utter religious convictions protect certain spheres of human life from the intrusion of rules of economic efficiency on grounds of human dignity and equality (Okun, 1975: 6, 10). The hypothetical results of an efficient allocation of resources and life chances are "distorted" by principles of distribution. This sounds strange, but why shouldn't an economist suggest trading voting rights or the right of the defendant to an elaborate trial so as to enhance the overall social utility? (Okun, 1975: 6). But non-tradeable rights do not contain either the entitlement of the individual to veto any change in the given set of distribution. Whereas, as we have seen, money mobilizes property rights for the sake of efficiency, it is the law which mobilizes non-tradeable rights for the sake of maximizing public welfare (at the expense of the holder of the right). It compatibilizes the safety of non-competitive rights with the requirements of adapting public policy to changing conditions in the same way as money does for the property rights. Both "compatibilizers" respond to the specific traits of (tradeable and non-tradeable) rights: to the trait of self-interest (personal preferences) and its innate principle of irresponsibility towards society at large by equating individual interest and that of society at large on the basis of monetary value; the model is expropriation in exchange for just compensation. Or the society responds to self-interest through legal regulations, that is, by stipulating sanctions for the transgression of the law in such a way as to make the consequences of obedience or disobedience to the law a calculable factor in the individual balance of self-interests (non-tradeable rights). In both cases overall societal utility or public welfare is internalized; it has become an element of rational interest calculation and by this means has been made compatible with individual self-interest. The same applies to the other trait of rights, their non-reciprocity: the universality of money and law dissolves particularistic collectivities in which the exchange of goods and services takes place by virtue of status relationships and in which brotherhood balances the reciprocal obligations. Since money and law are universally present and facilitate relations between strangers, there is no further need for any innate balance and justice of rights because the universal and abstract character of law and money makes them a common denominator of all individual actions and thus establishes an abstract community in which responsibility for others is performed by reacting to monetary incentives and by compliance with the law.

IV. The Distributive Rights of the Welfare State

Does the welfare state change the concept of rights? As I stated above, rights are the pivotal bourgeois means of achievement for the institutionalization of the capitalist market exchange (see also Ewald supra). They are the safe fundaments of the overall uncertainty of market competition and serve the efficient allocation of scarce resources. They protect the individual's self-interest, i.e. the pursuit of personal rather than external preferences, and they are non-reciprocal. In contrast, the inherent ideas of the welfare state are those of just distribution and egalitarianism (and by that the recognition of external preferences) and its exchange pattern is redistributive (rather than market exchange). Is it justified to speak of a new structure of rights, at least of those which are typical of the welfare state and which I call distributive rights?

Distributive rights are interests which are satisfied through the performance of corresponding duties on the part of the government or any other party. In this there is no difference from any other right. But they are different in one important respect: they interfere with the process of efficient allocation of goods and services, protect the employees; the consumers; the clients; the tenants etc. against the power of the employers; the producers; the landlords etc. and alter — directly or indirectly — the reward structure of the capitalist economy. In other words, they are based on governmental interventions which encompass compulsory measures (like prohibition of children's work; safety rules for workers; prohibitions on polluting the water or the air etc.); in-kind provisions (like the supply of kindergartens; schools beyond elementary education; universities; health services) and cash transfers. If I speak of intervention into the reward structure of the capitalist economy, one clarification may be welcome. The point of reference is the capitalist market exchange which is often regarded as an unregulated economy. But there is no such thing as an unregulated economy. The system of voluntary exchange and efficient allocation has societal preconditions which allow authoritative regulation: the institutionalization of property rights affords the prohibition and sanction of theft and robbery; the efficient allocation of scarce resources affords competition and hence anti-trust laws (Thurow, 1980; 128). The production of (positive or negative) externalities — like external or domestic defense or air pollution — affords the distribution of payments or damages/benefits by authoritative regulation because voluntary exchange does not work in this area (Thurow, 1977: 85, 87). Certainly these are traditional rationales for governmental interference with market exchange which do not pose problems for most critics of the welfare state. Nevertheless, it is necessary to discriminate between authoritative interference which preserves the preconditions of an efficient resource allocation of the capitalist economy and interference which serves other goals because these are subject to different logics. Apart from creating the institutional and economic framework of the market through government regulation and expenditure there is still the influence on individual economic competitors either by imperative means (orders and prohibitions) or by so-called 'indicative' incentives which appeal to the interest of the economic subject in undertaking some desirable or in abstaining from some undesirable action. The positive or negative incentives for individual economic actors are created by the government's, or the legislator's, or the Federal Reserve Bank's manipulations of aggregate economic quantities such as tax rates; the rate of government spending; of national debt or of the interest rates. The creation of incentives and disincentives for individual economic action by manipulating aggregate economic quantities may be seen as the main trait of Keynesian economic policy.

Both Keynesian economic policies and authoritative regulations have undergone considerable change in the last thirty years. Although the Keynesian demand approach was primarily devised as a solution to the capitalist crisis of the twenties and early thirties it was certainly not a distributive policy approach which intentionally subordinated capital interests to the economic and social claims of the working class. Yet it was a far-reaching consequence that individual economic action now became indirectly amenable to political decisions. The gap between the economic policies of the capitalist state and the socialist demands of the working class organizations had become smaller – and it was bridged by the institutionalization of a competitive party system which could compatibilize the economic claims of the working class with the requirements of a 'planned capitalism' (Offe, 1983: 225) and transmit them into the political system of decision-making. Not surprisingly, step by step the distributional effects have become independent goals of governmental policy-making. Cash transfers became an important instrument in bringing about an optimum distribution of income.

On the other hand, politics have become economized. There is not only redistribution, but much regulation by orders and prohibitions, including interventions into private contracts. To be sure, the regulatory state is not just a phenomenon of the 20th century; remember the extensive regulations for the protection of the factory workers in the 19th century or the housing regulations providing a minimum standard of hygiene and safety in the industrial urban centers. Undoubtedly these had distributional effects, but they were not devised to alter the distributive pattern of the society; they were rather acts of policing the public order and they presupposed the underlying social and economic order to be just. I am not sure, if for instance, the regulations in the Weimar Republic which stipulated rent control and restrictions on giving notice have to be interpreted as an intentional distribution policy or as reactive attempts to mitigate the concrete misery of the masses especially in urban centers. Be that as it may, governmental regulations are today widely regarded as distributive acts of giving one group (e.g. tenants; consumers; apprentices; handicapped) what has been taken from another (e.g. landlords; producers; employers; tax payers). The advantages and disadvantages are calculated in terms of monetary costs and regarded as parts of individual income (see also Habermas infra). Now it comes full circle: market incomes have become an object of distributive justice and policies, and regulations, which in the pre-Keynesian period served to preserve public order and were based on the assumption of the justice of the social order, have become an element of individual income.

Economic policies with the aim of increasing mass spending power and protective regulations would, as a matter or fact, benefit the economic and social situation of the masses — but these benefits would be exposed to economic and political cycles and hence would remain very uncertain. The transformation of actual favorable conditions into rights establishes the corresponding duty of the government not to alter the distributional pattern once it is attained. To have a right means to enjoy the exemption of interests from the uncertainties of the economic cycle and economic competition, its rationale consists in the independence of its claims from any balancing against competing and possibly more urgent interests — they are non-reciprocal and justified as such. To put it more pointedly: it is an abstraction vis à vis the real socio-economic situation of the allocative functioning of the market, although its satisfaction is dependent upon it. Rights are 'irresponsible' although redistribution is based on solidarity and therefore implies the principle of responsibility. From the point of view of the market economy, distributive rights are no less paradoxical: certainty is established in the domain of genuine uncertainty — the competition for scarce resources as the source of individual income — and rules of distribution codetermine the process of efficient allocation which by this means loses its alleged apolitical and neutral character.

Of course, distributive rights do not create absolute security against any infringement of the underlying interest; they can be restricted or abolished by changing the law or constitution. The welfare state has established a very specific relation between the law and rights. According to its ideal concept, the law was abstract and general; that is, it applied to all cases and persons in an abstractly circumscribed category of social situations. The most prominent examples are the laws which stipulate the preconditions of market exchange such as legal capacity; the conditions of acquiring and having rights and owing duties; contract and tort law etc.. These institutionalize the framework for the market allocation, whereas public laws are general and abstract in that they protect the public order and abstain from intentional distributional goals. I do not want to deal with the questions of whether there ever was such a thing as an abstract and general law, since it is undoubtedly true that the non-reciprocal and socially abstract character of rights afforded laws which provided a certain constancy and calculability of the conditions of market competition. The uncertainty of market competition was to some degree compensated for by the security and constancy of rights and law. By way of contrast, the achievement by distributive rights of some security in competition is paid for by an increasing inconstancy of the law and uncertainty of rights, especially of property rights. Distributional policies are based on egalitarian principles of compensating economic and social inequalities which are regarded as incompatible with the 'natural' equality of all men and which have been 'artificially' brought about by the market system. This entails that the laws become evermore selective vis à vis different segments of the population and social situations and thus became concrete and special. All legal regulations of this selective type affect not only the distributional pattern by taking from one group what is given to another (Thurow, 1980: 122) but also provoke the attempts of all groups to transform their interests into rights, thus limiting more and more the scope of distributional politics. Whereas in the realm of allocative politics — of the neo-classical as well as of the Keynesian type — the law provides for constancy or at least for an institutional compatibility between self-interested action and the political framework: the very special and concrete shape of the law in the distributive order presses the actors to look for security in the realm of rights. But this turns out to be economically and socially counter-productive. In economic politics the government is less and less able to manipulate the aggregate quantities since rights restrict the scope of disposable factors and distributive arguments of justice increase the political obstacles to restricting or abolishing rights in precisely these situations in which flexibility is most afforded. Socially, policies of equalizing the life situations of different social groups also afford free distributive play to overrule vested interests and this is made either impossible or extremely difficult if they have been transformed into rights.

V. Difficulties in the Underlying Assumptions of Distributive Rights

It was said above that distributive rights are 'just' claims because they are justified by moral principles of distributive justice. Conversely, they have the legal structure of the original 'allocational' concept of rights in that they are non-reciprocal. They combine the balancing principle of justice and the 'responsibility' of redistributive exchange with the unbalanced practice of 'unjust' and 'irresponsible' rights of market exchange. Rights in the latter sense protect interests and favorable social positions against their redistribution for the sake of principles of social justice; they do not obligate the holder of the right to any social mutuality. In contrast, redistributive rights are apportioned according to the principle of solidarity and mutuality (see also Ewald supra); they serve the compensation of different need situations in time, space and life situations. Speaking of the ancient empires, Polanyi states that "in large countries differences of soil and climate may make redistribution necessary; in other cases it is caused by discrepancy in point of time, as between harvest and consumption" (Polanyi, 1971: 254). Most modern social security systems are shaped according to this principle. They organize systems of solidarity between the generations or between the able and less able participants of the labor market and thus recognize and compensate for the differences in time segments and life situations of the rightholders. Against this the abstraction of non-reciprocal rights from the institutional patterns of social life tends to equalize all life segments and situations on the basis of a homogeneous time continuum in which each segment of the past, the present and the future has equal significance for the lives of the individuals. The common denominator is monetary income and the trading of free time or family life for monetary income is only one, if a wellknown, trait of this process of equalization of individual life situations.

We have to distinguish very sharply between these two types of 'equalization'. The redistributive equalization tends to compensate differences in time, space and life situations by the principle of mutuality, i.e., by connecting these discrepancies and the respective segments of the population with each other. Nonreciprocal rights, by way of contrast, tend to equalize life situations by abstracting from their very specific traits and differences by safeguarding benefits independent of time, space and life situations and irrespective of more urgent needs of other members of the community. Thus mutuality and self-interest are the very different bases of the two modes of 'equalization'.

It certainly comes as no surprise that I hypothesize that many problems of the modern welfare state are caused by the combination of these two strategies of equalization, (which, by the way, I regard as hardly avoidable). I refer to the many distributive rights (apart from the social security) rights which are not based on mutuality but on the principle of substituting for a non-available market income, such as transfers for housing; education; farmers; the handicapped; the poor; etc. The equalization of life situations on the basis of non-reciprocal rights is incidental to the establishment of market income as the means of need satisfaction, thus dissolving virtually all goods into sources of income. This entails that the typical risks of life — lack of nutrition, shelter and protection — which in precapitalist societies were risks of the collectivity, have become individual risks. They have been supplemented by some new risks which could only arise in the area of the individualization of life situations: lack of medical care; joblessness; helplessness in old age or due to accidents. In pre-capitalist societies, individual life situations were inseparably connected with the economic, military, social and cultural fate of the collectivity which protected the individual against the typical risks of society (cf. Friedman supra). Since income is exposed to the uncertainties of market competition, security could only be achieved by rights which substitue for the embeddednes of the individual in protective social institutions. A distributive right is a surrogate for a safe income, i.e. it combines spending power (which is typical of the market income) and safety (which is not). Market income is independent of and not responsive to criteria of justice and to principles of reciprocity and mutuality and so is its surrogate, the right to cash or in-kind transfers by the government. There is yet another trait of the market income which is worth mentioning here. Both the inherent tendency of the competitive market to increase the supply of consumer goods and the insecurity of the market income force individuals to strive for a maximization of their incomes. Does this also apply to distributive rights which substitute for market income?

Theoretically, the answer is far from clear. Since income is spending power for (the demand of) consumer goods we can assume that the tendency of the capitalist market to increase supply entails the demand for an increase of income to buy these supplied goods. On the other hand, we should assume that the safety of rights makes the strife for income maximization dispensable, because the individual can trade income increase for income safety. This assumption would mean that the safety of rights curbs the inherent tendency of the individual to always increase his income. Hence both the affirmative and the negative answer to the question seem to be plausible. However, empirical evidence shows that there is growth in the number of distributive rights as well as in the amount of the transfers which serve as income for an increasing proportion of the population. The former phenomenon can be explained by the need for safety in the frame work of an economic system whose functioning is based on individual insecurity; but the latter is only partly explicable by the income function of rights and their connection with the growth of the market supplies. Observing the income policies of the unions of civil servants in Germany, it must be stated that they reject any trade-off of income increase for income security. Although of course the income claims of civil servants are not distributive rights, they are comparable in that the income claims disconnect them from the risks of the economic cycles. Is the safe income exposed to the dynamics of the unsafe one? This is a matter of empirical research which I did not undertake. What I can do is to suggest a hypothesis which tends to give an affirmative answer to this question. The non-reciprocity of distributive rights favors a purely self-interested attitude on the part of the individuals towards the obligated government (or respective distributing agency) since security is clearly not connected to the well-being and solidarity of a community and is not based on common moral convictions and mutual trust. In other words, security is not a public good but is a favorable market position. The equalization of life situations by the abstract quality of rights does not only cause the abstraction of claims from principles of mutuality but also from concrete risk situations like illness, joblessness, lack of shelter etc. Rights to compensation for lack of market income in specific situations is transformed into the right to an equal income irrespective of changing economic and social situations. This equalization is an important consequence of the abstract levelling of all (individual) life situations by the capitalist economy which is institutionalized by rights. Due to this abstraction, distributive rights also have the inherent tendency to being maximized — the trait of market income applies to its surrogate. To rephrase this, the transformation of the need for security into a right to income exposes distributive rights to the same dynamic of growth which applies to market income itself.

Another argument may be worth considering. Distributive politics are exposed to arguments of social justice. They are justified by principles of solidarity and mutuality and serve the goal of bridging discrepancies in the social situations of different segments of the population. Of course we must not overestimate the influence of the rhetorics of social justice on the real functioning of the welfare state. But they can become efficient if there are corresponding institutional mechanisms to transform ideologies into politics. The ideology of self-interest has become a powerful social reality to the degree that the rights to individual freedom and pursuit of self-interest have been institutionalized. There is no doubt that people do not only have (self-interested) preferences about preferences or, as Hirschman (Hirschman, 1982: 69) puts it, second-order preferences, by which they very often express desires about the well-being of their fellow citizens. The economist Thurow, (for example), argues that "the same reasoning that leads us to equality in voting rights might lead us to equality in medical care rights" (Thurow, 1977: 93) and that generally, "individuals do seem to have preferences about their neighbours' consumption of particular goods and services" (Thurow, 1977: 90). And the institutions of mass democracy, especially the competitive party system and its function of aggregating a wide range of individual preferences to politics, to a certain degree give way to the consideration and political relevance of arguments of social justice. But here, too, individual-societal preferences (as Thurow terms them in contrast to private-personal preferences which refer to private utility) do not establish mutual connections and obligations between the better-off and the worse-off, but simply satisfy the goal of social equality and solidarity through the institutionalization of rights which, as I have stated, are abstractions from any mutuality; they promise security by income rights, thereby institutionalizing equality without mutuality. Thus distributive rights combine the inherent tendency towards income maximization with the distributive and expansive principle of equalizing individual incomes irrespective of an inherent balancing counterweight. This works in a growing economy where distribution is not a zero-sum-game. When it is, the built-in dynamic of the modern welfare state which made it one of the most successful socio-political systems becomes the source of its crisis.

VI. Strategies to Overcome the Dilemmas of the Welfare State

Finally I shall make a few observations about the political and legal strategies which aim at solving the dilemma which results from distributive rights being based on the abstraction of interests from the underlying socio-economic situation — and by this guarantee individual social security — without disconnecting them from the economic development. The key problem is social responsibility: how can rights be reconciled with the requirements of the social order after the demise of the Keynesian welfarism?

1. A simple answer would be to abolish those distributive rights which are regarded as impediments to the allocative function of the market. This would re-establish bourgeois class hegemony and expose the working class to the destructive forces of the market and probably — if we look at Chili — permit the establishment of some sort of political dictatorship. No serious person would propose that.

2. Another strategy — within the institutional framework of constitutional democracy — could be the transformation of substantive rights into procedural ones (for different accounts of "proceduralization" see Wiethölter infra). This would mean that individuals do not have a claim to a certain share of the gross national product but rather the right to participate in the process of distribution, to argue their case, to influence the distributive preferences, and hence to trade rights for participation. This forces them to take into account competing interests and the functioning of the whole distributive system; in other words, to become responsible for public welfare. There are good reasons to assume that this proceduralization of rights would entail the establishment of a competitive market at the institutional level of interest articulation and aggregation with all its well known consequences. It would privilege those interests and groups which dispose the resources necessary for efficient organisation and politicization and hence disfavor those segments of the population which depend heavily on the regard of their fellow citizens because they do not have the power to pursue their interests efficiently.

3. There are different lines of argument which aim at the construction of a 'responsible right': a structural pattern is Art. 18 of the German *Grundgesetz*, which stipulates the forfeiture of some constitutional rights on grounds of their improper use. "Improper use" means "dysfunctional" use, namely the use irrespective of the bad consequences for the constitutional system as a whole. This concept entails a separation of the legality of a right from its legitimacy and hence causes the grave problem of the establishment of two competing legal orders. As a result, this might well lead to a devaluation of legal claims without really solving the problem of compatibilizing and reconciling the welfare state with the institution of distributive rights.

4. A more viable answer to this problem might be the concept of "reflexive law" which has been developed by Gunther Teubner (Teubner, 1983: 239 and infra). It aims at the constitutionalization of an "organizational conscience" of social organizations which have to respond to social demands. This would mean the institutionalization of processes of learning and adapting to "external" demands and to the functions and performances of other sub-systems. Responsibility would be organized within a self-regulatory mechanism which, could only work if social asymmetries of power and information are abolished. This concept is not just a proceduralization of subjective rights, but a more comprehensive theory of restructuring the process of interest bargaining on the basis of social equality (see also Willke infra). In this model, the organization is substituted for the market as a mechanism for distributing social rewards. Whether mutuality and responsiveness can be institutionalized in these self-regulating processes or if this remains a utopian goal is an open question which will be answered by our social practice.

References

ABENDROTH, Wolfgang (1967) "Zum Begriff des demokratischen und sozialen Rechtsstaates im Grundgesetz der Bundesrepublik Deutschland," in W. Abendroth, *Antagonistische Gesellschaft und politische Demokratie*. Neuwied: Luchterhand.

BARBER, Bernhard (1977) "Absolutization of the Market. Some Notes on: How We go from There to Here," in C. Dworkin *et al.* (eds.), *Markets and Morals*. Washington, London: Wiley.

BOMBACH, Gottfried *et al.* (1976) *Der Keynesianismus. Theorie und Praxis keynesianischer Wirtschaftspolitik*. Berlin: Springer.

DWORKIN, Ronald (1978) *Taking Rights Seriously*. Cambridge, Mass.: Harvard University Press.

FLATHMAN, Richard E. (1976) *The Practice of Rights*. Cambridge: Cambridge University Press.

HABERMAS, Jürgen (1981) *Theorie des kommunikativen Handelns*, Vol. II. Frankfurt a. M.: Suhrkamp.

HELLER, Hermann (1971) "Rechtsstaat oder Diktatur?" (1929), in Heller, *Gesammelte Schriften*, Vol. II. Leiden: Sijthoff.

HIRSCHMAN, Albert O. (1977) *The Passions and the Interests. Political Arguments for Capitalism before its Triumph*. Princeton: Princeton University Press.

— (1982) *Private Interest and Public Action*. Princeton: Princeton University Press.

HOBBES, Thomas (1978) *Leviathan or the Matter, Form, and Power of a Commonwealth Ecclesiastical and Civil*. Indianapolis: Bobbs-Merrill.

HOHFELD, W. N. (1923) *Fundamental Legal Conceptions as Applied in Judicial Reasoning and Other Legal Essays*. New Haven: Yale University Press.

HOPKINS, Terence K. (1971) "Sociology and the Substantive View of the Economy," in K. Polanyi *et al.* (eds.), *Trade and Market in the Early Empires*. Chicago: Gateway, Regnery.

HORWITZ, Morton J. (1977) *The Transformation of American Law 1780–1860*. Cambridge, Mass.: Harvard University Press.

- (1980) "The Crisis of Legal Theory in the Regulatory State". Unpublished Paper, Cambridge, Mass.

LANE, Robert E. (1978) "Markets and the Satisfaction of Human Wants," 12 *Journal of Economic Issues* 799.

LUHMANN, Niklas (1970) "Zur Funktion der 'subjektiven Rechte'," in 1 *Jahrbuch für Rechtssoziologie und Rechtstheorie* 322, 325.

— (1972) *Rechtssoziologie* 2. Reinbek: Rowohlt.

MAUNZ, Theodor, Günther DÜRIG, Roman HERZOG, and Rupert SCHOLZ (1983) *Grundgesetz Kommentar*. München: Beck.

OFFE, Claus (1983) "Competitive Party Democracy and the Keynesian Welfare State: Factors of Stability and Disorganization". 15 *Policy Sciences* 225.

OKUN, Arthur M. (1975) *Equality and Efficiency. The big Trade-off*. Washington D.C. The Brookings Institution.

POLANYI, Karl (1957) *The Great Transformation*. Boston: Beacon Press.

POLANYI, Karl *et al.* (1971) *Trade and Market in the Early Empires*. Chicago: Regnery.

PREUSS, Ulrich K. (1979) *Die Internalisierung des Subjekts*. Frankfurt a. M.: Suhrkamp.

REICH, Norbert (1983/84) "The Regulatory Crisis: American Approaches in the Light of European Experiences," *American Bar Association Research Journal* 693.

SCHMITT, Carl (1958) "Nehmen/Teilen/Weiden," C. Schmitt (ed.), *Verfassungsrechtliche Aufsätze*. Berlin: Duncker u. Humblot.

TEUBNER, Gunther (1983) "Substantive and Reflexive Elements in Modern Law," 17 *Law & Society Review* 239.

THUROW, Lester C. (1977) "Cash or In-Kind Aid?," in C. Dworkin *et al.* (eds.), *Market and Morals*. Washington, London: Wiley and Sons.

— (1980) *The Zero-sum Society. Distribution and the Possibilities for Economic Change*. New York: Basic Books.

VOIGT, Rüdiger (1983) "Soziale Homogenität als Voraussetzung des demokratisch-sozialen Wohlfahrtstaates — eine vergessene Erkenntnis?," in *Festschrift für Hermann Heller*. Baden Baden: Nomos.

WIEACKER, Franz (1967) *Privatrechtsgeschichte der Neuzeit*. Göttingen: Vandenhoeck und Ruprecht.

Legal Discourse in the Positive State: A Post-Structuralist Account*

THOMAS C. HELLER
Stanford

I. Structuralist Form and Structuralist Practice: Critique and American Legal Structure

A structural critique of phenomenological grammar constitutes an historically necessary moment within the development of an adequate post-structuralist account of any cultural institution, including law. The relevance of this point for legal theory becomes apparent upon recognition of the centrality of subjectivist categories within the dominant American legal discourse. Critical theory argues that the structurally defined elements of legal discourse have produced an implicit constitution — a legitimating and legitimated set of principles of social order. In turn, this constitution of legal rights and legal-political institutions has, through a transformative syntax, generated an interestingly coherent collection of more concrete legal practices. If the structuralist critique is to be generally effective, the apparent diversity of existing legislative, administrative, and judicial practices must be reducible to the limited components of the structural grammar.

The fundamental contradiction at the core of liberal theory, according to structural critique, is the phenomenological claim that institutional order originates in the action of speakers or subjects whose being is presocially or asocially given. Subjective discourse denies its own structural character

* This essay, first prepared in Florence in 1983, constitutes a portion of a longer article entitled "Structuralism and Critique" which appeared in Volume 36 of the *Stanford Law Review*. The full discussion includes a far more detailed account of the author's usage of the terms structuralism, phenomenology, discourse and post-structuralism. While those seeking such explanation may refer to the entire article, the familiarity of European readers with these categories will, I hope, make worthwhile those portions of my argument specifically concerned with legal theory.
I wish to thank the Stanford Law Review for their kind permission for allowing me to reprint my article here.

by tracing its genesis to the instrumental projects of its naturally existent constituents. To speak of a phenomenological structure is to deconstruct either the logic of structuralism or the antilogic (narrative) of spirit. In this sense a structural critique of phenomenological discourse must be theoretically uncompromising.

To analyze American legal categories as a structural discourse is to describe objectively a phenomenon that claims it ultimately has no order other than the chronicle of the aggregated wills of its members. Structural analysis calls forth the imagery of a culture whose system of differentiations (including legal rights) creates the specific concept of individuality. This concept of individuality is transposed by a ruling subjectivist ideology into the putative asocial source of institutional principle (cf. Broekman supra on the "dogmatics of individual subjectivity"). To name an object is to take power over it (Foucault, 1980: 96). Structuralism as critique names that structure which denies it has a name of its own. In showing that which hides itself in its own illusions, structural critique places the power of American legal discourse in issue.

I will not attempt to work out a detailed account of the determinative relations among structure, institution, and practice[1] for American legal discourse, though I have argued above that there are various possibilities.[2] This elaboration is properly the agenda of those who wish to propagate the existing liberal legal structure. Certainly, the great bulk of legal scholarship is aimed, though not self-consciously, at the specification of practices representing the competent use of the dominant transformational syntax. If Critical work becomes obsessed with working out the details of a systematically rationalized legal practice in order to demonstrate that the liberal legal structure exists, it will be deflected from its own reconstitutive task. It is sufficient for Critical theory to locate the categories of traditional legal analysis within the dominant phenomenological discourse, as long as

[1] While advocates of law and economics are busily trying to elaborate a relatively vulgar structuralism in which the determinate results of cases can be derived from structural principles, the standard legal response to the problem of structure and practice is more interesting. The world of possible cases usually is divided into two qualitatively distinct classes. Easy cases are those in which concrete outcomes clearly can be derived by applying the legitimating principles of the legal structure. Hard cases are those exceptional or aberrational situations in which results are not so easily derived. Law students encounter only hard cases since, presumably, they are more challenging. But the ideological value or meaning of the legal order is contained in the structure and its derivative easy case.

In practice the legal system depends on the existence of easy cases of a different type. A case is easy when particular settled practices are reproduced across time without theoretical re-examination. But the heart of legal critique is to show that there are no easy cases in the sense that practice flows directly from legitimating principles. *See* Heller (1979: 183).

[2] *See* text notes 26—30 (Heller, 1984).

it avoids representing the legal system in too vulgar a fashion. The legal order is laced with contradictions and complexities, and these should become a focus of inquiry. In an analysis seeking a path beyond structuralist determinism, as well as a displacement of the prestructuralist subject, it may be that less emphasis on the need for coherence in theory, and more attention to the incoherence of the production of practice, would be instructive.

Structural critique understands American legal theory and practice as an account of legal institutions that expresses the orthodox liberal commitments to subjective autonomy and objective method. The standard narrative of American law begins with presocial or naturally given individuals. These individuals voluntary associate in civil society and contractually create the state to further their individual life projects. In the standard narrative, reference to an underlying deep legal structure permits the correction of any discordant legal practices that remain as vestiges of the preliberal legal order or that result from technical failures in the process of institutionally reproducing liberal theory. While there is no need to show that each legal practice represents an appropriate institutionalization of legal structure, there exists the general sense that American legal history is characterized by a gradual evolution toward a perfected liberal order.

The working out of a legal theory adequate to liberal structure has involved the progressive reformulation of structurally appropriate principles of jurisprudence. Earlier conceptualizations of such principles suggested that legal discourse was largely autonomous from the discourse of other social subsystems.[3] More recently, under pressure from Realist attacks on pure legal conceptualism, the most sophisticated and exemplary reconceptualization of liberal jurisprudence has emerged in law and economics. The virtue and attraction of law and economics is its clear and persistent reiteration of the structural grammar of subjective intent and objective technique, its integrated and continuous history of the American legal order, and its consistency with the evolutionary and functionalist (purposive) tone of American social theory.

The principal symbolic significance of American law is its reproduction of the categories of phenomenological discourse and its ideological centerpiece, the existentially free subject. This figure is imagined as a being conscious of its autonomously selected normative principles and adept at the employment of instrumental reason in carrying out projects oriented

[3] There are also strong professional interests in the preservation of the autonomy of the legal subsystem. The capacity of any set of institutions to preserve and exercise power will depend in part on the clarity of the boundaries between subsystems organized around separate domains of expertise or local knowledge. To admit the relevance to a problem of a form of knowledge dominated by another group is to surrender hard-won professional ground. *See* note 15 *infra*.

to these norms. The autonomous self-definition of the subject by means of its projects is the source both of the moral respect accorded to, and the legal responsibility attendant upon, choice.[4] The phenomenological subject appears as a set of differentiations (legal rights) that define the space in which, and the instruments with which, the subject may freely act. The theory of property rights is essentially a structural code that defines the physical and intellectual arena, as well as the material resources, available to a legal actor in pursuit of his or her normative ends. To trespass this differentiated ground is, in a serious sense, to invade the personality of another. For modern legal economics, property is more than a matter of material rights — its categories construct a world by marking off the boundaries between self, others, and environment.

To complete a phenomenological account of law, it is necessary to derive the content of this system from a presocial origin. The subject must precede chronologically, as it does discursively, the social order which it constitutes to facilitate its intentionalistic projects. The legal order, like language and other aspects of this social order, must be derived from the will of its constituents. The metaphorical form of this precedence of subject over society is, of course, the social contract. Grammatically, the phenomenal subject cannot itself be an artifact of the legal (cultural) system without losing its discursive character.

Especially in the United States, accounts of the genesis of property rights display a somewhat ill-defined conjunct of ontological and theological propositions bunched under the concept of natural rights. In early liberal thought, the adjective "natural" expressed the extrasocial character of subjectivity. It referred variously to a Christian image of the divine infusion of spirit or to the philosophically generalized preconditions of knowledge and action that emerged as Kant's transcendental subject. In the subsequent intellectual retreat from theology and ontology, liberalism has experimented with both analytic and empirical alternatives to establish a theory of rights.[5]

4 "To know all is to forgive all" is the proverbial expression of the argument made here. If one is aware of the structure and of the operations of the structure that determine the subject's behavior, moral blame is not an appropriate response to an externally determined product. Conversely, if one has no science that can predict the behavior of the free subject in an *ex ante* fashion, then must not that subject be held accountable for behavior which need not have been?

5 Rights theory is the historic, though not logically necessary, form of Western liberal individualism. While many reformist approaches to legal change concentrate on the elaboration of new rights with transformed substantive content, the retention of a rights-based legal theory remains a structurally conservative strategy of limited cultural meaning. A fuller post-liberal legal theory would have to look beyond the organizing categories historically associated with the liberal social order. The most important of these are "man" as an existentially unique being who can know with certainty the conditions of his own existence, "rights" as the legal expression of this special ontological status, and "nation" as the collective aggregation of political identity.

One analytic example is the utilitarian attempt to derive property rights from presumptively technical principles such as the maximization of wealth.[6] In a similar, more sophisticated effort, Rawls, like Kant and Rousseau, locates the origin of social order in the hypothetical, rational choice of the pure expression of subjectivity denuded of all attributes that constitute the historic individual.[7]

Other theoreticians have given up the effort to ground rights theory in reason and have sought a noncollective foundation in empirical propositions. Three recent suggestions are: (1) that of sociobiology, which asserts that property systems develop naturally to facilitate the reproductive success of species (Demsetz, 1967: 347), (2) that of economists influenced by Hobbes, who consider the distribution of entitlements an historical remnant of preexisting anarchistic struggles abandoned when the costs of further acts of predation exceeded the marginal gains (Buchanan, 1974: 53), and (3) that of legal commentators who have attempted to place the genesis of basic rights in an historical agreement among individual subjects to respect some order of established endowments (for accounts of the development of "rights" see also Preuß, Ewald supra).

I do not believe that any of these accounts can dispel the structural counterclaim that a cultural or linguistic system of differentiations constitutes the concrete theory of the subject. However, a *liberal* social order must reflect the bifurcated grammar that is expressed in classical Western philosophical commitments. The dominant legal discourse must originate in the twin representations of a knowable, objective (natural and logical) world and direct subjective (phenomenological) apperceptions of norms originating only in individual volition. Liberal method denies the epistemological value and the political legitimacy of any *collectively* imposed ordering of propositions that are normative in the sense that they are not exclusively derived from analytical or empirical statements. Any such

[6] *See, e.g.*, Posner (1980: 487, 1981: 775). But see Markovits (1983: 667).

[7] In Kant, this dehistoricized experience of pure subjectivity, from which analytical reason can begin to derive the principles of social order, locates identity in a transcendental capacity for apperception. *See* Wilkerson (1976: 45).

In Rousseau it is the general will. *See* Talmon (1960: 38). In Rawls it is that which remains behind the veil of ignorance, which screens out all knowledge of concrete historical attributes, Rawls (1971).

A recent account of the nonparticularized subject, represented at the core of liberal legal theory, is given by Luhmann. Luhmann suggests that the legal subject is the potential for action freed of all its social roles. The subject defines itself through its engagement with functionally differentiated subsystems such as the legal or the economic. But since liberal societies are at a stage of social evolution in which functional differentiation has produced too many subsystems for a single subject to engage, the subject must be conceived as that which has the potential to choose among them. Luhmann (1982).

imposition would imply the existence of a substantive hierarchy of normative claims or a social ranking of the experimental apperceptions of some subjects over those of others. Liberal theory must therefore demonstrate that legal and political institutions can be built up solely from some combination of true non-normative propositions and the aggregated expressions of the wills of its constituting subjects. Nevertheless, each such liberal argument can be deconstructed by showing that it does not meet its own methodological criteria for validity.

Empirical theories justifying rights lack legitimating power precisely because they do not incorporate a Kantian norm which founds social arrangements in freely exercised subjectivity. Instead, Hobbesian and sociobiological accounts begin *in medias res*. Discovering the content of the entitlement system in a prior history of natural conflict, they incorporate in legal institutions the moral character of a history that displayed no respect for the subjective capacity of others. Beginning *in medias res* may be a virtue in Homer, but it is the negation of a theory of liberal justice.

The resolution offered by theories that refer to some historic convention of subjects is equally unsatisfying. Even if such a convention were valid, it would be necessary to hypothesize a continuing series of ratifications by successive generations. Such an ongoing consensus quickly assumes attributes of fictional construction unacceptably remote from any reasonable empirical or analytical propositions.

If empirical accounts of liberal rights fail largely because they remain trapped in the unfairness of preliberal history, accounts based on a historical reason fail because they incorporate normative propositions not derivable from individual expressions of will. Utilitarian argument falls back on intersubjective comparisons of well-being to set up its rights theories. These comparisons usually presume a psychological equality among individuals not traceable to logic, empirical fact, or historically agreed-upon convention. Yet, without such basis, the system is technically indeterminate (Heller, 1976: 385 and 438).

Rawls uses a criterion similar to Paretian optimality to mitigate the problem of intersubjectivity. But in order to specify even a minimal substantive content for the original distribution of entitlements, he is forced to rely on contestable empirical propositions including a universal sense of risk aversion among the hypothetical subjects. (Rawls, 1971: 65) In contrast to empirical theories of liberal order, such an analytically founded theory has the virtue of being normatively consistent with the subjectivist categories of phenomenological discourse. What it loses in dehistoricizing the subject, and thereby removing the taint of exploitative history, is the capacity to particularize the formal theory of rights it evolves. Such particularization is achieved only through the importation of collective norms that provide the character of subjectivity with content. But such imported norms are precisely the social orderings that a structuralist critique would identify as the materialist system that constitutes the phenomenological subject (compare the accounts of Ewald and Broekman supra).

Despite this shortcoming, there remains great value in the clarity with which the analytical genre of liberal theorizing displays the pure subject as the abstract moment of the immediate consciousness of self. The unmitigated expression of phenomenological experience in a political discourse founded upon a transcendental or nonparticularized subject provides the core cultural representation of this system of order. The ideological power of liberalism lies in the syntactical significance given to choice and responsibility as interpretive canons in constituting meaning from chaos, and in the potential application of these elements to the resolution of any disputed concrete legal or political practice. I will return to this point at the end of the article to consider its consequences for the enterprise of delegitimation.

If, as I have asserted, the phenomenological representation of the constituting subject in law is the theory of property rights, then the institutional rules governing all departures from the original legal position must reflect and ratify the legitimacy of those rights to freely constitute the self. Illegitimate change thus would be defined by the collective imposition, upon protected individual space, of the normative desires of other constituting individuals. Since any collective ranking of norms would conflict with the proposition that individual action is the sole source of value, liberal theory necessarily recognizes methodological limitations on public or governmental behavior.

Within these limitations, voluntary contract, represented in classical private law doctrine as the meeting of subjective wills, is the paradigmatic example of a social change that does not exceed the expressed intentions of the individuals affected by the change. The contractual exchange of legitimately held property requires the consensus of all those whose projects will be disturbed or aided by the transaction. Such private reorderings of property can be extended into generalized markets which, when operating ideally, retain unanimity or Paretian optimality as their legitimating principle. Perfect markets are institutions whose method of operation accords with liberal principles because they rely only upon the empirically verifiable display of volitional choice. The function of markets is to aggregate intentions (revealed preferences) by analytical processes, best represented mathematically, so as to maximize the ability of autonomous subjects to create their preferred worlds within the space allotted to them. In orthodox liberal American law, normative legitimation is firmly rooted in subjective desire. The normative power of the market is derived from the grammatical commitment to independent will.

It should now be evident how economic theory could emerge as an exemplary representation of liberal legal categories. Microeconomics, the core image of which expresses the cultural meaning of neoclassical theory, is itself a straightforward expression of phenomenological discourse. Since economics treats individual preferences as exogenous to its analysis, consciously held intentions are not reduced within economics to any structural order. Preferences appear instead as the products of autonomous choice, the narrative starting point of a phenomenological account. The operations of the market, on the other hand, reflect only analytical and empirical propositions legitimated by reference to their truth in an objective world. And normative statements are validated by reference to the fact that they are confessions of intent espressed directly by subjects through the price system. Property and contract — preferences and market — represent the integrated legal order of phenomenological discourse.

What remains to be described in the elaboration of the subjectivist legal order is the theory of the state or the public sector. As economic inquiry evolved, it became evident that private activity did not lead to an optimal level of protection for legitimated property rights because of negative externalities and lack of market competition. Moreover, unregulated markets did not maximize individual welfare because certain classes of goods and services possessed the technical characteristic of nonexclusive consumption and thereby produced free rider problems. In the liberal subjectivist order, legal institutions can, in theory, correct these difficulties. An activist public sector implies no discontinuity or structural break with the liberal tradition. The object of the modern state remains that use of resources, within the legitimated distribution of property rights, which would have resulted from the consummation of all consensual transactions in the absence of market failure.[8] The role of the state is residual because it acts only when private arrangements are insufficient to achieve this unchanging ideal of social order.[9]

The consistency of this description with liberal principles may be noted as well in the methodological prerequisites for proper governmental action. Public institutions act legitimately when they (1) force the internalization

[8] The apparently coercive action of the state is, in this view, illusory. Individuals *are* forced to do things such as pay taxes, but if the tax/expenditure system is properly conceived, this coercion is only necessary to overcome the free rider tactics of self-interested citizens. Absent such tactical behavior, taxed citizens should, in theory, consensually choose the collective goods they thereby purchase.

[9] A semiotic analysis of law school curricula illustrates the point. In spite of the emergence of the interventionist state as a market corrector, the first year of law study remains, with the exception of constitutional and criminal law, almost exclusively dedicated to the classical private law fields. This arrangement conveys the structural message of the legitimacy of the subject as rights bearer within the liberal order. Courses concerned with culturally less significant matters such as market organization (antitrust), information failure (securities; consumer protection), externalities control (environmental law) or redistribution (tax; labor) are relegated to later years when socialization has been completed and attention has waned.

of external costs that, in unregulated private markets, would otherwise lead to the expropriation of recognized property rights; (2) aggregate the preferences of consumers for social goods, revealed through political rather than market mechanisms, to increase the value of available resources; and (3) restructure market institutions to allow private activities to proceed in an undistorted fashion. In each case, the state must legitimate its behavior through the correctness of its analytical operations, the accuracy of its perceptions of individual intentions, and its respect for original entitlements.

While normative justification remains exclusively in the conscious acts of those subjects who constitute the state, the transformational syntax of the liberal structure has over time become remarkably more intricate. As phenomenological discourse has developed, the increasingly complex operations by which structural principles must be reduced to legal practices have produced an expansion of the public sector (regulatory or welfare state) and generated the illusion of qualitatively disparate forms of modern liberalism. In fact, however, the essential categorical differentiations and epistemological commitments that define the liberal structure have remained stable.[10] (See also Broekman supra.)

[10] I will not discuss in this article particular structuralist critiques of the phenomenological account of legal practices. For purposes of illustration, however, I will describe two general types of delegitimating argument. First delegitimating may concentrate on internal structural contradictions in order to demonstrate that the production of practice within a structure cannot proceed in accordance with its self-defined principles of justification. Such delegitimation advances the logical argument that, when examined sufficiently closely, a structure collapses of its own weight. For example, in the nineteenth century, the relative inactivity of the state allowed social change to go forward principally through markets. Consequently, as a matter of methodology, liberal institutions aggregated the empirically verifiable desires of economic actors that were represented in market prices. At the same time, because of market failures, this system did not permit the realization of many legitimate individual projects. In the twentieth century, the state has assumed a more active role in order to improve property protection and maximise welfare. But because an adequate mechanism for ascertaining consumer preferences through nonmarket institutions has not been developed, all government action has become of ambiguous character. That is, modern public action is based upon highly imperfect empirical indications of volition. Thus, collective controls may as easily be interpreted to be the illegitimate output of an exploitative government as to be the legitimate perfection of the liberal order. Due to the contradiction between the discursive referent (subjective intent) and the objectivist methodological principles (analytical/empirical) on which legitimated action can rest, there is a pervasive indeterminacy within contemporary liberalism about the propriety of public intervention. Liberalism is left to choose between, on the one hand, the nineteenth-century figure of the methodological coherence of economic markets and an acknowledged economic inefficiency and on the other hand, the twentieth-century figure of the methodological incoherence of political markets and the uncertainty as to whether efficient regulation is possible. (In the nineteenth

II. Poststructuralist Directions for Reworking Legal (and Other) Theory

There exists within the liberal legal structure a multiplicity of theoretically inconsistent legal practices, peculiar to particular regions of legal doctrine. These practices ought not to be explained as persistent mistaken transformations of structure or as exceptional (if temporary) aberrations within a legal system that is relatively autonomous of, but ultimately unified with, a deeper social structure. Instead, as this part will argue, irreconcilable practices are better described as the normal condition of a poststructuralist order, reflecting an underlying system of mutually deconstructive discursive representations of experience. Contrary to structuralist theory, each such symbolic representation is incapable of producing an objectively correct determination of legal practice. But, contrary to liberal theory, poststructuralism must incorporate the structuralist critique of subjective autonomy, and must not refer to personalized, autonomous decisionmaking (interpretation), in order to specify how legal practice emerges from the more abstract rules of alternative legal discourses.

In order to avoid restating exhausted formulations of the problem of legal method, a poststructuralist, Critical account of the law must rework the orthodox conception of the relationship between theory and practice.

century, some commentators perceived the serious problem in liberal theory due to the methodological necessity for objective legal observation of subjective states of mind. For example, Holmes, at times, wished to ban all subjective discourse and reconstitute law in collective, pragmatic terms. Other, more orthodox, constitutional analysts have tried to banish the contradiction between discourse and method by dividing the theory of the state into political and legal branches. Arbitrary actions (i. e., nonobjective, collective, coercive judgments) would be permitted in the legislature. Liberal purity of method (neutral principles) would be limited to the courts. This bifurcated approach led to a restriction of judicial review of legislative action but was essentially unsatisfactory, since an adequate subjectivist theory of the state requires a unified legal politics or constitution. Removing arbitrary action to the realm of politics seems only to defend the restricted turf of jurists.)

Second, delegitimation can follow a strategy external to structure. By attacking the central distinctions within what claims to be a naturally existent or externally referential language, Critical analysis, demonstrates the contingent historical production, and the constructed character, of a set of ordering categories. For example, subjectivist theory represents the subject preceding diachronically the social institutions which are its tools. In pre-twentieth-century legal theory, it was understood that entitlements were not assigned by the state but rather were the natural ontological attributes of individuality. With the contemporary development of new categories of social conflicts, such "natural" boundaries of individuality are no longer discernible. Complex environmental, distributional, and informational "rights" have come to be viewed as dependent upon political decisions by the state. Modern individuality is thus increasingly exposed as the artifact of public action, rather than being that which creates government and defines the range of the state.

Within a legal system producing and reproducing theories and practices, the role of legal structure should be reconsidered in a nonhierarchical fashion. Structure is neither irrelevant to, nor determinative of, the production of practice. The specific nature of the relationship will differ in local subsystems.

In a sense, we may speak of a need to dislocate both self and structure. Poststructuralism remains antihumanist to the extent that it sees consciousness as one of many possible states of representation, deserving no special priority. On the other hand, it is nonstructuralist in that explanatory theory is but another practice, valid in itself, but no more privileged than other representations within such a system. The production of theoretical practice is, like the production of more concrete practices, an act of systematic play not to be taken too seriously. Neither self nor structure, subject nor object, will disappear in poststructuralism. These discourses are simply the perceptions that result from looking at a complex system of experience from differing viewpoints within that system.[11]

The precedence of theory over practice comes from the utopian wish in both structuralism and phenomenology for unmediated and certain knowledge. To deprivilege theory is to give up this image of a positive truth, whether of subject or structure, and to lash out at all centralized political systems that base their claims to generalized power on the privileging of one representational form as universally valid. Poststructuralist thought refocuses concern on the unceasing production and reproduction of practices in multiple local systems neither free of their own histories nor determined in their courses (for an analysis of self-productive social systems see Luhmann, Teubner, infra). It suggests that the specific content of our personal identities and of the categories of collective organization are not established realities which we bring to politics. Rather, in redescribing consciousness and structure as projections back upon our own histories of the products of ongoing systems differentiating themselves through political competition, we may leave behind the modernist alternation of discourse that I criticized elsewhere (see Part II, Heller).

A. Theory and Practice in Complex Legal Systems

To reproduce a structural critique of standard subjectivist legal categories is no longer enough. Structuralism itself has been subjected to the criticism that it simultaneously under- and overdetermines practice. Any purely structuralist account of a uniform production of legal practices would miss the complexity of the legal landscape, and paint so false a picture of the reproduction of theory in practice that it would strain the credibility of

[11] See my postscript *infra* for a preliminary program to develop a poststructuralist discourse centered on the evolution of complex systems.

the entire account. Such thoroughgoing objectivism invites the reintroduction of an existential subject to compensate for its tedious simplicity in denying the indeterminacy of theory, an indeterminacy that characterizes our experiences of the production of legal practice. To avoid such a retrogressive step, it would be preferable for Critical theory to experiment with different representations of the relationship between legal theory and legal practice.

The positive science notion that theory and practice form a unified and integrated system should be reconsidered. The actual practice of the law is complex, local, and filled with contradictions when examined relative to any comprehensive theory. For example, although the dominant American legal discourse centers upon subjectivist categories that speak of undetermined action, there are numerous instances therein of determinist or objectivist discourse. Children, the insane, primitives, women, and blacks have been treated as less than autonomous subjects. They have been at times absolved of responsibility for their behaviour and made the objects of public interventions that overrode their interests such as they had defined them.[12] The legal development of an objectivist discourse examines

[12] One political explanation of this phenomenon is that structural discourse is no more than a rhetorical device used for taking power over the "Other." The privilege of responsible action is reserved for those like us. The Other is a homogeneous classification produced by social collectivities such as race, culture, or genetic underdevelopment. As suggested vividly by Edward Said, to apply a discourse of the Other is to subjugate by repressing the diversity of the particular. *See* E. Said (1979). This argument, though attractive, can itself be represented as a romanticization or subjectification of the relationship between language and power. In phenomenological terms, Power is a primary expression of desire realized through acts of political choice. Actors use discourse as an instrument in the project of taking power. In a structuralist account, however, this concept of power is no more than a necessary element produced within the grammatical system of phenomenological discourse. In other words, only where a subjectivist discourse is spoken is such a hierarchical understanding of the relationship between self and others imagined.

In a phenomenological grammar, the self is the speaker which creates meaning through its internal projects. It is thus at the origin or center of the semiotic system, and precedes discourse in a logical and chronological sense. The self is a being possessed of pure freedom or potential which assigns signifiers to others. Percy writes:

"For me, certain signifiers fit you, and not others. For me, all signifiers fit me, one as well as another. I am rascal, hero, craven, brave, treacherous, loyal, at once the secret hero and asshole of the Cosmos.

You are not a sign in your world. Unlike the other signifiers in your world which form more or less stable units with the perceived world-things they signify, the signifier of yourself is mobile, freed up, and operating on a sliding semiotic scale ..." Percy (1983: 107).

This discursive depiction of the self as the origin of the semiotic system creates the liberal "self without qualities" described by Robert Musil. *See generally* Musil(1965). The privilege of selfhood arises in the linguistic positioning of self. The Other is then

reductively the sources of human action and acknowledges the likelihood of the unintended consequences of choice, both of which are generally ignored by a phenomenological account of law. Structuralist legal discourse that deconstructs the subject is not invariably repressed within a liberal legal order. Contradictory linguistic practices do coexist within a single legal system without delegitimating the legal order itself.

The essence of daily legal activity is the reproduction of legal practices within the localities where they actually function. The simultaneous presence of contradictory legal discourses is not the heart of the problem for the liberal legal system. Instead, the difficulty lies with keeping these contradictions from spilling over their boundaries and destabilizing established legal practices. In this sense, there is no global or unifying legal structure that can determine legal practice. Law is essentially a cognitive and professional, rather than a normative, discipline, referring to theory only in the liminal case where the content of settled practice comes into

defined by its assigned qualities, a set of reified signifiers made concrete by a limited and limiting set of artifactual products. In order to proceed, the self must construct an objective world, even though the signification given to the Other imposes a form of enslavement upon it. At the same time, the psychological emptiness of the phenomenological self generates the urge to take others and appropriate their semiotic content. As a cannibal takes the exemplary qualities of those he consumes, so does too the subject give itself substance by exercising power over those upon whom it has conferred significance that must be returned. In this way, to take power is neither a choice nor an act. It is a consequence of the structure that is phenomenological speech.

If power can both produce language and be produced by it, understanding power may depend on differentiating the established configuration of linguistic practices in which phenomenological and structural constructions are found. In a world of multiple discursive practices, how can the discourse of the Other be limited to the description of certain sectors of humanity? In what principled way can the Other be distinguished from the self? What allows us to categorize with stability the line between us and them? Why doesn't objective discourse absorb our account of ourselves in law as it does in orthodox psychoanalysis? It must be that some other set of categorical distinctions allows each understanding of the exercise of power to focus on a limited set of objects. Here, we are led toward an exploration of analogical or metaphorical categorization to account for nonlogical differentiations. The status of subjectivity and narrative time may be reserved for those with whom we are more familiar and those who are relatively closer to us in species, in space, and in time. It is the stranger who lacks (or to whom we deny) the attributes of individualized identity. The metaphorical bounds of proximity to the center or likeness to the self coincide with the bounds of the use of a discourse and replace within a metastructure the concept of discourse itself. But if this treatment of discourse alternatively as rhetoric and as a practice within a figurative structure does no more than restate the dichotomy of subjects and objects at a more abstract level, must there not be some more fertile representation of this issue? For reference to a third representation of power, see my postscript *infra*.

crisis (see Habermas infra).[13] In other words, the practice of law primarily consists of the hermeneutic reproduction of that which already exists. Though the boundaries of settled legal practice do shift at the margin as mutually deconstructive accounts of events are juxtaposed in the form of

[13] The idea of theory as "liminal" to the routine reproduction of practice is borrowed from Turner's account of symbolic systems in primitive societies. *See* Turner. (1967:93) Turner analyzes rites of passage in which young men would withdraw from daily life at prescribed periods of their lives, be secluded in sacred places, and consider the meaning of their traditional forms of social organization. While there is a priestly class for whom the production of liminal content is routine, there is nevertheless a marginality, though not less importance, ascribed to the realm of the sacred that distinguishes its practice from the unanalyzed world of the profane.
The metaphor of "liminality" may also be useful in dealing with the place in contemporary society of institutions that produce symbolic structures of organization. There is, for example, a certain spatial and temporal marginality of the university system, where much contemporary theorizing is concentrated. The law also has liminal characteristics. In our secular society, in which meaning is depicted without reference to a true sacred object, the legal system has become a principal institution for the representation and reproduction of ideology. This imposes a curious duality on the nature of law schools and law courts: Both incessantly confuse functions related to the normative, theoretical representation of the legal system with those related to the reproduction of settled legal practice. The systematic reproduction of legal practice has an abnormal (compared to, say, linguistic practice) internal organization which produces a too frequent confrontation with theory. Ligitation, when not simply a form of debt collection, is designed to upset settled practice, invoke the search for meaning in legal reason, and present deconstructive rhetorics to adjudicators. This radical feature of the law has led to a certain ostracism of litigators within the profession and produced a series of procedural doctrines designed to keep litigation from undercutting any pretense of legal logic.
The concept of liminality has recently been explored in Da Matta (1983: 66). When he discusses the Brazilian Independence Day celebration, which is dominated by military imagery, Da Matta emphasizes the ordering function of liminal re-considerations of daily life which reinterpret the collection of existing practices as structurally unified. Another Brazilian holiday celebration, Carnaval, appears to be a recognition of chaos or of the dissolution of all normal practice in the celebration. It is possible to argue about the significance of either of these two festivals, but the important point is the politically and socially open nature of liminal systems, including the law. In this sense a law school's reconsideration of the normally unexamined practices that constitute the law's daily life may either express a theoretical ordering of such practices into structure or expose a deconstructionist denial of any possibility of meaningful order. I believe that much of the psychological discomfort experienced by many law students results from their lack of desire for any type of nonpractical approach to law. To the extent that education must be liminal, it seems clear that the style and spirit of law schools is more conducive to celebrations of hierarchy than to the staging of carnivals.
The disjunction of liminal experience into Independence Day and Carnaval mirrors Nietzsche's opposition of the Appollonian and Dionysian. But note that Nietzsche suggests that the post-Socratic impoverishment of Western culture stems from the loss of the Dionysian. *See* Nietzsche (1956: 1, 3–11, 76–96).

contending legal rhetorics, there is no structural logic to the occasions of this change. Each practice is theoretically overdetermined, and each theory is indeterminate of practice. To preserve the concept of a legal order as more than a haphazard collection of local exercises of power, a legal system must keep the contradictions of mutually deconstructive discourses from disturbing the reproduction in legal *theory* of its dominant symbolic representations of social organization.

I would suggest that a poststructuralist account of the law treat any existing set of legal practices as a succession of theoretically arbitrary signs. Like language games or forms of life for Wittgenstein (Pitkin, 1972: 132), such practices are reproduced across time as unanalyzed ways of being in the world.[14] The core of the training and work of lawyers is to learn these practices and how to manipulate them. In situations where legal practices are disturbed, the resettlement of an altered practice is not determined positively by the logical application of theoretically coherent rules, but rather proceeds alogically, or analogically, and may involve some mode of reference to contemporaneous competing theoretical practices.[15] At any

[14] I suspect that this concept of practice, which I take from Heidegger's notion of practices being "at hand" for use, *see* Heidegger (1962: 102) is the most important aspect of what Weber was getting at with his category of traditional legitimation. *See* Weber (1978: 215). However, to the extent that legitimation implies a consideration of the nature and source of a proposition prior to the acceptance of its authority, most human activity does not involve legitimation at all. The reproduction of practice is quite apart from the traditionalist rationality of Edmund Burke and the English common law. Traditionalist rationality explicitly questions and reaffirms tried solutions either out of mannerist fears of disorder or the sense that what lasts must by definition be superior. My notion of daily legal and political practice as unanalyzed or unexamined pushes, rather, toward the idea that legitimation itself is an exceptional or liminal event and of limited use in understanding social behavior. *See* note 18 infra.

[15] Resettlement of disturbed practice within a given system of practices is always system-specific. In other words, the rhetorical figures that have persuasive value in pushing back the threat of disorganization will differ in coexisting institutional orders, and the point at which a system's resettlement processes will appeal to practices drawn from other systems is a historically contingent event. In the American legal system, controversy is commonly closed off through reliance on the common law trope of analogizing the disputed practice to an uncontroverted practice. Thus unprincipled appeal for quiet succeeds only in the sense that it denies that a problem ever existed. At a middle level, legal institutions struggle to maintain their systemic autonomy and still resettle cases by invoking a set of substantively empty maxims such as "reliance," "legislative intent," "proximate cause," "balancing interests," and the like. Such ritualized recitations may incorporate generalized references to fundamental liberal categories, such as subjective intent, aggregation of volition, and efficiency, with a vagueness sufficient to create the appearance of doctrinal autonomy. Only in periods of severe re-evaluation of the system will fully articulated references to extrasystemic and ideologically dominant theoretical/structural practices of reorganization be made. The re-expression of law as economics in the postrealist period has many of these more extreme characteristics. Arguably, much of the ferment caused by this re-

given time, we should expect to discover contradictory (though arguably linked) discourses coexisting within the systems of both legal theory and legal practice. These render the nature of systematic reproduction complex.

This image of law leads away from the idea that the legal theory of the subject — the subject of structuralism's delegitimative analysis — unequivocally determines legal practice. It suggests instead that structuralism be seen as an assault of theory upon theory within the institutions where theory is produced. To argue that the scope of delegitimation in a poststructural analysis is limited is not to deny the deconstructive power of structural analysis. However, the impact of delegitimation will depend on the relationship between the separate institutional systems in which the practice of legal theory and the practice of law occur.

A similar integrated view of the relationship of theory to practice characterizes both structural and phenomenological discourse. Practice is connected to theory in the former by the logic of the structure, and in the latter by the instrumental action of the subject. Once we disrupt these relationships, the legal theory of the subject can no longer be held to produce any unified set of legal practices. Instead, our attention is drawn to the reproduction of the theory of the subject as a practice of theory, so to speak, in which the world is given a particular representation or meaning. What is necessary for the reproduction of theoretical practice is not control of the full run of legal outcomes, but rather continuing domination over paradigmatic or semiotically central events. For example, the legitimacy of

construction, when understood from a systematic perspective, derives from its ambiguous implications. On the one hand, law and economics is radical precisely because it breaches the bounds that traditionally have separated the legal system from coexisting and competing networks of institutions. To turn to an external system in order to resettle disrupted internal theoretical practices is to signal an essential breakdown in the reproduction of the practices that defined that system's exercise of power. Consequently, numerous recalcitrant traditionalists continue to urge the relatively exclusive study of doctrine to defend a closed or wholly internal realm of legal discourse and deny that a reconstruction of jusrisprudence was required by Legal Realism's assault on orthodox theory.

On the other hand, law and economics is conservative because it seeks to resettle disturbed legal practice by reference to an ideologically dominant, politically established system of liberal theoretical practices. As a consequence, the movement has attracted an amalgam of enthusiasts that includes both political critics attracted by its exposure of the structural unity of the legal system and political apologists attracted by the overt re-embedding of legal theory within the core set of representations offered by economics. However, such an extrasystemic response is professionally embarrassing and necessarily short-lived. Like ideology, which is most effective when not consciously worked through and when buried beneath layers of (usually incoherent) subideologies, the true nature of an integrating, structural legal theory is best not exposed. The emptiness of indeterminate and overdeterminate theories simply leads back to, at best or worst, an undergrounded prayer for the restoration of order. *See* Jacobson (1978: 137).

contractual bargain in labor transactions is founded on the attributes of autonomous subjectivity, but these attributes were progressively withdrawn from children, women, and lower class immigrant workers by social legislation early in this century. What remained untouched was the core wage bargain of white native males which held out the utopian image of free subjectivity to which others, after maturation, could aspire. Thus, legal practice reflected an objective discourse appropriate to the historical condition of ideologically marginal groups, while legal theory centered on the representation of the pure subject, a representation that continued to confer meaning upon the social order.

The legal form of the subject drawn from a phenomenological grammar is consistent with other dominant representations within systems of theoretical and symbolic production in this country. It is the ego of existential psychology, which has risen above its structural antagonists, the id and superego. It is the achievement-oriented figure, escaped from premodern social systems which formerly ascribed an identity to it, at the core of American social science in Parsonian action theories (Parsons and Shils, 1951: 53). In literature, it is the singular misanthropic (Western) hero who overturns bureaucratic (social or Eastern) barriers to discover truth. It reappears in the genre of a simple narrative recitation of events performed repeatedly on television and in other popular media.

A discourse of pure subjectivity characterizes, then, the symbolic ordering appropriate for a society that claims to have outgrown culture (determination) and to have reached the end of ideology (Bell, 1962: 392). But daily life, like daily law, is too difficult a jumble of contradictions for ideology or discourse to dominate. Only in the limited number of liminal, exceptional instances when the question of meaning or the ordering of society is examined must ideology control. And it is only in these situations, in which orthodox theory represents meaning as a utopia of existential subjectivity, that structural criticism may have force.

Structuralism provides an appropriate basis for critique in the United States because it contradicts the underlying liberal pretensions of autonomy, which are taken for more seriously in America than elsewhere in the West.[16]

[16] The very strength with which these ideological pretensions persist in American theory is worrisome. It appears that a mere restatement of some altered discourse of the subject, designed to escape the limitations of structuralism, would render critique politically ineffective in the United States. In Europe where the undergrounded subject has always been received with skepticism, a Nietzschean recreation of the subject as romantic hero, or the image of the posttherapeutic subject as free communicator (Habermas), may have political utility. Against the European intellectual backdrop that speaks easily of estate, class, national culture, and structure, and distrusts liberalism as ideology, perhaps critique may fruitfully refer to speech/act theory or to some ironic reinterpretation of the classical ontology of individuality. In America, such reference has begun to produce. I fear, only, a manneristic and dangerous re-

In a poststructuralist understanding, however, it is not yet evident what such an apt form of delegitimation would accomplish. It could be said that the domination of certain symbolic representations of order leads to a general acceptance of current institutional arrangements of power. This is the classic Weberian notion of legitimation (Weber, 1967: 1), which may explain some political behavior on those odd occassions when political life is thought through in places other than the institutions in which political theorizing occurs. But more typically, structuralist deconstruction, if it truly contradicts rather than complements phenomenology, would play an important role only within institutions specialized in theory production. Delegitimation, thus, would represent an assault on the self-characterization of members of a theory elite that could create internal confusion and yield some measure of satisfaction to their more irreverent colleagues.

This result, however, falls far short of the original project of a delegitimative politics of law. On the assumption that practice followed directly from theory, the delegitimation of legal theory was intended to alter daily legal practice. Phenomenological and structural discourses assert that when practice needs to be reformed, reference is necessarily made to theory. Conversely, when theory comes into crisis, so do its positively derivative practices. This logic rests on the existence of a hierarchical relationship between the system that produces theory and the institutions that produce practice. In a poststructural order this hierarchical arrangement becomes wholly problematic.[17]

commitment to the same institutional practices we have always known. It is manneristic because the spirit of natural individuality is gone and only the fear of anarchy remains to support continuing adherence to the form of the subject. It is dangerous because it is so easy to confuse the transvalued, postmodernist subject with the traditional subject that continues to dominate popular consciousness, the subject as natural being. To maintain a firm separation between the classical liberal subject and the transfigured subject that fills the space opened within structural critique requires a degree of subtlety that politics does not achieve. Such subtlety may delight the intellectual left, but its effects will likely be conservative.

17 I am concerned that the limitations I express about the role of theory may be confused with traditional anti-intellectual distinctions between thought and the "real world." I am not arguing that theoretical practices are somehow divorced from reality or that they particularly distort the actual nature of experience. Theoretical practices have the same relation to the chaos of unordered "reality" as does any other set of practices. I personally find the practices concerned with the production of meaning or the symbolic ordering of experience to be esthetically pleasing. But theoretical practices exist and are reproduced within systems that have no natural hierarchical precedence over other institutionalized orders. The special relationship of the practice of theory to other practices is associated with the exceptional (liminal) occasions on which reference is made to theory because the routine of established practice is somewhat upset. It does not derive from the positive capacity of theory to determine practice. The claim to a metastatus for theory may be seen as a claim to institutional power for the practitioners of theory or as a desire for a utopia of closed knowledge. To

To summarize, then, my description of some elements that may figure in a refounded Critical account of law and politics, I would stress the following points. The legal system should be understood as a self-reproducing set of theoretically unintegrated practices which refers to legal theory only when some local practice becomes unsettled. The continuing presence of contradictory practices is not a consequence of mistaken judgments to be corrected by a more competent application of structural principles but a normal and stable condition of the system (see also Luhmann supra). Theory, only exceptionally involved in the legal system, is represented by a complex system of seemingly competing symbols that have only an analogical and indeterminate bearing on the resettlement of disturbed practices.

Structuralist delegitimation is a critique aimed at an ideologically dominant representation of theory. But symbolic systems are marginal to daily life. The resettlement of disturbed theoretical practices is an esoteric activity concerned with metaquestions about the symbolic reorganization of symbols. A crisis in theory may be disruptive within the particular institutions where theoretical practice is shaped, but its wider effect on the reproduction of political and legal practice is indirect and unclear. What seems more clear is that neither orthodox nor Critical accounts of the hierarchical relationship of theory to practice now adequately describe the impact of the delegitimation of theory on political and legal practice.

B. Relocating Knowledge

The origin of the Critical theory of ideology lay in the search for an answer to the question posed by Marx of why workers do not perceive their species interests and overturn established social order. Weber generalized the inquiry to ask why men accorded authority to social orderings that he assumed could not exist by means of the exercise of repression alone. Repression occurs at the level of specific practices, and if legitimating ideologies acted for Weber as a substitute for repression, then those ideologies would seem to operate at that level too. Delegitimation analysis, based on reversing the mechanisms of authority, presumes it will alter political or legal practice by tearing away the theoretical justification that Weber suggested shielded practice from the consequences of Marx's teleological argument that human nature would lead to revolt. Yet, in fact, the delegitimation of theory, though well and often advanced, seems too peripheral to political life.[18]

admit this does not delegitimate theory; it decenters it. On these last points, see Cavell (1979: 191); Rorty (1979: 3).

18 One must avoid confusing the distinct levels of political practice to which the concept of legitimation may be pertinent. I disagree with the assumption that legitimation acts directly in the sustenance of ordinary political life. This perspective ignores the

It could be that structuralist critics do not effectively delegitimate liberal society. It could be said they only express an objectivist discourse which alternates with subjectivism to form the real constitution of liberalism. It could also be argued that it is the dehabilitation of structuralism by its own methodological limitations that has led to a readoption of phenomenological discourse in the poststructuralist period. I believe that in deconstructing a universalist subjectivism with a global structural theory, delegitimation restricts its impact to a realm beyond political action, if not political theory. Delegitimation derives its Critical force from its structuralist logic. This logic contrasts the contradictions within the existing social order with some perfected image of a unitary knowledge able consistently to relate a single theory of society to a rationalized practice. Yet, like postmodernist esthetics, a viable Critical politics as its natural condition must tolerate, if not seek, contradiction between practices and between theories.

When Aristotle referred to man as a political being, his referent was the *polis*. Plato's prescription for the *polis'* optimal size was 5400. The evident lesson is that political life is local and not global. Modern global theories operate within local centers of power, explain and justify the domination of those centers, and create the appearance of mass involvement. Political practice, like legal practice, remains local and theoretically indeterminate. Delegitimation, like the universalizing claims of liberal subjectivist equality which it assaults, contributes to the myth of the structurally unified or extended political organization. Ultimately, it risks deflecting analysis and attention to institutions of theory only marginal to the institutions of legal and political practice where power is actually produced and reproduced.

The unified image of man projected by structuralist theory must dissolve and carry with it the reverie of a unified science of human affairs.[19]

unthought nature of normal practice, and assumes such practice needs, or can be given, justification. Weber properly discerned the problematic nature of authority that can resettle practices that have been brought into crisis. But here, ideal categorizations of authority types constructed upon analytical reason may be misleading. Substantive and formal rationality always refer to theoretical structures of under- and overdeterminate character. Consequently, resolutions of disturbed practice, or *ex post* correct interpretation, must emerge either through a recognition of the authority of the fathers (which Weber called traditional legitimacy) or through the acceptance of the arbitrary pronouncements of some other voice that speaks aptly in particular historical circumstances (Weber's charismatic legitimation). *See* Weber (1964: 324). A hypothetical account of the psychological and dramatic elements of the reconstruction of sacred or theoretical practices out of the crises of disorder — a reconstruction that matches the collective embrace of one arbitrary order and the sacrificial repression of the symbols of linked (twin) alternative orders — is presented in Girard (1979).

[19] It has often been suggested that the quest to discover or impose coherent meaning is the essence of the special claims of Western civilization. It is also asserted that the suppression of contradiction is a necessary consequence of our struggle with our

But there must be no falling back upon a discourse of the unremitting fragmentation of the civic order. Refashioning a cultural representation that imagines that meaning can be gleaned from individual projects, and that immediate consciousness of the presence of self can be more than an empty echo of our own speech, is reactionary. Given the decentralized and ongoing production of communities, it is *local, depersonalized*, and *public* history that should appear as the centerpiece of theory. Such history should reject both the power of global theory and the validity of concentrated power. Mass politics, like the dream of a timeless or personal knowledge, should be seen as oxymoronic. Power is always local in its exercise. To indulge the illusion that it can be legitimately delegated or administratively banished is to give up politics for manipulation.

One possible step toward a Critical theoretical practice might be the development of a poststructuralist "architecture" of complex systems, which would accept the inevitability of inconsistency and contradiction in the everyday life of legal and political theory and practice.[20] At the level of nontheoretical practice, it is necessary to describe in detail the network of established practices within functioning legal institutions and to understand the reproduction of unanalyzed ways of going about the world. The logic (or analogic) of reproduction must take into account that existing practices may be continually reformed because they are constructed in systematic processes that may refer to multiple discursive representations of experience. In terms borrowed from biology and cybernetics, the internal life of the system must be autopoetic, or capable of selfprogrammed reproduction. At the same time, the evolution of practice can be responsive to interactions with other subsystems of practice, including those which produce theoretical practices. How these relations will best represented is difficult to predict (for a tentative formulation see Teubner infra).

At the level of theory, global theory is to be replaced by a local set of theoretical practices. Theory must be analyzed as nothing more than one system of practices among others, with dynamics of reproduction and environmental interaction similar to those of nonsymbolic practices. In displacing the hierarchical superiority over other levels of practice that is claimed by the pretense of theory to a determinate knowledge of self and

potential schizophrenic dissolution. However attractive this defense of consistency may be, it is threatened by the converse propensity to indulge in delusive wish fulfillment. Perhaps, for us, as for the ancient Greeks, some moderation in our mixing of psychoses is now advisable.

[20] The metaphor of a complex, contradictory, poststructuralist architecture is borrowed from the antimodernist criticism made by architects such as Venturi and Portoghesi. This architecture, with its insistent stress on the importance of global history, typifies the poststructuralist problem through its embodiment of the promise inherent in the development of a variety of communities and the threat inherent in a sterile reproduction of an exhausted past.

others, there is at least a symbolic expression of the desire to decenter the political power that has, in our era, been linked to that pretense.

I am aware that a discourse that speaks of the architecture of unpredictable systems could be recast in the terms of either a phenomenological or a structuralist grammar. The disordered evolution of system could be read as the narrative of some transfigured, collective spirit. The categories that distinguish one system from another could be read as the differentiation of a metastructure. But why retrace this now barren ground?[21]

Summary Questions

Whatever value this account of structuralism may have, it surely raises more questions than it lays to rest. There remain the political tremors that we properly experience when confronting the noncritical application of global objectivizing structures. To the extent that structuralism is too flawed an analysis of consciousness, must not its derivative accounts,

[21] A related point:

"... All arguments between the traditional scientific view of man as organism, a locus of needs and drives, and a Christian view of man as a spiritual being not only are unresolvable at the present level of discourse but are profoundly boring — no small contributor indeed to the dreariness of Western society in general. The so-called détentes and reconciliations between "Science" and "Religion" are even more boring. What is more boring than hearing Heisenberg's uncertainty relations enlisted in support of the freedom of the will? The traditional scientific model of man is clearly inadequate, for a man can go to heroic lengths to identify and satisfy his needs and end by being more miserable than a Calcuttan. As for the present religious view of man, it begs its own question, the question of God's existence, which means that it is not only useless to the unbeliever but dispiriting. The latter is more despressed than ever at hearing the good news of Christianity. From the scientific view at least, a new model of man is needed, something other than man conceived as a locus of bio-psycho-sociological needs and drives.

Such an anthropological model might be provided by semiotics, that is, the study of man as the sign-using creature and, specifically, the study of the self and consciousness as derivatives of the sign-function." Percy (1983: 81).

There are, of course, obvious reasons to object to the persistent use of the imagery of the autonomous self if it is, as structuralism asserts, false or illusory. There would also be political reasons to become depressed if the existence of a liberal self were proved true. My sense is that, at this point, the relevant question is no longer whether the predominant narrative of autonomous selfhood is true or false. Rather, autonomous selfhood is increasingly seen as one of a related series of possible accounts that describe and organize experience in the world. It is the unceasing recitation of this discourse and its complements, recognized as discursive phenomena and transformed by this recognition, that is esthetically unsupportable. On one hand, ennui may not seem to offer a standard on which to base political or social critique. On the other, one computer theorist has suggested that boredom is the principal quality that still distinguishes human from artificial intelligence.

including that of delegitimation, be flawed also? Nevertheless, the problem of what to do after the structuralist argument has been understood and internalized interests me most.

If there exist a multitude of structuralisms and a multitude of possible practices consistent with each, how does one "choose" among them to produce explanation or prediction? Are we compelled to reintroduce the notion of the autonomous subject, at least in the guise of author, analyst, or reader? How can such a reintroduction be possible, given the telling assaults of historical materialism, psychoanalysis, and linguistics on the "natural" conception of individuality? And is not my account of the movement between structuralist and phenomenological discourses in language and other fields simply a prelude to (another) universal metastructure of discursive differentiations? If so, must not my implicit structuralism itself be subject to a poststructuralist attack on its indeterminacy and overdetermination? If we now rediscover the subject, do we not expose ourselves to a potentially infinite alternation of discourses, going nowhere ever more rapidly?

I believe the answer to all these questions is a confused and disturbing assent. I also suspect that the path beyond the limits of these discourses lies neither in retreat from, nor in embracing with the perverse pleasure of resignation, the paradoxes they establish. As with all games built upon true paradox, in spite of the wondrous levels of complexity at which they can be played, in the end the game grows tiring and we must simply put it to one side.

Post Script

The program I wish to see developed would deny neither the reality of the experience of consciousness nor the validity of explanatory structures. Rather, it would presume to clarify the boundaries between discourses and properly resituate these contradictory representations within a more general system of information. The purpose of such a reconstruction would be threefold. First, it would lessen the confusion that currently exists due to the conflation of concepts and procedures appropriate to one type of discourse in discussions of some alternative grammar. Second, in emphasizing that the particular symbolic orderings within any single discourse are historically produced, a reconstruction of theory would invite reconsideration of terms and relationships often accepted as natural and necessary. For example, to view phenomenology as one among many possible discursive practices, ought, at the same time, to call attention to the myriad possible accounts of subjectivity within phenomenological discourse.

Most importantly, to relocate contending discourses within a more comprehensive topography of possible expressions would transform how we understand the politics of knowledge. My thesis is that contending discourses never touch one another. Instead, they are images drawn from distinct vantage points within complex information systems. Neither the unique experience of indeterminacy which we label self-consciousness nor the symbolic orderings that we use as determinative explanatory structures has a privileged claim to constitute any particular discursive event. Both the specific transformation of the grammatical rules within any spoken discourse and the more general discourse (e. g., structural or phenomenological) that is actually used to constitute any particular event are themselves the outcomes of an ongoing process that Foucault has called, for lack of a better term in our present speech practices, the exercise of power. *See* Foucault (1982: 108). Power is neither individual nor collective; it is the historical emergence of voice that founds both consciousness and structure. The constellation of discursive practices at any given time is literally a *regime du savoir* since any particular claim to knowledge is installed through the exercise of power. The object of understanding is to trace the trajectory of the system that at once generates the possibility of discourse and constrains the evolution of its practice.

We can speculate about some results of the application of this reformed perspective to the discourse with which we have become familiar. The claim of hermeneutics — the empathetic apprehension of the intentions of self or others — to present the sole method appropriate to phenomenological knowledge must be resituated. Consciousness is not a unique attribute of mankind. It is rather the representation of one level of a complex system to itself. We appear to ourselves to be special because we have access only with respect to our own position to the odd viewpoint afforded by reflexivity (for an account of reflexivity see Luhmann supra, Teubner infra). Reflections through which the higher and lower levels of the complex system in which we participate are represented to themselves are simply unavailable to us. There is, however, a coherent discourse appropriate to every such reflexive phenomenology. It is the discourse whose method is confession or *Verstehen*, whose politics speaks of rhetoric or persuasion, whose revision lies in therapy, whose genre is narrative, and whose authority is charismatic.

Alternatively, we must resituate structuralism's claim to produce a scientific knowledge that affords a complete, determinate, causal, and timeless account of the particular. Such discourse is appropriate either to a system's representation of the more complex system of which it is an element or to its representation of the lower levels of system which, in turn, compose it. Structuralism is the expression of our attempts to step outside our own position, ranging up and down through the multiple levels of the complexity in which we are enmeshed. This effort to escape the confines of reflexivity yields symbolic or collective orderings that fashion messages out of randomness and restrict the ultimate freedom from order that is entropy. These structural orders are theoretical practices that describe the coherence or internal logic of alternative representations of system. Such symbolic practices frame and shape the production of nontheoretical practices. The method of structural discourse is positivist: its explanatory form privileges the un- (or super-) conscious; its authority is rationality.

To resituate discourse within the wider topography of a complex system is to dwell on its self-contained character or epistemological limits. From the standpoint of structure, all nontheoretical or individual practice is inexplicable and, in a way, uninteresting. In the epistemology of a discourse of systems, we can have knowledge of experience only at the collective level of representation. All symbolic ordering or theory is probabilistic generalization from the aggregation of the particular. There is no science of the individual, nor should we treat as meaningful each particular event, behavior, or practice. Rather, the particular is randomly distributed in relation to the symbolic order that affords meaning. Only from the standpoint of reflexive consciousness does such randomization appear as intentionality.

Theory and practice, meaning and individual action, are terms drawn from different discourses. The dream of their unification is empty. Individuals may be persuaded or coerced; we cannot know one another as conscious actors. But symbolic orders are never the static, idealized forms to which our Platonic longings aspire. Viewed from a systematic perspective, culture itself is an institutionally produced aggregation of local practices. The symbolic practices that I have called knowledge, theory, identity, level of representation (i. e., what is termed collective or particular), and discourse (i. e. viewpoint on the system) are themselves constantly contestable and indeterminate in the process of their reproduction. In developing a broader discourse of system, we must see theory and practice, structure and consciousness, as equifinal states within an evolving network of possible messages. All these messages are local and represent permutations of the information sets that preceded their generation. The historical production of new information is the exercise of power, and it is all that we have to share.

In this latter sense, to explain and elaborate a discourse appropriate to the description of autopoietic systems is to resituate politics at the center of our being. The essential attribute of a self-referential system is its evolutionary history of continual internal differentiation of newly organized patterns of information out of its preexisting states. Variations in the construction of these differentiations are functions of a self-programming system's operating instructions, and are therefore unrelated through predictable rules to alterations in the extrasystemic world. The genesis and maintenance of codes of symbolic order arise in the course of organizing the process of systemic reproduction. Typical differentiations within contemporary systems include the attributes of personal identity, such as economic preferences and legal rights, and the categories of collective organization, such as race, nation, class, culture, and structure. Objective and subjective discourses are equally artifacts of system differentiation that represent indeterminate outcomes of its evolutionary process. However, from the reflexive perspective of conscious actors within the more complex system, the outcome of system is not random. The process of differentiation is perceived as political struggle over the establishment of practice. At the same time, the set of alternative differentiated outcomes (practices) made possible within the trajectory of the system is reified by participants in politics and mistakenly understood to be the inputs of political conflict.

My argument is that we have neither fixed subjective identities nor determined ascribed memberships in particular corporate groups prior to the generation of those attributes in the local histories of systems. These differentiated categories of identity that we take on randomly in the process of political competition afford organization to our lives only when they are reified and reprojected back over our personal histories prior to the conflict. Each particular account of identity produced is framed by the local evolution of systems as they move among the many potential levels of system representation to rework the architecture of established claims to knowledge. Legal rights, legal identities, and legal theories arise in ongoing, indeterminate production of legal practices specific to systems in existing Western social orders. Describing the boundaries of those systems, the nature and ontogenesis of the categories of their internal organization, and the practices that exist at any moment is the task of poststructural legal theory. Active participation in accessible political competitions (local public life) is the only way to gain whatever identity or knowledge we may have a poststructural order.[22]

References

Bell, Daniel (1962) *The End of Ideology*. New York: Free Press.

Buchanan, James M. (1974) *The Limits of Liberty*. Chicago: University of Chicago Press.

Cavell, Stanley (1979) *The Aim of Reason: Wittgenstein, Skepticism, Morality and Tragedy*. New York: Oxford University Press.

Da Matta, Roberto (1983) *Carnavals, Bandits et Heros: Ambiguities de la Société Bresilienne*. Paris: Seuil.

Demsetz, Harold (1967) "Toward a Theory of Property Rights", 57—2 *American Economic Review* 347.

Dreyfus, Hubert L., and Paul Rabinow (1982) *Michael Foucault: Beyond Structuralism and Hermeneutics*. Chicago: University of Chicago Press.

[22] For discussion of developments in physical science and artificial intelligence, where autopoietic systems have become prominent, see generally von Foerster (1981: 2); Dupuy (1982); Luhmann (1982). For speculation about the resituation of consciousness within more complex systems, see Hofstadter and Dennett (1981: 149).

DUPUY, Jean-Pierre (1982) *Ordres et Desordres: enquêt sur un nouveau Paradigme.* Paris: Seuil.
FOUCAULT, Michel (1980) *Power/Knowledge: Selected Interviews and other Writings 1972—77.* New York: Pantheon Books.
— (1982) "Afterword" in H. Dreyfus and P. Rabinow, *Michel Faucault: Beyond Structuralism and Hermeneutics*, Chicago: Universites of Chicago Press.
GIRARD, René (1979) *Violence and the Sacred.* Washington: John Hopkins University Press.
HEIDEGGER, Martin (1962) *Being and Time.* Oxford: Blackwell.
HELLER, Thomas (1976) "The Importance of Normative Decision Making: The Limitations of Legal Economics as a Basis for a Liberal Jurisprudence — As Illustrated by the Regulation of Vacation Home Development". *Wisconsin Law Review* 385.
— (1979) "Is the Charitable Exemption from Property Taxation an Easy Case? General Concerns about Legal Economics and Jurisprudence" in D. Rubinfeld (ed.), *Essays on the Law and Economics of Local Governments.* Washington DC: Urban.
— (1984) "Structuralism and Critique", 36 *Stanford Law Review* 127.
HOFSTADTER, Douglas R., and Daniel C. DENNET (1981) *The Mind's I: Fantasies and Reflections on Self and Soul.* New York: Basic Books.
JACOBSON, Richard (1978) "Absence, Authority, and the Text", 3 *Glyph* 137.
LUHMANN, Niklas (1982) "The Autonomy of the Legal System", in N. Luhmann *The Differentiation of Society.* New York: Columbia University Press.
MARKOVITS, Richard S. (1983) "Legal Analysis and the Economic Analysis of Allocative Efficiency. A Reply to Professor Posner's Reply", 11 *Hofstra Law Review* 667.
MILLER, James D. (1975) "Holmes, Pierce and Legal Pragmatism", 84 *Yale Law Journal* 1123.
MUSIL, Robert (1965) *The Man without Qualities.* New York: Capricorn Books.
NIETZSCHE, Friedrich W. (1956) *The Birth of Tragedy and the Genealogy of Morals.* Garden City, N. Y.: Doubleday.
PARSONS, Talcott, and Edward A. SHILS (eds.) (1951) *Toward a General Theory of Action.* Cambridge: Harvard University Press.
PERCY, Walter (1983) *Lost in the Cosmos: The Last Self-Help Book.* New York: Farrar.
PITKIN, Hanna F. (1972) *Wittgenstein and Justice: On the Significance of Ludwig Wittgenstein for Social and Political Thought.* Berkeley: University of California Press.
POSNER, Richard (1980) "The Ethical and Political Basis of the Efficency Norm in Common Law Adjudication", 8 *Hofstra Law Review* 487.
— (1981) "A Reply to Some Recent Criticisms of the Efficiency Theory of the Common Law", 9 *Hofstra Law Review* 775.
RAWLS, John (1971) *A Theory of Justice.* Cambridge, Mass.: Harvard University Press.
RORTY, Richard (1979) *Philosophy and the Mirror of Nature.* Princeton: Princeton University Press.
SAID, Edward W. (1979) *Orientalism.* New York: Times Books.
TALMON, Jacob L. (1960) *The Origins of Totalitarian Democracy.* New York: Praeger.
TURNER, Victor W. (1967) *The Forest of Symbols: Aspects of Ndembu Ritual.* Ithaca, N. Y.: Cornell University Press.
VON FOERSTER, Heinz (1981) *Observing Systems.* Intersystems Publications.
WEBER, Max (1964) *The Theory of Social and Economic Organizations.* Glencoe, Ill.: Free Press.
— (1966) *On Law in Economy and Society.* Cambridge: Harvard University Press.
— (1978) *Economy and Society.* Berkeley: University of California Press.
WILKERSON, Terence E. (1976) *Kant's Critique of Pure Reason.* Oxford: Clarendon Press.

IV

Perspectives of Legal Development

Law as Medium and Law as Institution

JÜRGEN HABERMAS
Frankfurt

I have explained elsewhere* the symptoms of reification appearing in developed capitalist societies by the fact that the media controlled subsystem of economy and state intervene in the symbolic reproduction of the lifeworld by monetary and bureaucratic means. According to our hypothesis, however, a "colonialization of the lifeworld" can come about only:

- when traditional forms of life are so far dismantled that the structural components of the lifeworld (culture, society and personality) have been, to a great extent, differentiated;
- when exchange relations between subsystems and lifeworld are regulated through differentiated roles (for employment at organized work places and the demand for the (consumer) of private households, for the relation of clients to government bureaucracies and for formal participation in the legitimation process);
- when the real abstractions – which make the labour power of the employed available and make possible the mobilization of the vote of the electorate – are tolerated by those affected as a trade off against system-conforming rewards;
- whereby these compensations are financed according to the welfare state pattern from the gains of capitalist growth and are canalized into those roles in which, withdrawn from the world of work and the public sphere, privatized hopes for self-actualization and self-determination are primarily located; namely in the roles of consumer and client.

Now statements about an internal colonialization of the lifeworld are at a relatively high level of generalization. This is not so unusual for social theoretical reflections, as can be seen by the example of systems functionalism as well. But such a theory, always exposed to the danger of over-

* Jürgen Habermas (1981) *Theorie des kommunikativen Handelns* Frankfurt: Suhrkamp. Translated from the German by Iain Fraser and Constance Meldrum. This paper is taken from Bd. 2: 522–547. We acknowledge permission from Beacon Press to translate and publish this extract.

generalization, must be able to specify at least *what type* of empirical approach is appropriate to it. I shall, therefore, illustrate with one example the evidence by which the thesis of internal colonialization can be tested: the juridification of communicatively structured action areas. I choose this example because it offers no particularly serious problems in method or content. The development of law belongs to the undisputed and, since Durkheim and Weber, classical research areas of sociology.

If it is true that the symbolic reproduction of the lifeworld cannot be radically reoriented towards the foundations of systematic integration without pathological side effects, and if precisely this trend is the unavoidable side effect of a successful welfare-state program, then, in the domains of cultural reproduction, social integration and socialization, an assimilation to formally organized domains of action areas will take place under the conditions mentioned above. The social relations we call 'formally organized' are those that are first constituted in forms of modern law. Thus it is to be expected that the change-over from social to system integration would take the shape of juridification processes. The predicted reification effects would have to be demonstrated at this analytical level and, indeed, as being the symptomatic consequence of *a specific kind* of juridification.

I shall analyze this specific juridification process using the examples of family and school law. It is only the late off-shoot of a juridification process that has accompanied bourgeois society since its beginnings. The expression 'juridification' (Verrechtlichung) refers quite generally to the tendency towards an increase of written law which can be observed in modern society. We can distinguish here between the *expansion* of law, i.e. the legal regulation of new, hitherto informally regulated social situations, from the *densification* of law, that is the specialized breaking up of global statutory definitions (*Rechtstatbestände*) into more individuated legal definitions (Voigt, 1980: 16). Otto Kirchheimer introduced the term *Verrechtlichung* into academic discussion during the Weimar Republic. At that time he had in mind primarily the institutionalization of class conflict through collective bargaining law and labour law, and in general the juristic containment of social conflicts and political struggles. This development towards the social welfare state, which found expression in the participatory social rights (*soziale Teilhaberrechte*) of the Weimar Constitution and received great attention in the constitutional law theories of the time (above all from Heller, Smend and Carl Schmitt), is but the last link in a chain of juridification thrusts. Roughly outlined, we can distinguish four epochal juridification processes. The first thrust led to *the bourgeois state* which, in Western Europe, developed during the period of Absolutism in the form of the European state system. The second thrust led to the *constitutional state* (*Rechtsstaat*) which assumed an exemplary form in the monarchy of 19th-century Germany. The third thrust led to the *democratic constitutional state* (*demokratischer Rechtsstaat*) which spread in Europe and in North America in the wake of the French Revolution. The last stage (to date) culminates in the *social and democratic constitutional state* (*sozialer und demokratischer Rechtsstaat*), which was achieved through the struggles of the European workers' movement in the course of the 20th century and codified, for example, in Article 21 of the Constitution of the Federal Republic of Germany. I should like to characterize these *four global thrusts of juridification* from the social theoretic standpoint of the decoupling of system and lifeworld and of the conflict of the lifeworld with the self-dynamics of autonomous subsystems.

a) The European development of law during the phase of Absolutism can basically be understood as an institutionalization of the two media through which the economy and state were differentiated into subsystems. The *bourgeois state* formed the political order within which the transformation of early modern feudal society into capitalist market society was effected. On the one hand, relations among individual commodity owners were subjected to legal regulation in a code of civil law tailored to strategically acting legal persons who enter into contracts with one another. As we have seen, this legal order bears the features of positivity, generality and formality, and is constructed on the basis of the modern concept of statutory law as well as of the concept of the legal person, as one who can enter into contracts, acquire, dispose and bequeath property. The legal order has to guarantee the liberty and property of the private person, the certainty of the law (*Rechtssicherheit*) and the formal equality of all legal subjects before the law, and thereby the calculability of all legal-normed action. On the other hand, public law authorizes a sovereign state power with a monopoly on coercive force as the sole source of legal domination. The sovereign is absolved from orientation towards any particular policies or from specific state objectives and becomes defined instrumentally, i.e. only in relation to the means of the legal exercise of bureaucratically organized domination. The means of effective power allocation turns into the only objective.

With this first thrust of juridification, "civil society" was constituted, if we use this expression in the sense of Hegel's philosophy of law. The self-understanding of this phase found its most fully developed expression in Hobbes' *Leviathan*. This is of special interest in our context. Insofar as Hobbes constructs the social order exclusively from the system perspective of a state that constitutes civil societies, he defines the lifeworld negatively – it encompasses everything that is excluded from the system and left to private discretion. The lifeworld is that from which civil law and legal domination emancipate the citizen; its essence lies in the corporatively bound, status-dependent conditions of life which had found their particularistic expression in feudal, laws concerning person, profession, trade and land. What remains of this in the bourgeois state is attributed to the sphere of the private, which indeed can now only be characterized privately through a minimum of peace which ensures physical survival and through the unfettering of the empirical needs of isolated subjects who compete for scarce resources in accordance with the laws of the market. The lifeworld is the reservoir, not to be more precisely determined, from which the subsystems of economy and state extract what they need for their reproduction: performance at work and readiness to obey (Preuß, 1980; Neumann, 1980).

The Hobbesian construction hits exactly the level of abstraction at which the innovations of the bourgeois state namely, legal provisions for the institutionalization of money and power can be characterized. Hobbes, in abstracting from the historical substratum of premodern life forms, anticipates in his theory what Marx will later ascribe to reality as "real abstractions". Without this lifeworld substratum, the state in its absolutist form could not have found a basis for its legitimation, nor could it have functioned. Certainly, the bourgeois state accelerated the dissolution of this substratum on which it tacitly fed. However, out of the exhausted traditional life forms, and out of institutionalized life relations in the process of dissolution, there arose — at first in class specific forms — the structures of a modern lifeworld, which Hobbes could not see because he exclusively adopted the system perspective of the bourgeois state. From this perspective, everything that is not constituted in the forms of modern law must appear *formless*. But the modern lifeworld is no more stripped of its own structures than are historical life forms. The *subsequent* juridification thrusts can be understood in these terms: a lifeworld which at first was placed at the disposal of the market and absolutist rule little by little makes good its claims. After all media such as power and money need to be *anchored* in a modern lifeworld. Only in this way can the bourgeois state gain a non-parasitic legitimacy appropriate to modern levels of justification. Ultimately, the structurally differentiated lifeworld, upon which modern states are functionally dependent, remains the only source of legitimation.

b) The bourgeois constitutional state found a prototypical form in 19th century German constitutionalism and was conceptualized by theoreticians of the *Vormärz* period (1815—1848) such as Karl von Rotteck or Robert von Mohl (Boldt, 1975), and later by F.J. Stahl[1]. Used as an analytical term, this concept refers to more general aspects of a juridification thrust

[1] See Maus (1978: 13) The famous definition is: "The State should be one based on the rule of law (Rechtsstaat): that is the slogan, and is truly the developmental thrust of modern times. It should precisely define the paths and limits of its efficacy, and the free sphere of its citizens, by way of the law, and unswervingly guarantee these: it should not realize (enforce) moral ideas through the state, i.e. directly, any further than is proper to the legal sphere, i.e. only as far as the most necessary demarcation. This is the concept of the *Rechtsstaat*; not that the state should merely manage the legal order without administrative objectives, or merely completely protect the rights of the individual; it does not at all mean the goal and content of the state, but only the ways and means of realizing this." See Stahl (1963: 137).

that by no means coincides with specific legal developments in Germany (Böckenförde, 1976: 65). This second thrust means the constitutional regulation of executive authority, which up to then was only limited and bound by legal form and the bureaucratic means of exercising power. Now, as private individuals, citizens are given actionable, public subjective rights against a sovereign — though they do not yet democratically participate in forming the sovereign's will. Through this kind of constitutionalization of the state (*Verrechtsstaatlichung*), a bourgeois order of civil law system is coordinated with the apparatus for exercising political rule in such a way that the principle of administrative legality can be interpreted in the sense of the "rule of law". In the citizens' sphere of freedom the administration may interfere neither *contra* nor *praeter* nor *ultra legem*. The guarantees of life, of liberty and of the property of private persons no longer arise only as functional side-effects a of commerce institutionalized by private law. Rather, with the idea of the constitutional state, they achieve the status of morally justified constitutional norms and put their mark on the structure of the order of domination as a whole.

In terms of social theory, this process can again be seen from two sides: from the perspectives of the system and of the lifeworld. The absolutist state had understood itself exclusively as an agent of subsystems that were differentiated through money and power: it treated the lifeworld, pushed into the private sphere, as unformed matter. This legal order was now enriched by elements that acknowledged the entitlement to protection of the modern lifeworld of the citizen. Viewed from the outside, one can also understand this as a first step by which the modern state acquired a legitimacy in its own right-legitimation *on the basis* of a modern lifeworld.

c) The *democratic constitutional state* first took shape during the French Revolution and, since Rousseau and Kant, has occupied political theory up to the present day. I again use the term analytically to refer to the juridification thrust in which the idea of freedom already incipient in the concept of stratutory law (*Gesetzesbegriff*) as conceptualized by the natural law tradition was given constitutional force. Constitutionalized state power was democratized and the citizens, as citizens of the state, were provided with rights of political participation. Laws now come into force only when there is a democratically assured presumption that they express a general interest, and that all those affected would have to agree to them. This requirement must be met by a procedure which binds legislation to parliamentary will-formation and public discussion. The *juridification of the legitimation process* is achieved in the form of general and equal sufferage as well as the recognition of the freedom to organize political associations and parties. This heightens the problem of the separation of power, i.e. of the relation between the functionally differentiated state institutions of legislature, executive and judiciary. Within the constitutional state this problem was posed only in the relationship between executive and judiciary.

In terms of social theory, this thrust of democratization parallels the previous constitutionalization. Once again the modern lifeworld asserts itself against the imperatives of a structure of domination which abstracts itself from all concrete life relations. With this, the process of anchoring the medium of power in a rationalized lifeworld, i.e. one no longer only differentiated in the bourgeoisie, comes to a definite end.

The first juridification thrust constitutive of bourgeois society was still dominated by those ambivalences which Marx exposed in the example of "free" wage labour. The irony of this freedom was that the social emancipation of wage labourers, i.e. the freedom of movement and voluntariness upon which labour contracts and organizational membership are based, had to be paid for by the proletarianization of the labourer's mode of life, of which normatively no account at all was taken. The next two juridification thrusts were already carried forward by the pathos of bourgeois emancipation movements. The *unambiguously* freedom-guaranteeing character of legal rules reveals itself along the lines of the constitutionalization and the democratization of a bureaucratic domination which first appeared in absolutist form. Civil formal law loses the ambivalence of the realization of freedoms bought with destructive after-effects wherever it visibly accentuates demands of the lifeworld against bureaucratic domination.

The *social welfare state* (which I need not characterize once again) which developed in the framework of the democratic constitutional state continues this line of *freedom-guaranteeing juridification*. Apparently it tames the economic action-system in a fashion similar to the way in which the two preceding thrusts of juridification tamed the administrative system. In any case, the achievements of the social welfare state were politically fought for and vouchsafed in the interest of guaranteeing freedoms. The parallels leap to the eye: in the one case the inner dynamics of the bureaucratic exercise of power, in the other the inner dynamics of economic accumulation processes were reconciled with the obstinate structures of a lifeworld that had for its part also become rationalized.

The development toward a *social and democratic constitutional state* can actually be understood as the constitutionalization of a social power relation anchored in the class structure. Classic examples would be the shortening of working hours, freedom to organize unions and bargain for wages, protection from layoffs, social security, etc. These are instances of juridification processes in a world of work previously subordinate to the unrestrained power of disposition and organization that was exercised by private owners of the means of production. Here too we are dealing with power-balancing juridifications *within an* area of action that is *already constituted by law*.

Norms which contain class conflict and shape the social welfare state have, from the perspective of their beneficiaries as well as from that of democratic lawgivers, a freedom-guaranteeing character. However, this does not apply unambiguously to all welfare state regulations. From the beginning on, the *ambivalence of guarantees* of and *denials of freedom* have adhered to the policies of the social welfare state (Guldimann *et al.*, 1978). The first juridification thrust constitutive of the relation between capital and wage labour owed its ambivalence to a contradiction between the social emancipatory intent of the norms of bourgeois civil law and its socially repressive effects on those who were forced to offer their labour power as a commodity. The net of welfare state guarantees is meant to cushion these external effects of a production process based on wage labour. Yet the more closely this net is woven, the more clearly appear ambivalences of *another sort*. The negative effects of this — to date, final — juridification thrust do not appear as side-effects; they result *from the structure of juridification itself*. It is now the very means of guaranteeing freedom which endanger the freedom of the beneficiary.

In the area of *public welfare policy* this situation has met with wide attention under the title "juridification and bureaucratization as limits to welfare policy" (Reidegeld, 1980: 275). In the case of social security law it has been shown repeatedly (Ferber, 1967) that although legal entitlements to monetary income in case of illness or old age and the like definitely signify historical progress when compared with the traditional care of the poor, this juridification of life-risks demands a remarkable price in the form of *restructuring interventions in the lifeworld* of those who are eligible. These costs ensue from the bureaucratic implementation and monetary redemption of welfare entitlements. The structure of civil law dictates the formulation of welfare state guarantees as *individual* legal entitlements under precisely *specified* general legal conditions (Tatbestände) (see also Preuß and Ewald supra).

In social security law, *individualization* — that is, the attribution of entitlements to a strategically-acting legal subject pursuing his private interests — may be more appropriate to life situations that require regulation rather than, for instance, to family law. Nevertheless, the individualizing definition of, say, geriatric care has burdensome consequences for the self-image of the person concerned, and for his relations with spouse, friends, neighbours etc.; it also has consequences for the readiness of mutual aid communities to provide subsidiary assistance. Considerable compulsion toward the redefinition of everyday situations proceeds above all from the *specification of legal conditions* — in this case, the conditions under which social security will compensate:

An insured case is normally understood as the 'appearance of the particular contingency against which social security is supposed to provide protection'. Compensation is made in the event of a valid claim to benefit." The juridification of social situations brings along with it the incorporation into the business of economic and social distribution of the if-then structure of conditional law that is 'foreign' to social relations, to social causes, dependencies and needs. This structure does not, however, allow for appropriate, and especially not for preventive reactions towards the causes of the situations requiring compensation (Reidegeld, 1980: 277: see also Willke infra).

In the end, the *generality* of legal conditions is tailored to *bureaucratic implementation*, i.e. to the administration which deals with the social problem as it is expressed through the legal entitlement. The situation to be regulated is embedded in the context of a life-history and of a concrete way of life; it has to be subjected to violent abstraction not merely because it has to be subsumed under the law but in order that it can be handled administratively. The implementing bureaucracies must proceed very selectively and *choose* those instances of social needs which, using the means of a legally-proceeding bureaucratic rule, can be brought under the legal fiction of the compensation situation. This, by the way, meets the requirements of a centralized and computerized handling of social exigencies by large distant organizations. These organizations add a spatial and temporal element to the social and psychological distance of the client from the welfare bureaucracy.

Moreover, the life risks that have occurred are usually paid off in the *form of monetary compensation*. In such cases as reaching retirement or losing a job, the typical consequent problems and changes in life situation cannot as a rule be subjected to consumerist redefinition (for the development of a similar view see Preuß supra on "distributive" rights). To balance the inadequacy of these system conforming compensations, *social services* have been set up which give *therapeutic assistance*.

With this, however, the contradictions of welfare state intervention are only reproduced at a higher level. The form of the administratively prescribed treatment by an expert is for the most part in contradiction with the aim of the therapy, namely, that of promoting the client's independence and self-reliance. "... the process of providing social services takes on a reality of its own, nurtured above all by the professional competence of the public official, the framework of administrative action, biographical and current 'states of mind', the readiness and ability to cooperate of the person seeking the service or being subjected to it. In these areas too there remain problems connected with a class-specific utilisation of such services, with the assignments made by the courts, the prison system and other offices, and with the appropriate location and arrangement of the services within the network of bureaucratic organizations of the welfare state; but beyond this, such forms of physical, psycho-social and emancipatory aid really require modes of operation, rationality criteria and organizational forms that are foreign to bureaucratically structured administration" (Reidegeld, 1980: 281).

The ambivalence of the last juridification thrust, that of the social welfare state, is shown with particular clarity in the paradoxical consequences of the social services, which are really a therapeutocracy. This extends from the prison system through medical treatment of the mentally ill, of addicts and of the behaviourally disturbed: through the classical forms of social work and the newer psychotherapeutic and group dynamic forms of support, of pastoral care and the formation of religious groups, and goes as far as youth work, public education and the health system and general preventive measures of every type. To the degree that the welfare state goes beyond the pacification of class conflict arising in the immediate sphere of production and spreads a network of cliental relationships over the spheres of private life spheres, the more strongly appear the anticipated pathological side-effects of a juridification, simultaneously signifying a bureaucratization and a monetarization of core areas of the lifeworld. The *dilemmatic structure of this type of juridification* consists in the fact that, while the welfare state guarantees are intended to serve the goal of social integration, they nevertheless promote the disintegration of life relations. These become separated, through legalized social intervention, from the consensual mechanisms that coordinate action, and are displaced into such media as power and money. In this sense, R. Pitschas speaks of the crisis of public welfare policy as a crisis of social integration[2]. (Cf. this view with Aubert and Friedman supra).

For an empirical analysis of these phenomena, it is important to clarify the criteria on the basis of which the aspects of guarantee and withdrawal of freedom can be separated. From the legal viewpoint the first thing that presents itself is the classical division of fundamental rights into liberties and participatory rights; one might presume that the structure of bourgeois formal law becomes dilemmatic precisely when these means are no longer used to negatively demarcate areas of private discretion, but are supposed to provide positive guarantees of membership and participation in institutions and benefits (see also Aubert supra on promotional function of law). If this presumption were proved true, then indeed one would already have to expect a change from the guarantee to the denial of freedom at the third (democratizing) juridification thrust and not only at the fourth, social state thrust. There are indeed indications that the *organization of the exercise of civil liberties* considerably restricts the possibilities for spontaneous opinion formation and discursive will formation through a segmentation

[2] "In the area where Rechtsstaat and Sozialstaat meet, social policy which uses an "active" social intervention through state organization of freedom threatens to overwhelm the individual's right to help himself. The state benefit system thereby not only dissolves the distribution of responsibilities between state and society. By its shaping of social benefits, it moulds *whole patterns of life*. If the citizen's life is insured in legalized form agains *all* vicissitudes, from before birth to after death, as the law of the survivor's pension system teaches, then the individual fits himself into these social shells of his existence; he lives his life free of material worries, but simultaneously suffering through an excess of state provision from a kind of fear at their loss". See Pitschas (1980: 155).

of the voter's role, through the competition of leadership elites, through vertical opinion formation in bureaucratically encrusted party apparatuses, through autonomized parliamentary bodies, through communication networks etc. that become distorted by power. But such arguments cannot be used to deduce aspects of withdrawal of freedom from the very *form* of participatory rights, but only from the bureaucratic ways and means of their *implementation*. The unambiguously freedom-guaranteeing character of the *principle* of universal suffrage can hardly be disputed and these include also freedom of assembly, of the press and of opinion – which, under conditions of modern mass communication, must also be interpreted in the sense of democratic participatory rights.

A different criterion, more socio-legal in nature and capable of social-theoretic interpretation, takes us further: that is, the classification of legal norms according to whether they can be legitimized only through procedure in the positivist sense, or are capable of substantive justification. If the legitimacy of a legal norm is brought into question, it is, in many cases, sufficient to refer to the formally correct genesis of the law, judicial decision or administrative act. Legal positivism has conceptualised this as legitimation through procedure, though of course, without seeing that this mode of legitimation is insufficient in itself, but merely points to the legitimizing state authorities' need of justification. However, in the face of the changing and steadily increasing volume of positive law, modern legal subjects content themselves in actual practice with legitimation through procedure, for in many cases substantive justification is not only not possible, but is also, from the viewpoint of the lifeworld, meaningless. This is true of all cases where the *law* serves as a *means for organizing media-controlled subsystems* which have, in any case, become autonomous vis-à-vis the normative contexts of action oriented towards reaching understanding. Most areas of economic, commercial, company and administraive law are significant here: the law is combined with the media of power and money in such a way that it itself takes on the role of a *steer*ing medium. *Law as a medium*, however, remains bound up with *the law as an institution*. By legal *institutions* I mean legal norms that cannot be sufficiently legitimized by the positivistic reference to procedure. Typical of these are the bases of constitutional law, the principles of criminal law and penal procedure, and all regulation of those criminal offences close to morality (e.g. murder, abortion, rape etc.). As soon as the validity of *these* norms is questioned in everyday practice, the reference to their legality no longer suffices. They need substantive justification, because they belong to the legitimate orders of the lifeworld itself and, together with the informal norms of conduct, form the background of communicative action.

We have characterized modern law through a combination of statutory and justificatory principles. This structure simultaneously makes possible the positivistic prolongation of the methods of justificatory reasoning and the moralizing intensification of the justification problematic, which is shifted into the foundations. We can now see how the decoupling of system and lifeworld fits into this legal structure. Law used as a control mechanism is relieved of the problem of justification and is only connected through formally correct procedures with the body of law whose substance requires legitimation. As against this, legal institutions belong to the social components of the lifeworld. Like the other norms of conduct not covered by sanction authority of the state they can become moralized under appropriate circumstances. Admittedly, changed bases of legitimation do not directly affect the stock of legal norms; but they may provide the impetus for a legal (or, in the limiting case, a revolutionary) change in existing law.

As long as the law functions as a complex medium, bound up with money and power, it extends to formally organized domains of action which, as such, are directly constituted in the forms of bourgeois formal law. Against this, legal institutions have no *constitutive* power, but only a *regulative* function. They are embedded in a broader political, cultural and social context; they stand in a continuum with moral norms and remould communicatively structured areas of action; they give the already informally constituted domains of action a binding form backed by state sanctions. From these viewpoints, we can also distinguish processes of juridification according to whether they are linked to the antecedent institutions of the lifeworld and juridically remould socially integrated areas of action, or whether they merely increase the density of the legal relationships that are constitutive of systemically integrated areas of action. Here, the question of the appropriate mode of legitimation may serve as a first test. The technicized and de-moralized areas of law that grow along with the complexity of the economic and administrative system, must be evaluated with regard to functional imperatives and in accordance with higher-order norms. Looked at historically, the continuous increase in statutory law mostly falls into this category and simply indicates increased recourse to the medium of law. The epochal juridification thrusts are, on the other hand, characterized by *new legal institutions*, which are also reflected in the legal consciousness of everyday practice. Only with respect to this second category of juridification do questions of normative evaluation arise.

The first juridification thrust had a freedom-guaranteeing character to the extent that bourgeois civil law and a bureaucratic domination exercised by legal means at least meant emancipation from premodern power and dependence relations. The three subsequent juridification thrusts guaranteed an increase in freedom to the extent that they were able to tie down, in the interest of the citizens and of private legal subjects, the political and economic dynamics which had been released by the legal institutionalization of the media of money and power. The step-by-step development towards the social and constitutional democratic state is directed against those modern relations of power and dependence that arose with the capitalist enterprise, with the bureaucratic apparatus of domination and, more generally, with the formally organized domains of action of the economy and the state. The self-dynamic of these action systems also takes place in the organizational forms of law, but in such a way that law here takes on the role of a steering medium and does not supplement the institutional components of the lifeworld.

In its role as a medium, existing law can be more or less functional; but beyond the horizon of the lifeworld it is meaningless to question the freedom-guaranteeing or freedom-reducing character of norms. The ambivalence of guarantee/withdrawal of freedom cannot be reduced to a dialectic between law as an institution and law as a medium, because the alternative between guarantee and withdrawal of freedom is posed only from the viewpoint of the lifeworld, i.e. only in relation to legal institutions.

So far we have proceeded on the assumption that law is used as a medium only within formally organized domains of action, and that as a steering medium it remains indifferent vis-à-vis the lifeworld and to the questions of substantive justification that arise within its horizons. Welfare-state interventionism has since rendered this assumption invalid. Public welfare policy has to use the law precisely as a medium in order to regulate those exigencies that arise in communicatively structured action areas. To be sure, the principle of social participation and of social compensation is, like freedom of association, a constitutionally anchored institution, informally attached to the legitimate order of the modern lifeworld. But social-welfare law, through which social compensation is implemented differs from, for instance, the laws governing collective bargaining, through which freedom of association becomes effective in one important respect: measures of social-welfare law, (as a rule, compensatory payments) do not, like collective wage and salary agreements, intervene in an area that is *already* formally organized. Rather, they regulate exigencies which, as lifeworld situations belong to a communicatively structured action area. Thus, I should like to explain the type of reification effects that can be shown in the example of public welfare policy by the fact that the *legal institutions* that guarantee social compensation become effective only through *social-welfare law used as a medium*. From the standpoint of action theory, the paradox of this legal structure can be explained as follows: as a medium, social-welfare law is tailored to domains of action that are first constituted in legal forms of organization and that can be held together only by systemic mechanism. At the same time, however, social-welfare law extends to situations embedded in informal lifeworld contexts.

In our context government welfare policy serves only as an illustration. The thesis of internal colonialization states that the subsystems of economy and state become more and more complex as a consequence of capitalist growth, and penetrate ever more deeply into the symbolic reproduction of the lifeworld. It should be possible to test this thesis sociologically wherever the traditionalist padding of capitalist modernization has worn through and central areas of cultural reproduction, social integration and socialization become drawn undisguisedly into the wake of economic growth and, therefore, of juridification. This applies not only to such themes as ecological conservation, nuclear reactor security, data protection and the like, which have been successfully dramatized in the public sphere. The trend towards juridification of informally regulated spheres of the lifeworld is gaining ground along a broad front — the more leisure, culture, recreation and tourism recognisably come into the grip of the laws of the commodity economy and the definitions of mass consumption, the more the structures of the bourgeois family clearly become adapted to the imperatives of the employment system, the more the school manifestly takes over the functions of assigning job and life prospects etc.

The structure of juridification is characterized in school and family law by ambivalences similar to those in the area of social-welfare law. In the Federal Republic of Germany these problems, which dominate discussions of legal policy, have been worked out for particular aspects of the development of school (Laaser, 1980; Richter, 1973; 1974) and family law (Simitis *et al.*, 1975; Finger, 1979; Beitzke, 1979). In both cases juridification means, in the first place, *enforcement of constitutional principles*: the recognition of the fundamental rights of the child against his parents, of the wife against her husband, of the pupil against the school, and of the parents, teachers and pupils against the state school administration. Under the headings of "equal opportunity" and "the welfare of the child" the authoritarian position of the paterfamilias, still anchored in, among others, matrimonial-property law in the German Civil Code, is being dismantled in favour of a more equal distribution of the competencies and entitlements of other family members. To the juridification of this traditional, economically-grounded, patriarchal power relation in the family, there corresponds, on the part of the school, the constitutionalization of the special power relation that persisted into the 1950s between government bureaucracy and school. While the core areas of family law (marriage, maintenance, matrimonial property, divorce, parental care and guardianship) have been reformed through courts and legislature the bringing of the school under the rule of law, i.e. the legal regulation of areas outside the law, as specified in the official prerogatives of the schools, was initially stimulated by case law and then carried forward by the government educational bureaucracy through administrative channels (Laaser, 1980: 1357). The bureaucracy had to ensure that educational procedures and school measures, as far as they were relevant to the pupil's later life and the parents' wishes, took on a form in which they were accessible to judicial review. It is only more recently that the judiciary has called up on the legislature to act so as to guide the overflowing bureaucratic juridification into statutory channels (Laaser, 1980: 1357).

The expansion of legal protection and the enforcement of fundamental rights in family and school called for a high degree of differentiation of specific legal conditions, exceptions and legal consequences. In this way, these domains of action are opened up to bureaucratic intervention and judicial control. In no way are family and school formally organized spheres of action. Were they, *at root*, already constituted in legal form, the densification of legal norms could lead to a redistribution of money and power without altering the basis of social relations. In fact, however, in these spheres of the lifeworld there exist, *before any* juridification, norms and contexts of action that from functional necessity are based on communication as a coordinating mechanism. Juridification of these spheres means, therefore, not the densification of an already existing network of formal regulations, but rather legally supplementing a communicative context of action through the superimposition of legal norms, albeit not through legal institutions but through law as a medium.

The formalization of relationships in family and school means, for those concerned, an objectivization and *removal from the lifeworld* of the (now) formally-regulated social interaction in family and school. As legal subjects they encounter one another in an objectivizing success-oriented attitude. Simitis describes the complementary role played by the law in socially integrated areas of action: "Family law *supplements* a morally secured system of social rules of conduct, and to that extent is strictly complementary" (Simitis, Zenz; 1975a: 48). The same is true of the school. Just as the socialization process in the family *exists prior to* and conditions legal norms, so too does the pedagogical process of teaching. These formative processes in family and school, which take place via communicative action, must be able to function independently of legal regulation. If, however, the structure of juridification requires administrative and judicial controls which do not merely *supplement* socially integrated contexts with legal institutions but *convert* them to the medium of law, then functional disturbances arise. This is the action-theoretic explanation for the negative effects of juridification stressed in juristic and socio-legal discussions.

Simitis and his collaborators have have carried out empirical research on the dilemmatic structure of the juridification of the family in connection with child custody laws (Simitis *et al.*, 1979; Zenz, 1979). The group has concentrated on the decision-making practices of wardship courts. The protection of the welfare of the child as a fundamental right can be implemented only by giving the state possibilities to intervene in the privileges of parents, once regarded as untouchable. It was the dialectic of this juridification that inspired Simitis to undertake his study:

However indispensable state services may be, they not only bring advantages for individual family members, but simultaneously bring about increasing dependence. Emancipation within the family is achieved at the cost of a new bond. In order to constitute himself as a person, the individual family member sees himself compelled to make claims on the assistance of the state. What, therefore, at first sight is sometimes presented as an instrument for breaking up domination structures within the family, proves on closer examination to be also a vehicle of another form of dependence (Simitis, Zenz, 1975a: 40).

The study shows that the wardship judges surveyed gave judgment on a basis of insufficient information, orienting themselves predominantly towards the child's "physical" rather than "spiritual" well-being. The proven psychological shortcomings of judicial decision-making practice result, however, not so much from an inadequate professional training of jurists for this task, as from a juristic formalization of situations that require a *different type* of treatment

Initiatives ... to ascertain the facts or to suggest better ways of resolving conflicts are scarcely to be found. There are perhaps reasons for this on the side of the parents themselves; but it is also a result of their position in respect to the legal process which tends to turn them into "objects" of negotiation between the judge and the youth-welfare office and thus to make, them 'subordinated subjects of the proceedings' rather than 'participants' in them (Simitis *et al.*, 1979: 39).

In almost all cases one can see "how little the judge is able to accomplish with his specifically juridicial means, whether it is the question of the communication with the child that is essential for the proceedings, or of understanding the factors important to the child's development" (Simitis, Zenz, 1975a: 55). It is the medium of the law itself that violates the communicative structures of the sphere that has been juridified.

From this viewpoint, one can understand the legal-policy recommendation that the legislator should restrict to a minimum the state interventions necessary to protect children's rights. "Among the various possible solutions, the one to be preferred is that which leaves the judge the least amount of discretion in taking decisions. Legislative regulation, therefore, ought not to favour far-reaching judicial intervention, as has hitherto increasingly been the case. On the contrary, it must first and foremost, do everything possible to de-judicialize the conflict" (Simitis, Zenz, 1975a: 51).

Of course, replacing the judge by the therapist is no panacea. The social worker is only a *different* expert, who does not free the client of the welfare state bureaucracy from his position as an object. The re-modelling of wardship law in a therapeutic direction would merely accelerate the assimilation of family law to child welfare law:

In this para-law of the family, it is a governmental authority, the Division of Child Welfare, which sets the tone. Here child-rearing takes place under state supervision, and parents are held accountable for it. The language, particularly of many older commentaries, shows better than any regulation what the goal is. State intervention compensates for disrupted normality (Simitis, Zenz 1975a: 36).

Nevertheless, the intuition that underlies the paradoxical proposal to de-judicialize juridified family conflict is instructive: the juridification of communicatively structured areas of action ought not to go beyond the enforcement of principles of the rule of law; beyond the legal institutionalization of its *external* constitution, be it of the family or of the school. The place of law as a medium must be replaced by procedures for settling conflicts that are appropriate to the structures of action oriented towards communication – discursive processes of will-formation and consensus-oriented procedures of negotiation and decision-making. This demand may seem more or less acceptable for private realms like the family, and it may well be in line with the educational orientations specific to the middle class. For a public realm like the school, the analogous demand for de-judicialization and de-bureaucratization meets with resistance[3]. The call for more strictly pedagogical approach to instruction and for a democratization of decision-making structures is not immediately compatible with the neutralization of the citizens' role (Scheuner, 1973: 61), and still less with the economic system's imperative to decouple the school system from the fundamental right to education and to close-circuit it with the employment system. From the perspective of social theory, the present controversy concerning the basic orientations of school policy can be understood as a fight for or against the colonialization of the lifeworld. However, I want to confine myself to the analytical level of juridification; and this manifests itself no less ambivalently in the school than in family.

The protection of pupils' and parents' rights against educational measures (such as promotion examinations and tests, and so forth), or from acts of the school or the department of education that restrict fundamental rights (disciplinary penalties), is bought at the expense of a judicialization and bureaucratization that penetrates deeply into the teaching and learning process. On the one hand, responsibility for problems of educational policy and school law overstrains government agencies in a similar way as the responsibility for the child's welfare overstrains the wardship courts. On the other hand, the medium of the law comes into collision with the form of educational activity. Socialization in schools becomes broken up into a mosaic of legally contestable administrative acts. Subsuming education under the medium of law brings about the "abstract grouping together of those involved in the educational process as individualized legal subjects in a system of achievement and competition. The abstractness consists in the fact that the norms of school law apply without consideration of the persons concerned, of their needs and interests, cutting off their experiences and splitting up their life relationships" (Frankenberg, 1978: 217). This must endanger the pedagogical freedom and initiative of the teacher. Compulsion towards litigation-proof certainty of grades and over-reg-

[3] In this connection L.R. Reuter speaks of a "reconstruction of the educational mission in the educational responsibility of the pedagogical institutions". See Reuter (1980: 130).

ulation of the curriculum, lead to such phenomena as depersonalization, inhibition of innovation, breakdown of responsibility, immobility and so forth (Reuter, 1980: 126). Frankenberg has studied the consequences of the juridification of teaching practice from the viewpoint of how teachers, as norm addressees, perceive the demands of law and react to them.

There are structural differences between the legal form in which courts and school administrations exercise their powers, on the one hand and an educational task which can be accomplished by way of action oriented to reaching understanding on the other. Frankenberg captures these differences well.

> We can take as dominant characteristics of the political-legal dimension of the teaching task: (1) a discrepancy between behavioural prescriptions and concrete action situations (2) a two-fold protection for the governmental "educational mandate", through the school administration's responsibility for setting guidelines, and through the authority of administrative courts to interpret and specify general norms; (3) an unclear demarcation of the teacher's pedagogic scope for action; and (4) the possible threats, whether open or disguised, of sanctions for behaviour that conflicts with the norms. To the opacity of the normative complex school law this adds the incalculability of the normative demands that are decisive for educational practice (Frankenberg, 1978: 227).

These structural differences leave the teacher insecure and evoke reactions that Frankenberg describes as over- or under-utilization of the pedagogical scope of action — that is, as over-attention to or concealed disobedience of the law.

The constitutionalization of the special power relation of the school removes some relics of absolutist state power. However, the normative remoulding of this communicatively structured action area is accomplished in the form of social-welfare state-interventionist regulations. Controlled by the judiciary and the administration, the school changes inperceptibly into a welfare institution that organizes and distributes schooling as a social benefit. As in the case of the family, the result for legal policy is the call to de-judicialize and above all to de-bureaucratize the pedagogical process. The framework of a school constitution under the rule of law, which transposes "the private law of the state into a genuinely public law", should be filled, not by the medium of law, but through consensus-oriented procedures for conflict resolution — through "decision-making procedures that treat those involved in the pedagocial process as having the capacity to represent their own interests and to regulate their affairs themselves [4]."

If one studies the paradoxical structure of juridification in such areas as the family, the school, social-welfare policy and the like, the meaning of the demands that regularly result from these analyses its easy to decipher.

[4] See Frankenberg (1978: 248); this is also the direction taken by the draft of a provincial law put forward by the Schulrechtskommission of the Deutscher Juristentag: (1981, Vol. I).

The point is to protect areas of life that are functionally dependent on social integration through values, norms and consensus formation; and to protect them from falling prey to the system imperatives of economic and administrative subsystems that grow with dynamics of their own. And finally to defend them from becoming converted, through the steering medium of the law, to a principle of socialization which is, for them, dysfunctional.

References

BEITZKE, Günther (1979) *Familienrecht*. München: Beck.

BÖCKENFÖRDE, Ernst, W. (1976) "Entstehung und Wandel des Rechtsstaatsbegriffs", E. Böckenförde, *Staat, Gesellschaft, Freiheit*. Frankfurt a. M.: Suhrkamp.

BOLDT, Hans (1975) *Deutsche Staatslehre im Vormärz*. Düsseldorf: Droste.

SCHULRECHTSKOMMISSION DES DEUTSCHEN JURISTENTAGS (1981) "Schule im Rechtsstaat", in Deutscher Juristentag (ed.), vol. I. München: Beck.

FERBER, Christian v. (1967) *Sozialpolitik in der Wohlstandsgesellschaft*. Hamburg: Wegner.

FINGER, Peter (1979) *Familienrecht mit familiensoziologischen und familienpolitischen Schwerpunkten*. Königstein/Ts: Athenäum.

FRANKENBERG, Günther (1978) "Elemente einer Kritik und Theorie des Schuldrechts". Dissertation, Department of Law, University of München.

GUILDIMANN, T., U. RODENSTEIN, U. ROEDEL, and F. STILLE (1978) *Sozialpolitik als soziale Kontrolle*. Frankfurt a. M.

LASSER, A. (1980) "Die Verrechtlichung des Schulwesens", in Projektgruppe Bildungsbericht (ed.), *Bildung in der BRD*. Hamburg.

MAUSS, Ingeborg (1978) "Entwicklung und Funktionswandel der Theorie des bürgerlichen Rechtsstaates", in Mehdi Tohidipur (ed.), *Der bürgerliche Rechtsstaat*, Vol. I. Frankfurt a. M.: Suhrkamp.

NEUMANN, Franz (1980) *Die Herrschaft des Gesetzes*. Frankfurt a. M.: Suhrkamp.

PITSCHAS, Rainer (1980) "Soziale Sicherung durch fortschreitende Verrechtlichung", in R. Voigt (ed.), *Verrechtlichung*. Königstein/Ts: Athenäum.

PREUß, Ulrich K. (1980) "Der Staat und die indirekten Gewalten", Lecture at the Berlin Hobbes Colloquium, 12—14. 10. 1980.

REIDEGELD, Eckart (1980) "Vollzugsdefizite sozialer Leistungen", in R. Voigt (ed.), *Verrechtlichung*. Königstein/Ts: Athenäum.

REUTER, Lutz-R. (1980) "Bildung zwischen Politik und Recht", in R. Voigt (ed.), *Verrechtlichung*. Königstein/Ts: Athenäum.

RICHTER, Ingo (1973) *Bildungsverfassungsrecht*. Stuttgart: Beltz.

— (1974) *Grundgesetz und Schulreform*. Weinheim: Beltz.

SCHEUNER, Ulrich (1973) *Das Mehrheitsprinzip in der Demokratie*. Opladen: Westdeutscher Verlag.

SIMITIS, Spiros, and Gisela ZENZ (eds.) (1975a) *Familie und Familienrecht*, Vol. I. Frankfurt a. M.: Suhrkamp.

— (1975b) *Familie und Familienrecht*, Vol. II. Frankfurt a. M.: Suhrkamp.

SIMITIS, Spiros (1979) *Kindeswohl*. Frankfurt a. M.: Suhrkamp.

STAHL, Friedrich J. (1963) *Die Philosophie des Rechts*, Vol. II. Hildesheim: Olms.

VOIGT, Rüdiger (1980) "Verrechtlichung in Staat und Wirtschaft", R. Voigt (ed.), *Verrechtlichung*, Königstein/Ts: Athenäum.

ZENZ, Gisela (1979) *Kindesmisshandlung und Kindesrecht*. Frankfurt a. M.: Suhrkamp.

Materialization and Proceduralization in Modern Law*

RUDOLF WIETHÖLTER
Frankfurt

This is a subject which lends itself to wordplay. The classical (civil law) formal law was ultimately substantive as a philosophy of freedom, and as a directive programme, oriented for its realization towards proceduralization. Moreover, there can simply be no materialization without form and without procedure. In order to keep my use of terms more or less clear from the start, I shall briefly outline the problem to be examined.

It concerns rationality of law as rationality of society: rationality understood as justice of the society in which one lives, and which is appropriate to its development. "*Proceduralization*" of law is, for me, a problem of the *justification of collision rules* as the institution of bindingness. This bindingness always relates both to a *thing as content* (= materialization) and to *conflict rules as form*. The very diverse usages in language, above all the transformations in language use, are, of course, determined by the material differences between law and social theories. My thesis is that from the "social science point of view", each individual (the human being as human being) who in the law, or at least in "civil" law, has the major role, does not exist (for differing views on the theoretical status of the individual see Ewald, Broekman, Heller supra). But it is not merely "legally" that living men defend themselves against the diverse presumptions of sociological reconstruction. For the law is (or at least was) connected with relatively eternal dreams and revelations such as justice or as liberty—equality—fraternity (in Germany now more fashionably seen as: liberty—justice—solidarity). Proceduralization may be a way of saving such promises and simultaneously of enduring the coldness of modernity while enjoying its fruits.

I shall first of all identify the problem (I), then outline a few developments and backgrounds (II), and finally deal in particular with the category of "proceduralization" (III).

* Translated from the German by Iain Fraser.

I.

1. In order to bring to mind the original conceptual unity between the formality, materiality and procedurality of law (at least of German civil law) I shall summarize an analysis of it as follows.

(i) "*Politically*", the presupposed and maintained separation of "state" and "society" is a guarantee of coexistence (politics, state) in peace (law, freedom). The state is a means to the goal of the realization of law as "certainty of freedom under law": universal, equal and definite law, publicity and private autonomy form its core elements and all individual legal categories (the prototypical examples are legal contract and administrative act) are rooted in it.

(ii) "*Economically*", competition on the market invisibly controls the inter-twining of consumption and production: the legal core element is the contract.

(iii) "*Socially*", the "civil" position is dependent on "having" (as a guarantee of lasting identification): "property" is the central legal category.

(iv) "*Scientifically*", explanatory programmes (decoupled from their preconditions) apply, relating to generalizable law-governed regularities as the essence of modern and progress-guaranteeing modes of work; "positivism" aims at the disclosing of the factual, of the given, of reality, rather than at metaphysical meaning or prophetic action.

(v) "*social psychology*" (cultural anthropology), gives "justice" and "prudence", basic categories originating in Scottish 18th-century moral philosophy, which represent the essence of conditions under which social identity can manage to "function" as free action under (legal) framework rules and as responsibility-related ("prudent", "proper", "appropriate") utilization of the freedom of manoeuvre.

On the whole, the citizen as voter (owner) and as consumer thus dominates the scene of political sociology, so that parliamentary legislation, market competition, contract and bankruptcy form the legal procedural centres. Consensus and normality (homogeneity) are here both the premises and the results of regulated social life. All forms of opposition (discontent) are reducible on these bases to intellectual (public) debate and commercial (market-oriented) competition as modes of permissible conflict. Constitutional law sets up the programme for a given — always provisional — period. The citizen as producer (worker, entrepreneur) belongs to the fundamental model only indirectly and at any rate not as a direct pillar of the system. His position is marked in the 19th century by "labour law" and "economic law". Since then constitutional law transforms itself into the welfare constitution that embraces both work and the economy. To the extent that there is inner social conflict, increasing pressure of problems, and rivalling authority claims, peaceful social relations are "re-politicized". The key problem becomes — and, not today for the first time, — the presumability (restorability) of fundamental consensus on goal orientations, modes of procedure, organizational forms, institutional forms of "peaceful coexistence" (nationally and internationally). Is "rational identity" (still) possible for a complex society? What share does "law" retain?

In the programme of law sketched out, law — in accordance with its self-conception — forms the decisive structure of society. Civil society is (as a private-law society = state under the rule of law) the installed and exercised (social, philosophical and historical) legal programme. From — or more exactly, as — natural law, law becomes positive.

2. A comparatively precise analysis of contemporary law is nowhere available. For a view of the extent of the changes and the rival efforts applying to them, I make use of the work of Franz Wieacker (Formalismus und Naturalismus in der neueren Rechtswissenschaft, Festschrift H. Coing, 1982, I, p 703—713), whose sovereignty in this field guarantees valid information in however abbreviated a summary. A brief reconstruction of Wieacker's analysis would be as follows:

a) Formalism: Imanuel Kant's ethics of freedom has remained, through/in Savigny's private law, confined to property law.

b) Naturalism: the following have asserted themselves as the three most powerful reform movements in modern German jurisprudence:

i) the modern penal law school (goal-oriented thinking)
ii) the liberal-law school (*Freirechtsschule*)
iii) interest jurisprudence (as a happy mixture of utilitarianism and obedience to law).

c) Relationship between formalism and naturalism: they are warring brothers representing two sides of a coin; both are decoupled from a legitimation of the law through pre-positive, general and substantive justice.

d) More modern approaches: all present legal theories aim at objectivisable criteria of justice:

i) unsuccessfully: pre-critical natural law; idealistic legal philosophy; institutional theory; material value ethics; neo-Hegelianism.
ii) unsuccessfully: logical empiricism; analytical linguistic theory.
iii) relatively successful rivals today: (a) the justification of projects on justice on the basis of social regulatory function ("systems theories") with "procedures" as their core; (b) justification of justice projects by social recognition ("practical legal philosophy") with, as their core, "consensus" and "communication".

Wieacker, whose inclinations evidently tend towards practical philosophy, closes on a sceptical note. In all camps of practical legal philosophy, questions of practical action are regarded as decidable by scientific means (viz. rational justification); though this conceals two unstated assumptions, firstly, an open society which would at all admit "discourse" and for another thing the expectation that social action could at all be motivated on the basis of practical reason.

3. In Wieacker, the unease in (and about) legal culture is quite unmistakable. Karl Marx was still confident in the eudaemonic, teleological hope of lasting satisfaction for all people equally; of reconciliation between (achieved) culture and (yet to be achieved) identity of interests. He therefore held the fundamental questions of political economy to be scientifically (that is to say, compelling acceptance) decidable.

In Max Weber's view however, since he no longer believed that the interests of people were reconcilable, there could be no reconcilability of culture (ideas) and needs. He therefore placed his (very limited) hopes in the bonds between those governmental and economic bureaucracies which had an awareness of their responsibilities. Social theory programmes have since striven towards a critical, constructive combination and/or transcendence of Marx and Weber. Programmes of so-called "critical theory" have so far regarded harmonies of interests *and* culture ("in the given circumstances") as unattainable, and consequently regarded revolutionary changes as historically legitimized and worth fighting for in practical politics. Such programmes have thus so far regarded such goals as never attainable anywhere: since all fundamental changes lead to unforeseeable and thus unjustifiable consequences, only medium-term strategies can be justified on the basis of experience to date. The approaches used by the other programmes have until now been regarded by programmes of so-called "systems theories" as over-burdened by "old Europeanism" and as unmodern, so that they have primarily aimed at developing more radical, more abstract, more indirect approaches (and only secondarily at institutionalizations and organizational forms). It seems that these alternative social theories and scientific methodologies, philosophies of action and systems sociologies have since become exhausted by prolonged trench warfare and that truces are being aimed at by way of more complex, longer term and more fundamental (and therefore also more reflexive) reorientations.

I go along with these efforts which use the categories of "proceduralization" (relating more narrowly to projects that are still action theory approaches) and "functionalizations" (relating more narrowly to projects that instead make exclusively systems theory approaches).

To such projects can be presented (if I am permitted this simplification as a stylistic recourse) as voters (owners) and as comsumers those sovereign ideal model citizens who once "constitutionalized" our law and today can be classified as "voters" needing interest representation and chances of identification; as "welfare clients' looking for care and protection; as "workers" looking — increasingly, even unsuccessfully — for work; as "consumers" demanding not only goods and services but also relief and need dispositions. At any rate it is no wonder that here legal formalizations provide stones instead of bread: though admittedly, to stay with this image, legal materializations might lead more to bread and circuses than to the "good life" and "just order", and legal proceduralizations and legal functionalizations are primarily only a means of diversion.

II.

In order to briefly sketch out the development and background of legal formation to date, I shall draw together a few associations.

1. Since the nineteenth century, a shift to social practice has taken place. This is, in turn, due to the fruitful insight that a (more exactly any) search for philosophical ultimate justifications as recognizable and practicable social theories – along the lines of classical speculation on overall orientations, from the same mould and binding for all – must necessarily and permanently remain hopeless, or at least unsuccessful in practice. According to the general recent trend, that now abandoned search should be replaced by historically teachable, i. e. practically fruitful, social theory; as learning social systems that prove themselves ever anew; as a shift from ideal rational systems to learning social systems; as a shift from causality to functionality; as a shift from theory to practice; as a shift from traditional transcendental subjects (God, absolute spirit, true nature of man etc.) or revolutionary classes (feudal, bourgeois, proletarian revolution etc.) to theoretical social sciences with directly practical conditions of application and effects of application. With the alleged achievement of "rational", i. e. consciously of this world, finite, historical, "real" and "positive" sociology (with society understood no longer as "nature", but as a social process in (system) contexts of action), there has been combined a simultaneous social process of crisis-ridden reference orientations of "theory" and "history" as determination of the relationship between philosophy, science, methodology, morals, practice and real system contexts of social stability and social change. Since the characterization of these modern (i. e. bourgeois, emancipatory, circular and pluralist) societies is their stable, lasting condition of change, a situation can today be described in which all efforts (right and left) are directed at the strategic task of longer term definitions of problems, so that capacities, machinery and procedures to deal with the problems can be plausibly and successfully set up and correspondingly translated into "constitution" and into "law". In traditional political language, the point is whether and how a "conflict" is conceivable and achievable between normative structures (i. e., to be historically specific – a bourgeois society as a "revolutionary" movement towards the complete meeting of its programmatic promises) and real functions (i. e., being

historically specific — a bourgeois society as an instituted, exercised, organized late capitalist industrial society). Conceivable and achievable in the language of categories: "logic" and "history" is a (conceptual) unity of social motion which, mediated through consciousness, tends to impose itself (this formula being short for "laws of history"). Its possibility, and thereby the possibility of a socio-historical law of development, is dominated above all by the complexity of the pressure of historical problems and the extent of the system crises that arise.

2. The characteristic, and the learning problem, of modern societies then, is their stable condition of permanent change. However, this is no longer so much oriented towards and involved in directions of change which are rivals and therefore decidable (and that always means "politicisable", i. e. coming under values, norms and programmes that still have to be defined (implemented)), rather it is much more strongly concerned with tendencies dangerous to the social system, which needs interpretation and is therefore structured (and that always means "legalised", i. e. coming under values, norms and programmes that are already defined (implemented)).

3. Our traditional concept of law presupposes (and sanctions) the exercise of freedom by individuals (as legal subjects) under general prohibitionary rules: action through contract and under the protection of tort, penal and procedural law on the basis of guaranteed social positions. Current programmes of materialization of law (especially programmes that do not guarantee social positions but rather grant (realise, produce) them,) are by contrast dependent — the more specific the more complex and productive they are (if the goals are set entirely abstractly, nothing changes) — on implementation of each programme by a continuous administration (instead of controls through occasional legal pronouncements, as in formalised legal programmes). A transition in principle from legal guarantee to political provision of social positions, which strikes to the root of the category of law, involves "legally" constituted societies in momentous system crises. From the rationality patterns via the institutionally organised procedures to the training and orientation of the problem-solving elites, not one stone is left in place. Here are the reasons why, most recently, legal programmes — beyond both formalization and materialization — have increasingly been reoriented towards proceduralization or, more exactly, aimed not at social guarantees (as "rights to freedom"), nor at provisions (as "political administration"), but at the conditions for the existence (and then organisation, procedure, implementing personnel) of such guarantees and provisions (as "reflexive", learning social systems). The consequences for substantive programmes, organisational forms or professional socialization are often less apparent here than are the social areas in which the problems manifest themselves.

4. The perceptible changes penetrate deep into the world of legal categories and can probably be understood only as changes in the legal structure itself (for an opposite view see Broekman, Heller supra). On the whole, it is no longer possible to set up, for instance, the kind of prohibitionary rules whereby restrictions on freedom (of the State and in society itself) were traditionally to be identified as forbidden forms of conduct (and thus as guidelines for free, permitted behaviour). Relatedly, the basic structure always presupposed therein (namely that by appealing to regulatory reservations in favour of community interests, political arrangements assure the justification of interventions, measures and plans vis-a-vis "private" freedom) is itself affected by decay or at least transformation. The point is, no doubt, that "goals" are so interwoven, i. e. "private" and "social" goals so interpenetrate that, in consequence, framework regulations and implementation have to be justified along with each other; notably through the social sub-systems equipped with competences for this, e. g. the courts, firms, associations. But then "freedom", for instance, does not (any longer) mean autonomy within definite limits, but rather collaboration, which gives entitlements, in perceiving the necessity of such limits (for a similar view see Ewald 45 supra).

5. Part of the tradition of our legal culture is — as its paradigm — the idea that it is the law that through its norms binds social values (interests, preferences, positions). The opposing position — which I share — insists that even the highest (e. g. constitutional) norms are in turn determined by social value preferences. Somewhat more exactly, since freed from this — crudely put — false alternative: the prevailing position is dependent on a concept of legal order as (goal-free) action of men under rules (procedures). Its core legal category is the contract; its politico-economic sphere is "distribution"; its necessary precondition is social consensus on its untouchable fundamentals, which it must at least understand as second-best institution and exercise of life in society. The counter-position is dependent on a concept of legal order as bound action of men under goal-means and/or rule-exception projects (plans, programmes) for "society" itself. Its core legal category is the organization; its politico-economic sphere is "production"; its necessary preconditon is social consensus as to conceptions and as to the realization of a possibly better situation than the existing one, which is regarded to that extent as inferior. Each of these positions is linked to a complicated network of substantive premises (goals) and formal rules.

6. As lawyers, we stand between "norms" and "reality" or, more generally, between theories and objects (experiences, history, practice). The classical alternative conceptions here are on the one hand, rationalist ("norm" decides — centrally: "God" does not deceive/betray us); and on the other

empiricist ("reality" decides – centrally: "Nature" does not deceive/betray us). Of these there has remained, in the passage through idealist and materialist schools of philosophy in the 19th century under the banner of "positivism", only the problematic material, i. e., the old questions and a search for new answers. The major lines of development since simply cannot be sketched out here, even extremely briefly, and are in detail probably not so important. Let the following alternative programmes serve as signposts and milestones.

Analytical programmes split their object areas into object (substantive) levels and meta-(procedural) levels, thereby reducing meta-theories to methodologies. Ultimately, their concern is for intellectual concepts to order reality as material in relation to definite *preset* categories, values or ideas, and for academic work to deal exclusively with that ordering. Methodologically, such theories aim at the production of hypotheses, at the securing of law-governed explanations as the basis for predictions and technologies or strategies.

Synthetic programmes rest on the perceived unity of their object areas and work methods. Three clear trends are distinguishable.

a) *historical materialist programmes.* By virtue of their due appropriateness to reality, rational concepts are in *practice* the real reality itself, as a perceived unity of analysis and strategy (= social work). Methodologically, such theories aim at social movements which, mediated through consciousness, tend to prevail.

b) *system functionalist programmes.* Through abstractions and cyberneticisations of networks of relationships, the social "subjects" become lost in the "substances" of the complexity in need of reduction. All system variations (mutations) and selections are rooted in institutionally remembered history and in the organisation of decision-making competences. Methodologically, such theories aim at so-called functional equivalents for each problem-solving task.

c) *social-critical theory programmes.* Evolutionary concepts of late-capitalist societies deal with problems of the genesis and validity of social change and of social legitimation. Methodologically, such theories aim at negotiating on problems (solutions) as the basis for forming rules by those affected by such rules.

Of course, no analytical theory is radically disinterested in (substantive) objects and no synthetic theory independent of procedures. Today, almost all concern themselves – more or less clearly – with the system connection of (substantive) theory and (formal) methodology. The differences of principle could be more clearly seen if comparative judgments over the system as a whole could be made possible; with the total systems, as unity of theory and methodology, in each case acting in relation to society as "nature" and as "history". But how, through what "method" or "theory", can this type of general meta-system work be done? Classical philosophy mastered these problems too, with the concept of the "concept". "Concept", was originally understood as mediation between idea and system, between principles and institutions: a "whole" (essence) which corresponded to this mode of mediation in all its parts (phenomena), and simultaneously made definable a specifiable relationship of "top" and "bottom", of "aims" and "means"; which – in short – made rationality (in the classical sense of reference to any invariance) possible and necessary. This concept of the "concept" is also the basis of any "*conceptual jurisprudence*". The *concept of law* here is – irrespective of whether it is made explicit or not – a connection in legal theory and legal practice between "life", "society" and "law" as a unit of rational reality and realized reason. Until now jurisprudence has stuck to this concept despite repeated changes in its self-designations (conceptual jurisprudence; interest jurisprudence; evaluative jurisprudence etc.), and must do so if and as long as it wishes to maintain the claim to simultaneously guarantee "positive law" as right "law". This mixture is in fact nothing other than philosophy and history becoming "practical". Interest jurisprudence, evaluative jurisprudence (or indeed "free law") can escape this vicious circle only at the expense of giving themselves up.

7. With the change in perspective from "*history*" (i. e., translated into legal terms: solution of cases in accordance with "laws", given or to be made, as interpretive material (or more briefly, orientation towards "texts")) to "*society*" (translated into legal terms: solution of cases in accordance with "laws", maintained or to be maintained, as hypothetical material (or more briefly, orientation to "reality")), the methodological Wars of the Roses today being waged between "analytical" (methodological) and "dialectical-hermeneutic" (practical) conceptions of science are for the first time, and even tardily, invading jurisprudence too. My thesis on this is that legal theory deals with social contents only as "political" legal theory. All the differences lie in these contents and in the procedures; neither "natural or rational law" nor "conceptual jurisprudence" nor "legal positivism" nor "interest or evaluative jurisprudence" allow reliable approaches; these can only be attained through the "positivity" of law with an irrenounceable claim to realization of "right" law (as availability, changeable within "system" and "social" limits, of rules of procedure for the handling of problem material by lawyers) and the professionalization of lawyers (as social recruitment, socialisation through vocational training and professional practice of the producers of interpretations of "law").

The terms here are irrelevant. The core problem is a timeless relationship between legal *norms* and legal *concepts*, and it is only from their agreement that something like legal *pronouncements* in legal *cases* can be formed. It is not by chance that possible methodological answers here amount to concepts of substantively binding "value orders" as pre-suppositions, which everyone would then like to fill in in his own sense and with his own purposes. In the underlying constitutional theories, accordingly there are only two rival conceptions. For some, constitution is nothing but the supreme (pure) *legal norm* (legal order of politics). They have the advantage of being able to combine clear "principles" with clear "deductions", but have the disadvantage of no longer being competent in the overall relationship between "law" and "politics" (social reality). For others, constitution is a *political order* of law, admittedly with a very different material content of the political. They have the advantage of being able to *integrate* "law" and "reality", but the disadvantage of not being able to do without *substantive positions* ("values") in order to legitimize law. In the course of the history of the Weimar Republic and German Fascism, therefore, this constitutional alternative – not surprisingly – developed into that between suicidal legalism and homicidal decisionism. In traditional language, the constitutional context sketched out is described as the relationship between "substantive reason" (= *possibility* of a "proper", "true" reality of society) and "social domination" (= "*reality*" of a society that is "rational" or else "irrational" in the light of such proper, true possibilities). In old European society, the problem was taken as solved; as being already brought to a harmonious constitution. Since Enlightenment philosophy it has ordinarily been interpreted as contrafactual: the point is alleged to be first and foremost to "realize" "real" reason against the irrational reality of domination. The major debates in social theory in our time are now carried on solely because those questions seem to some to be no longer at all useful, and to others to be timelessly so.

Answers to these questions can, of course, not be assembled by division into "conservative" and "progressive" camps. The matter of dispute is today split rather between "functionalists" on the one hand, who, following the Enlightenment idealist or Enlightenment materialist social action projects, want to make culturally traditional and recognized and/or self-adopted "rational" rules, as the foundation of social system games, into the *plan* for implementation programmes; and "functionalists" on the other hand, who, following social institutionalist social system patterns, want to disclose the "rational" rules already always (presup-)posed in society as the basis of social system games in the *structure* of developmental possibilities. The central dispute is thus on the "pre-ordained pressures" (or pre-existing premises briefly, the "structures") of functional performances according to their substantive qualities or to their institutional and organizational procedures; according to their epistemological (methodological) or to their social philosophical (theory of science) *paradigms*; and not least, obviously, according to their presuppositions and their effects in and on the consciousness and conduct of the human actor himself.

III.

It would seem as if the development of legal culture, as crudely sketched out above, is today coming up against increasingly fundamental, more abstract, more radical transformation (reproduction) projects. I shall discuss these below with the intention of dealing above all with the connection between materialization and proceduralization.

1. Although it concerns a dominant problem of the development of bourgeois legal culture, I shall not deal in detail here with programs which – theoretically – preach pure legal reforms and – practically – produce impure legal contents and thereby become ideologized. It is for good reason that "leftist" and "liberal" legal critics in particular warn against material realizations of "order" in "right-wing" formal legal projects. There are also "left" phenomena, close to legal "theology", but they have no influence. The point is almost always to maintain *one* material foundation idea as a social ordering project in the form of "permanent revolution" against resistances, thereby playing off the legitimations of a higher-level justification (as materialization) "procedurally" against the legalities of a lower-level justification (as formalization). To that extent, the theme would be the "strong state" and the "healthy economy"; or personalized, the legal theory of C. Schmitt; or more generally at least the specifically German legal development in the last two hundred years; or quite generally the legal developments of capitalist industrial societies.

Still less is it intended to place in the foreground here the numerous, very diverse approaches to adjusting formal law, by way of social compensations and/or "political administration", to developments and situations. From the adhesion contracts to class action, one could to that extent of course speak of "materialization" and/or "proceduralization: a broad field.

The centre here would, by contrast, be occupied by those approaches that, as it were, treat the former major alternatives as "exhausted". To put it briefly, the decisive alternatives were, that the subject was either radically superordinate to his environment, or was absorbed in it. If one defines the problem of "law" by referring to particular German philosophers: law as the rational idea and the form of (subjective) freedom (Kant); law as historically and socially "realized freedom" (Hegel); law as an obstacle on the path to the "true reality" of social freedom (Marx), all constitute for themselves, units of form, content and procedure. Present day "mediations" between ideas and interests of (individual or collective) reason and social realities (institutions, organizations, procedures), have assuredly not forgotten these predecessors but have "transcended" them. Accordingly, in the main schools that descend from them, the historical heritage can be found again; admittedly not in the old forms or the old contents, but instead in the content-dependent form of renewable *procedures* for the "mediation" issues concerned. Present day models and projects have behind them so to speak, all the historical experiences with "subject failure" as well as with "institutional failure". Current verbal coinages here are "market failure", "failure of politics". Briefly, what is meant by this is that crisis phenomena of capitalist societies (mass unemployment and excess productive capacity with rising prices) bring with them a dilemma for all "system" elements which is related to the traditional "form" of their activities. The dilemma of the system element "*state*" is that if it lags behind the combined requirements of the economy and the society, then it – i. e. the representative political and administrative leaderships – falls into just as much confusion and lack of control as if it – e. g. through reforms of all kinds – puts too much strain on those areas. The dilemma of the system component "*labour*" is to exercise restraint in economic slumps so as not to endanger possible booms and to exercise restraint in booms so as to prevent possible slumps. This means that, for instance, trade unions with structurally-oriented, major reform plans and policies aimed at mass movements come into conflict with "government" and usually also with "public opinion"; and with wage policies oriented solely to productivity increases, they come into conflict with their rank and file and with the opponents of the system. In the meantime, the whole world knows that the long-practised exercise of mixing "slight" inflation with "very little" unemployment does not (any longer) work. *Central banks* produce through their controls either "galloping" inflation or unemployment. *Entrepreneurs* decide on investments, prices and jobs in framework conditions set by the "welfare state" and "free collective bargaining". *Associations* are helpfully/helplessly exposed to concepts of "pluralism" or "corporatism". Here too, an increasing number of binding/non-binding *conduct agreements* are set up as control machinery e. g. among central bank, government, unions, associations, monopoly commissions, industry and trade; less along the lines of concerted "actions"; of planning "councils"; negotiating "rounds"; as by way of loudly silent mutual notifications of expectations and behaviour.

This gives rise to an all-round situation which is no longer characterized by high mountains and deep valleys, as in classical crisis periods, but instead by long-term entanglements of currency stability and employment crises, which are "connected" in parallel and thus each signals the up and down in a milder form. Catastrophic lows and heady highs are, as it were, in turn withdrawn from the market; creative self-destructive functions on free markets are replaced by power arrangements, through non-aggression pacts between the major combatants. Unavoidable inflation, particularly for reasons of the growing state share in money movements, combined with not (again) attainable full employment, for reasons of the "functionalisation" of "labour" in the "economy", brings about stagflation: a form of expression of political and economic permanent crisis which lives on the fact that precisely those political and economic cooperative forces that bring it about prevent other, sharper, traditional, cyclic crises. The fate of "planning" thereby opens up the dilemma of any "materialization". Originally anathema, for long still a strategic taboo, planning had imposed itself as a problem-solving strategy – "planning" though, understood not in the socialist sense but in the "organized capitalism" sense as "decision about the premises for decision" – as a strategy against the lack of consensus and time resources in particular. From the contemporary viewpoint, earlier waves of planning can be demarcated against each other: anarchic phases of pure distributive competition (fights for shares of the cake!) were followed by administrative system policies, which failed because of a failure to manage the trade cycle, and then by the more modern trend to "socializations" of planning processes (major problems: difficulties in securing clear objectives as control orientations (= "production" of consensus!); conflict potential and resistance movements against changes in "bureaucracies" and "interest groups" (= "production" of cooperation!); lack of finance, planning techniques, machinery (= "production" of resources!)). The collapse of planning euphoria has since provided the insight that lack of political subjectivity and substantive quality of social processes, from which and towards which all planning would have to go, cannot themselves be "planned". Almost all planning time and planning energy is then swallowed up, not in attempts to impose innovations against resistance, but to "clear up" such resistance, i. e. to explain why almost everything does not work, and to show that changing nothing would mean deterioration. It is no wonder that recent planning research has concentrated on the so-called self-paralysis of political and administrative planning processes. It is not so much that there is a lack of planning staff as that the whole planning strategy potential is playing on ice or sand: implementing activities are so blocked that either too-radical changes and questionings of any status-quo relationships become clear, or "grand rules" which have been introduced are (ought to be) broken. In both these alternatives of planning or reform, the approach "fails" almost "automatically"; the only remaining alternatives seem to be either to let the oppositions between goal and strategy potentials become intensified – as a rule a battle of David against Goliath – or else to see the reform energies become worn down in self-pitying, resignatory adaption processes or finally, to set out the *procedures* again – and that always means, of course, the contents as well as the forms – in a different way. Of course, all experience with the failure of politics or of the market does not, especially strategically, preclude the possibility of giving old forms new contents and/or new forms old contents. The centre of interest in each case is occupied by the *procedure*, in which the old is determined by the old, the new by the old, the old by the new or the new by the new.

The main schools of thought can therefore be divided into two groups:

a) "interests" should neither go to "markets" nor simply impose themselves "dominantly" nor be already "oriented" a-priori, but rather they must "legitimize" themselves. At bottom, all theory projects concerned with *procedures* of a "rational" rationality are like this.

b) It is only those "system" formations which "transcend" all out-of-date approaches (simultaneously increasing and reducing complexity) which make possible stabilities of conservation and development. At core, all theory projects concerned with *procedures* of a "systemic" rationality are like this.

In view of the formation of these schools of thought, it is interesting whether and how conclusions on changes can be obtained from the case-law of the highest courts in the problem areas concerned. Such areas are found in the political (economic) constitution as a combination of labour, economic and welfare constitutional law (as short-hand I call this "economic constitution"). In the view of governments in office, such an economic constitution is as a rule a comprehensive slogan for a long-term oriented, pragmatic systems policy. The theoretical opinion camps of "social capitalism" on the one hand and "democratic socialism" on the other, stand out here with stronger outlines. The former make promises of a future which is being squeezed out by the worse present: the latter make promises of a future which will squeeze out the worse present. In very radical simplification, the former call first for the restoration of an economic constitution of social and bourgeois rationality, and the latter for the introduction of such an economic constitution in the first place. In a triangle of practical politics and theoretical critique of irreconcilable camps of opinion and interests, so much mutual situational stalemate pressure has since accumulated that almost literally nothing can now take place by way of major, planned change, even if (or better, precisely because) everything is essentially possible (or at least, much is necessary). It is no wonder in such a situation that "en bloc" legal programmes are no longer possible; that neither "formal" nor "material" programmes can determine *social proportionality*. Nor is it any wonder that no slogan so dominates legal theory work on principles or legal systematic work on decisions as that of "proportionality". For the narrower partial area of "economic law" this abstract concept becomes concrete in a complementary system of market and planning elements with, at the centre, the law of stability; and in historical shifts in consumer sovereignty, with at centre the laws of competition (law against restrictions on competition and law against unfair competition). For the narrower partial area of "labour law" it becomes concrete in a complementary system of conflict law (central: free collective bargaining and labour struggle) and co-operation law (central: works constitution and participation). The policies which the law of stability makes possible, affect the framework and the extent of government action, then the financial constitution in particular and, finally, the two introduced major systems of measures. The most important consequence is that decision-making competence on prices and on investments comes into the strategic centre. For both of these, traditionally (and also very consequentially: contractual constitutional law!), market competition was prescribed as the solution. The most important consequence of this consequence effect: is that if and because – with changing consumer sovereignty – competition becomes increasingly a problem of the social guardianship functions of entrepreneurs (in this function therefore to be interpreted "politically"), and the successful entrepreneur's system performance therefore counts as a criterion and guarantee of the social market economy (slogan: competition as discovery procedure!), then political and economic price control (far less investment control) has in consequence no chance at all. As a further consequence, wage rates are to be determined which can be distributed – according to universal public pressure and through mechanisms of collective labour agreements (free collective bargaining) – as shares in productivity increases. If and because, – on the other hand, trade unions do not keep to their limitation to the sphere of circulation and distribution, they burst the fundamental social legal restraints (the production sphere is not to be included in the legal constitution) to great effect; their (labour) struggle hovers between being opposed to, or without, the law and becoming a new law. Debates on these issues are dominated by "participation" and "labour struggle". Again, it is no wonder that the most recent decisions of the highest courts in both areas play a part in determining "legal form" developments in the long term, at any rate by excluding some.

I shall therefore draw on the most important court-decisions in both these areas for the debate on "materialization" and "proceduralization".

2a) Co-determination

(Decision of the Federal Constitutional Court of 1. 3. 1979, BVerfGE 50, 290–381)

aa) In the co-determination dispute there was a rivalry between concepts of a "right-wing" materialization of the law (more exactly: the retranslation of a particular order of labour and the economy into legal and constitutional terms) and a "left-wing" legal formalization (more exactly, the opening up of creative freedoms for the legislator). The alternatives which were involved in these legal programmes can be seen by characterizing more precisely the fundamental rights programme mobilized in each case, on the basis of which the legislator's political creative freedom can be determined.

(1) Concepts of so-called negative (defending freedom) fundamental rights are aimed at protecting the stock of ("classical", *guarantory*) rights, with the courts as the guarantor of protection, and with legislation as free

competence for framework-setting within clear limits (namely the obligation of equality, the principle of proportionality).

(2) Concepts of so-called positive (participatory), "political" fundamental rights are aimed at the realization of ("social", *providing*) rights; all differences lie exclusively in the degrees and extents of the normative predeterminedness of such realisations. Substantive predetermination programmes reveal themselves clearly in, for instance, institutional and institute guarantees or in historical legal entitlements etc.; the less clearly that substantive predetermination programmes stand out and accordingly the more open that the procedural rules seem to be, the harder it is to grasp the substantiality of the pre-definitions, though in any case this is unavoidable and indispensable.

(3) In view of this situation (namely that nothing (more) can be brought about through formal partisanships but that not all the interests and needs which arise can be treated equally with substantive partisanships), interest in the co-determination decision concentrates on the central questions of to what (how, why) the (constitutional) legislator for his part is substantively bound; to what (how, why) the "constitutional" law as a social relationship relates; in what the functionality and proceduralization for relationships of politics, economy and the law consists.

bb) In the co-determination case, the complaining firms and employer associations (for short: the "attackers") based themselves above all on three points: the co-determination law allegedly would secure for workers on the whole a superiority over shareholders (accusation of hyper-parity); it would lead to fundamental changes in the economic system (accusation of constitutional amendment without a law to amend the constitution); it would not provide protection for the set of ownership, enterprise and coalition rights (accusation of infringement of individual rights). Those in favour of the attacked legislation (for short: the "defendants"), claimed against this that: worker participation rights were in every respect below parity; the law would introduce no essential essential innovations by comparison with existing forms of participation, with which good experience had been accumulated; no individual constitutional right would be infringed in its core content.

cc) The social and legal matter of dispute can be summarized under three headings.

(1) The point is the acquiring of historical laws of experience: in virtue of which (epistemological or sociological) criteria can one predict with certainty or even only with probability what a participation law will lead to, when only practical application of the law will show what character the law will have? We enter here on to very shaky ground of the general theory of knowledge, and are, as it were, in zones of political burden of proof: who has (and then, how and why) to show what effect as a planning

programme a law directed at the future has? How are such proofs to be supplied?

(2) The point is legitimation for prerogatives: who has the ultimate decision where there is political doubt about legal plans? Who even has the right in some circumstances to make historical errors? This also touches on the problem of responsibility for social change. Are the courts the highest agency of responsibility, since in each case they decide *ex post*, or even *ex ante*, what has become or will become false? Is academic political advice responsible, by "objectively recognizing" (what does that mean in that area?) what has been done rightly or wrongly? Or is the political legislature competent, since it introduces future-oriented innovations – perhaps riskily, but with democratic legitimacy?

(3) The point is the essential creation of unity and provisions of wholeness (a "system whole") of the constitution itself, from which alone can order be brought into a multiplicity of individual norms. However, how is such a gain in unity (order) possible? What is evidently at issue here is social theory in and for (and not least through) practice. If this stays too close to the status quo, modern problems remain unsolved; if it gets too much involved with modernizations and changes, acquired rights and customs will be left in suspension.

dd) The Federal Constitutional Court denies both the purely legal protection of existing ownership-, enterprise- and coalition- legal relations (and thereby also conceptions of exclusively formal liberal law), and also the far-reaching, unrestricted political scope of the legislator (and thereby simultaneously conceptions of exclusively substantive and social law). Instead, it combines and augments both directions in the form of a proceduralization: it concedes to the politically legitimized legislator the freedom to bring in innovations if he convincingly bases his legislation on *all* previous experience and the *totality* of available insights. The legislator thereby retains the forecasting prerogative (and therefore simultaneously the prerogative of error); admittedly he must correct his laws if reality turns out differently than predicted. The constitutional court binds all parties to the dispute (above all: employers and unions) by oath to the loyal and fair implementation of the plans, hopes, ideas and possibilities bound up with the co-determination law. Of course, such proceduralization of politics and law may be differently assessed. Trade-union criticism points out that old possibilities of labour struggle, indeed class struggle, are being lost. Employer criticism points out that concern for worker interests makes necessary decisions harder or impossible.

ee) The Federal Constitutional Court, explicitly rejected the criteria formulated by the "attackers" (namely that co-determination was "to be measured by the normative guarantees of the institutional context of the economic constitution"; it was in "contradiction to economic and labour constitutional law guarantees and to the order and protection context that could be deduced from the fundamental rights for the economic and labour constitution in the Basic Law"), and thereby rejected a conception whereby any particular status quo would be guaranteed as a body of law so that changes could be interpreted as infringements of the law. Its own criterion is that substantive differentiating of fundamental rights and the legislator's freedom for development are the legal situations to be protected: so that, while changes cannot be conceived of as observance of the law (as obligatory execution of the law), politics is possible without infringing the law.

This formulation of criteria, though it may still sound very formal, has its content made clear from the individual evaluations, in particular of Article 14, 9 I, 12, 9 III of the Basic Law, and can be summarized as follows:

(1) The legislator is free, if and because he acts to extend the protection of individual freedoms from dangers (of whatever kind, e. g. from the state, from society, from associations or trade unions). This core area of individual/subjective freedom (as a right and that (remaining) legislative freedom (as politics) are involved equally in constitutional and political protection of a social market economy, and of a democratic society oriented towards cooperation and integration. They constitute the general interest as unity of the constitutional order.

(2) The legislator is forbidden (specifically in labour constitution law) from making political formations "dependent" on circumstances not required by the *subject matter* itself, i. e. by the general-interest task of (one might add, "rational") making "working life ordered and peaceful". The legislator is in no way prevented from "appropriate extension".

(3) As far as content goes, functions of fundamental rights and legislative freedoms are determined by a combination of historical experiences, core contents of subjective-individual rights (in the sense of "classical" private rights) and prerogatives of the legislator, who must above all — in addition to the sum of experience and available knowledge — keep to the subject matter.

In the traditional language of "law" and "politics": substantive constitutional programmes are determined by the realization-effects of law through politics on *all* citizens. In other words fundamental rights theory and legislative policy are bound up with the replacement of *civil* law by politics in each case, which has to hold on to all experiences and all available insights. With this obligation, politics ("the State") can expand on previous developments only on the basis of universal (learned) consensus (cautiously and prudently) and likewise oppose newer developments (in a universally supportable and maintainable manner).

b) Co-determination

(Decisions of the Federal Court of Justice of 25.02.1982, BGHZ 83, 106 ff, 144 ff., 151 ff.)

According to the German Corporation Law (1965), arrangements, where not bindingly laid down by the law, may be determined by the corporate charter. In the Co-determination Law (1976) however, arrangements on "co-determination" are not *in general* arrived at via company law. In many such companies, decisions have been based on the charter in the last few years (by the general assemblies of shareholders competent thereto). "Shareholders" interpret these decisions as part of the *private autonomy to enact a charter*, while "workers" and "unions" interpret them as an *infringement of co-determination law*. The charter rules therefore prove to be material for far-reaching conflict.

aa) Does the Co-Determination Law decide on the Corporation Law or does the Corporation Law decide on the Co-Determination Law?

Is private autonomy under the "private-law" Corporation Law transcended by the social measures of the "political" Co-determination Law? The problem can be put still more generally. How can a *compatibility* of "private company law" and "political social constitutional law" be realized? What would legal conflict rules look like (and how would they be applied) that would make possible the reconcilability of irreconcilable (as being of different natures or different kinds) partial legal systems? The point at issue is in each case the relations between "old" and "universal" total codifications and "new" and "special" institutional design in individual areas. Rather more precisely: from the viewpoint of legal theory and legal doctrine, a relationship of so-called conditional programmes to so-called purposive programmes is concerned; from the viewpoint of legal methodology, case-law guidelines (above all in the courts) are concerned; from the viewpoint of political economy, the mutual adjustments of legal system and social reality (under conditions of a policy of limited change) are concerned. A total of four partial problems may thus readily be picked out.

(1) Mutual allocations of the "general" (primarily understood as liberal, and in the long term stable private law) and the "particular" (primarily understood as political control effective only in the short term): here the point is to find and apply synchronized evaluations (for "the whole"). This partial problem is a problem of the social meta-structure (as unity of its constitution) for "law" and "politics" simultaneously.

(2) Experience gained from accomplishing the implementation of so-called purposive (measure) laws: this partial problem is a problem of the possible goals (and the conditions of such possibility) of laws and of the law as such.

(3) The relationship of principle between prohibitions under general rules (traditionally counted as characteristic of "private law") and in-

structions in implementation of planned measures (traditionally regarded as characteristics of "politics" or of "governmental and administrative law"): this partial problem is a fundamental problem of the very relationship between law and society.

(4) The conflict about social models, social consciousness and decision-making machinery, above all in the ruling elites: this partial problem is a problem of the structuring (and constant restructuring) of social systems for purposes of regulatory steering and control formations, i. e., for institutional practice itself.

bb) By means of a substantive and procedural dual "transcendence", the Federal Court has of Jusltice rejected both the excessive legal hopes of capital owners for private autonomy under company law (i. e., by elimination of co-determination possibilities through rights to freedom in the articles of association) and the excessive legal hopes of the unions for participation-based changes in private law (i. e., for implementation through company law of the participation possibilities not achieved through the co-determination policy). At the same time, it transferred the priority (*sub-parity* for workers and unions) of "capital" over "labour" from the Co-determination Act fully into the law on corporate charters.

The parties to the conflict thereby become bound in everyday company law by the loyalty guidelines laid down by the legislator (more precisely, "proceduralized" by the Constitutional Court).

c) Labour conflict (lock-outs)

In the struggle over the law of labour conflict, especially the dispute on the law of lock-outs, there were two rival concepts. One was of a contractual constitutional law strictly confined to the sphere of circulation and distribution (more precisely, a law of labour conflict linked with law of labour peace (free collective bargaining)). The other was of an organizational constitutional law extending into the production sphere (more exactly, a parity of opportunity oriented towards the relationship between ownership of the means of production and dependent employment). In three fundamental decisions (of 10 June 1980), the Federal Labour Court proposed a comprehensive fundamental re-orientation of labour conflict law. Strikes will not (any longer!) be examined to see if their goals are justified, but declared unrestrictedly admissible as *freedom* to strike and thereby explicitly justified as a historically established measure of counter-power to the power primacy of employers as entrepreneurs. To curb hyper-parity abuses of such free power for the trade unions, freedom of lock-outs is legally admitted, but is limited by the socially-determined legal goal of justifying labour conflicts with a "*cause*" (= fairness in collective bargaining) (under the "superordinate principle of proportionality"). This (still very abstract) *functional definition* is made concrete in the *form* of "general and abstract rules" (for reasons of legal security; the most dominant term is "normative typification").

The rule concerned (as guideline, not definition of legal principle) is that if – in any bargaining area – less than 25% of the workers strike, then the employers may lock out up to a further 25% of workers; if more than 25% of workers strike, employers may lock out other workers until a total of 50% of all workers are out; with over 50% out there would "as a rule" no longer be a need for a lock-out (but the court has left this question undecided).

The *proceduralization rationality* set up here can be reconstructed as follows:

Trade-union strike strategies move between fronts of interests. The interest in gaining much but also, say, protecting one's own (strike) funds leads to so-called narrow (i.e. partial or localised) strikes. Such strikes however, affect employer solidarity in the form of interest in competition between firms. For either they show solidarity – and then they will (which is the core of the theory of entrepreneurial risk) not employ the non-striking workers (with cost consequences above all for the unions, since the "state" (the wage compensation funds) must remain neutral in a labour conflict); or they act *competitively*, as it were in an uncomradely fashion – then they should (by majority decision!) react according to labour conflict law, i.e. they ought to lock out. Proceduralization: in the long run, the burdens on union funds and the burdens of distortion of competition for firms are so much in balance that a labour struggle – if suitably strongly spread – rapidly and "properly" fullfills its function, not least because of the influence of "public opinion".

d) Entrepreneurial Risk

As a sketch of a "typical" set of interactions between goals: (medium sized) firms, which as suppliers of parts are dependent on "functioning" plant performance of the (big) firms that purchase from them and/or are in turn dependent on previous suppliers, fall into difficulties, say, in labour struggles (particularly strikes) where their purchasers or suppliers stop working, though they themselves are not affected by the strikes.

They may then, for instance, be interested in introducing short-time working. In the case of short-time working, the Federal Labour Office supplies public wage compensation for reasons of job maintenance. In labour conflicts, however, the Labour Office has to remain "neutral". Works councils have co-determination rights over the details of short-time working, except where their rights have to "rest" for reasons of labour conflict. There are strategic possibilities in such situations, for instance, coalitions of employers and works councils in order to secure public funds (= subventions!) for their firm; or labour struggle as a pretext for employers as entrepreneurs to "split" members and non-members of trade unions; or interest in short-time working as a cover-up for entrepreneurial failures; or co-determination by works councils in order to provide control over entrepreneurial decisions; the list could be continued. The Federal Labour Court has so artfully interwoven the "freedom" of all interest groups concerned (by limiting but not quite eliminating the works council's co-determination even in cases of labour conflict) that not only collaboration rights in plants, labour conflict "parity", "neutrality" of public funds, but also the relationship between entrepreneurial investment and price decisions on the employment structure in the plant are each accorded their place. The whole amounts to a stage direction for a multi-lateral, simultaneously "open" and "closed" play of self-interest and performance of social function, a "system" play of steering and control.

e) Summary

The Federal Constitutional Court proceduralizes legal rationality in such a way that universally consented (more exactly, consent-meriting because instituted by the legitimate legislator, oriented to loyal implementation and with medium-term reservations) transformations of social institutions, organizations and procedures can be brought about. The fundamental judgments in labour law proceduralize legal rationality in such a way that, by way of appeals that promise success to all the specific interests involved and concerned in each case, an indirectly guided and at the same time controlled "concerted action" in the medium term can be set up. Admittedly, it turns out that the limitations on trade unions act more effectively than those on employers. This results from the transformation of contract (labour) law into competition (economic) law. The hidden *materiality* (of the procedural investment plans) is a specific competition model. That is the only reason why (successful) labour conflict law can be "functionalized" in free collective bargaining and this collective bargaining can in turn be functionalized into a (macro-politicized, because "politics" and "economy" in their turn are blended into a single big market) concept of economic (constitutional) law, which in turn is to be interpreted as a substantive programme of legal theory as social theory.

On the whole, case law links legal events to realization of goals of the civil-law form (individual human freedom) through canalizations and/or interpenetrations of interest "parities" and through social functional definitions of such parities and interpenetrations. There is involved here a re-constitutionalization of contractual constitutional law (= ideal of the freely determined justice of exchange) as organizational constitutional law (ideal of universally limited impossibility as the justice of stability).

3. No direct, exclusive connection to particular camps of social theory can be seen in the newest patterns of case law from the highest courts. For

indirect and/or combined connections, interpretation would have to relate the legal development trends in detail to such theoretical projects. Picking out only the theoretical jumping-off points, in the language of functionalist evolutionary theories the issues would then be the position of law as a specific subsystem medium, as a partial medium in (all) subsystems and as an intermediary (meta-)medium, or at least as a "constitution" for media compatibilizations. In the language of normative critical evolutionary theories, the issue would be the position of law as system functionality but also as normativity in the life-world (in Habermas's language: law as "medium" and law as "institution" see Habermas supra). My support for the normative critical evolutionary projects is connected with the fact that approaches such as that of Habermas convince me more than purely functionalist programmes. Habermas has, in the most recent past, gone into media-theory (media understood as generalized communication) as integration of system and action theories. But he holds to the limited (limitable!) substitution of the universal medium (namely language) by systems. Such a transposition of the constitution of action from language to media controlled (and therein technologized) interactions, at the centre of which stand organization and procedure, is seen by him in power-controlled administration (more exactly, media power linked back to legitimation of rule) and in the money-controlled economic system (more exactly: money as a medium linked back to self-justified exchange) as irreversibly achieved and indispensable. He rejects such a transposition for a "life-world" of cultural reproduction, of social integration and socialization; more exactly: for a life-world determined through cultural traditions, institutional orders and "socialized" interior worlds (see also Habermas supra). In this life-world, it is precisely its ever-critical overall situation that sets free a rationality potential for linguistic communication which makes communicatively achieved consensus and communicatively regulated dissent dependent on intersubjective recognition of criticizable validity claims (truth, rightness, truthfulness, bounded by comprehensibility). At root, Habermas finds in "solidarity" and in "integrity" the leading substantive qualities of communicative actions. All practical philosophical social theories meet in dependency on substantive projects which are aimed at bindingness and/or rationality of practical statements. It is only with the "presentation" (by human beings) of a theory in practice, i. e. through the fact that men live for their "model", that the theory project becomes "proved" (or more modestly, is maintained).

More concretely, for (more exactly, in) a project oriented towards "rational" justificatory rules for practical legal pronouncements, what is necessary is *substantive impartiality*. For this, Scottish 18th century moral philosophy could find only secularized divine images (the well-informed and impartial spectator, appearing simultaneously as man within the breast) and Immanuel Kant could supply only an analysis, not to be striven for (any longer) as materiality, nor admittedly solely accepted as formality, but to be conceptualized as proceduraliry, i. e. as impartial justificatory procedures for legal conflict rules. However one looks at it, the fact remains that society and history can be "discovered" only by "acting", or more briefly, they are not anywhere simply given, but given as tasks. Here belongs the demand to provide, while defending good conditions reached in each case, better ones in the place of worse ones, i. e. "criticism" and "constructions". Those who do not (any longer?) base themselves on "god" or "market" and also do not (yet?) count on "self-referential systems", must go into the justificatory rules for practical legal pronouncements.

At bottom (the following takes off from the "Starnberg School", in particular E. Tugendhat), the issue for them is not a parallel to "scientific" establishment of truth. This cannot reach beyond an analytical status (more exactly, in and because of the identity of semantic (understanding of meaning) and pragmatic (understanding of justificatory rules) language rules always already "given"), but at the same time has and creates its impartiality. Instead, the issue is the creation of a *synthetic status*, which has to stand up for itself naturally and on a basis of principle from which scepticism cannot be excluded. The overcoming of scepticism as concretization of the justificatory (explanatory) procedure takes place in the unity of production and application of legal conflict rules; (as against this, the abstract procedure is for that reason universally recognized, because it is identical with the universalizability principle itself: norms are just (right) if and because all can agree with them).

Guidelines for this proceduralization project (as it were, the form of the object "proceduralization") can be obtained from a reconstructive stage theory of justificatory (explanatory) learning levels.

a) *First stage:* "Rigid" rational morality. "Law" is then freedom, grounded only on reason, and has absolutely no relationship to any kind of need (of legal subjects, societies, systems etc.). The "moral" core lies in man's agreement to taking the maxim of his action as a project for a universally applicable law. There are, in principle, no conflicts of norms, because the negative (perfect) duties of non-interference with the freedom of others take absolute primacy over the positive (imperfect) duties of substantive promotion of objectives.

b) *Second stage:* "Flexible" rational morality. "Law" then follows the universal relativization of absolute criteria; and in the shift of its reference from individual to intersubjectivity ("society") loses the formal reliability of the criteria but gains in exchange substantive (equality of interests or goals; in short, "empirical") links to criteria (for a similar analysis see Ewald supra). The idea of "impartiality" is as it were "relatively" saved by the fact that market and/or organizationally mediated partialities are equally probable for everyone, and universal amicable agreements on them can be conceived of. Admittedly, this theoretical strength is at the same time a practical weakness: the "authoritative" "decision" *procedure* (market? organization of system differentiations? game programmes? civil religion? all together or some of them in — arbitrary or definite — combinations?) is for its part no longer decidable. It is not hard to diagnose our contemporary law as "formalized", "materialized", "functionalized", "proceduralized", at this level. This observation is not meant as a reproach. For while a way out into the old conditions can certainly not be found, new conditions are — on assumptions of insecurity — still to be sought. Practical philosophy (in the classical centre of which stood: virtue as the guarantee of right practical goals, prudence as the guarantee of right choice of means) always had and has to do with practical comprehensibility (rationality). Admittedly, the classical final goal (happiness) has in modern times been replaced by methodology (Descartes), by legal forms as guarantee of security (Hobbes), by political prudence of leading elites (Vico), by laws of freedom (Kant). The extent of demands for change that are still to be taken up today springs to mind. A "mediation" of ideas (norms, values, guidelines, plans, programmes) and interests (needs) is still largely to be regarded as impossible. A social *universalization project*, "law and morals", is, however, oriented towards nothing less than such "mediation". Approaches to this can be summarized as the:

c) *Third stage:* "communicative" rational morality. "Law" is then put in a position of impartiality, to arrive at which admittedly there cannot (any longer) be any unambiguous procedure — or only at the expense of regressions. Law becomes reflexive. Just as in the first stage the principle *each man for himself* and in the second stage *each man for all* had to formulate the conflict rules, so in the third stage they can be arrived at only by there being a possibility of each putting himself in the position of every other — as precondition of any proceduralization of decision-making (*each with each*!), in order through the reflexively "transcended" partiality to determine the impartiality positions — thoroughly burdened with decision, but no longer to be obtained "more simply" (more rigidly, more formally). This positional determination is the current problem of autonomy.

Such stages do not arise by themselves, and they are certainly not produced. They are not historical law-governed regularities, and they guarantee neither "progress" nor "liberty". They may be reconstructively determined — e. g. in regard to crisis — and prospectively applied — e. g. in regard to "projects". The method inherent in this is "impartial" procedure for consensus as goal and for potential participation of all those concerned in decisions in cases of non-agreement (such participation to be at any rate regulative). To that extent, the way in which the Federal Constitutional Court does its "proceduralizing" (making possible legality based on historical experience, consensus loyalities etc.) has certainly more to do with "third-stage" approaches than the way the federal special courts go about proceduralizing. And quite obviously, "proceduralization" of the stage project sketched out is linked with a sociological model which seeks to keep open "rational life-worlds" – which are as yet outside system formations.

4. *Concluding Remarks*

a) By proceduralization of the law one may understand the transformation of a social context of legal freedoms (linked with rule-exception, or interest reconciliation, decision-making patterns) into a system of justification of the respective new social contexts of "ideas" and "interests". Such new creations – as stable change in permanence – are compelled by the state of socialization. This makes necessary a legal "administration" for which the important thing is less rules of application and implementation than criteria for guarantees of success and for procedures for replacing men and machinery in case of failure. Because of the substantive non-decidability of historical and social developments, competences are allocated for forecasting and for responsibility. Here the major role is assigned to the egislature, the judiciary and the associations, and above all the "entrepreneur" (of all levels and areas). The latter is understood as a universal manager of needs who "finds" the social possibilities and "allocates" the realizations. Control through intermeshing of "freedoms" simultaneously permits guidance, over and above form (= means) control and not going as far as content (= goal) control, to be oriented as "defensibility" control. It still remains to be discussed here whether the trend towards a neo-corporatism tends rather to encourage or to hinder freedoms and social stability. My assessment, in brief, is that the classical social consensus producers ("market" and "public") could for a while be seen as replaceable by parties and associations ("liberal pluralism"). The modes of application of the concept "neo-corporatism" (the career of which as a theme goes back to crisis conceptions of the type of "ungovernability") show a still more recent substitution development. A contractual constitution originally determined by the logic of exchange ("friendly" agreements among "corporations") has in turn been transformed into an organizational constitution determined by the logic of stability. Here, what can more readily be traced as neo-corporatism is general-societal (originally trust, but today) "concern" *strategies* rather than new social "ideologies" (= new social formations themselves, e. g. as renewal of the division of powers). Among the critical corporatism theories it is no doubt the block-formation interpretations ("selective corporatism" as splitting of society) that have the greatest convincingness.

b) Present programmes of legal development are correlated with (more exactly are one part of) so-called *positive* crisis theories (representative concept: capitalist interventionist democracy). Their thesis is that though coexistence of capitalism, democracy and bureaucracy may be wrecked in historical catastrophe, there is no practical alternative. Any alternative would have to combine a higher degree of social stability, political liberality and economic efficiency. The occurrence of crises is alleged to be dependent on – disrupted or erroneous – joint and pertinent assessments of the overall situation by the protagonists (those successfully leading their respective constituencies). In sum, political and economic ("negative") crisis theories (with their finding that systems come to a crisis at their end) are replaced by interactionist ("positive") crisis theories (with their finding that through learning capacity systems can reach stable permanent change). In the context of such crisis theories, law is neither a fatal product of ideology nor successful achievement of freedom, but (only) *one* element involved.

Present-day programmes of legal development "fit" because they are based less on normative assumptions than on procedural-functionalist exclusions of possibilities within structural systems – and "fit" too with the general trends in economic theories, systems theories, planning theories, competition theories, decision and game theories and development theories. All take as their theme a connection between (in each case restricted) structural possibilities and realizable freedoms. What needs justification here is, most notably, what can be determined (achieved) by excluding other (older? worse?) possibilities. It looks as if, in terms of the logic of research, a context of discovery is here becoming independent of a context of justification. A "practice as a discovery principle" would then, so to speak, have passed the "scientific" reliability tests simply in terms of "letting be" and "doing". A need for justification (namely: deductive, inductive, abductive, or at least analytical judgement) is alleged to have been replaced by the pragmatic virtue of always having synthetic judgments on "proofs" of the theory project available.

c) My support therefore goes to an understanding of proceduralization as a justificatory problem of "rational" practical action under "system" conditions (= justification of collision rules in the exercise of judgemental competences). The notion is of a sort of *forum*, before which negotiation on transformations of society goes on reconstructively and prospectively. This is a new type of concept of the correctness of positive law: no closed, correct, substantive ("rational", "natural") concept should prevail against a "false" reality; nor should any reality presume to an idea of correctness, but "society" – as restrictedly open – should expose itself to new experiences on the basis of its experience hitherto. Here one finds the endeavour, if not to rewrite history, at any rate not simply to pass from it to the specific order of the day. Within the context of a critical rationality theory, at any rate, proceduralization thereby becomes a logic of reconstruction. "*Social rights*", are understood as guarantees (guaranteeing of "having") and concessions (make possible "being able") under the law, i. e. not as pure securing of having (= formal freedom), nor as pure realization of participation (= materialization of a "directed" theory of history). They are dependent less on exclusively individual participation and/or collective welfare provision than on procedural qualities and procedural guarantees of each given "perception" (as short-hand for the activities in the "undertaking" of the "project of modernity"). They live from the guaranteed respect for the needs of "voters", "welfare clients", "workers", "consumers", and also from the freedom conceded in the "private sphere" and in "public". Participation and involvement as fundamental legal categories have admittedly still to be worked out.

d) Last but not least, an observation on the outstanding importance of "professional training for lawyers". If the issue in the law, in jurisprudence and for lawyers is simultaneously functionalities of the law and legitimations of the law, both in practice but with high claims to reflexivity, i.e. to abstraction, analysis and synthesis, then the demands on lawyers and on lawyers' professional training grow to an extent that was never at any earlier time so apparent as it is today. For the structural transpositions make legal thinking and acting (as re-acquisition of rationality) definable less on a direct plane of action than on a plane of *productivity of legal principles*, more exactly: of reflexive translation of legal pronouncements into situations of application and of reflective production of unavailable, or insufficiently available, legal pronouncements themselves.

This was the way the late Savigny saw the academic legal practioner. At the time, that meant, politically, that lawyers had to obtain and implement their orientations in that way if and because, in a time of social structural change, they were to be able to achieve influential and successful collaboration. The point today is, of course, not so much a return to Savigny but certainly comparable, and certainly on the whole more complex, challenges. For it is not a foundation alliance between rational law based on reason (Kant), and the needs and endeavours of capitalist economic development that is (any longer) up for discussion, but the question of the rationality guarantees of a late-capitalist bourgeois society which cannot (any longer) be helped by a uniform, closed, rationality pattern. Our position is, rather, characterized by a *dissociation of law*. One part of the law and lawyers is role-oriented, specialized and another part of the law and lawyers is abstractly and reflexively engaged with problems of justifying validity, with decisions on conflict rules, with production of legal principles. The most important consequence seems to me to be (or to be becoming) prone to criticism. There does not, for either part, exist a social legal average, that classical field of "regulated" and therefore "functioning" dogma on the basis of justificatory because justified systematic legal categories. For those "in the field", no universal orientations of action (any longer); at the "top", orientations of action which do not yet have an effect on the situations of action. Future legal work will have to take this phenomenon of dissociation of normative (universally rational) justifications from (practical and technical) situational assessments of and solutions to, everday practical problems as its major task, or else it will die a slow death as "legal" work. To be more concrete: that universal theoretical and practical bourgeois level of culture and interest which was once brought into the constitution is today not (any longer) effective as a unit that creates such a rationality, as a category, as a basis for validity, for the justifiability of practical (legal) principles, nor is it in practice legitimizable. "Proceduralization of law" might be the contemporary manifestation of a bourgeois society which, while it does not (yet?) give up its institutional hopes (synthesis of individual and societal needs, reconciliation of achieved "culture" and realizable "interests"), does start to follow different paths to that institutionalization.

Law as Critical Discussion

Antonie A. G. Peters*
Utrecht

Model

Two views of law. Law is characterized by a polarity between finality and provisionality, closedness and openess, which find expression in two opposed views of law. In one view, probably the dominant one among jurists and laymen, law is associated with order, unequivocal meaning, settlement of disputes *lites finiri oportet*, enforcement of rules. It is a view which emphasizes the decisive role of statements by authorities: legislators, courts, especially, especially supreme legislators and supreme courts; but also prevailing doctrines and official opinions, which congeal normative options as positive facts by placing them in an established context of government, power, interests and ideology. This conception appeals to a traditional mentality of deference to the status quo; it feeds on man's inclination towards regularity, his need of certainty, his complacence. As is often said, law is a form of social control.

In the other contrasting view law is associated with liberation from existing restrictions, with the possibility of improvement, critique of authority. Emphasis is on justification, not only of deviations from established norms and opinions but, in the case of deviance or contestation, of these norms and opinions as well. The distinctive feature of a "legal" order is not its official confirmation of a *status quo* but its recognition that things can be changed, that there is always a multiplicity of meanings that law lends itself to quite different interpretations and uses. In this view, legal life embodies the belief that social reality is faulty but that it can be reformed. The remarkable thing about the judgment of a court of justice, for example, is not that it puts an end to a dispute, but the way a court does this and the form which its judgment takes. In court the dispute-character of a conflict is articulated (even the devil gets his advocate); the issuing judgment reveals the reasoning on which it is based thereby

* I thank my friends Paul Moedikdo Moeliono and Paul van Seters for their continuous encouragement, criticism and help.

exposing itself to criticism; in some legal systems court judgments are accompanied not only by the arguments that support them, but also by counter-arguments which are published at the same time in the form of dissenting opinions. All order is seen as provisional, valid for the time being, until it will be contested and altered. The existing legal system is understood to be problematic as a matter of principle, because it represents a structure not only of guaranteed interests, rights, liberties and equality, but also of inequalities, deprivations, repressed material and ideal interests, a structure, that is, of denied alternatives. A legal system is appreciated for the ways in which it may facilitate the improvement of given social order.

The operative reality of all positive law lies somewhere in between these extremes. In some systems there is more emphasis on law enforcement and obedience to given rules, whereas other systems are more "constitutionally" oriented and lay more stress on principles which keep the process of law-making open. In the latter, controversies about form and substance of the law are an essential part of legal life, an it is thought imperative that such controversies never be ended, for that would mean the end of legal life itself. This model of law as "open debate" should be distinguished from freedom to express opinions about law which have no consequences for the legal system. Such freedom is fully compatible with the other, positivist, model of law as a socially sanctioned system of normative facts. In this case too, not everybody is supposed to agree with the existing law, since it is only natural that different groups and individuals have different ideas about justice and about what would be good law. These opinions, however, have no status in the system itself, which they do have in the other model. There is another important difference. In the first view law is mainly the responsibility of legal specialists, whose authority is based on their expertise in handling received doctrines and set procedural routines and whose activity is, on the whole, subservient to established power. The second view embraces a broader conception of legal life. This is appreciated especially in its progress, its continuous self-transcendence. Law is not seen as the exclusive domain of professional jurists, but as the inalienable responsibility of all citizens. Very important, in this perspective, is the role played by non-professional legal critics: intellectuals, individuals and groups who contest the established social order. Not only the enforcement and application of existing law, but also the struggle — legal and illegal, parliamentary and non-parliamentary, reformist or revolutionary — against the law, for a different law, is part of legal life. It is, more truly, its very essence. Legalization means that a social activity is provisionally validated. It recognizes the important function of social critique and accords constitutive significance to the reflexive dimension in human affairs. Particular political and legal institutions may give room for critical reflection and further it, in which case law works as an agent of emancipation. However, they can also obstruct critical reflection, restrict its scope, or even cut it out altogether, so that law becomes an agent of repression.

In the structure of legal discourse, the conflict between freedom and domination, between potentialities and restrictions, becomes manifest in this tension between openness and finality. A closed legal discourse is imperative, official and unequivocal. *Unequivocal meanings* and precise definitions of right and wrong, legal and illegal, mine and thine are contrary to a notion of law as tentative, as project, always in the making, as sensitive to shifting social meanings, premised on fallibility. Law's *official status* comes easily into conflict with the notion of law as serving man in coping with his problems. Official law tends to become the law of officials. Lastly, law as *imperative* is contrary to the postulate of reciprocity in human relations: law as expression of mutual expectations; a system of primary *and* secondary rules instead of the gunman situation writ large (Hart, 1961). It is because of the open structure of law that Illich (1973) is able to conceive of legal procedure as a "tool for conviviality", something which people can use to resist the structural violence of facts.

Legalization. The two views of law are not arbitrary but reflect an essential dynamic in all systems of positive law. I shall try to illustrate this by looking at what happens when things become regulated by law. Legalization, inevitably, implies a certain cognitive and evaluative "elaboration" of social reality, as a result of which this social reality undergoes a change, comes to be seen in a different perspective, and obtains a new, modern, structure.

A first characteristic of legalization of a social activity, relationship, or problem is, that its meaning is made more precise. The essentials are specified and named. This happens, for example, when a custom is recorded. It is impossible to write down the entire custom as it lives in people's experience with all its nuances and contextual details. For here essentials and accidentals are interwoven, and the relations at issue are often diffuse and inseparably related to other customs. Only when a custom is to be codified or when it must be specified in the case of a dispute, does one become conscious of these matters. Then not all aspects appear as relevant and not all elements are considered to be of equal importance; one has to choose what is part of the custom and what is not. The legally ratified aspects are accorded a higher, "official", status which sets them off against other aspects which, though initially not distinguished from the former, are now relegated outside the law. In this way legalization brings a new dimension into social reality. Specification, definition of essentail elements, formulation, all this implies a great many interpretative choices: choices in the legal reconstruction of social reality. Such choices will often, almost inevitably, invite criticism and call for explanation and justification. Thus a completely new problematic situation arises with respect to the original social reality, which gives rise to new kinds of legitimizing activities. These activities can be manifold: appeals to Divine will or to existing authority, to nature or to the public interest; etc. Legitimation may also consist in obfuscation of choices made, as if there were no options, so that no special reasons need to be given. The choices that are made may exhibit conflicts of interests which, until then, had not been there, or had remained latent. This is one reason why legalization may not always be considered opportune.

Legalization makes explicit what had been implicit. Choices must be accounted for. Criticism has to be answered. In this process of explicating, explaining, distinguishing, criticizing and justifying, there emerges a new, rational, intersubjective consciousness of social reality. There is a novel awareness of grounds, ends and means; a clearer understanding of motives and interests at stake. In this way legalization contributes to the transparency of social reality and to rationality in social action. It is possible to go one step further in this characterization of legalization and recognize it as a rational reconstruction of social reality. Elements of this reality are detached from their context and, after being explicated and rationally conceptualized, reinserted into it. Law loosens before it binds, uproots before it confirms. In a legal contract, which determines mutual rights and obligations, parties are opposed to one another, interest versus interest, claim against claim, all sorts of conflicts and forms of bad faith are anticipated, in order to re-unite parties in one legal relationship which gives shape to a common activity. Because of this antagonistic, or rather antagonizing, aspect people may prefer not to regulate their relations by means of a formal contract (Kawashima, 1963, 1974; Macauley, 1963). We encounter this principle of reconstruction inherent in legalization also in criticism of the notion of "customary law" as an artificial product of legal conceptual thought and political decision (Weber, 1921).

So this is my point of departure: in the process of legalization, social relationships, activities, interests and purposes are rationally conceived or re-conceived; they are defined and means are selected for their realization. At the same time, what is legalized is incorporated in a larger project, ultimately that of society, or even humanity as a whole. It is, indeed, only in the process of legalization that society comes to be understood as *project*. To this argument I shall return.

Legalization's paradox is that by bringing clarity and certainty, it also suggests the possibility of alternatives and, thereby, communicates uncertainty. In representing social reality as subject to interpretation and regulation, the legal reconstruction of the world becomes manifest as political choice. Those who regulate may well wish to suppress this latter meaning but they will never be able to do so completely since their own action testifies to the contrary. In principle, legalization contains these three messages: this is something that can be regulated; we do this in this particular way; but it could also be done differently. A certain reality and normative direction are posited, but, at the same time, the possibility is indicated of a different reality and a different normative direction.

These features of legalization — choice, need of justification, critique and controversy, elucidation of interests, political manipulation, communication of alterability — are special because they often go against the primary intentions of those who want to legalize. They will be interested in unequivocalness certainty, change perhaps, but only in the direction and to the extent envisaged by them. The characteristics of legalization noted here should not, therefore, be understood in terms of the intentions of legalizing subjects, but rather as the unintended consequences of legalizing action.

Procedural dimension. I have tried to explain how legalization alters social reality. As soon as an activity or state of affairs is legalized, i.e. reconceived in legal terms, no matter whether this is done in statutory, contractual or other formal documentary form, through litigation and adjudication, or in social protest which denounces this activity or state of affairs as "injustice" and demands cessation or reform as a matter of right, the social meaning of such an activity or state of affairs is no longer the same. A new, critically reflexive, dimension has been added to it. I call this dimension procedural, since it constitutes a typically procedural space of communicative interaction, in which people may litigate, deliberate in legislative style, put forward alternative interpretations, discuss questions of execution and practical consequences (cf. various accounts of the procedural dimension in this volume, Habermas, Wiethölter, Teubner).

This may be illustrated by Piaget's (1932) classical study of the development of moral judgment in children, especially his analysis of their understanding of the rules of the game of marbles. Very young children are guided by the pleasure they take in their own movements and the rules which they follow have nothing obligatory about them. In this first phase *le plaisir du régulier* prevails. In a subsequent phase the children learn from older children the true rules of the game. These rules they regard as absolutely obligatory and immutable. Any thought of possible alteration is absent. It is a regime of strict, readymade rules to which they have to submit. The rules are sacred: behind them stands the authority of the older children and the world of the adults. All this changes again in a later phase when the rules lose their necessary and coercive meaning. As children grow older they discover that different rules are followed in other neigbourhoods and in other schools; they may learn from their parents that in former times the game was played differently; hence, they become aware that the rules, as they have learned them, "ain't necessarily so". They now feel free to change the rules if other children agree. Established and newly proposed rules are evaluated in terms of fairness — do they promote reciprocity and equal chances? — and purposiveness — do they make the game more interesting? In addition to their interest in the game itself, children develop a new "juridical" interest in the rules of the game. They spend much time dicussing the rules they will follow, deciding what sanctions should be applied in case of infringement, and they "seem to take a particular pleasure in providing for all sorts of cases and in codifying these". Orthogonally related to the original interaction-system of the game, a new interaction-system has come into being in which the children participate as equals who share sovereignty with respect to the game. Within this latter context the rules of the game — the orginal interaction context — are decided upon, the meaning and validity of various moves are discussed, etc. There are no longer "older children" whose opinions are decisive, and the strong discuss on equal footing with the weak. By virtue of the existence of this new dimension of interaction, the game can be interrupted at any time — point of order! — to question the validity of an act or the fairness of a particular application of a rule. It is important to see that here we have to do with a new, distinct type of interaction which has come about in the transition from rules as regularity of behaviour via externally imposed rules to free legislation (cf. as well Febbrajo supra). This interaction-system is of an order different from the previous one and appeals to different human capacities — the best player is not necessarily the one who excels in legal discourse and in arguing questions of fairness. At the same time the original interaction-system is considerably qualified by the existence of this second one. The meaning of the game has changed. A game which can be interrupted at any time for the sake of discussing the fairness of the way it is played, is very different from a game in which no such possibility exists.

The value added by law should not primarily be seen in its confirmation of social order through official recognition and power-backed sanctions. Rather, it has to be sought in the procedural dimension added to social interaction, in which questions of propriety, fairness and desirability can be brought up. In this perspective, the legal certainty often valued by jurists and laymen is of a very special kind. It is the certainty that the *uncertainty* of social order, of statutes, official decisions, legal judgments, contracts and other legally confirmed social facts, can, at any time, be made salient.

The distinctively *legal* (Selznick, 1968) may thus be seen in a special, deliberative, critically-reflexive dimension which it adds to social interaction. Institutionally, this dimension is given form in a regime of principles which are to govern the practice of rule-making, interpretation and application, and in the designation of a forum where one can litigate and proceed to alter established rules and have new ones adopted. This is how I think we should understand Hart's (1961) definition of law as a union of primary and secondary rules. The first are of a prescriptive, obligatory nature, telling people how to behave. Secondary rules tell people how to deal with the primary rules: they indicate how these are to be applied, interpreted and changed.

The concept of a forum is essential in this connection (see also Wiethölter supra). It is for good reasons that so much emphasis is given, in national and international legal instruments for the protection of human rights, to *habeas corpus*, judicial review of administrative acts and legislation, and to the right of individuals to have access to an international court of justice when they consider that they cannot obtain justice in their own country. The significance of such provisions lies in the possibility they open for a free and critical assessment of decisions by authorities in an institutional context which shields such assessment from domination by any power bent on suppressing criticism or controlling the discussion and its outcome. The pre-eminent importance of a forum where the propriety of the uses of power can be criticized is endorsed by the value which, in a Rechtsstaat and under the rule of law, is traditionally attached to an independent judiciary. It also explains how seriously allegations of corruptibility of judges and accusations of class justice and discrimination in legal administration are usually taken. Judicial independence expresses the idea that the use of power, whether or not legally dressed up, ought to be reviewable in terms of principles of fairness, in an environment which is protected from the pressure of surrounding social forces. Where no forum exists, people may create one — in legal or quasi-legal form, sometimes in "wall-papers" or an underground press, frequently in international public opinion. Organizations like Amnesty International and the International Commission of Jurists address this latter tribunal on behalf of the many who have no access to a regular, independent court of justice. The same is done by all sorts of national groups — the Crazy Mothers of the Plaza de Mayo in Argentina, the Legal Aid Institute of Jakara. Often, however, even access to this court of international public opinion is closed.

Citizenship. The example of children discussing, or perhaps fighting over, the game of marbles shows that we have to do with two kinds of interaction. There is, first, the interaction taking place within the context outlined by the rules of the game. Then there is interaction in which this rule-confirming activity is deferred or interrupted and the rules themselves become the subject of discussion and critical evaluation. What could be taken for granted and remain implicit in one context, becomes problematic, susceptible to re-interpretation and revision in the other. As we have seen, in the latter context two issues typically come up for discussion. The first one concerns the fairness of the rules and their application; the second has to do with the usefulness of the rules: do they make the game interesting? These two questions indicate two potential functions of law-as-critical-discussion: to guarantee fairness and contribute to the purposiveness of social intercourse.

This discussion constitutes the political dimension of social life: people participate in it as citizens. The two kinds of interaction and participation correspond to two kinds of social identity: one deriving from the place a person occupies in the social division of labour; and another, that of citizenship, deriving from membership in a political community. (I shall not now consider a third social identity which derives from primordial "givens" such as ethnicity, race, and religion). The coexistence of these two kinds of social interaction and identities may be illustrated by the example of the ancient Greek polis (Arendt, 1958: ch. 2). The polis was characterized by a juxtaposition of two sharply differentiated spheres, the private sphere of the household and the public sphere of politics. In the household, life was subjected to the laws of economic necessity and the will of its master. The public sphere, however, was the realm of free political discourse which centered on public meetings where those who were citizens came together to discuss the affairs of government.

In modern times the private and the public no longer exist as separate spheres. However, analytically the distinction is still significant. We may no longer be able to designate concrete activities as either public or private, yet we can distinguish private and public aspects or dimensions in, theoretically, all social relationships, at home and at work, as well as in politics. In modern society all relationships have acquired a "citizenship-" dimension and all relationships lend themselves to political decision making, including the most intimate ones. When my little daughter reminds me of my earlier promise to take her to the swimming pool, she addresses me as a fellow citizen of our household who holds me to my word. Much of politics, on the other hand, has come to be dominated by private aspects. Many people are "in politics" because it means an attractive job, a good salary, interesting intercourse, that is for motives of private consumption, which may inspire a great deal of their public activity as well.

One socially important development of the last decades has been the growing recognition in the Western world of workers' rights of citizenship in industry. From this point of view, Works Council Acts, such as exist in Holland and Germany, constitute attempts at introducing a principle of free deliberation into the sphere of production, which seems inescapably ruled by economic laws, technological dictates, organizational rationality and hierarchical authority. When the Works Council meets, work is interrupted and becomes the subject of discussion; management is questioned on the soundness of its policies; persons in command are held accountable for the way in which they exercise their authority. A procedurally demarcated social space is created in which, theoretically at least, surrounding organizational constraints, external pressures of work, and individual differences in function, learning and status, are suspended. Inside the domain of "the private" a public sphere is established, where matters of general interest may be debated, the wisdom of given organizational rules and the fairness of their application may be called into question, and where the administration of the organization may be criticized. I do not want to overstate the case of the Works Council as an institution that carries the potential for changing the basic authority structure of the industrial enterprise[1]. The point I want to argue is that inside the "given" interaction-system of the industrial enterprise, which operates on the basis of a functional division of labour and under the dictates of class-based hierarchical rule, another interaction-system is set up, which operates on the basis of very different principles, yet is critically related to it. Important conditions for the realization of this critical relationship are publicity, independence and competence. *Publicity* means that everybody may see how affairs are conducted, hear the arguments, know what is at issue. Publicity in this sense implies access. As a matter of principle, there can only be "open meetings" where everybody has "standing", may make his views known and is entitled to have them seriously considered. *Independence* means that discussions are not to be dominated by external conditions, particularly forces in the interaction-system the normative premises of which are in debate. Much is demanded of the civic *competence* of participants. Often a certain kind of attitude seems to be required – distrustful, inquisitive, stubborn, vindicative – that goes against existing expectations. When we consider these conditions in the context of the forces that work in opposite direction, it may become apparent how precarious they are. The setting of a capitalistic enterprise imposes obvious restrictions on the potential development of any scheme of "industrial democracy". Yet the capitalistic enterprise only exemplifies, albeit in stark fashion, the power of antagonistic conditions that exist quite generally, even in societies with a pronounced democratic ethos. Seen in this light, a true political community of citizens may never be more than an aspiration. As such, however, it constitutes an essential normative assumption of most of our legal and political institutions, and inspires much of our thought and action. Short of full achievement, variations in the direction of its realization determine in an important sense the human quality of social life.

With respect to civic competence there is one question which deserves more particular attention. Does citizenship require specialized knowledge?

[1] In this respect, I agree with Fürstenberg (1958) who, referring to the German experience, has pointed to the typical dangers of the Works Council's isolation from the body of workers, ritualistic performance, and development into an extension of the plant's personnel division, thus emphasizing the Works Council's institutional weakness. However, he also recognizes a certain effect of the Works Council in relaxing the authoritarian command and communication structure of the enterprise by constituting an instance of appeal.

The assumption of the Dutch Works Council Act that workers who are elected as members of a Works Council need training in order to be able to function effectively in that role, may not be unrealistic, but is it correct? And if it is, what kind of training, what special knowledge, would citizens need, in order to make democracy work? These questions are as old as democracy itself. In the ancient Athenian polis political life was based on the assumption that all citizens were equally qualified to participate in government. However, this assumption was not undisputed. In Plato's dialogue *Protagoras* the question is the subject of debate between Socrates and Protagoras. Could all citizens be supposed to possess the necessary knowledge or virtue for taking part in the conduct of public affairs? And if they did not, was this something that could be taught to them? The ensuing dialogue is useful as an elucidation of some of the implications and problems of the notion of "law as critical discussion". Particularly relevant is the distinction made between technical judgments, which can only be made by persons who by virtue of expert knowledge are especially qualified to make them, and political judgments. In Socrates' own words:

> I hold that the Athenians, like the rest of the Hellenes, are sensible people. Now when we meet in the Assembly, then if the State is faced with some building project, I observe that the architects are sent for and consulted about the proposed structures, and when it is a matter of shipbuilding, the naval designers, and so on with everything which the Assembly regards as a subject for learning and teaching. If anyone else tries to give advice, whom they do not consider an expert, however handsome or wealthy or nobly-born he may be, it makes no difference: the members reject him noisily and with contempt, until either he is shouted down and desists, or else he is dragged off or ejected by the police on the orders of the presiding magistrates. That is how they behave over subjects they consider technical. But when it is something to do with the government of the country that is to be debated, the man who gets up to advise them may be a builder or equally well a blacksmith or a shoemaker, merchant or shipowner, rich or poor, of good family or none. No one brings it up against any of these, as against those I have just mentioned, that here is a man who without any technical qualifications, unable to point to anybody as his teacher, is yet trying to give advice. The reason must be that they do not think this is a subject that can be taught (Guthrie, 1956).

From this exposition I want to retain the thesis that in political matters, including questions of justice and legal fairness, everybody is held to be competent of judgment. It may indeed be argued that there is a valuing in law and democracy of non-expertise, and that this has a potential for preserving a moral quality of human affairs. In the dialogue the question whether civic virtue can be taught remains open. Surely, it cannot be taught like any kind of technical knowledge, even though familiarity with some of the pitfalls and tricks of law and politics might not be wasted on anyone. (For purposes of demystification sophistry may yet have educative utility). However, the real answer to the question concerning civic education lies in Socrates' life-long endeavour to empty the minds of his fellow-citizens of false knowledge and in his continuous search, in critical dialogues, for general moral principles about which all persons, once they had "discovered" them, could agree.

Legal discussion. In the concept of law as critical discussion, discussion *about* law is part of law itself. No line can meaningfully be drawn between inside and outside. Every contest, every vindication, legal or illegal, has legal import. Even the struggle against law has, inescapably, legal meaning. For sake of clarity I want to detach the idea of law as critical discussion from another manner of speaking of law which recently has gained some popularity, viz. the notion of law as a (closed, established) juridical discourse. In the words of an adherent of this view, such discourse is "an ensemble of linguistic acts, organized according to certain principles" (Broekman, 1978; 1979 and supra; cf. also Heller supra). In this view, the most important characteristic of an established juridical discourse is that it keeps all legal thought imprisoned within bounds determined by a limited number of central presuppositions which are dictated by the dominant ideology of the surrounding social environment. The established juridical discourse, then, expresses in stark and concentrated form the dominant ideology which, in turn, finds its confirmation in it. According to this theory, this is not merely a matter of law being *dominated* by the ruling ideal interests which would still leave room for deviant and oppositional legal thought and action; rather, law is to be understood as a function of those very interests. Juridical discourse can only be carried on in such a manner that certain truths are always confirmed. These truths, since they constitute the foundations of juridical discourse and condition all its categories and patterns of thought, cannot themselves be called into question. One such "truth" is the principle of individualistic atomism according to which society can only be seen as a getting together of individuals and the other person as the boundary of my liberties (Broekman, 1978, 1979 and supra). Now, this juridical discourse is thought to impose itself in an obligatory fashion; its rules are to be obeyed by everybody who takes part in legal life. Legally one can only make sense by expressing oneself through the ways and means in which the established truths lie moored. In the words of Foucault (1971), to whose ideas much of this can be traced, "one may speak the truth in the space of a savage exterior; but what one says can only *be true* if one obeys the rules of a discursive 'police' ... which one must reactivate in each of one's discourses".

Are we really so stuck to established ways of thought, reasoning and discussion that we are unable to call dominant truths into question? I do not want to minimize this problem. I have already pointed to the need for a critical discussion to be independent of forces in the environment. In reality such independence may never be fully attained, if only because people continue to speak the same language and do not undo their socialization in established meanings when they shift from one interaction-system to another. Moreover, there is the authoritarian appearance of the official administration of justice. Legal disputes are typically dealt with in the monumental setting of a *palais de justice* or an equivalent intimidating setting, under the authority of magistrates who represent the established order and who appear as official experts in matters of right and wrong. In this discourse, presided over by authority, only such kinds of criticism are admitted, that have no consequences for the status quo; only those questions can be raised the answers to which have already been formulated. Perhaps there is no language available (not in the formal language of official law) in which protest and moral indignation can be expressed and in which human worth can be vindicated. Perhaps these can only be expressed in the nonlanguage of absenteeism and riots. With respect to the possibility of legal criticism, however, I want to make three observations.

(1) A distinction has to be made between a discourse which admits only a certain kind of question, which can accommodate only a certain kind of problem and knows only a certain kind of truth, and discourse aimed at uncovering such limitations, aspiring towards liberation. There is, for example, the theoretical and political counter-discourse constituted by the researches of Foucault and others, which presents critical reinterpretations of established modes of understanding and which continues the various "dispersed and discontinuous offensives" against official truths: in anti-psychiatry; in attacks by prisoners and others upon the legal and penitentiary system; in the "insurrection of subjugated knowledges" (Foucault, 1980a: 80); in the attempts at "countering the grips of power with the claims of bodies, pleasures, and knowledges, in their multiplicity and in their possibility of resistance" (Foucault, 1980b: 157); in the search for a new, anti-disciplinarian and non-authoritarian form of right (Foucault, 1980a: 108) — "the 'right' to life, to one's body, to health, to happiness, to the satisfaction of needs and, despite all the oppressions, or 'alienations', the 'right' to rediscover what one is and all that one can be" (Foucault, 1980b: 145); in the discourse, too, of the intellectual "against the forms of power that transform him into its object and instrument in the sphere of 'knowledge', 'truth', 'consciousness', and 'discourse'" (Foucault, 1977: 207):

(2) Positive law, as it is created and continuously recreated in an ongoing discourse, is not a homogeneous system. It contains authoritarian *and* liberating meanings (cf. Habermas supra 209). This is especially true for the law of present-day Western societies which must maintain a precarious compromise between universalistic values of citizenship, and the interests of capitalism and class domination. The legal system inevitably reveals the contradictory nature of social life itself. Next to the dominant, integrative logic of capitalism it has been forced, as a consequence of class struggle, to accommodate elements of an antagonistic logic which point in the direction of socialism and freedom (cf. Basso, 1975).

(3) The meaning of legal categories, patterns of reasoning and acting, is not fixed or inherent. It depends on the interests which call for justification, on the manner in which the law is invoked and the legal process used and integrated in social action and political struggle. It would be a mistake, also historically, to think that critical legal discussions can, or should, only take place in parliamentary style. If the dominant discourse has monopolized the parliamentary forms of debate and if alternative views and vital interests are systematically excluded, real discussion can only come off in a different manner. If legality has become subjugated by established interests and subordinated to the needs of power, legal criticism will have to take on illegal form. The struggle for justice may have to be conducted with illegal, sometimes even violent, means. There are the obvious historical cases of revolt against systems of colonial domination, of armed resistance against foreign military occupation, of illegal strikes by the working class in the early phases of capitalism, of the political illegalities to which people often heroically resort under totalitarian regimes. In all these cases there is no room for disputing the rights of power in a legal way. However, such room may be quite narrow as well in systems which are formally democratic. The squatters movement, for example, which in the past decade has developed in several West-European countries, has brought about a discussion that had not been possible within the limits set by legality. Through illegal occupations of empty houses this movement has forced a discussion upon the system in which use value claimed right of priority over legally protected exchange value, interests of neigbourhood were defended against city-development, and spontaneous, grass-root organization confronted an alienated system of government. This line of argument gives rise to problems of tactics and strategy. The language of protest and struggle must be understood not only by comrades, but also by "the system"; proposed solutions should not only be radical, but also practicable. However, the closer one sticks to the rules of established discourse, the more futile may be the attempts to communicate something significant; and the more practical one's proposals the less chance there may be that they will contain something new.

I want to illustrate this with the example of criticism of the criminal law. Two types of legal critique may be distinguished; technical and what I shall call social legal critique. In the former the ends of the law are not at issue, in the latter they are. Technical critique of law stays within the boundaries of law as a specialized social function; it is concerned with the question to what extent this function realizes the purposes that have been attributed to it. With respect to the criminal law, for example, it asks how the tasks assigned to this branch of "the administration of justice" might be fulfilled in a better way. This kind of technical critique of law is standard. Social critique of law, however, is less common; it judges law in the light of general human values. Mostly this critique is not the concern of professional jurists, the technicians of right and wrong. However, it sometimes is, as in the case of Professor Louk Hulsman of Rotterdam who criticizes the practices of criminal justice from an abolitionist point of view. The intention underlying this critique is "to renew completely the global discourse on what is called the phenomenon of crime, and on the social reaction which this calls forth" (Hulsman, 1982). Hulsman considers criminal justice to be an inhumane and harmful social practice whose abolition is a matter of moral urgency. In his own words:

> If, in my garden, I remove the obstacles which prevent sun and water from fertilizing the soil, plants will grow up the existence of which I had not even dreamt of. The disappearance of the punitive system of the state may, likewise, result in a conviviality which will be more sane and more dynamic, and which will open up ways that may lead toward a new kind of justice.

Such views have not been appreciated within the legal establishment. According to one of its representatives: "with this abstract utopianism the author places himself outside the sphere of serious discussion" (Remmelink, 1980). One is advised not to listen: There are two grounds for this rejection of abolitionism. First, since it is too radical, it is not practicable. Secondly, by subjecting the most fundamental premises of criminal justice to criticism, including the special role of jurists, and by presenting this criticism as a problem of practical morality, which, in principle, is the concern of all men, this critique transcends the boundaries of regular juridical discourse. This cannot fail to irritate *serious* people, who, in the words of Simone de Beauvoir (1947), call nothing in question:

> The serious man calls nothing in question; for the military officer, the army is useful; for the colonial administrator, the road that must be built; for the serious revolutionary, the revolution; army, road, revolution, products of man becoming inhuman idols to which one will not hesitate to sacrifice man himself.

Problematic Reality

Society as project. The model of law as critical discussion is closely related to modern society's "modern" character, that is, its *man-made* aspect. Law itself reflects this aspect, for critical discussion is possible only about what is made by man and what can eventually be changed by man. On the other hand, this meaning of modern society, as the work of man, can only be kept alive through continuous critical discussion. The special contribution of law lies in the fact that it offers patterns of questioning and demanding, a structure of accountability for the conduct of social affairs. From this man-made aspect of modern society follow several important constitutional characteristics of modern social reality.

First, modern society is inherently "unfinished". Society as it actually exists is experienced as not quite valid. Many things in it need to be changed. There is no government that is not busy pursuing change and there is no political party that is not committed to the same. It is not society as it *de facto* exists that is valid, but society as it ought to become. Orientation towards change has become a structural characteristic. Social reality can be understood only in terms of the tension between its actual state and an ideal state which is projected into the future. It is inconceivable that this will ever be different. Modern society is doomed to remain an unfinished project.

A second characteristic is uncertainty. Even though we strive for a future, we are not sure about the ways in which that future may be reached. Not only the meaning of the present but also the meaning of the past has become uncertain. In modern times we see a continuous rewriting of history, which forces us to modify established images of the past. Certain knowledge no longer exists. If there has ever been a belief that sure and objectively valid knowledge of social reality could be obtained and that social science could discover its "laws", later developments and controversies in social theory have evaporated this illusion. One cannot very well imagine that there will ever be a sociological certainty which will not be contested.

A third structural characteristic of modern society is its controversial nature. What is valid and not valid in a concrete situation, what ought to be changed, how the future is to be, which means must be used to reach that future, all this is subject to controversy. Here again, we cannot imagine that this will ever be otherwise. Even the interpretation of existing reality, of what "social facts" are, is controversial, dependent on the material and ideal interests which are invested in that reality.

The uncertain and controversial nature of modern social reality gives rise to two sorts of conflict. Uncertainty is difficult to bear; people crave for certainty. As soon as the old gods are dead, new ones are created. There is a permanent temptation to escape from the unescapable. At issue is the very essence of modern society. Recent times have witnessed many instances of massive denial of modernity and of irrational flight into the pseudo-truths of blood, soil, religion, ideology, nation, progress, and what not. The same choice presents itself at the levels of institutional and personal life: whether or not to accept the modern condition of uncertainty, ambiguity, relativity. A second kind of conflict is associated with the contradictory interests, material or ideal, that different classes or groups of people have invested in the existing reality and in particular futures. Everybody may agree that many things ought to be changed. But different classes and different groups have different ideas about what ought to change and how. All this testifies to the precariousness of modern society's most fundamental attributes. There are forces which tend to obliterate them. There are people who want to convince others and themselves that things are not man-made, that they are as they only can be, and that this is not a matter of choice and political decision. They will appeal to religious belief, to science, to research which has proved this or that, to lessons of the past, to destiny. We find this problematic character of modern society clearly demonstrated in the works of the founders of sociology. I shall briefly consider Durkheim's ideas on this.

As is well known, Durkheim was especially interested in the question of how a society is kept together. What is the integrating element, the social force binding people together into a group or society which, to them, becomes a source of identity and meaning? What makes society more than a mere aggregate of individuals? Durkheim's major concern was the problem of modern industrial society which, according to him, showed many pathological developments when compared with the traditional agrarian societies of the past. In modern society "community" could no longer be taken for granted. Because of his preoccupation with this question, Durkheim has sometimes been criticized for attaching too much importance to social integration and control. This criticism does not do him justice. The way he dealt with the problem and the answers be came up with show clearly that he was not concerned with social cohesion, integration and control as such but, more crucially, with the question of their quality.

"Society" was for Durkheim a highly normative concept, corresponding to a phenomenon which could only be understood in terms of its normative structure. He saw the normative character of social reality and social "facts" not as something added from outside but as its constitutive element, its integrative principle, its very essence. The operational value of this principle varies; it does not work automatically but only through the committed activities of men. The division of labour, for example, has created a need for rules that may guide the exchange of goods and services on which social life has come to depend (Durkheim, 1893). Such rules, however, do not always come about spontaneously. Besides, if these rules are to give institutional form to a true "contractual solidarity", which would be necessary for them in order to command people's loyalties, they must be just. And just rules mean rules that promote fairness in contractual relations. This justice is not something that stands above man, but that is human, open to rational inquiry.

Here we see three notions of social order united in one dynamic concept of social reality: (1) actual contractual practices, that is, practices of exchange of goods and services, inevitably brought about by the social division of labour, a phenomenon which sociological positivism might recognize as "social facts"; (2) the law of contracts which, though insufficiently, provides a normative framework for these contractual practices, legal rules which legal positivism might recognize as valid law; and (3) an evolving notion of what constitutes a "just contract" which, as value-to-be-realized, serves as model for law-making and, indirectly, for the contractual practices themselves. This ideal is, of necessity, only insufficiently realized and calls for continuous legal reform. In this multi-layered normative structure of social reality we may recognize the distinction, made by Hart (1963), between positive morality ("the morality actually accepted and shared by a given social group") and critical morality ("the general moral principles used in the criticism of actual social institutions including positive morality"). I want to emphasize the element of criticism. Critical review of social practices and institutions has become *the* most conspicuous feature of modern society's moral life. In this conception a special task devolves upon intellectuals, those, as Sartre (1972) has said, who meddle with what does not regard them: to constitute a social conscience (Durkheim, 1898). Even the state, seen not as embodiment of power – Durkheim (1915) scorned Treitschke's dictum *Der Staat ist Macht*, but, above all, as parliament, is to be valued as institution of critical reflection: "Properly speaking everything in the life of the state goes ... in deliberations ... The state is strictly speaking the very organ of social thought" (Durkheim, 1950). As is well known, Durkheim saw modern society as deficient in terms of its own ideals, hence, in need of reform. Again, this work of reform is not to be considered as something imposed upon social reality, but as an integral part of it.

Reification and dereification. A critical understanding of social reality assumes (a) a notion of positive reality "as it is", e.g., prevailing contractual practices, (b) general concepts, such as a notion of what constitutes a "true" or "fair" contract, and (c) some space, whether or not institutionalized, in which reality and general concepts can be related to each other. The third assumption implies that "reality" is experienced as "problematic" and that general concepts are not taken as absolutes but as meaningful only in critical application to the "reality" (cf. Teubner 302 infra). Discussion is critical only if it has practical consequences. This concept of law stands in radical opposition to the notion of law as buttress of established social order. The opposition may be formulated as law on the side of reification *versus* law on the side of dereification. This may be clarified by briefly considering two analyses by Marx of the function of law in the process of historical change.

A large part of Marx's sociology of law is devoted to the analysis of the rise of capitalist private property as an exclusive jurisdiction of the owner, freed from the customary restraints of social purpose and participatory rights of others. In the first volume of Capital (1867), following the chapter on the expropriation of the English peasants, Marx describes the "bloody legislation" against the expropriated. This process of expropriation had been extremely cruel and violent and law had been part of it. Marx's analysis gives insight into the role of law as a coercive device in the course of social development. In periods of institutional change, i.e., change from one "pattern of normalcy" to another "pattern of normalcy", law plays an important role as an instrument of force, to drive people, so to speak, from one pattern to the other. This is the case when there is a change from a pattern of communal use of the land to a system of exclusive jurisdiction over the land by a single proprietor. Another example is provided by the transition from the traditional master-servant relationship to a contractual relationship between capitalist and worker based on wage and a hierarchical organization of the labour process. Such a transition must, in a very real sense, be forced upon people. Initially, there may have been a need for criminal law sanctions to remind the worker of his contractual obligations[2], and the capitalist may have needed "a penal code of his own" to fight loafing on the job and to discipline the workers[3]. Likewise there was a need for anti-union legislation to prevent workers from collectively resisting the new system, and, often, anti-press laws to prevent critical public discussion. Once the new system was firmly established, however, it became compelling by its own logic. Being the dominant force in shaping people's behaviour and expectations, it generated its own self-perpetuation. As Marx observed, direct force was hardly necessary any more to discipline the workers. Modern industrial organization has in many respects perfected its inherent powers of control. Rational organization of labour, Taylorism, minute classification of functions with corresponding wage-differentials, sometimes supplemented by "promotion-"tracks, job-evaluation systems, etc., have made the penal code of the factory superfluous. In the words of Marx, "the organization of the process of production, once fully developed, breaks down all resistance." Involved is a process of habituation, in which the working class gradually grows accustomed to the new conditions and adjusts its moral expectations. The new social relations come to be seen as "natural", even "inevitable"; they become reified, i.e., they come to be seen as "things". This reification of man-made social arrangements and the rise of new patterns of normalcy and reasonable expectations have two important consequences. First, law loses much of its saliency in upholding social order. To the extent that it provides rules for social interaction, like the law of contracts, it becomes part of established routines and is, therefore, largely "self-executing". The use of law as a means of social control can be limited to exceptional situations and to cases of deviance. In the second place, it becomes clear what the importance is of historical analyses like those carried out by Marx, in which these processes of reification are exposed, and of revolutionary thought and practice in which they are undone. Ultimately, what is at stake here, is the modern, i.e. man-made, nature of modern society itself.

[2] Compare Capital I (Modern Library Edition) 464—465, the footnotes by Engels about the *initial* need for criminal law enforcement of the workers' "contractual" obligations.

[3] English edition p. 219. Elsewhere (p. 464) Marx speaks of the overlooker's book of penalties which in the modern factory has taken the place of the slave driver's lash.

Not only social reality but ideas, too, run the risk of reification. The classicial analysis of hypostatisation of legal concepts and their alienation from actual life is to be found in Marx's (1843a) discussion of legal and political emancipation. He criticizes the legal concept of citizenship in which citizenship is relegated to the isolated sphere of "politics" so that it loses all relevance in social and economic relations. In the view of Marx, political emancipation, i.e. the acquisition of equal rights of citizenship, *may* constitute an important step on the way towards real, social emancipation, but it can never be more than that. On the contrary, when emancipation remains limited to the sphere of law and politics it easily becomes a substitute for real emancipation, because it allows inequality and forms of coercive domination to continue in social and economic life. This is what has actually happened in modern history; man has come to live a double life: "He lives in the political world, where he regards himself as a social being, and in society, where he behaves simply as a private individual, using other people as means, degrading himself to the role of a mere means, thus becoming the plaything of alien powers." Marx uses the concept of "true man", man as he is according to his "essence". He speaks of man as "species-being", that is, man considered in terms of his specifically human qualities, which he shares with all other men and by which he distinguishes himself from animals. In historical reality this human essence of man is in many ways denied and violated. Marx saw people who use others as their instruments and those who are thus used as alienated from their true human nature. For him this alienation was epitomized in the degradation of the worker under capitalism. It is clear that by itself formal recognition of the liberty and equality of men in a legal constitution does not eliminate from social reality the prevailing patterns of negation of man's true nature. Real emancipation, according to Marx, can only take place when the ideals of political citizenship — equality, liberty, rule of law, and the like — are extended to the sphere of actual social life, especially in the field of economics. As long as this does not happen, the ideals of citizenship are no more than vain abstractions, "creations of fantasy, dreams"; deceptive and dangerous illusions, for they blur our view of reality and divert our attention and energy from the real work we have to do.

Emancipation demands that the concept of political freedom comes to govern social reality. However, the opposite has happened: politics has become subservient to the forces that dominate society; the citizen has entered into the service of the bourgeois. In actual social life man lives an a-political, egoistic and passive existence, yielding to external forces and giving way to his immediate, privatized and sensual feelings. Man's true nature is projected on the abstract level of political and legal rights where it remains an empty category. Real emancipation, according to Marx, can only be achieved when these two — meaningless life and lifeless meaning —

are brought together. It is true that for Marx ideas did not determine the course of history. With respect to legal ideals his enterprise was, on the whole, one of debunking. Yet, he recognized the value of some ideal concepts — including legal principles — as clues to man's true nature and to a just society. The *truth* of these ideals, as he saw it, could only be redeemed by transforming them into practice: "The critique of speculative legal philosophy cannot remain within its own sphere, but leads on to tasks which can only be solved by means of practical activity." (Marx, 1843b).

Legitimacy. In the procedural concept of law advanced here, a central role is assigned to rational justification of rules and decisions. Law is seen as institutionalizing the conditionality of positive law and order in a procedurally created space in which prevailing rules and authority are, actually or virtually, suspended and room is made for questioning their validity. Here again the modern character of society is at stake; we are confronted with the task of freeing ourselves from irrational restrictions on our thinking, feeling, appreciation and action. In this sense the progress of law is tied up with the emancipation of man. In this progress the problem of power comes to the foreground. By making social order and the structure of authority transparent, power becomes visible and persons who by their decisions wield power are identified. This calls up the question of the legitimacy of this power and of these decisions. In traditional societies authority and the exercise of power were mostly embedded in firmly established social and moral contexts. Under these conditions all power was, in principle, legitimate power; its *regular* use could not give cause to dispute. In modern times power has been loosened from contextual constraints and has come to connote autonomous action. In the words of Leonard Krieger (1967), "by general consensus, the problem of power as we know it is coeval with the modern period of history." The most important forms of modern discretionary power are the institutions of capitalist private property and the modern power state with its proper *raison*. In modern time legitimacy has typically become an unstable and *variable* quality of power. The model of law as critical discussion provides only one of several possible answers to this *chronic* problem of legitimacy. This may be schematically indicated as follows[4]:

[4] I want to dispense with a comparative discussion of these modes of legitimation. The general idea of each may easily be understood. The scheme summarizes some of the theoretical notions of Weber (1922), Luhmann (1969), Selznick (1969) and Habermas (1973).

Modes of Legitimation

	conformist	critical
static	confirming to existing social expectations, to what is customary	formal compliance with established law or accepted principles
dynamic	creation of willingness to accept through involvement in proceedings instituted for that purpose	justification through rational arguments in critical discussion

Legitimation through critical discussion has the same structure as legal reasoning and moral justification generally. This structure shows the following characteristics: (a) contradictory interests, ideal or material; (b) option of normative regulation; and (c) concepts which transcend the concrete situation and constitute a normative framework for interpretation and justification. Discussion and contention are possible with respect to each of these elements. The fact that there are contradictory interests makes the question of legitimacy salient. However, in cultures which set a high value on social harmony and a consensual approach to problem solving, conflict may be denied or suppressed. Such cultural preferences are often quite stable since they tend to be favoured, and enforced, by governments and power elites. From a traditional religious point of view certain institutional arrangements may be interpreted as sacred so that man is not free to alter them. On the other hand, technocrats may argue that there is only one technically correct solution, hence no choice. Further, those who seek legitimacy will try to monopolize generally accepted ideas for their interests, like the bourgeoisie representing its interests as those of humanity, governments identifying the public interest with their own, etc. Moral justification involves an understanding of factual and normative assertions in terms of more general concepts. These general concepts are the fruits of an ongoing work of creative interpretation of received legal and moral ideas in the light of ever-changing social conditions. They are conditionally accepted as a normative framework for legal and moral reasoning. Unlike the case of legitimation through formal compliance with law or accepted principles, in this model norms and principles have no fixed value. Like all normative claims, assertions with respect to the meaning and validity of these principles and concepts are also subject to re-interpretation and re-evaluation. The value of concepts for critical discussion derives from their transcendent quality, their "excess of meaning" (Marcuse, 1964), which points beyond positive reality to fuller social achievements and which enables us to disengage ourselves morally from positive reality and criticize it. Concepts like contract, rule of law, fair trial, human rights, democracy, etc., lose their transcendent quality when they are reduced to their operational meaning. Their referential value is then limited to the status quo and they can no longer be used to contradict the validity of prevailing practice. In recent times there has been no shortage of analyses, especially by Marcuse (1964), of the tendencies in advanced industrial society to annihilate all possibility of critical thought.

The implications of the model of legitimation through critical discussion have been clarified in several studies by Jürgen Habermas (1962; 1963; 1973). In these studies Habermas has elaborated a theory of "legitimation in terms of publicly discussed and rationally justified purposes" (Habermas, 1963) through extrapolation of legal principles and modes of justification implicit in rule-making, legal procedure and the idea of law generally (cf. also Habermas supra 212). What Habermas calls *herrschaftsfreier Diskurs* indicates a model of critical discourse, free from domination and irrational restrictions, in which only the better arguments count[5]. According to Habermas, the Western institutions of parliamentary democracy and rule of law are based on such a model of open, free, informed, and rational discussion. This model, of course, is nowhere fully realized; prevailing political and legal practices are at best approximations of it. The model specifies several normative requirements. In the present context two of these deserve special attention.

(1) Discussion ought to be "removed from contexts of experience and action." This can be taken to mean two things. First, it refers to the external position we may take, outside the concrete context of social action, in order to reflect on it and discuss its normative validity and wisdom generally. Secondly, it points to the *veil of ignorance* that characterizes the "original position" of John Rawls' theory of justice. According to Rawls, just principles of social order are those principles that free and rational persons, meeting in an initial position of equality, and concerned to promote their own interests, would accept as normative terms for their social interaction. Those principles would have to be chosen behind a "veil of ignorance":

[5] Habermas (1974: 107) defines this model as "that form of communication that is removed from contexts of experience and action and whose structure assures us: that the bracketed validity claims of assertions, recommendations, or warnings are the exclusive object of discussion; that participants, themes and contributions are not restricted except with reference to the goal of testing the validity claims in question; that no force except that of the better argument is exercised; and that, as a result, all motives except that of the cooperative search for truth are excluded".

> No one should know his place in society, his class position or social status, nor (should) anyone know his fortune in the distribution of natural assets and abilities, his intelligence, strength, and the like ... The principles of justice are chosen behind a veil of ignorance. This ensures that no one is advantaged or disadvantaged in the choice of principles by the outcome of natural chance or the contingency of social circumstances (Rawls, 1971: 11).

That is to say, if we were to decide what would be the constitutional rights of ethnic minorities, we should abstract from knowledge about our own ethnic affiliation, for taking such knowledge into account would certainly make our judgment biased. In practice, of course, people always have such knowledge, and it may be too difficult for them not to use it. Yet this does not detract from the validity of the concept of an original position as an ideal to be approximated in constitutional discussions. Indeed, we tend to ascribe greater moral validity to rules, principles and policies when these are not visibly motivated by the self-interest of those who advocate or decide them.

(2) There can be no a priori validity of normative claims, for example, the claim that a particular policy should be followed or that a particular rule should apply. The validity of such claims can only be established in critical discussion. Society, of course, is not a debating club and social life would come to a standstill if all normative demands had to be first put to the test of a critical discussion. It is important, however, that normative claims can be criticized when there is doubt about their validity — point of order! — and that they then need to be justified with rational arguments. The model implies the concept of free and rational man: man as a competent citizen, who feels that he does not have to accept things because he is commanded to do so or to obey rules only because they conform to established practice or issue from instituted authority, but who at all times feels free to question the righteousness of any demand imposed on him and who feels entitled to rational and convincing answers which he is then willing to accept as normative premises for his own action; the citizen, indeed, with a sense of sovereignty.

Legitimation through critical discussion leads to legitimation "in depth". The concept *legitimacy in depth* has been introduced by Philip Selznick (1969) to denote justification in terms of arguments that reach beyond formal legality to underlying rationale. It contrasts with *gross* legitimation which consists in the justification of a law or a decision by tracing it to an authoritative source, for example the king or parliament, whose own legitimacy is deemed to need no justification and must therefore be obeyed. Legitimacy in depth means that, legality of origin notwithstanding, particular decisions and policies may be queried as to their rationality, their rightfulness and their wisdom in view of larger values and purposes (Selznick, 1969: 30). Questioning the validity of a rule or a particular interpretation and demanding clarification about its rationale promotes the development from concrete rules to more general principles and purposes as terms for justification of decisions. In this way general interests gain priority over particular interests. For in a free and rational discussion only those norms and policies can be accepted as legitimate which can be demonstrated to be in the interest of all, specifically including the most deprived groups. Put differently, only those interests can have normative validity that could be the interests of anybody, if we abstract from particulars that could have no status in Rawls' original position.

These tendencies – toward legitimation in depth, from rules to principles and purposes, and from the promotion of particular to the promotion of general interests – point in the direction of a rational and universal political morality (Habermas, 1973). The first of these tendencies relates to the mode of civic participation in society's normative order; the second concerns the nature of this normative order, especially its potential for rationality and its moral depth; the third pertains to the exclusiveness or inclusiveness of this order.

It is obvious that in reality this model of legitimation does not prevail. Actual legitimation falls short of the model's demanding assumptions. However, exposing such discrepancies as may exist constitutes a necessary part of a critical legal discussion and political practice which aims at reconstructing society along the lines of those ideals.

Countervailing Tendencies

The ideal and the actual. In the foregoing I have sketched a model of law as critical discussion which is highly normative. My assumption is that this normative quality cannot be dismissed as merely an arbitrary notion of "good law". The criteria of moral propriety which it contains derive from and are part of positive legal reality as an ongoing process. I do not consider, therefore, this normative concept to be any less empirically valid than positivistic definitions of law, even though it emphasizes aspects that are frequently honoured in the breach only.[6] I have tried to ground this concept of law as critical discussion in the theory of modern society. In doing so I have emphasized society's normative structure, that is, its orientation toward an ideal of the good society or "real society". This ideal aspect, too, is not taken to be something arbitrarily attributed to the factual

[6] In this view legal ideals, moral notions of propriety, legal doctrines, principles, etc. have the status of social phenomena which ought to be included in social analysis no less than "behaviour". This is so because in studying legal action, no matter whether of individuals, groups, institutions or legal officials, we have to take account of the intentions and interpretations of the acting subjects, and also of the ideal notions which inspire legal action, and the historical and social conditions which have given rise to these notions.

but as constituting an essential dimension of social reality, its truly social significance. Stress has been laid on the affinity between law and modernity. This would seem to be in accordance with the theoretical insights of Max Weber (1921) whose sociology of modern society has brought out the crucial role in modernization of legal rationality, both as dominant style of organization and as form of legitimation. It would seem to be in agreement also with the later evolutionary theories of Talcott Parsons (1966) and Niklas Luhmann (1967). According to Parsons the transition of a society to the modern stage of evolution is marked by the development of a legal system. This legal system has to meet certain requirements. Under the modern conditions of societal complexity and change law can only function as a general system of social control when it is organized around universalistic principles and when it assigns primary importance to *procedure* as distinguished from substantive precepts and standards: "Only on the basis of procedural primacy can the system cope with a variety of changing circumstances and types of cases without prior commitment to specific solutions" (Parsons, 1966: 26). Luhmann (1967) has stressed the fact that in modern society "the validity of law has been made completely dependent on organized decisions and in this manner has become the responsibility of a differentiated, specialized social system." (cf. also Luhmann 111 supra) These theories may explain how within the legal system a sphere of freedom and reflection is established which enhances society's adaptive capacity, rationality, and powers of self-control. This new freedom and reflexivity, and these new powers are attributes of social organization, of the social system. In this essay I have been concerned with the question of freedom, reflexivity, etc. not in the social system but in the interaction of men. Can freedom and modernity only be achieved by organizations or can they be appropritated, re-appropriated perhaps, by people? Modern social systems can and do function without modern men and in doing so they may make effective use of authoritarian law. The model of law advanced here is premised on man's capacity for modernity. In this perspective law is not appreciated for its instrumental and integrative functions but for its anti-systemic potential and its unsettling modus in the service of the emancipation of man. We live in a world which is in many ways dominated by this conflict between the emancipatory needs and aspirations of people and the demands of system. This statement can be made more specific by considering briefly some of the forces that work against critical legal discourse.

As I have argued, there exists a continuity between the concept of law as critical discussion and modern society's man-made aspect which finds expression in the rational reconstruction of social reality. Both critical law and society's man-made aspect, though implied in modernization, are precarious because of tendencies which ensue from a basic human need for security and a stable social environment, from the dynamics of social interaction and institutionalization, and from the very process of modernization.

There are, first, the countervailing forces in the practice of law itself. In part these draw on the other, authoritarian model of law, which belongs as much to the Western legal heritage as critical law. The authoritarian model certainly has the advantage of historical plausibility: its record in the service of dominant political and economic interests. In the light of this tradition critical legality may never be more than a cultural "counterpoint" (Wertheim, 1964, 1972). Countervailing forces inevitably inhere in the processes of institutionalization which continuously turn means, selected to promote values, into ends served for their own sake. Legality thus easily degenerates into legalism. This process of rigidification has been referred to as a "natural pathology of institutionalization"; it stands in contrast to a moral order which remains truly governed by aspirations, in which specific duties are seen as means to larger ends and subject to rational reassessment (Nonet and Selznick, 1978).

As has been pointed out by Marion Levy (1966: 26), all societies know the difference, as well as the discrepancies, between the ideal and the actual. It is possible to advance plausible functionalist arguments for such discrepancies. They may, among other things, serve to legitimize social hierarchy. The dynamics of any society or social group may in part be explained with reference to the differences between the ideal and the actual. Yet the problem of modern society is special in at least two ways: (a) the ideal has been permanently projected into the future; and (b) the ideal criteria in terms of which the actual is evaluated have lost their firm status in living traditions and have themselves become subject to political choice. A morality which demands that the modern qualities of our social reality — its imperfection, uncertainty, openness — and the political responsibility which follows from these qualities be recognized and upheld is more difficult to bear than any traditional moral code, and it is continuously in danger of being replaced by more comforting ideological substitutes and authoritarian patterns of social order.

The Welfare State as an adverse condition. In conclusion I want to consider briefly three tendencies in today's state of social affairs, more specifically in the practice of the Welfare State, which have an adverse effect on critical legal discourse. These tendencies were already well understood by Rousseau.

> The citizen of the well-governed city goes to council-meetings as fast as his legs will carry him. Under a bad government, by contrast, every last citizen begrudges the steps that carry him toward the meeting-place, for the following reasons: (a) the business transacted there excites nobody's interest, (b) the citizen knows beforehand that the general will is not going to prevail, and, finally (c) everyone's time is completely mortgaged to his domestic concerns. (Rousseau, 1762: III, 15).

Without stretching the meaning of Rousseau's terms too much we may translate these negative factors to our own time as: (a) alienated bureaucratic dealings, (b) the belief that ideas about the good society and about justice are merely a matter of subjective personal preference and that such ideas carry no weight in view of hard social facts, and (c) a weakening of political commitment and privatization of the meaning of life. As the quotation from Rousseau indicates, these tendencies did not originate in the Welfare State, but they have been enormously reinforced by it.

In the Welfare State the concept of right has lost much of its constitutional significance. From a guaranteed "inalienable" sphere of discretion, a sovereignty, a power of creation, an attribute of man as producer, it has become an entitlement to care and benefits, an attribute of man as consumer (see Ewald, Habermas, Preuß supra). This *privatization of right* is documented by the transformation of the Western labour movement fighting for the emancipation of the working class to an encorporated organization representing mainly consumer interests. This transformation, in which membership in society was stripped of its political meaning, has been implicit in the Welfare State from the beginning. The intellectual father of the Welfare State, Bismarck, wanted to see "moderate Conservatives who would offer the people material benefits in place of those who thought only of formal guarantees". In 1871 he wrote: "The action of the state is the only means of arresting the Socialist movement. We must carry out what seems justified in the Socialist programme and can be realized within the present framework of state and society" (Taylor, 1955: 162). The so-called social rights of citizenship (Marshall 1965: 78) have not come about through re-uniting the political and the social as Marx had wanted it. Instead, these have been driven further asunder and the unemancipated state of man has, consequently, been confirmed.

The Welfare State has not only brought material benefits and social security but also a proliferation of consultative procedures and participatory devices. These have had effects which are quite the opposite of critical legal discourse. Through them people are coopted behaviourally into the system and they are alienated from their own reasoned convictions. The classical analysis of the various interactional processes and psychological mechanisms by which this *bureaucratic entrapment* is effectuated has been given by Luhmann (1969). The participation which takes place is not autonomous political action but organizationally induced activity. Organization is no longer an interaction-system like the game of marbles, the rules of which can be discussed and freely agreed upon by the participants. Rather it is an all-embracing on-going process into which one is willy-nilly drawn and inside of which it has become ever more difficult to make some room for constitutional thought and deliberation. Because of the important role which bureaucratic organizations play in the administration of the Welfare State a large part of culture has come to be dominated by bureaucratic modes of cognition and understanding (see Habermas supra). There is a continuous output of bureaucratic communication which holds whole populations in its grips and which makes autonomous thought and authentic dialogue virtually impossible. This bureaucratic mode of cognition "comes to constitute the things known and done themselves" (Wolin and Schaar, 1970: 86). Bureaucratic communication is not primarily a linguistic means of understanding between subjects who are on an equal footing. It is, rather, a quasi-language which serves the function of symbolic representation of officialism, bureaux, organization, system. We are witnessing daily the production of a consciousness which lacks all potential for critical opposition. What seems to be stifled here is the possibility of common discursive communication in which people can take part as subjects and in which human responsibility for the conduct of social affairs can be vindicated.

The "democratic" Welfare States of the West have seen an enormous expansion of individual freedom: freedom of expression, freedom to follow unorthodox life-styles, freedom from all sorts of traditional inhibitions of morality and the criminal law. The relative ease with which these new freedoms have come about shows how harmless they are for the dominant structures of power and interest. Instead of advancing the cause of emancipation, they seem to signify a new kind of expressive alienation: the *subjectivization of critical thought*. The new freedoms have been taken in by the prevailing mode of private consumption. Each is entitled to his own critical views about the meaning of life, about the good society, about justice, etc. In the words of Marcuse (1965: 94): "Within the affluent democracy, the affluent discussion prevails, and within the established framework, it is tolerant to a large extent. All points of view can be heard: the Communist and the Fascist, the Left and the Right, the White and the Negro, the crusaders for armament and for disarmament. Moreover, in endlessly dragging debates over the media, the stupid opinion is treated with the same respect as the intelligent one, the misinformed may talk as long as the informed, and propaganda rides along with education, truth with falsehood." What seems to be obscured here is objective meaning. As I have suggested, ideals which transcend the actual social situation are a necessary condition for critical discourse. However, ideals lose all critical significance when they become thus privately appropriated in the form of personal preferences, for which an ever more liberal law grants the rights.

References

ARENDT, Hannah (1958) *The Human Condition*. Chicago: University of Chicago Press.
BASSO, Lelio (1975) *Gesellschaftsformation und Staatsform*. Frankfurt: Suhrkamp.
BEAUVOIR, Simone de (1947) *Pour une morale de l'ambiguité*. Paris: Gallimard.
BROEKMAN, Jan M. (1978) *Recht en Anthropologie*. Antwerpen: Standaard.
– (1979) *Recht en taal*. Praeadvies Koninklijke Notariële Broederschap. Deventer: Kluwer.

DURKHEIM, Emile (1898) "L'individualisme et les intellectuels", *Revue bleue,* 4e série 10.
– (1915) *L'Allemagne au-dessus de tout: La mentalité allemande et la guerre.* Paris: Colin.
– (1950) *Leçons de sociologie.* Paris: Presses Universitaires de France.
– (1964) *The Division of Labor in Society.* New York: Free Press.
– (1973) *On Morality and Society: Selected Writings,* edited by Robert N. Bellah. Chicago: University of Chicago Press.
DURKHEIM, Emile, and Guglielmo FERRERO (1942) *The Principles of Power.* New York: Putnam.
FOUCAULT, Michel (1971) *L'ordre du discours.* Paris: Gallimard.
– (1977) *Language, Counter-Memory, Practice: Selected Essays and Interviews.* Oxford: Basil Blackwell.
– (1980a) *Power/Knowledge: Selected Interviews and other Writings.* New York: Pantheon.
– (1980b) *The History of Sexuality* I. New York: Vintage.
FÜRSTENBERG, Friedrich (1958) "Der Betriebsrat: Strukturanalyse einer Grenzinstitution", 10 *Kölner Zeitschrift für Soziologie und Sozialpsychologie* 418.
HABERMAS, Jürgen (1962) *Strukturwandel der Öffentlichkeit.* Neuwied/Berlin: Luchterhand.
– (1963) *Theorie und Praxis.* Neuwied/Berlin: Luchterhand.
– (1973) *Legitimationsprobleme im Spätkapitalismus.* Frankfurt: Suhrkamp.
– (1974) *Legitimation Crisis.* Boston: Beacon Press.
HART, Herbert L. A. (1961) *The Concept of Law.* Oxford: Clarendon Press.
– (1963) *Law, Liberty and Morality.* Stanford: Stanford University Press.
HULSMAN, Louk, et J. BERNAT DE CELIS (1982) *Peines perdues: le système pénal en question.* Paris: Centurion.
ILLICH, Ivan (1973) *Tools for Conviviality.* New York: Perennial Library.
KAWASHIMA, Takeyoshi (1963) "Dispute Resolution in Contemporary Japan", in Arthur T. von Mehren (ed.), *Law in Japan: The Legal Order in a Changing Society.* Cambridge, Mass.: Harard University Press.
– (1974) "The Legal Consciousness of Contract in Japan", 7 *Law in Japan* 1.
KRIEGER, Leonard (1967) "Power and Responsibility: The Historical Assumptions" in Leonard Krieger and Fritz Stern (eds.) *The Responsibility of Power.* Historical Essays in Honor of Hajo Holborn. Garden City, N.Y.: Doubleday.
LEVY, Marion J. Jr. (1966) *Modernization and the Structure of Societies.* Princeton: Princeton University Press.
LUHMANN, Niklas (1967) "Gesellschaftliche und politische Bedingungen des Rechtsstaates" in N. Luhmann (ed.), *Studien über Recht und Verwaltung.* Köln:
– (1969) *Legitimation durch Verfahren.* Neuwied/Berlin: Luchterhand.
MACAULEY, Stewart (1963) "Non-Contractual Relations in Business: a Preliminary Study", 28 *American Sociological Review* 55.
MARCUSE, Herbert (1964) *One-Dimensional Man.* Boston: Beacon Press.
– (1965) "Repressive Tolerance" in Robert Paul Wolff *et al. (ed.), A Critique of Pure Tolerance.* Boston: Beacon Press.
MARSHALL, Thomas H. (1965) *Class, Citizenship and Social Development.* Garden City, N.Y.: Doubleday.
MARX, Karl (1843a) *Zur Judenfrage.* In: Karl Marx und Friedrich Engels (1974) *Werke,* Band 1. Berlin: Dietz.
– (1843b) *Zur Kritik der Hegelschen Rechtsphilosophie.* In: Karl Marx und Friedrich Engels (1974) *Werke,* Band 1. Berlin: Dietz.
– (1867) *Das Kapital.* Erster Band. In: Karl Marx und Friedrich Engels (1972) *Werke,* Band 23. Berlin: Dietz.
– (1963) *Capital.* New York: Modern Library.
NONET, Philippe, and Philip SELZNICK (1978) *Law and Society in Transition: Toward Responsive Law.* New York: Harper & Row.

PARSONS, Talcott (1966) *Societies: Evolutionary and Comparative Perspectives*. Englewood Cliffs, N.J.: Prentice Hall.

PIAGET, Jean (1932) *Le jugement moral chez l'enfant*. Paris: Alcan.

PLATO (1956) *Protagoras*. (Translation by W. K. C. Guthrie). Harmondsworth: Penguin Books.

RAWLS, John (1971) *A Theory of Justice*. Cambridge, Mass.: Harvard University Press.

REMMELINK, Jan (1980) *Aktuelle Stromingen in het Nederlandse strafrecht*. Amsterdam: Noord Hollandse Uitgeversmaatschappij.

ROUSSEAU, Jean-Jacques (1762) *The Social Contract*. (1954) Chicago: Regnesy.

SARTRE, Jean-Paul (1972) *Plaidoyer pour les intellectuels*. Paris: Gallimard.

SELZNICK, Philip (1961) "Sociology and Natural Law", 6 *Natural Law Forum* 84.

– (1968) "The Sociology of Law", in *International Encyclopedia of the Social Sciences*. New York: Macmillan & The Free Press.

– (1969) *Law, Society, and Industrial Justice*. New York: Russell Sage Foundation.

TAYLOR, Alan J. P. (1955) *Bismarck: The Man and the Statesman*. New York: Vintage Books.

WEBER, Max (1922) *Wirtschaft und Gesellschaft*. Tübingen: Mohr (Siebeck).

– (1954) *On Law in Economy and Society*. Cambridge Mass.: Harvard University Press.

WERTHEIM, Willem F. (1964) "Society as a Composite of Conflicting Value Systems" in W. F. Wertheim (ed.), *East-West Parallels: Sociological Approaches to Modern Asia*. The Hague: van Hoeve.

– (1972) *Evolution and Revolution: The Rising Waves of Emancipation*. Harmondsworth: Penguin Books.

WOLIN, Sheldon S., and John H. SCHAAR (1970) *The Berkeley Rebellion and Beyond: Essays on Politics and Education in the Technological Society*. New York: The New York Review.

Three Types of Legal Structure: The Conditional, the Purposive and the Relational Program

HELMUT WILLKE
Bielefeld

I.

Still the nation state seems to be the central locus of collective identity and the main agent of societal guidance. In spite of all efforts to move beyond it to international levels and in spite of increasing economic interdependency between nations, the focus and unity of societal processes still revolve around the nation state. In fact, contrary to much theorizing in state and in legal theory, some developments not outside but rather within the nation state seem to undermine its very function: its capacity to plan, decide upon and implement programs and so to represent the unity of society.

In the course of its history there have been many challenges to this function of the state, ranging from socialist to liberal concepts. However, the rise of the welfare state within highly complex societies poses a drastically different problem: it is not that of the reduction or even the vanishing of the state (and its medium of action, the law) through its becoming increasingly superfluous, but instead, that of the failure of state and law to manage and guarantee the governability of complex democracies.

The success and the specific accomplishments of the state in establishing a welfare society turn out to be the conditions of its subsequent overload and crisis. For Western Europe, M. Crozier observes two basic characteristics of the probelm of governability which cut across the widely different practices and forms of the different countries:

> The European political systems are overloaded with participants and demands, and they have increasing difficulty in mastering the very complexity which is the natural result of their economic growth and political development... The bureaucratic cohesiveness they have to sustain in order to maintain their capacity to decide and implement tends to foster irresponsibility and the breakdown of consensus, which increase in turn the difficulty of their task. (1975: 12).

It should be stressed here that the "participants" are not only individuals. More important seem to be the demands of organized participants which have long developed under the control and protection of the state and which have now become serious competitors of the state for societal guidance. Parties, labour unions, big banks and corporations, voluntary associations and societal subsystems such as the health service or university system have grown into complex and powerful societal actors. It becomes a question of how far, in what respect and at what cost they will comply to state control and containment.

To be sure, this new situation poses a challenge and it is at the same time a risk. There is no evolutionary law which states the functional supremacy of the state and law in guiding societies. But if the function and the role of the state is to change, state and legal theory had better do some re-thinking and pre-thinking, lest they lose contact with reality.

On a rather general level, we can distinguish three processes which converge in overloading the guidance capacity of the state in highly developed societies:

Firstly: the increasing internal complexity of modern societies. The breaking up of feudal structures in Western Europe opened up developmental pathways towards markets, cities, science and technology, and other societal subsystems. The emerging "division of labour" and functional differentation of society transformed the relatively homogeneous, hierarchically ordered, community-type (*Gemeinschaft*) societies into increasingly complex, internally differentiated and interdependent association-type (*Gesellschaft*) societal systems. The "Great Transformation" (Polanyi) and its underlying "process of rationalization" (Weber) resulted in a degree of internal complexity of modern society which basically altered the conditions and consequences of societal development and guidance.

Secondly: the increasing world complexity and the emergence of lateral world systems.

Today, it is quite evident that this process towards increasing internal complexity was accompanied by the co-evolution of external complexity. The relations and interdependencies between modern societies have multiplied as has the potential for conflict and for emergent gains. In a very precarious sense the state becomes outdated, out of step with societal evolution. It is caught between two frontiers: the rise of societal *sub*-systems on the one hand and the emergence of functionally specialized *supra*-systems (world systems) in the areas of the economy, science, religion, labour movement, art and aspects of popular culture on the other; and today also the peace movement and "alternative" life-styles. State and law, designed to control and guide nationally organized societies, are therefore confronted with a qualitatively new situation; their coercive power and guidance capacity can be challenged by resourceful subsystems and can, in addition, be evaded by "going international".

Thirdly: the temporal horizon and the operational perspective of system guidance are shifting to a future-orientation.

Modern positive law, as man-made voluntaristic rule-making, reflects this shift from tradition to future-orientation and it advocates the legitimacy of an active interventionist state. The preconditions and consequences (including the costs) of this shift in temporal orientation are not well understood in state theory, legal theory, or, for that matter, in sociology. Understanding, modelling, and implementing the purposive guidance of complex social systems is still mostly guesswork — although the possibilities of errors are enormous. "The state of the art of ameliorating societal problems is dismal." (Warfield, 1976: 1). Law-making is still governed by short-term considerations and constraints and the forms and procedures of law are out-moded. It is not surprising then that modern societies which cannot solve their problems postpone them for the future. But this means that even the future becomes over-burdened and that the problem pressure of future present-times escalates (Luhmann, 1976). Even at present, law and state are in a defensive position; they merely supply a superficial and vulnerable coherence between the emancipated societal subsystems, thus virtually inviting *paradox interventions* of the self-conscious and resourceful actors, who are supposedly governed by law.

II.

The possible implications of high complexity in social systems were shown clearly and dramatically by Forrester, Meadows and other researchers. They show that the aggregated and combined effects and feedback-effects of dynamic processes, even within modestly complex relationships, are beyond intuitive human understanding: *complex systems behave counter-intuitively*:

> (A) downward spiral develops in which the presumed solution makes the difficulty worse and thereby causes redoubling of the presumed solution. The same downward spiral frequently develops in government. Judgement and debate lead to a program that appears to be sound. Commitment increases to the apparent solution. If the presumed solution actually makes matters worse, the process by which this happens is not evident. So, when the troubles increase, the efforts are intensified that are actually worsening the problem (Forrester, 1972: 203).

The law forms of the present are simple forms. They were designed to regulate relatively simple — mostly bi-polar — problems, and they work within relatively simple — mostly tripartite — procedures, and all this generally on the level of the individual. Thus, it is not altogether surprising, that these traditional structures of law fall prey to the fallacy of forced simplicity (see Weaver, 1948). An adequate understanding of modern welfare societies and their guidance problems presupposes willingness and capacity to face the fact of *organized social complexity* — that is, the fact that these societal and social relations are "made up of a large number of parts that interact in a non-simple way." (Simon, 1965: 63). In order to examine more closely what has happened here, we shall look at the types of interaction between the whole of society (represented by the state) and its parts. This is important because we have to admit that complexity of social relations is not an entirely new phenomenon. Particulary in the economy, a considerable degree of complexity had developed quite early in the 19th century. However, this complexity did not "show up" outside the economy and therefore did not appear as a political guidance problem. It was contained within the economy by the liberal formula of subsystem autonomy and the *subsidiarity* principle. So that although a high degree of internal complexity and conflict was possible and permissable within the economic (or religious, health or science) subsystem, the state was not involved except in setting legal frameworks and normative standard procedures. The principal guidance form was *self-regulation* with minimal central interference. Therefore, the main danger of this format of societal guidance today is a centrifugal tendency of over-differentiation and ensuing disintegration.

The social and societal costs of this arrangement led socialist thinkers (and later on, practitioners) to reverse the complexities: to de-differentiate, unify and homogenize the subsystems by transferring the bulk of conflicts and complexities to the central unit of state administration, the party. As far as societal guidance is concerned, however, the results are even less convincing that those of the liberal concept. The principal guidance form is *central guidance*; and as a principle it definitely contradicts the necessity to process high loads of complexity (Willke, 1979). Its tendency towards over-integration ensues in the danger of regressive de-differentiation.

Beyond liberal and socialist formulas, the emerging *welfare state* is bound to find and establish new guidance principles. As an integral part of a democracy it cannot drastically reduce the internal complexity of the differentiated subsystems. This new problem of the welfare state — a post-modern structure which is characterized by the high internal complexity of its parts, as well as high external complexity in the relations between the different parts of society — constitutes *the guidance problem of the welfare state*.

If the overriding problem is the processing of high loads of organized complexity within and between the specialized parts of society, then we can no longer rely on the two classical problem-solving techniques:

- direct central guidance by organization or plan, and
- self-regulation trough various types of markets.

Instead, we have to elaborate a third way. Here the ideas of "reflexive law" (Teubner, 1982 and infra) and "relational programs" (Willke, 1983) come into play.

Within the present structures of law the guidance capacity of the state is severely limited by the combination of several constraints:

1. State activity by means of law is geared towards definite decisions. It is structurally unfit for reflective and responsive decision-making (see Nonet/Selznick, 1978, for a more practical treatment and Luhmann, 1979: 8, for a more theoretical treatment of this term). This was inconsequential as long as a relatively low degree of societal complexity permitted guidance through action. Highly complex systems, however, are opaque and resistant to straight-forward action. As Forrester (1972: 205) puts it:

> First, social systems are inherently insensitive to most policy changes that people select in an effort to alter the behaviour of the system. In fact, a social system tends to draw our attention to the very points at which an attempt to intervene will fail ... A second characteristic of social systems is that all of them seem to have a few sensitive influence points through which the behaviour of the system can be changed. These influence points are not in the locations where most people expect.

2. In complex societies the state is remarkably unable to control its action in the dimension of time. The long range consequences of political action seem to remain uncontrollable, not just because of the lack of knowledge, (within limits this could be improved), but because of structural inconsistencies between the time horizon of pluralistic politics and the time horizon of systemic politics (Schick, 1969). This quite familiar situation could even escalate to ungovernability and the regression of systems, if various apparently small and unrelated disturbances cumulate into positive feedback loops. For example, nobody can predict any more (this is a problem of knowledge and therefore certainly could be helped) and no politician can care any longer (and within the given structures and guidance mechanisms this seems inevitable) whether or not programs against unemployment, for securing old-age pensions, and for humanizing industrial production will interact negatively, positively or even cancel each other out.

3. Probably the most important constraint on the efficiency of the legal guidance of societies is to be seen in the highly developed self-consciousness and indispensability of the specialized, differentiated societal subsystems: e.g. voluntary organizations; labour unions; corporations, the organized pressure groups in the health system; the educational system; the cultural or the science system (for a similar definition of the problem see Wiethölter supra).

These three points, taken together, may show that traditional legal structures are incongruent with the reality of the welfare state. It therefore becomes necessary to develop adequately complex guidance instruments. It is the purpose of this paper to outline a "relational program" as an adequately complex legal guidance instrument. Its blueprint will follow some lines of thought put forward in a few outstanding studies on the conditions and consequences of societal and administrative responsiveness (Etzioni, 1968; Steiss/Daneke, 1980); studies on possible ways to handle excessive loads of organized complexity (La Porte, 1975; Warfield, 1976);

and studies on the prerequisites of discursive rationality (Habermas, 1981: I, 367). The studies converge in taking the societal problem of organized complexity seriously, and in avoiding simple solutions.

In order to approach the idea of a relational program, it is necessary to specify the functional prerequisites and logic of positive law as the medium of action of the state. Positivity of law means (1) that legal rules are enacted in a law-making procedure and that the legitimacy of any man-made law rests upon this very procedure; (2) that the possibility of changing a law is organized by routine procedures; and (3) that finally, all participants of this process are conscious of the contingency of any law. Contingency here means

> that being depends on selection which, in turn, implies the possibility of not being and the being of other possibilities. A fact is contingent when seen as selection from other possibilities which remain in some sense possibilities despite a selection (Luhmann, 1976a: 509).

The reasons for substituing positive law for traditional, religious or natural law lie of course in the necessity to increase the contingency and complexity of legal rules in the evolutionary context of the growing contingency and complexity of the emerging, primarily functionally differentiated modern society. The observation that this co-evolutionary adaptation has been immensely successful in shaping the"legal state" (Rechtsstaat) and a rational bureaucracy and administration has led to characteristic linear extrapolations: more law, more rationality and bureaucratic efficiency. For example, Luhmann states:

> Law does not restrict societal evolution any more, since all needed structures (if they can be determined safely enough) can be juridified (Luhmann, 1972: 212).

In contrast to this position, I want to argue (and illustrate with an empirical example) the thesis *that the program-structure of modern law hampers the further evolution of highly complex societies and that therefore it is necessary to design new forms of legal programs.*

Our starting point is an understanding of the *welfare state* as the condition and consequence of societal guidance problems and their repercussions in law. In order to bring the connection of welfare state and adequate legal guidance forms into perspective, it is useful to stress the covariation and co-evolution of three factors:

1. structural principle of society
2. function of the state, and
3. types of law or legal programs.

An old and continuous sociological tradition links the evolution of societal formations and the emergence of new types of law (Durkheim, Weber, Luhmann, Habermas). The contemporary welfare state has not yet found its adequate legal form. One of the main problems seems to be in assessing the *type of differentiation* which may be imposing itself on a

Table 1: Co-evolution of societal structure, role of the state and legal form

structural principle of society	role of the state	legal form	type of rationality
segmentary differentiation	— — —	archaic, religious law	magic reciprocal
stratificatory differentiation	repressive state	customary, natural law	material substantial
functional differentiation	liberal state	secular, 703positive law	formal procedural
organized differentiation	welfare state	reflexive law	systemic discursive

Note: The underlying evolutionary principle is *additive*, not substitutive. Therefore post-modern societies include all four types of differentiation, all four types of legal forms and rationalities etc. What changes during historic evolution is the primacy of certain types.

saturated functional differentiation and which may be gradually growing into a primary structural feature of welfare societies. I suggest calling this evolving type of differentiation "*organized differentiation*". Following the primacy of segmental differentiation in archaic society, of stratificatory differentiation in premodern society, and of functional differentiation in modern society (see Luhmann, 1982); organized differentiation of post-modern welfare societies indicates a movement towards a new "architecture of complexity" (Simon, 1965) — the formation of building-blocks which encompass functionally differentiated parts in a specific problem field. An outstanding example of this is the trend towards neo-corporatist inter-mediation in the economic sphere (Schmitter/Lehmbruch, 1979; Lehmbruch/Schmitter, 1982). Other examples are cross-sectoral con-certation efforts in health or science policy, in regional or city development, even in fields as traditional and specialized as budgeting (Schick, 1980; Lynch, 1981).

What conclusions can be drawn from this for the design of an adequate legal program structure?

III.

It is well-known that the "openness" of human response and activity is ordered by certain behavioural programs which secure congruent expectations and the expectancy of expectations. During the evolution of positive law the first major form or structure of binding norms has been the *conditional program:* rules of an if-then-structure. The simple relationship between cause and effect, normative conditions and consequences of conditional programs made this type of program extremely successful in regulating simple problems and routine conflicts. In criminal law as well as in civil law conditional programs are the "standard operating procedure" for social control in simple individual relationships (e.g. offender – victim or buyer – seller).

With increasing complexity of social relations, however, a new program type emerges: the *purposive program*. Here the rigid connection between the factual preconditions of a norm and its consequences are loosened. One or several regulatory goals are predominant which can be pursued by a variety of legal means. Examples for this legal program type are economic policy laws (*Stabilitäts- und Wachstumsgesetz*); regional and communal development laws (*Städtebauförderungsgesetz*); social policy laws (*Arbeitsförderungsgesetz*) or planning laws (*Finanzplanungsgesetz*). Obviously this program type is connected with the rise of the interventionist state which in itself is a reflection of a series of economic and social crises after World War I that left the state with the task of guiding a variety of social and societal processes which had hitherto been considered self-regulating (see Aubert; Broekmann, Luhmann supra; Teubner infra).

It is important to realize that this change in state activity – although historically a continuous process – has fundamentally altered the role, the structure, and the guidance capacity of state and law. State and society have become interlocked in a way which has forced the law to step down from its throne of splendid isolation, generality and impartiality and enter the arena of societal and social purposes (see Hanf/Scharpf, 1978 and Ewald; Febbrajo supra).

On the other hand, of course, the purposive program is a more powerful guidance instrument than the conditional program. It permits a degree of flexibility in state actions and reactions, it introduces a limited learning capacity into the law (e.g. choice of means and intensity of means), and it certainly expands the time perspective of law from the present structure to future processes. Thus, it cannot be denied that the purposive program is better fitted to the conflicts which characterize modern industrial societies.

Nevertheless, there is no reason for contentment. We probably all still underestimate the forces and dangers of the existing societal complexity.

West Churchman (1968: XI) wrote: "The systems in which we live are far too complicated as yet for our intellectual powers and technology to understand." If this is only in part true, we must expect some surprises: for example, those that have resulted from the research of the systems dynamics approach of the Forrester-Meadows group. By combining just five variables which are usually treated separately, they came up with completely unexpected and thoroughly disconcerting results. (Variables: populations, capital investment, natural resources, fraction of capital devoted to agriculture, and pollution))Meadows *et al.*, 1975).

In a similar way, modern technological and industrial societies have reached a level of *organized social complexity* which far surpasses the intellectual capacities of individual actors. Myriads of specialists concentrate on small segments and limited aspects. But we have lost control, it seems, over the interrelation of these aspects and segments and over the combined effects of the many elements. I shall briefly retrace what has happened.

For sociological purposes it is convenient to distinguish three stages in the evolution of modern societies: a primitive level characterized by segmental differentiation (aggregation of same parts): a mezzo level characterized mainly by class differentiation; a modern level characterized by functional differentiation (see Table 1). Functional differentiation in its developed form is a product of the process of occidental rationalization, as analysed by Max Weber. It means that certain aspects of communal life such as economic, political, scientific, technological, religious, educational and other activities are increasingly separated from each other; become more and more specialized; produce separated occupational roles, professions and specialists. Finally, they become incorporated into relatively autonomous, functionally differentiated and specialized subsystems of society. All these subsystems develop their own partial rationality: their own partial options and demands, goals and means, functions and products (see Luhmann supra). Together, all this makes for a very strong centrifugal dynamic of modern societies. The parts drift apart and the question is, what is left to preserve and integrate the whole of society. This is, in my opinion, the central question and the central problem of modern western societies.

The traditional answer, of course, is, that it is the state which unites and integrates the whole of society. It must be accepted however, that the state and the traditional political system (parties, parliaments and administration) seem to have reached the limits of their guidance capacity. The main subsystems of economy, science, technology, health and educational system are far too complex to be guided by the simple means of law and money. The internal complexity of these subsystems; their capacity for self-authorization and production of specialized options; their time perspectives and planning horizons are beyond the limited rationality of the political sub-system.

A tidal wave of interrelated problems rolls against the (bureaucratic) walls of the welfare state – and it appears that its present legalistic and inflexible form induces positive feedback processes (Forrester, 1972) instead of helping to stem the flood. Balancing the budget; fighting drug criminality; designing mental health policies; deciding on atomic energy; implementing environmental protection programs; inducing sufficient investment; integrating discontented youth and protest movements; adapting the social security system; deciding on new weapons system; promoting growth industries; fighting the production of an academic proletariat; fostering chances of disarmament are just a few examples of the problems and contingencies produced by societal subsystems *which the present welfare state must handle and cope with.* This is a crucial point: the dissociation of problem-producing and problem-processing arenas in modern society simultaneously

1. increases the guidance load of the state because it is the state, and the state alone, which can legitimately decide for society as a whole on questions of societal concern (see Mayntz, 1975); and
2. decreases the guidance capacity of the state because its actors and units cannot understand and manage the diverse complexities of the specialized subsystems. These – because of their interdependence – increasingly produce problems with far-reaching implications for the whole of society (see Etzioni, 1977: 619).

We seem, therefore, to be confronted with an apparently inescapable paradox:

> (I)n the complex modern societies, the less foreseeable the future, the more foresight is required; the less we understand, the more insight is needed; the fewer the conditions which permit planning, the greater is the necessity to plan. (Ruggie, 1975: 136).

Yet a comprehensive model of systems steering or societal guidance is too complex for our simple minds and policies; and the incremental model is too simple for our complex societies. There seems to be no way out of this trap.

It is not impossible to invent a theoretical way out of this paradox. If the overall problem is one of exceedingly high complexity, then the overall solution must lie in complexity reducing and complexity processing mechanisms and institutions. And if the specific problems are consequences of the functional differentiation and specialization of various subsystems, specific solutions must consist in the creation of interlinking structures and intermediating processes which make compatible and reintegrate the divergent sub-rationalities of the different parts.

The question is: can we transfer these exigencies of highly complex systems into an adequate structure of law, into a new type of legal program?

My contention is that we should at least try. What seems to be necessary is to design a program which permits a higher degree of flexibility and learning capacity than the purposive program without losing the directive capacity of the law form. Its main characteristic therefore, lies in a built-in two level structure: first, the formulation of legislative guidance goals analogous to the purposive program, possibly enriched with general standard decision programs for prototypical cases; and secondly, an explicit provision for discursive and decentralized decision-making. As a decision-making structure this legal program reflects Etzioni's (1967) model of "mixed-scanning" as a third approach to decision-making.

The problematic part, of course, is the second. Its function is to preserve the complexity of the different rationalities of those actors or subsystems which are affected by the specific guidance problem. This built-in discourse is meant to induce mutual learning processes between the relevant interdependent actors, to activate their specialized information, and to initiate self-binding, consensus-building processes among the affected interests. This provision seems to be necessary because, in complex decision fields like economic policy, technology assessment, health policy or science policy, the state cannot decide authoritatively. Instead, the state becomes dependent upon using and activating the power, information processing and problem solving capacities of the relevant societal actors to arrive at adequate decisions *and* to arrive at adequate implementation. The state has to go beyond the means of traditional law to provide for adequate guidance. In these highly complex decision fields structural flexibility is mandatory. There is a need to combine normative and cognitive learning processes, to combine a normative frame with room for the discursive fine-tuning of complex relations. I shall call this type of legal structure a *relational program*.

The relational program is designed to help accomplish two objectives simultaneously:

1. to enable and facilitate self-regulating processes within specific problem areas (e.g. economy, science, health system). Here the relational program implies a legislative self-restraint from substantive regulation (see also Teubner infra). It seems to me that at this point an adequate *legislative science* would have to take seriously Herbert Simon's (1979) idea of a progression from substantive to procedural rationality when the problem-situation becomes too complex for central substantive decision-making.
2. to provide for the formulation of indicative legislative goals which reflect overall societal needs or requirements. The main problem is that these goals or purposes cannot be set authoritatively by the state. They might, however, be formulated within *discourse systems* where representatives of centrally affected interests are procedurally guided towards finding their common cause, their "common sense", their "generalizeable interests" (Habermas, 1973).

Table 2:

Three structural types of guidance program

1. The conditional program — causal guidance
(proto-type: if-then-norm)

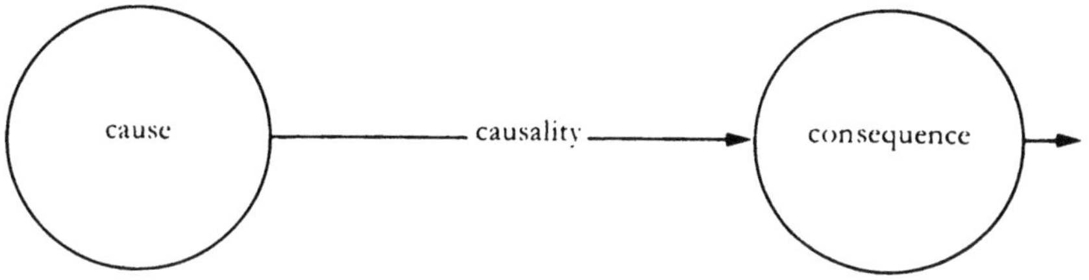

2. The purposive program — instrumental guidance
(proto-type: directive norm)

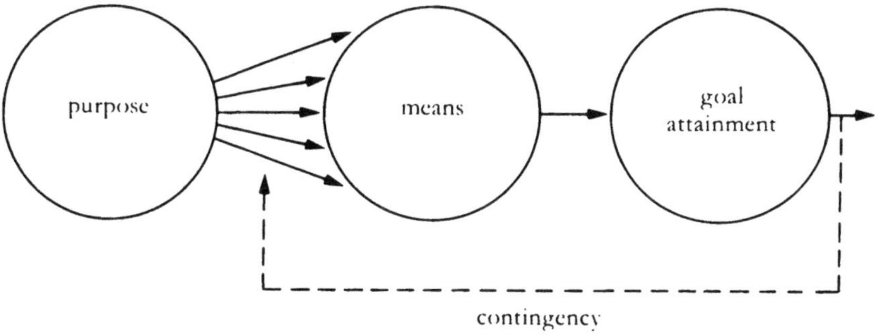

The combination of self-regulating, relatively autonomous processes within the various subsystems and self-restraining, reflexive accordation of options within societal discourse systems is designed to achieve that type of decentralized re-integration of complex societies which prevents overintegration on the one hand, and disintegration on the other, or in Etzioni's terms: overmanagement and drifting (1968: 466). The point of the relational program is to enable self-regulation of the parts, but at the same time to concert and guide these processes of self-regulation by agreed-upon and self-imposed common goals. It is a program structure for problem areas where the collective capabilities of different participants are essential for effective problem-solving *and* where general policy considerations require guiding interventions into the self-regulation of the societal subsystems.

(Table 2: Continue)

3. The relational program – responsive guidance
(proto-type: coordinative norm)

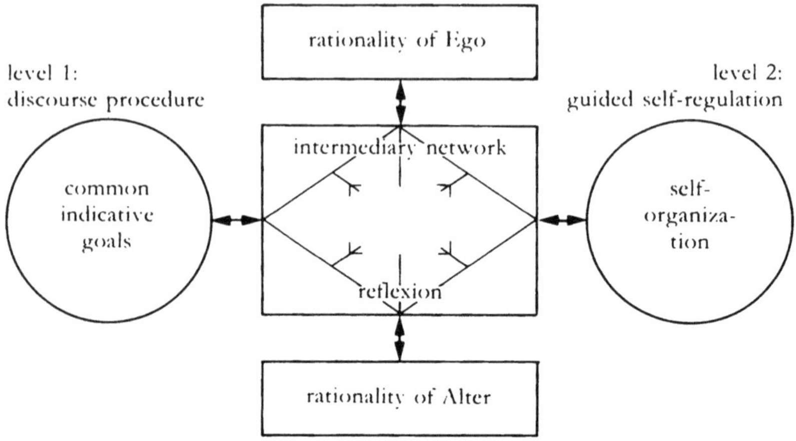

Its main purpose is to increase the guidance capacity of law by involving the subjects of regulation in the consensus-building and fine-tuning part of the decision-making process. Its main problem seems to be that the concept of "law" becomes rather "fuzzy", and that the continental idea of "Rechtsstaatlichkeit" seems to be endangered. However, in a situation where even a classically strict and logical discipline like theoretical mathematics develops ideas about "fuzzy sets" and "fuzzy systems" it might – in an evolutionary perspective – be permissable to put even the idea of *Rechtsstaatlichkeit* to the test.

In order to illustrate the different types of guidance structures a schematic representation might be helpful.

Even the purposive program, as a relatively simple form of feed-back guidance, creates problems for traditional state action – action according to the rationality of legal authority. Working with purposive legal programs includes estimating the degree of goal attainment and, if necessary, readjusting operative methods. This means that purposive control and consideration of consequences are built into the operation of law – and this contradicts the traditional exigency that law should be unambiguous and calculable. This necessary contradiction has caused a proliferation of vague legal terms of general clauses or even the opportunistic choice among possible justifications of decisions. The problem is far from being new. Max Weber delineated it in detail and he has named the two major reasons for modern law shifting from conditional to purposive programs: the social demands of democracy on the one hand, and the regulatory demands of social law on the other (Weber, 1967: 336).

Moving towards relational programs increases these difficulties. However, what seems to be an attack on the formal rationality of law from a legal perspective, has quite different implications within a sociological one. Here law is only a contingent means of societal and social guidance. The focus is not on dangerous developments which shake the foundations of legal formal rationality. Instead, it focusses on the costs and consequences of a mismatch between the operational capacity of the present forms of legally programmed state activity and the pressing need for a more efficient and responsive guidance program.

Luhmann is sceptical about considerations of consequences (*Folgenberücksichtigung*) in law. He states:

> (C)onsequent purposive decision programs need a much more intricate, professionally and functionally differentiated organizational form than the legal system is able to offer at the present time (Luhmann, 1974: 39 and supra)

This statement can be read, however, as the description of the decision form which would match present and foreseeable conditions for the guidance of complex social systems. We indeed need a much more intricate, professionally and functionally differentiated guidance program. It must be able to relate specialized sub-rationalities in a legally organized process. Its outlined two-step structure permits the combination of "remote control" and responsive fine-tuning. In developed democracies state action is bound by law and legal procedure. In this sense, all modern democracies are legalistic (*rechtsstaatlich*). However, when existing law forms show signs of overloading even under routine purposive guidance demands then even legalistic pathos can no longer suppress the question of how the human achievements of the legal state may be preserved whilst still reducing the social costs of an outdated guidance system.

The demand for relational programs develops as self-determination ceases to be the prerogative of the state. As other societal subsystems reach a relative autonomy, self-generated complexity and systemic indispensability, they become able to counteract legal guidance imperatives of the state with their own options. In this sense, all theories of an economic determination of society necessarily presuppose that the economic subsystem commands a guidance capacity superior to that of the state. And the theories which assume the coming of the technotronic or scientific society then postulate a functional supremacy of the science subsystem. Although these concepts are quite problematic, they correctly point to a qualitatively new situation: the state is confronted with a growing number of competitors for societal guidance. Their strength is difficult to judge; but their propensity for self-determination is evident. Therefore, on the level of societal guidance, differentiated subsystems with diverging rationalities exist and interact on the basis of functional interdependence and indispensability. Their interaction can no longer be guided by binding legal orders or authoritative goal-setting. Instead, the state seems to be *forced to operate with new types of responsive guidance programs if it wants to guide at all.*

Of course, this statement does not imply that existing legal programs have become obsolete. They are still adequate for the vast area of everyday conflicts. But they are insufficient for the newly-emerging complex conflict areas which are characterized by requiring continous learning, readjustment, and decentralized self-regulation in the face of substantial uncertainty. This is the case, for example, in the areas of determining the priorities and problems of economic, scientific or cultural production; of deciding on military or technological major projects; on basic questions of social policy, health policy or industrial policy; of guiding the complex relationships between big organizations, corporations, etc., which produce societal externalities that need to be controlled.

An empirical example might illustrate this rather abstract outline: I shall use that of "Concerted Action" in West Germany.

IV.

"Concerted Action" was instituted by law (§ 3 *Stabilitäts- und Wachstumsgesetz vom* 8. 6. 1967). The legislative goal was to create a formally voluntary discourse system where the main actors in economic policy-making — the state, labour unions, and the employers associations — were brought together to work out mutually compatible policies. The state took part in this process of problem-solving not in a leading or authoritatively deciding role, but as an equal — a primus inter pares at best.

Concerted Action was an offspring of the recession of 1966-69, and after lengthy discussions, mainly within the unions, it was established in 1967 when the Social Democrats were part of the governing coalition and a Social Democrat was Minister of Economics. Concerted Action was designed to play an intermediate role between the autonomy of the economic system (i.e. the autonomy of the participants of collective bargaining) on the one hand, and the increasing necessity for the state (that is the leading administrative and executive actors of the political system) to intrude into those areas of autonomy for the purpose of guiding and planning overall social requirements.

The idea was to introduce *societal responsibility* into a central area of economic decision-making. The main conceptual target was to combine comprehensive ("global") guidance of economic macro-relations with a decentralized decision-making in the area of micro-relations. Operationally this idea was implemented by involving the relevant actors in a procedural setting of self-binding commitment to mutually compatible policies. In order to achieve this, the state was placed between the proponents of collective bargaining — not as an arbiter, but as a third interested party (see also Febbrajo 134 supra on "game analogy"). That third party's function was to introduce into the process of collective bargaining those aspects and interests which could no longer be treated as externalities to it: for example, national and international economic policy; middle-range planning and budgeting; or the problems of the social side-effects of some economic policies such as pollution or unemployment.

Concerted Action, to be sure, was designed as a voluntary discourse system without competence for binding decisions. However, there was strong pressure on all participants to redefine their terms of interaction. The proponents of collective bargaining, labour unions and employer's associations, were confronted with a situation in which they became involved in overall societal responsibilities. Both interest organizations had to realize that there were limits to conflict; limits imposed by considerations of interdependencies within the complex system of society.

The problem of Concerted Action – and the main reason why it ended after ten years of activity – was its asymmetrical structure. The formal structure of the discourse system does not show that asymmetry. It is hidden in the logic of economic policy within a capitalistic society. The state, even a welfare state with a ruling social democratic party, cannot escape the imperatives of capitalist reproduction for long and thus it has a built-in tendency to favour policies which are welcomed by the employers' side and to demand sacrifices from the unions.

This structural and procedural difference creates an asymmetry of power-dependence relations between unions and employers' associations. It is important to realize that neocorporatist discourse systems such as Concerted Action, even if their actors are highly corporated, are not to be understood as mechanisms whose institutionalization alone changes the power relations in a given society. On the contrary, if they are meant to be instruments of political guidance and more rational policy-making, then their function is to bring into the open existing power differences, to articulate conflicts, and then to look for areas of compromise and cooperation. Societal discourse systems thus play a "mixed-motive game", as Thomas Schelling has put it, that is to say, a game with a "mixture of mutual dependence and conflict, of partnership and competition." (Schelling, 1970: 89).

It seems that the state here is confronted with the task of learning a new role: the role, not of arbitrator, but of mediator and moderator. Where the traditional forms of conflict, such as strike and lock-out are counterproductive and much too simple for complex dependence relations within and between societies, this new, more modest and yet more demanding role of the state might prove to be a crucial part of more adequate forms of societal guidance. Possibly this type of guiding intervention in predominantly self-regulating processes is a more adequate and promising form of action for the *welfare state* than the increasingly costly and futile activity of directing individual welfare. It seems to fit well with Drucker's (1978: 232) point that contemporary governments ought to *do* less and to *guide* more.

In the specific case of Concerted Action the state has not been very successful. After ten years of activity the Concerted Action ended in 1979. However, it is still worthwhile to look closely at this instrument and scrutinize both its weaknesses and its more promising features.

The *leitmotif* of Concerted Action is still valid — and increasingly so: to institutionalize the incentive for societal responsibility in a discourse system whose operational principle is to infuse societal commonsense into the "corporatist exchange logic" (Lehmbruch). "Societal common sense" is an opaque term — as vague as e.g. generalizable interests (Habermas) or "ethic of whole systems" (Churchman). However, this is necessarily so: the purpose of societal discourse systems is to improve the guidance capacity of exceedingly complex societies. From organizational and planning experience, we know that neither comprehensive directive control, nor incremental "muddling through" solve the problem of guiding highly complex social systems. Neither the central prescription of *substantive goals* nor the pluralistic belief in the self-organizing and self-directing capacity of *formal instruments* (mainly: markets and procedures) seem to suffice. Instead, discourse systems embody the idea of a *systemic rationality*. Conceptually, the idea of systemic rationality is based on the attempt to combine procedural rationality of formal legal framing of decentralized decision-making (legally guided self-regulation) with the "reflexive rationality" (Teubner, 1983 and infra) of built-in responsiveness of the parts (i.e. the functionally differentiated subsystems of society) to the overall exigencies of the whole.

Procedural rationality becomes appropriate — as Simon has convincingly shown — when decision domains

> "are too complex, too full of uncertainty, or too rapidly changing to permit the objectively optimal actions to be discovered and implemented." (Simon, 1980: 33; for a somewhat different account of "proceduralization" see Wiethölter supra).

And reflexive rationality plays its part when the centrifugal impetus of functional differentiation endangers the unity and coherence of society. Of course, the crucial question is how to operationalize and implement systemic rationality. The case of Concerted Action shows the difficulties clearly. It began as a relatively small, highly corporated circle of 32 participants representing 9 institutions and it ended as a "big band" of 79 members representing 24 institutions (Groser, 1980: 125). It started with the premise and promise of "social symmetry", clearly aiming at possible combinatorial gains of neo-corporatist exchange logistics for the participants; and it ended because of the real asymmetry of power relations between capital and labour that tended to distort the intended exchange logic of a corporatist discourse system.

Much more important, however, seems to be the fact that Concerted Action was installed as an instrument of short-term crisis management without taking the trouble to

1. provide a coherent theoretical concept of its preconditions and functions as an integrative device on a societal level.
2. to coordinate and make it compatible with other instruments regulating economic processes, mainly the structures of collective bargaining on the mezzo level and the institutions of co-determination on the micro level of the individual corporation; and
3. to provide the regulatory means — legal programs, organizational designs, informational procedures — indispensable for working out the difficult problem of a societally responsive guidance of the economy.

Again it should be stressed, that this type of guidance must not be confused with central directives or even central planning. It is a much less ambitious attempt to activate the problem-solving capabilities of self-regulating societal actors by simultaneously involving them in a discursive process of discovering and promoting common interests. Here we are mainly concerned with one aspect of a complex of societal guidance problems; that is, with outlining a relational program as the type of legal program best suited to the task of societal guidance of complex problem domains. The relational program can be seen as proto-typical for "reflexive law". And Concerted Action can be understood as an almost heroic attempt to institutionalize, prematurely and without due preparation, a discourse system structured by a relational program.

Surprisingly similar to the American experience with introducing PPBS in 1965, the hasty establishment of Concerted Action tended to magnify its shortcomings and hide its merits. Not the least of its merits was to experiment with a relational program as opposed to central state guidance on the one hand, and incremental self-organization on the other. Its guidance structure aimed at combining decentralized autonomous self-regulation (mainly: consensus-building and implementation processes within unions and employers' associations) with overall societal regulative ideas (mainly: consideration of long-range effects; redistribution and internalization of external effects; safeguarding learning capacities within the relatively autonomous subsystems). In spite of its shortcomings, it did begin to put into practice the idea of "reflexively regulated autonomy" (Teubner, 1982: 25) or reflexive re-integration of differentiated subsystems — which is the core element in discursive rationality and societal guidance by reflexive law.

References

CHURCHMAN, West (1979) *The Systems Approach*. New York: Delta.

CROZIER, Michel (1975) "Western Europe", in M. Crozier, *et al.* (eds.), *The Crisis of Democracy*. New York: New York University Press.

DRUCKER, Peter (1978) *The Age of Discontinuity*. New York: Harper Colophon.

ETZIONI, Amitai (1967) "Mixed-Scanning: A Third Approach to Decision-Making", 27 *Public Administrative Review* 385.

FORRESTER, Jay (1969) "Planning under the Dynamic Influences of Complex Social Systems", in E. Jantsch, (ed.), *Perspectives of Planning*. Paris: OECD Publications.

GROSER, Manfred (1980) "Konzertierte Aktion zwischen Korporatismus und Pluralismus, in E. Boettcher *et al.* (eds.), *Neue Politische Ökonomie als Ordnungstheorie*. Tübingen: Mohr.

HABERMAS, Jürgen (1973) *Legitimationsprobleme im Spätkapitalismus*. Frankfurt: Suhrkamp.

HANF, Kenneth and Fritz SCHARPF (eds.) (1978) *Limits to Coordination and Central Control*. London: Sage.

KÜLP, Bernhard (1980) "Theoretische Grundlagen der Konzertierten Aktion", in E. Boettcher *et al.* (eds.), *Neue Politische Ökonomie als Ordnungstheorie*. Tübingen: Mohr.

LA PORTE, Todd (ed.) (1975) *Organized Social Complexity*. Princeton, N.J.: Princeton University Press.

LEHMBRUCH, Gerhard and Philippe SCHMITTER (eds.) (1982) *Patterns of Corporatist Policy-Making*. London—Beverly Hills: Sage.

LUHMANN, Niklas (1972) *Rechtssoziologie*, 2 Vol. Reinbek: Rowohlt.

LYNCH, Thomas D. (ed.) (1981) *Contemporary Public Budgeting*. New Brunswick—London: Transaction Books.

MAYNTZ, Renate (1975) "Legitimacy and the Directive Capacity of the Political System", in L. Lindberg *et al.* (eds.), *Stress and Contradiction in Modern Capitalism*. Lexington, Mass.: Heath.

MEADOWS, Donella *et al.* (1975) *The Limits to Growth*. New York: Signet.

NONET, Philippe and Philip SELZNICK (1978) *Law and Society in Transition. Toward Responsive Law*. New York: Harper.

RUGGIE, Gerard (1975) "Complexity, Planning and Public Order", in T. La Porte (ed.), *Organized Social Complexity*. Princeton, N.J.: Princeton University Press.

SCHICK, Allen (1969) *System Policy and System Budgeting*. 29 *Public Administration Review* 137.

SCHMITTER, Philippe and Gerhard LEHMBRUCH (eds.) (1979) *Trends Toward Corporatist Intermediation*. London and Beverly Hills: Sage Publications.

SIMON, Herbert (1965) "The Architecture of Complexity", 10 *General Systems Yearbook*, 56.

— (1979) "How To Decide What To Do", 27 *Economic Impact* 28.

STEISS, Alan and Gregory DANEKE (1980) *Performance Administration*. Lexington, Mass.: Lexington Books.

TEUBNER, Gunther (1983) "Substantive and Reflexive Elements in Modern Law" 17 *Law and Society Review* 239.

WARFIELD, JOHN (1976) *Societal Systems. Planning, Policy and Complexity*. New York: Wiley & Sons.

WEAVER, Warren (1948) "Science and Complexity", 30 *American Scientist* 536.

WEBER, Max (1968) *Economy and Society*. 3. Vol. New York: Bedminster Press.

WILLKE, Helmut (1979) *Leitungswissenschaft in der DDR*. Berlin: Duncker & Humblot.

After Legal Instrumentalism?

Strategic Models of Post-Regulatory Law*

Gunther Teubner
Bremen, Firenze

I. Concepts, Models, Theories

1. Rechtsbegriffe

To construct *Rechtsbegriffe* (concepts of law) raises suspicion in the scientific community of today. When legal theorists dealing with the function of law in the welfare state present ambitious constructs, such as instrumental versus expressive law (Ziegert, 1975), autonomous versus responsive law (Nonet and Selznick, 1978), purposive versus procedural law (Unger, 1976; Wiethölter, 1982 and supra), or, to use my formulation, substantive versus reflexive law (Teubner, 1983a, 1984), they have to face the accusations of violating the basic norms of scientific discourse. Special zeal in this policing function is demonstrated by authentic legal sociologists (e. g. Black, 1972; Blankenburg, 1984). In the name of science and with the sharpened tools of modern social science methodology they charge the construction of *Rechtsbegriffe* as being against the letter and spirit of the canons of social research methodology.

To begin with minor offences, conceptualizations are too vague and operationalizations extremely cloudy. The phenomenon in question is not identified properly. Is the law itself formal, substantive, reflexive? Or is it legal consciousness (of whom? the profession? the law professors?)? Are we dealing with theories about law, general principles behind the law, or with doctrinal constructions within the law? Is it law in the books which is supposed to unfold an autonomous logic of development, or is it law in action (Friedman, supra)? In addition, there is operational negligence: How are broad concepts to be translated into precise measurement procedures for empirical research? How is one to decide whether, at a certain

* This is a revised version of an article which originally appeared in *International Journal of the Sociology of Law* 12 (1984) 375–400. I wish to thank the editrice for permission to reprint.

historical time, law was formal, or material, or procedural, or reflexive? (Rottleuthner, 1983, 1984).

A more grave offence in the eyes of the science police, is that those constructs do not appear to produce theories in the sense of a generalized set of assumptions from which testable hypotheses could be derived. Rather, they represent vague "concepts", ideal-typical configurations of legal elements revealing some obscure sort of legal rationality. Worse, they are speculative: they seem to be interested in ideas, rather than in facts. How far are they concerned about a methodologically sound empirical proof of their broad generalizations? Worst of all, they are hopelessly normative since they not only analyze a certain potential development in law but argue more or less openly for a conscious realization of this potential (Ietswaart, 1983). In short, rather than being good theories about law, these are bad ideologies for lawyers. No question, they serve the function of covering the social interests behind such rhetoric by some quasi-distanced meta-theory. And, if not intentionally, they do this at least sub-consciously via a "projection" of normative purposes and similar pathologies (Blankenburg, 1984: 274,284).

Legal theorists in turn might defend their *Rechtsbegriffe* rather defensively. One way is to adapt their constructs as far as possible to meet the rigid standards of social science methodology. Normative elements are either denied or reduced or at least neatly detached from the core analytical-empirical elements. Outright speculations are transformed into more technical hypotheses disciplined by their theoretical derivation. And those hypotheses are formulated so that they can be tested by elaborate empirical methods (see Rottleuthner, 1983; 1984). Unfortunately, as a result of this tailoring the intellectual constructs are cut off from much of their explanatory and creative power.

Another defensive defence is to play the game of soft science as against hard core science. In this one might protect *Rechtsbegriffe* by referring to the relative weakness of scientific methods in regard to the complexity of their object (Hayek, 1972), to a non-empirical logic of theoretical reasoning (Alexander, 1982), to the inherent normative qualities of scientific research activities (the German *Werturteilsstreit*), to pragmatism and legal naturalism (Selznick, 1973), or to "anything-goes"-pluralism (Feyerabend, 1975). Unfortunately, in this game of soft science one loses many of the insights of modern theory of science.

2. Theory or Strategy?

In contrast to the defensive arguments, I will try a more offensive defence of formal, substantive, instrumental, expressive, reflexive etc. law. In my view, it is a grave error to subsume *Rechtsbegriffe* under the specific logic of scientific inquiry since, in the strict sense they are not scientific theories but are strategic models of law. Strategic models are, at the same time, both more *and* less than scientific theories. They incorporate sociological theories of law but transform these into legal constructions of social reality. In addition they incorporate normative evaluations and strategic considerations. My thesis is that *they represent legal "internal models" of law in society their main function being to use the self-identity of law to produce criteria for its own transformation.* In this sense, legal theory does not only form part of the subject matter of the scientific enquiry but also forms part of the legal system and thus orients legal practice. What appears, for orthodox legal sociology, to be the private vice of legal theorists might turn out to be their public virtue: the ability of legal theory to produce normative criteria for a conscious self-transformation of the law.

For this interpretation of how and why legal theory constructs its *Rechtsbegriffe*, I rely on the following intellectual traditions:

(1) *General model theory* (Stachowiak, 1965; 1973). This theory develops an understanding of scientific theories, legal doctrines, political action programs as being the internal models of specific social systems and explains the differences between them in terms of their purpose, function and social context. The crucial point is that internal models do not function as passive receivers of external information but as active designers of the system's environment. More particularly, this theory permits the distinction between different sub-models within legal models of reality and the analysis of the relations between them (empirical, prospective, operative sub-models) (Teubner, 1978; see below sub. 3).

(2) *Cybernetic theory of adaptive systems* (Buckley, 1968). This approach identifies "internal models" of external reality as being the main adaptive mechanisms which map parts of the environmental variety and constraints into the internal organization as structure. Thus, the evolution of complex adaptive systems to higher levels depends on successful mapping as a selective matching of system and environment.

(3) *The concept of self-reflection of a social system* (Luhmann, 1981a:198; 1981b:419 and 125 supra). The main function of self-reflection is the use of a system's identity for its self-substitution. Especially, to define legal theory as the law's reflective theory identifies its function for orienting legal transformation.

(4) *Theory of self-referential systems* (Maturana, 1970; 1975; Varela, 1979; Maturana and Varela, 1980; Zeleny, 1981; Hejl, 1982a; 1982b). Concepts of self-observation and self-consciousness of systems are developed in which systems can be seen to represent themselves and to interact with those representations. In the case of law, this leads to the necessity of a social orientation within the law (in the sense of a consensual description of experience), in which the social situation of the producers of the description is always presupposed. Consequently it makes no sense to attempt a critique of lawyers' ideologies in the name of science but rather one should formulate

those constructs in terms of competing social models according to the social context in which they were created.

What is the relation of strategic models to scientific theories? As stated above, concepts of formal and substantive law are not to be identified as theories. However, they are not unscientific uncontrolled ideologies as our science police suspects (Blankenburg, 1984). Rather, they incorporate sociological theories and must be compatible with scientific developments. To take an ironical formulation seriously, they are "more or less empirical theories with practical intentions" (Rottleuthner, 1983). In particular, if the models ascribe certain social functions to law, they have to deal with sociological theories about the relations of law and society. If legal "formality", for example, means setting a framework for autonomous economic and social action, further if "materiality" means social guidance through law and "reflexivity" means a generalized form of legal control of social self-regulation (Teubner, 1983a), then obviously, sociological theories have something to offer.

Nevertheless, it would be erroneous to describe this relation as a contrast between lawyers' ideology and social reality. There is no direct access to social reality, there are only competing system models of reality (Stachowiak, 1973:97). Therefore, one has to see this as a problematic relation between legal and social models of reality; each having its own rightful claims. There is a fundamental difference between the analytical-empirical environment of science, the perception of which is due to more or less severe restrictions, and the world constructions of legal theory which have quite different restrictions.

The same holds true for the dynamics of motives. The motives and value premises of legal constructions of reality are different from those of scientific constructions (e. g. scientific rationality, experience orientation, scientific discourse procedures). That means we have to accept different "cognitive conditionings" (Stachowiak, 1973:97) as premises of operational processes in law and in science. In short, the differences between scientific theories and strategic models refer to the selection of the model variables, the procedures of model construction, the methods of testing, the criteria of certainty and the requirements for success.

This implies complications for the relationship between scientific theories about law and strategic models in law. Historical accounts of legal developments or empirical sociological analyses are not — as some would like to see it — intrinsically superior to legal conceptualizations of law in society, due to their closer access to social reality. A higher degree of isomorphy (structural and material approximation of model and original) is not yet an argument for the superiority of an alternative model.

In particular, science is not in a position to authoritatively define models of external reality. Science produces only hypothetical models which can be tested in their capacity for strategic purposes. Science can serve only as stimulation not as notification (Habermas, 1976:107). In a precise sense, one cannot speak of an incorporation of theories into legal models, or of a legal reception of sociology. Rather, one has to see them as competing constructions of reality which allow for comparison of their relative strength.

It is possible to see this relation as a problem of power: who has the power to force his construction of reality upon others? (Hejl, 1982a:320). I, however, would prefer to see it as a problem of compatibility, of possibilities of analogization and of mutual learning. Legal history and legal sociology produce results which may be either rejected by lawyers or which may lead to profound changes in legal model construction. At best, there is a productive mutual penetration in the sense of scientific "subsidies" (Luhmann, 1981a: 134) of grand concepts of law in legal theory. In sum, it is the precarious double character of legal models influenced by internal legal "ideologies of legitimacy" and external sociological "functional analyses" which forms our understanding of specific types of legal rationality.

How are these models to be tested? When we label them as legal "models" and not as theories, we have their action orientation in mind. If their function is to produce criteria for the self-transformation of law, they go beyond scientific theories which are tested by empirical falsification of hypotheses. At the same time they are more than just choices of decisions or strategies for the law. We are dealing with competing intellectual constructs that contain different "empirical" assessments of society, as well as their "normative" evaluations and subsequent "strategic" decisions. The premises, structures and consequences of all those models can be analyzed and discussed. The „experimentum crucis" takes place only when they reenter social reality. Since there exist no scientifically proven laws of sociolegal development it is only legal practice which can decide on the success of those competing models. The models can be tested if they are institutionalized and exposed to the competitive markets of scientific discourse, legal doctrinal controversies, conflicts of social movements and to institutional decisions. Experience can be gained only in the form of social experiments in which those legal models are tried out.

3. Elements of Strategic Models of Law

What determines the selectivity of such strategic models — in other words according to what principles are model variables chosen? In terms of general model theory (Stachowiak, 1965, 1973) models are intentionally defined by three elements:

1. projective element: models are always representatives of originals which, in turn, may be models themselves;
2. selective element: models represent in principle only specific attributes of the original;

3. pragmatic element: models are not defined per se; they fulfill their representation function a) for certain subjects, b) within a given time interval, c) restricted to certain intellectual or factual operations.

The extension of such a concept is extremely wide. By varying and recombining the three elements, however, a meaningful model typology can be formed. This typology ranges from graphical and technical models, via semantic models at different levels, (among which there are even poetical and metaphysical models), to scientific models (theories in the narrower sense) and planning and decision models (Stachowiak, 1973).

Now, it would be too esay to subsume our "grand concepts" of law under one of these model types, e. g. the "socio-normative" model or the "imperative" model (Stachowiak, 1973:234). This would not take into account that in strategic models qualitatively different model operations take place, different with regard to the choice of attributes and the method of their symbolic manipulation. In other words, we are faced with selections in different dimensions which cannot be accommodated within one model type. This suggests that they may be thought of as complex models composed of three sub-models: an empirical, a prospective and an operative sub-model. Thus, one gets close to the construction of planning models in politics which differ from scientific models in the above-named elements, i. e. projective, selective and pragmatic elements (Stachowiak, 1973:269). The parallel is obvious. However, it needs some re-formulation in order to grasp the specific properties of strategic models of law as opposed to general planning models.

The *empirical* sub-model is the model type with the largest distance from action orientation. The degree of selectivity is rather low, as well as the transformation of the original data into other symbolic systems. The empirical sub-model concerns the social fields regulated by law, i. e. empirical theoretical statements about social structures, functions and development tendencies in the regulated areas, and interrelations between legal norms and social structures. The *prospective* sub-model defines the dimension of normative evaluation and strategic goals. It refers to fundamental principles which justify the specific way that legal norms should govern human actions. It has to do with statements about the purposes of law, means-end-relations, and evaluations of legal and social consequences. The *operative model*, finally is closely oriented to action and shows the strongest degree of manipulation of the original data. It has to do with the internal conceptual and procedural structure of law and the systematization of doctrine.

We do not gain an adequate understanding of those sub-models if we see their relation simply as additive, as a mere cumulation of otherwise independent empirical, normative and strategic elements. Rather, we have to take into account their mutual interdependence. All three sub-models are highly selective and the problem is how to define their criteria of selectivity. The thesis is: *Criteria of selectivity are to be found in a circular relation, in the mutual limitation of the three sub-models, finally, in the self-reference of the legal system*. If we want to understand why certain assumptions about the social world within these models differ from scientific theories in terms of testing procedure and criteria of certainty we have to see that they are determined by the normative and strategic context of the prospective and operative sub-models. And if we want to understand what makes the difference between a "concept" of, for example, formal law and a mere technical recommendation of normative generality and conceptual precision, then we have to realize that such a "concept" is informed by underlying theoretical assumptions and normative evaluations which are formulated in the empirical and prospective sub-model.

To sum up, when in legal theory "grand concepts" are produced such as formal, substantive, reflexive law, they do not represent external scientific theories but internal strategic models of law. Strategic models are highly selective legal constructions of social reality. Their selectivity is defined by the social context and the criteria of selectivity result from the mutual limitation of their empirical, prospective and operative sub-models. Their ultimate test is re-entry in social reality. Their social function is the self-identification of the legal system as a criterion for its own transformation.

II. Competing Strategic Models in the Regulatory Crisis

All these elements of our definition can be identified if one looks at emerging concepts in the current socio-legal discussion of the regulatory crisis in the modern welfare state (Mayntz, 1979; Mitnick, 1980; Reich, 1984). Regulatory law — the most ambitious, modern, goal-oriented, sociologically informed type of law representing a political mechanism of social guidance — is said to be in deep crisis, or at least in a state of institutional failure. Out of this diagnosis emerge three concepts of law which deserve the name of strategic models. They all use the identity of law as a criterion for its post-instrumental transformation. But they differ widely in regard to their empirical, prospective and operative sub-models and their interaction with each other. Depending on what problems of regulatory law in relation to regulated fields are perceived as relevant and how positively or negatively the instrumentalization of law through the political system is evaluated, very different types of solutions are arrived at.

1. Implementation

The implementation approach represents a strategic model in the empirical dimension of which the crisis of regulatory law is identified as a problem of effectiveness (e. g. Mayntz, 1980). The starting point is the guidance intention of the political system and law is analyzed as ineffective insofar as it turns out to be an unsuitable instrument to fulfill those intentions in social reality. Background theories are theories of societal guidance through political processes (e. g. Etzioni, 1968). These are closely related to the prospective dimension. A society is envisaged in which the political system takes over the responsibility for unresolved social problems of society. Compensatory state intervention is supposed to react against the undesirable side-effects of the modernization processes. The normative goal is an increase in social welfare through democratic processes and political decisions. Law is politicized in the sense that it serves as one of the main mechanisms towards the realization of the welfare state. It belongs to the inherent logic of this model that, in its operative dimension, the crisis of regulatory law is to be cured by *increasing its instrumental effectiveness* (Clune, 1983). If the problem of regulatory law is its implementation, then effective implementation mechanisms have to be designed. The point will then be to strengthen cognitive, organizational and power based resources in such a way that the law can cope in practice with its control function. In this sense, legal doctrine will have to shift from being primarily concerned with juridical conflict resolution to more of a legal policy orientation (Nonet and Selznick, 1978). Legal science will see itself as a part of the social sciences, which produce control-knowledge (Ziegert, 1975). Law would then primarily be social technology (Podgorecki, 1974). Economic and sociological analyses will be brought in, with a view to efficiency. This means, at the same time, that the law must take into account its own implementation in social reality and the social consequences (implementation research and consequence control, e. g. Wälde, 1979, Mayntz, 1980).

2. Re-formalization

In the diagnosis of the regulatory crisis, the selection of attributes for the empirical sub-model is quite different. The crisis is mainly identified with the economic and social costs which regulation creates. State interventionist law is supposed to be one of the main obstacles to reaching the goal of allocative efficiency. Background theories are various liberal and neo-liberal theories, the concept of "interventionist constructivism" being a prominent and ambitious example (Hayek, 1972). In the prospective dimension the maximization of freedom is the main normative goal. The function of law is to define a general framework for social freedom insofar as it establishes a sphere for autonomous activity and fixed boundaries for the property rights of private actors.

In the operative dimension, strategies aim at a certain *de-legalization*, an ordered retreat of the law from the "occupied" areas of social life, either by a complete withdrawal of its regulatory function ("de-legalization" in the strict sense), or by concentrating its forces on the secure bastions of formal rationality ("re-formalization", Grimm, 1980). In this connection, particular interest attaches to the re-privatization of state tasks and also to the abandonment of interventionist constructivism in favour of general law, in a conception of law as a set of rules of the game (Hayek, 1973; Hoppmann, 1972; Mestmäcker, 1978; see also Febbrajo supra).

3. Control of Self-Regulation

As alternative solutions transcending the distinction between formal and substantive law, strategies are discussed that amount to a more abstract, more indirect control through the law. The law is relieved of the burden of direct regulation of social areas, and instead given the task of the active control of self-regulatory processes (e.g. Bohnert and Klitzsch, 1980). Empirically, the crisis of regulatory law is identified as an incompatibility of the internal logics of different social systems. It has been demonstrated that regulatory law programs obey a functional logic and follow criteria of rationality and patterns of organization which are poorly suited to the internal social structure of the regulated spheres of life (Reidegeld, 1980: 281; Pitschas, 1980: 150). In consequence, law as medium of the welfare state either turns out to be ineffective or it works effectively but at the price of destroying traditional patterns of social life (Habermas, 1981 II: 531 and supra).

Scientific background theories are as a rule current macro-social theories; either the theory of functional differentiation or variants of critical theory or diverse attempts of a selective accommodation between them. Prospective orientations of those concepts are highly diverse according to the range of macro-theories to which they are connected. However, they have in common the normative problem of how to achieve social integration; how to define the identity of society, given the ubiquitousness of disruptive conflicts between the different rationalities of highly specialized social subsystems (Habermas, 1975 and supra; Luhmann, 1982 and supra). Clearly, this social integration cannot be achieved by the state imposing unified norms on society. Nonetheless, social integration is still seen as a political problem in which the legal-political-system — however indirectly — plays a critical role.

In the operative dimension, "*proceduralization*" is offered as a formula for the role of the law in promoting and controlling the setting up of "social systems with a learning capacity" (Wiethölter, 1982 and supra; Mayntz, 1983b; cf. as well Brüggemeier, 1982:60 and Willke supra). The empirical basis is in a whole variety of new forms of non-directive legal interventions (Winter, 1982:9). This approach emphasizes the design of self-regulation mechanisms, combining competition, bargaining, organization and countervailing power (Hart, 1983:22).

There are essentially three issues at stake: (a) the guarantee of life-world autonomy by an "external constitution" (Habermas, 1981 II:544 and supra);

(b) structural preconditions of effective self-regulation, for instance, by way of "external decentralization" of public tasks (Lehner, 1979: 178; Gotthold, 1983) or in the sense of internal reflection of social effects (Teubner, 1983a; Hart, 1983); (c) canalization of inter-system-conflicts through "procedural regulation" (Mayntz, 1983b; Streeck and Schmitter, 1985) or "relational programs" (Willke, 1983:62 and supra), or by semiformal procedures of "practice as a discovery method" (Joerges, 1981, 1985), or by an institutionalized co-ordination of different system rationalities (Scharpf, 1979; Assmann, 1980; Ladeur, 1982, 1984).

III. Self-Referentiality as the Criterion?

Is there a reasonable way to choose between those competing strategic models? As we said earlier, the ultimate test for success is their re-entry into social reality. But this does not exclude evaluating them in terms of higher or lower plausibility. In my view, a plausible choice can be made: that of concentrating intellectual attention and institutional energy on the third strategy, the legal control of social self-regulation. I find criteria of plausibility in the theory of self-referential systems.

Why make use of the theory of self-referential systems? Why should legal sociology use insights of psychocyberbioepistemology (Beer, 1975). This newly developed theory has been formulated by biologists (Maturana, 1970; 1975; Maturana et al., 1974; Varela, 1979; Maturana and Valera, 1980; Zeleny, 1981) and transferred to the social sciences (Beer, 1975; Hejl, 1982a; 1982b; Luhmann, 1981a, 1984; Teubner and Willke, 1984). There is not as yet general agreement that it is a fruitful paradigm. Thus, we shall use it in a more experimental manner as a strictly heuristic device. What follows for our problematic law and society relation if we reformulate them in terms of self-referentiality? What hypotheses, what recommendations for political-legal action are implied?

The message of self-reference can be clearly distinguished from older versions of systems theory. While classical notions of system concentrated on the internal relations of the elements, searching for emerging properties of the system ("the whole is more than the parts"), modern theories of "open systems" reject the "closed system approach" and stress the exchange relations between system and environment. One *Leitmotiv* is requisite variety (Ashby, 1975:207). How can the system cope with an over-complex environment? Another is contingency theory (Lawrence and Lorsch, 1967): How can we explain internal structures as a result of environmental demands? A third one is the input/output model (Easton, 1965): In what way are inputs processed into outputs through an internal conversion process? These are the guiding questions of the open system approach.

In a sense, the theory of self-referential systems seems to return to the concept of a closed system, even to a radical concept of closure. *A system produces and reproduces its own elements through the interaction of its elements* (Maturana et al., 1974:187) – by definition, a self-referential system is a closed system. However, what makes the theory more promising than both its forerunners is the inherent relation of self-referentiality to the environment.

Self-referential systems, being closed systems of self-producing interactions, are, necessarily at the same time, open systems with boundary trespassing processes (Hejl, 1982b:57). And it is precisely the linkage between internalizing self-referential mechanisms and externalizing environment exchange mechanisms which makes the concept of self-reference more fruitful and more complex than its predecessors with their somewhat sterile alternative of closed versus open systems.

If we are using self-referentiality as the criterion to judge competing strategic models of post-instrumental law, two directions of analysis seem to be fruitful. One concerns the question about what effective *limits* the self-referential structure of social systems sets to legal intervention. The second direction of analysis concerns the *social knowledge* which is necessary if law acting within those limits seeks to cope with self-referential structures of the regulated areas. Thus, we arrive at the following theses if we reformulate the premises of the competing strategic models in terms of that theory:

1. *The Regulatory Trilemma:* The implementation strategy will ultimately run aground on the internal dynamics of self-referential structures of both the regulating and the regulated system. Without taking into account the limits of "structural coupling", it inevitably ends in a trilemma: it leads to either "incongruence" of law and society, or "over-legalization" of society, or "over-socialization" of law. Moreover, the models of causal linearity which the implementation strategy uses seem to be insufficient for the social knowledge that is required for the "regulation" of autopoietic systems.

2. *Social Self-Closure:* The re-formalization strategy neglecting in its turn the need of self-referential systems to externalize, develops no obstacles against the dynamics of social self-closure. An increase in subsystem rationality may be the result, but with possibly disastrous effects with regard to the coordination with the system's environment.

3. *Response to Self-Referentiality:* In contrast, the third strategic model seems to be compatible with self-referentiality. As we have seen, for the control of self-regulation, theorists have developed a broad range of rather diverse recommendations about the way to "proceduralize" the law. Now, in the light of self-referentiality, what seem to be obviously heterogeneous recommendations can be interpreted as complementary strategies. The maintenance of a self-reproductive organization needs societal support. The

recommendations can be read as strategies to make compatible the self-referentiality of various social sub-systems. "Proceduralization" represents society's response to the needs of self-referentiality: "autonomy", "externalization", and "coordination".

If we translate our problem of legal regulation into the language of self-reference, a decisive difference becomes apparent. Models of regulation and of implementation, even if they are developed in the open system framework, deal with the implicit assumption of basal linearity. This means, that they see the relation between the regulating systems (politics and law) and the regulated system (functional subsystem, organization, interaction) as a relation between environment and system in which the regulating systems maintain and control the goals and the processes of the regulated systems. Deviant behavior is supposed to be controlled and corrected by the regulated system. This holds true even for recent reformulations of implementation theory (Mayntz, 1979:55; 1983a:7; Bohnert and Klitzsch, 1980: 200). While it is true that they abandon a purely instrumentalist model and take into account autonomy in the regulated area and complicated interaction processes in the implementation field, they still have no adequate concept of what constitutes the autonomy of the regulated system. They still conceive of the regulated system as "allopoietic", as dependent on the actions of the regulating system.

In contrast, a theory of self-reference would define the regulated area as a system consisting of elements which interact with each other in such a way that they maintain themselves and reproduce elements having the same properties as a result of repeating the self-producing interaction (Hejl, 1982b:56). They are systems that keep their reproductive organization constant. To be sure, their concrete structures can be influenced and changed by regulation, but only within the limits of that reproductive organization (see Maturana, 1982:20). As Beer puts it, regulations do not at all change social institutions, they produce only a new challenge for their autopoietic adaptation (Beer, 1975). Any external regulatory influence which leads to a new internal interaction of elements not maintaining its self-reproductive organization, is either irrelevant or leads to the disintegration of the regulated system (cf. Hejl, 1982b:58).

The picture becomes more complicated if we take into account that the regulating systems, politics and law, are themselves self-reproductive systems. We have then to reformulate the hierarchical relation of regulation into a circular interaction between three self-referential systems (law, politics, regulated subsystems). The limits of regulation are then defined by the threefold limits of self-reproduction. *A regulatory action is successful only to the degree that it maintains a self-producing internal interaction of the elements in the regulating systems, law and politics, which is at the same time compatible with self-producing internal interactions in the regulated system.* This threefold compatibility relation may be called "structural coupling"

(Maturana, 1982:136). Thus, we can formulate the ***regulatory trilemma***: If regulation does not conform to the conditions of „structural coupling" of law, politics and society, it is bound to end up in regulatory failure. There are three ways regulation can fail:

(a) "incongruence" of law, politics and society

The regulatory action is incompatible with the self-producing interactions of the regulated system — the regulated system reacts by not reacting. Since the regulatory action does not comply with the relevance criteria of the regulated system, it is simply irrelevant for the elements' interactions. The law is ineffective because it creates no change in behaviour. However, the self-producing organization remains intact, in law as well as in society. This is what one might call the "symbolic use" of politics and law (Edelmann, 1964).

(b) "Over-Legalization" of Society

Again, the concrete self-producing interactions within law, politics and within society are not compatible with each other. In this case, however, the regulatory action influences the internal interaction of elements in the regulated field so strongly that their self-production is endangered. This leads to disintegrating effects in the regulated field, well-known under the heading of "colonialization" (Habermas, 1981:542 and supra). The regulatory programs obey a functional logic and follow criteria of rationality which are poorly suited to the internal social structure of the regulated spheres of life. Law as a medium of the welfare state works efficiently, but at the price of destroying the reproduction of traditional patterns of social life.

(c) "Over-Socialization" of Law

A third type of regulatory failure should be taken into account. Once again incompatibility of self-production is the result of regulation, but in this case with the difference that the self-producing organization of the regulated area remains intact while the self-producing organization of the law is endangered. The law is "captured" by politics or by the regulated subsystem, the law is "politicized", "economized", "pedagogized" etc. with the result that the self-production of its normative elements becomes overstrained. Overstrain of the law in the welfare state may be the effect of its political instrumentalization (Luhmann 122 supra), but it may also be the law's "surrender" to other sub-systems of society at the cost of its own reproduction (Nonet and Selznick, 1978:76). The "over-socialization" of law may take on many forms.

All in all, these three types of regulatory failure which each show very distinctive features have one thing in common. In each case, regulatory law turns out to be ineffective because it overreaches the limitations which are built into the regulatory process: the self-referential organization of these systems, of either the regulated field, or politics or the law itself. The effects are likewise problematic, being either irrelevance of regulation or disintegrating effects in the self-reproductive organization of law, politics or society.

Up to now we have been concerned with the effective limits which the self-referential organization of regulated social areas sets to the implementation strategy. Now we focus on the question of social knowledge. The question is: Does the implementation strategy apply adequate internal models of social reality in order to cope successfully with the self-referential organization of the regulated subsystems? As we have seen above, the implementation strategy works with purely instrumentalist models which differ more or less only to the degree of their complication and refinement. In its most simple form a political goal or a political program is defined as purpose and the question is scrutinized if legal norms as means do reach this purpose. It becomes more complicated if one enriches the factual situation in the implementation field in order to more successfully assess the chances for realization. Another possibility is to ask for side-effects and dysfunctional consequences. Basically, however, the model is limited to linear causality: the goal determines the program, the program determines the norm, the norm determines changes of behavior, those changes determine the desired effects.

It would be erroneous to insist that such model of linear causality are bound to fail totally if applied to self-referential systems. The basal circularity of self-reference does not mean that any contact between systems is ecxluded. Rather, a limited mutual "understanding" is possible: albeit in a very complicated fashion. For "understanding", one social system has to internalize the self-referentiality of the other. This is a complicated process which suggests how limited causal models are for the intervention into self-referential systems. The simple model of "political goal — legal norm — social effects" would have to be enriched with social knowledge of how self-referential systems receive regulatory information and how they process it according to their autonomous rules of internal interaction. This presupposes profound knowledge about general regularities of a self-closed structure and its effects in particular cases which is generally not at hand. Law would have to store social knowledge about the general self-referential circularity in different social sub-systems and their particular effects, a knowledge which even for social science is not available.

It is precisely this lack of social knowledge which was the reason why Renate Mayntz (1983a) the leading researcher in implementation in West-Germany, demanded a theoretical re-orientation of the whole of implementation research. According to Mayntz, implementation research is at present not in a position to develop coherent middle range theories about political programs and their social effects in the implementation field. It runs aground on the complexities of the regulated area. What is possible is at best conceptualization, typologies and particular case studies. The non-generalizable case study seems to be the only method available of collecting knowledge about causal relations in the implementation fields. Cautious inductive conclusions from established experience to future regulation determine the potential and limits of causal models in regulatory law.

What have we gained up to now from using the concept of self-referentiality? We utilized it as the criterion to judge the potential and limits of the implementation model. It led us to the regulatory trilemma as the basic limitation of the implementation strategy and within this limitation to the limited use of linear causal models. If it is true that instrumental law founders on the structures of self-referentiality, so that its absolute and relative limits are easily reached, then the question emerges if and how law can cope with self-referential systems (cf. also Luhmann, 1985). Would this not mean that law has to retreat to its own basal circularity concentrating on internal interaction of its own elements — norms, decisions, doctrines — and leaving outside effects to their own fate? This is by no means only a rhetorical question. Perhaps it was the hidden wisdom of "autonomous law" that it did not care for ethical, political, economic and social considerations. However, before one indulges in a resignative new justification of the old formalism, one should scrutinize strategic models of post-instrumental law, which might compete with the implementation model in being better suited to respect the absolute limits of self-referentiality and by producing norms within these limits that are not a priori counter-productive. Again, we are using self-referentiality as the criterion in two directions: (1) limits of self-production, (2) social knowledge required for coping with self-reproductive organization.

IV. Three Dimensions of Reflexive Law: Some Illustrations

It seems there are needs of a self-referential system which all stem from the necessity of maintaining its basal circularity. Regulatory processes can interfere positively and negatively with those needs. They can sabotage them, they can neglect them, or they can support, even facilitate them. The external support of self-referentiality is precisely the place at which one should localize recent efforts to translate the intentions of regulatory law into "reflexive" models of the control of self-regulation.

At first sight, they seem rather diverse and heterogeneous. But they are seen to support each other if one re-interprets them in the light of self-referentiality. One way to interpret them is rather modest and only negative: they can be read so as to avoid the regulatory trilemma and by designing legal interventions in such a way that the self-referential structure of law, politics and society are not infringed. Another interpretation is more ambitious and more positive: they attempt to define certain basic needs of self-referential systems and to design a law which is responsive to those needs.

To be sure, self-referentiality is a highly abstract concept. If it is supposed to serve as a criterion to judge the social adequacy of legal interventions, everything depends on its respecification in concrete contexts (Joerges, 1983:14). Thus, one of the most important tasks for this theory will be to identify the concrete mechanisms of self-referential closure and openness and the linkage between them (see as an important step in this direction, Luhmann 113 supra).

1. Autonomy: School Law

Jürgen Habermas (1981:522 and supra), in his discussion of recent trends of juridification, develops a remarkable sensitivity in this direction. His ambivalent attitude toward legal welfare-state interventions in the "life-world" can be interpreted as reflecting the dilemmatic structure of law in its double capacity to infringe and to facilitate self-productive interactions in the spheres of socialization, social integration and cultural reproduction. Habermas considers legal regulation as destructive of the very nature of such relations. This is only one aspect, however, and one misses the crucial point when one interprets Habermas as postulating "to keep any sort of legal regulation our of interactions that require spontaneous social communication" (Blankenburg, 1984:281). This is to misrepresent Habermas as a partisan of a naive communal de-legalization movement. Habermas has a strongly normative interest in the law as such, especially in its emancipatory potential as a universalization mechanism (Habermas, 1962:91, 242; 1963:82; 1973:123; 1976:260; 1981: 322, 364, 522 and supra). In the case of welfare state law, he searches for criteria which would allow one to distinguish at least analytically between the law's capacity to guarantee freedom and its capacity to destroy it (Habermas, 1981:534 and supra). He comes up with the distinction between law as medium and law as institution, the test being the justifiability through moral norms of the "life-world". As a medium, law is a functional socio-technological steering instrument through which the subsystems of economy and politics are "colonizing" central areas of cultural reproduction, social integration and socialization. Only when law is restricted to an "external constitution" of the "life-world" spheres, can it serve as an "institution" facilitating rather than disintegrating "consensus oriented procedures of conflict regulation" (Habermas, 1981:546, 544 and supra).

In our interpretation, this concept of law as "institution" shows signs of adequacy to self-referential structures within certain social contexts. Take the example of school law which Habermas uses: by protecting children's and parents' basic rights against the school administration, the law tends to free the education process from bureaucratic and administrative constraints. However, as a medium it is, in itself, in conflict with the form of pedagogic action if it is not restricted to the mere "frame of a legal school constitution". In the past the function of the "school constitution" was to secure its freedom from administrative pressure. And its future function could be — if we may extrapolate from Habermas' argument — to defend it against those bureaucratic processes which translate the "economic system imperative to de-couple the school system from the basic right of education (*Bildung*) and to close-circuit it with the occupation system" (Habermas, 1981:545 and supra). It is only within such a sphere of autonomy protected by a legal "external constitution" that the educational system has a chance of defining on its own in what respect it will depend upon its environment in self-referential processes. An external constitution thus facilitates internal reflection on the basic orientation of education: balancing environmental demands of performance — knowledge, skills — against its proper social function — *Bildung*, learning how to learn (see Luhmann and Schorr, 1979:18).

Of course, this is a precarious process. It is a paradoxical technique: fire to fight fire. And there are no guarantees against burning down the whole area, against an almost total legalization and judicialization (Blankenburg, 1984:288). But at the same time there is no reason to believe that a blind automatism is at work. Rather, it is a matter of political commitment and careful institutional design. Habermas himself shows this sensitivity to the problem by sympathizing with the paradoxical suggestion of Simitis and Zenz (1975:51): to dejudicialize legalized conflicts.

Such a retreat of the law from a regulation of whole life areas to the mere guarantee of their autonomy has effects not only for the areas concerned but for the law itself. If the law is relieved from its regulatory function, it is relieved at the same time of constructing models of social reality. Such a law concentrating on securing social autonomy does not need to utilize ambitious models of causal relations between legal norm and social effects. It is sufficient to develop a very general and rather vague understanding of self-regulatory processes in the social areas concerned. Since its function is the enablement of freedom within delimited autonomous areas, no knowledge is needed about their internal processes.

As useful as Habermas' concept of the external constitution is, there are two points which show the necessity of reformulating the argument. One is its generalization and re-specification; the other shows that an external constitution in this sense is a necessary but not a sufficient condition for "reflexive law".

The effect of legalization processes disintegrating reproductive structures is not limited to the spheres of the "life-world". Any social system with a self-referential structure can be endangered by outside interference in the self-productive interaction of its elements (Hejl, 1982b:58). Even the "systems" of economy and politics can be partially paralyzed by legalization. This is again a problem of self-referentiality. Economic and political processes will be paralyzed if their self-productive and reproductive capacities are infringed. Thus, the concept of "colonialization" needs to be generalized and applied to any inter-system relations.

This is the point at which the crucial task of re-specification begins for a theory of self-referentiality to define for any social system the specific self-productive mechanisms that need to be shielded from outside interference, whether it be a great functional system (politics, economy, education, religion, family, etc.), or be it a large organization or a small interaction. Of course, in this operation one abstracts from the difference between system and life-world which is crucial for Habermas' normative intentions. However, those intentions need not be given up; they can be re-introduced at a more general level through the concept of responsiveness to human needs, which would cut through the system/life-world difference and be applicable to any social system.

2. Externalization: Corporate Social Responsibility

This re-specification is necessary if "reflexive" legal action is to go beyond the mere securing of autonomy (see Teubner and Willke, 1984). Autonomy is a necessary, but not a sufficient precondition of self-referential processes. It does not guarantee their success. Self-referentiality is a precarious structure. It is always in danger of self-closure and self-referential systems need outside support to develop certain externalizations. The political system, for example, tends to operate too selectively and to concentrate on the complicated games of politics, thereby neglecting problems of its social environment (Luhmann, 1981a:57). In a similar way, the economic system works selectively via the language of monetary action and is not able to adequately re-translate its environmental consequences into its own language (Willke, 1982 and supra; see also Preuß supra).

Insofar as systems cannot develop sufficient externalization on their own, outside pressures are needed to impose structures on them which avoid self-closure. This is not to say that law or politics are the only, or even the main, outside mechanisms of enforcing externalization. Law can serve only as one among other compensatory institutions of society which compensate for the self-reference of social systems. Compensatory institutions have to operate under the double constraint of integrating environmental demands into the system while not disintegrating its conditions of self-production and reproduction.

"Corporate social responsibility" is a good case in point (see Teubner, 1983:34, 1985). If it is meant to go beyond a managerialist ideology and to be taken seriously as a compensatory institution which builds social side-purposes into economic action (Willke, 1982:17 and supra), then powerful outside pressure supported by political-legal measures is necessary. However, it has been demonstrated again and again how easily "external" regulations run aground on the regulatory trilemma (Stone, 1975:93; 1984).

The most promising approach seems to be "internal" regulation: strategic intervention into certain characteristics of the organization's decision-making process; the so-called structural, as opposed to the duty-approach (Teubner, 1983:48; 1984; Wedderburn, 1985). Their success, however, depends upon their taking into account the self-referential structure of economic organizations. For example, they have to follow what Krause calls a "profit-threatening strategy" (Krausé, 1984).

As the example shows, this poses problems of power. Political and social power is needed to exert external pressure on established social systems to externalize their self-reference. The imposition of an "external constitution"; the re-distribution of property rights to hitherto excluded constituencies; the redesign of decisional procedures; all constituting the core elements of "reflexive law", aim at a power change within the subsystem in question and demand strong power support from outside (Teubner, 1983a:254, 273, 276). Historical examples — the legal institutionalization of collective bargaining and of co-determination of labour — show that the role of law in influencing power relations is not simply marginal. Rather, law is one of the major mechanisms to change social power relations inside the organization (IDE, 1979). Formalizing property rights which are backed by the sanctioning power of the state clearly does not create social power, but it stabilizes social power rendering it to a certain degree independent of the fluctuations of shifting power and market relations.

Thus, reflexive law depends on political power and, in this respect, does not differ from regulatory law. In situations of social power relations, the success of both legal forms depends on the extensive use of political power resources. There is, however, a decisive difference. The difference concerns the strategic use of power as a limited resource. Regulatory law, working with detailed regulation and a sophisticated implementation machinery, is bound to liquidate a large amount of political power. Techniques of reflexive law, however, tend to minimize that liquidation by restricting themselves to certain strategic organizational and procedural key-variables. Galanter (1974) makes this point very clearly. Concerned with the problem of how to use the law to reduce social inequality in conflict situations, he considers a whole range of strategic variables (legal rules, institutions, lawyers, parties). Under the perspective of effectiveness he clearly prefers organizational variables over material legal rules. It makes for a more economic use of scarce power resources to concentrate them on strategic changes of the organization rather than dispersing them in permanent regulatory efforts.

It should be stated clearly, however, that power equalization is not the primary aspect of "reflexive law". As important as it is in the public control of private government (Macaulay, 1983) it does not make sense to tie the concept of "reflexive law" too closely to power-equalization within social subsystems, especially private organizations. The minimization of power is not a reasonable normative end in itself, it is an instrumental device for achieving certain social goals. Strategies of power-equalization make sense only if those goals are expected to be achieved through symmetrical power relations. This is not immediately apparent. Power-equalizing strategies are well suited to situations of zero-sum-games: gains in power on the one side mean losses of power on the other. The optimal state is a precarious power-equilibrium. The law's role in private organizations would be to control misuse of power and to stabilize the equilibrium. This is the classical view of the law's role toward power. However, a change from equilibrium models to growth models of organizations would drastically change the law's relation to power: "The division of power is not the thing to be considered but that method of organization which will generate power" (Lammers, 1967). In a growth model, power is seen not as a constant but as a variable phenomenon. In consequence, power-equalization only amounts to a "distributive-regressive" solution of the organization problem while the "productive-progressive" solution would be an increase of collective need satisfaction through *mutual power-increase* and power distribution (Hondrich, 1975:55).

Within this perspective, power is not primarily seen as a source of inequality and injustice but as a social instrument for an effective transfer of decisions. The task of the law then is still to control power abuses, but the central problem becomes rather to design institutional mechanisms that mutually increase the power of members and leadership in private organizations. Lammers (1967:201), for example, concludes in "Power and Participation": "Managers and managed in organizations can, at the same time, come to influence each other more effectively and thereby generate joint power as the outcome of a better command by the organization over its technical, economic and human resources".

That means, among other things, that power-equalization is not suited to use as a criterion for distinguishing between conservative and progressive forms of "reflexive law", centrist and radical views of decentralization (Unger, 1983). Moreover, being bound to static equilibrium models, power-equalization appears itself as a conservative strategy. If we are looking for normative criteria to judge social institutions, responsiveness to human needs (Hondrich, 1975) is what is required and not neutralization of power. Dynamic, flexible institutions with strong asymmetric power relations can, under certain conditions, be more responsive to human needs than self-closed, power-symmetrical, equilibrium institutions.

More important than the issue of power is the question of the kind of social knowledge that is necessary to enable the law to intervene successfully in self-referential systems (cf. Luhmann, 1985). What is the use of increasing power resources if the cognitive resources are lacking, or if they are so insufficient that they guide power resources in the wrong direction? Indeed, reflexive law clearly needs more and different social knowledge than a law which restricts itself to an "external constitution". This might suggest that reflexive modes of social guidance overload the cognitive competences of the law. However, it should be seen as well that the reality models needed in a reflexive law have considerably lower requirements than those needed in comprehensive planning models of regulatory law. As in the case of power resources, reflexive forms of law aim at an "economic" use of cognitive resources. A profound "understanding" of the total self-referential structures and processes in the implementation field is not necessary. As Hayek (1972; 1973) has convincingly demonstrated in his critique of constructivist interventionism, even science is not in a position to achieve such a profound understanding of particular processes in complex structures; much less able then is politics or law. However, predictions are possible as soon as the specificity of the autopoietic organization is understood. This knowledge can be acquired through system theoretical analysis and used by politics and law (Beer, 1975). The "economic" advantage of reflexive law is that it requires only general knowledge of the self-referentiality and needs not to control specific effects. It is sufficient to restrict "understanding" to the strategic structures according to which reflexion processes take place within the social subsystem concerned, since reflexive law intends only to change those general forms of procedure and organization. If it is true, for example, that in the economic system, reflexion takes place at the general level of monetary policies, then it would be sufficient to use social knowledge about the banking sector and its political processes in their general structure in order to achieve changes. One would not need models for the total economic system and its particular processes. Another example: If the reflexion center of an economic organization can be localized in its board system then corporation law could utilize rather simple models about the internal decision-making in order to influence reflexion processes through norms of organization and procedure.

3. Coordination: Concerted Action

Up to this point, we have discussed how law reflects two basic needs of self-referential subsystems: the need for autonomy and the need for externalization. A third dimension becomes apparent if one takes into account that not only social subsystems but also the encompassing society as a whole constitutes a self-referential system. The interaction of the functional subsystems, politics, economy, law, education, religion, family etc. can be seen as a self-producing interaction between elements of a larger system. Each of these subsystems contributes to the maintenance of societal self-reference. The law's contribution in this respect is the resolution of inter-system-conflicts by a specific "procedural regulation" (Mayntz, 1983b). Helmut Willke (1983 and supra) has developed a concept of a legal program aiming at this function: the "relational program". As opposed to the typical programs of formal law (conditional program) and of instrumental law (purposive program), the function of relational programs is to make compatible different purposes and rationalities of social subsystems by committing political and social actors to discursive procedures of decision-making. He identifies the emergence of this new type of legal program in diverse inter-system-coordination mechanisms, such as the Concerted Action (Konzertierte Aktion) or the Science Council (Wissenschaftsrat) in the Federal Republic of Germany. As Mayntz puts it: "It is in fact an aim of procedural regulation at the supra-organizational level to set up such networks or to provide platforms for such coordination which, where no hierarchical relationships of dependence are involved, will mainly proceed through bargaining" (Mayntz, 1983b; cf. as well Streeck and Schmitter, 1985).

One promising mode of understanding the working of such "relational programs" can be found in the theory of "black-boxes" developed in the context of cybernetics (Glanville, 1975). Self-referential systems – social systems like law, politics and regulated subsystems – are "black boxes" in the sense of being mutually inaccessible to each other. One knows the input and the output; the conversion, however, remains obscure. Now, black-box-techniques do not aim at shedding light onto this obscure internal conversion process, but circumvent the problem by an indirect "procedural" activity. They concentrate, not on the internal relations within the black box, but on the interrelation between the black boxes. Black boxes become "whitened" in the sense that an interaction relation develops among them which is transparent for them in its regularities. So law still cannot intervene directly into the economy; legal access consists in the relation between law and economy. It is the peculiarity of relational programs that they regulate internal processes in systems indirectly so that they concentrate on the relations between the systems. That means again to drastically decrease the requirements of cognitive capacities of law and politics, since they no longer attempt to directly influence economic action but to influence only the "concerted action", whose internal structure is for them much more transparent.

It is crucial that between the interaction relation and the regulated system (in our example, between concerted action and economy) consists a dense connection which is the source for guidance effects. This is to be expected from two mechanisms. One is the commitment of economic actors in the concerted action and the other is that the concerted action as such develops cognitive modes of the economy which may be more adequate than those of politics and of law. This whole way of thinking is quite close to what Lindblom called the combination of social knowledge and interaction (Lindblom and Cohen, 1979). According to Lindblom, one has to give up concepts of comprehensive social planning since they are utopian and unrealistic and replace them by more realistic models in which limited and strategic knowledge is combined with social interaction, that is in our concept the interaction between the two black-boxes in order to reach guidance effects within one of the black-boxes.

Autonomy, externalization and coordination – these are three dimensions in which reflexive law responds to the basic needs of self-referential systems. These dimensions have been analyzed by different legal theorists with the intention of pointing out the developmental tendencies of post-instrumental law. With the concept of self-referentiality I have tried to demonstrate that they represent complementary rather than competing approaches. "Proceduralization" of the law (Wiethölter, 1982, and supra; Mayntz, 1983b), as opposed to formalization and to materialization is one formula which captures what they have in common. Another, with slightly different nuances, is the "constitution of organization" (Brüggemeier, 1982) as opposed to the constitution of status and of contract. A third would be "relational program" or "reflexive law", stressing the aspect of legal prerequisites for social self-regulation (Teubner, 1983a; Willke, 1983, 1984). Clearly, those formulae invite misunderstanding (Blankenburg, 1984). If they are arbitrarily separated from their theoretical background (functionalist or "critical" macro-theories) and are equated with just any type of procedural and organizational law, for example, in a stratified society, they become rather meaningless. It is then easy to ask: What's new?

More serious questions have to be raised about the relation of procedural elements to formal and material elements in post-instrumental law. Again, in any type of law all these three elements can be identified, though with different weight and different functions. After all, classical "formal" law had specific content and specific procedures (Teubner, 1983a:252; Wiethölter, supra). What are the material orientations of post-instrumental law?

The answer can only be very tentative. Material orientations of procedural law aim at nothing less ambitious than a bridging of functionalist and critical approaches to social theory. Wiethölter argues explicitly for an understanding of "proceduralization as a justificatory problem of 'rational' practical action under 'system'-conditions". The goal is to create a "forum, before which negotiation on transformations of society goes on re-constructively and prospectively" (Wiethölter, supra). I agree with the general intention. I would, however, prefer to point to the limited potential of practical philosophy beyond the sphere of morality in personal interaction and so stress the aspect of enhancing specific learning capacities in decentralized social subsystems. These learning capacities should be oriented toward re-introducing the consequences of actions of social sub-systems into their own reflexion structure. Setting such a context of discovery – would that satisfy our need for a material orientation of reflexive law?

References

ALEXANDER, Jeffrey C. (1982) *Theoretical Logic in Sociology, Vol. 1, Positivism, Presuppositions and Current Controversies.* Berkeley: University of California Press.

ASHBY, William R. (1975) *An Introduction to Cybernetics.* London: Methuen.

ASSMANN, Heinz-Dieter (1980) *Wirtschaftsrecht in der Mixed-Economy. Auf der Suche nach einem Sozialmodell für das Wirtschaftsrecht.* Frankfurt a. M.: Athenäum.

BEER, Stafford (1975) "Preface to Autopoiesis" in: H. Maturana and F. Varela, *Autopoietic Systems,* Urbana: University of Illinois Press.

BLACK, Donald (1972)"Book Review: Philip Selznick, Law, Society, and Industrial Justice, 1969," 78 *American Journal of Sociology* 709.

BLANKENBURG, Erhard (1984) "The Poverty of Evolutionism. A Critique of Teubner's Case for 'Reflexive Law,'" 18 *Law & Society Review* 273.

BOHNERT, Werner, and Wolfgang KLITZSCH (1980) "Gesellschaftliche Selbstregulierung und staatliche Steuerung. Steuerungstheoretische Anmerkungen zur Implementation politischer Programme," in R. Mayntz (ed.), *Implementation politischer Programme.* Königstein: Athenäum.

BRÜGGEMEIER, Gert (1982) "Wirtschaftsordnung und Staatsverfassung" – "Mischverfassung des demokratischen Interventionskapitalismus" – "Verfassungstheorie des Sozialstaates". Drei Modelle der Verflechtung von Staat und Wirtschaft?," in V. Gessner and G. Winter (eds.) *Rechtsformen der Verflechtung von Staat und Wirtschaft.* Opladen: Westdeutscher Verlag.

BUCKLEY, Walter (1968) "Society as a Complex Adaptive System," in W. Buckley (ed.), *Modern Systems Research for the Behavioral Scientist.* Chicago: Aldine.

CLUNE, William H. (1983) "The Political Origins and Political Process of Regulation: What We Can Learn From A Positive Political Analysis," in: D. Trubek (ed.), *Reflexive Law and the Regulatory Crisis.* Madison.

EASTON, David (1965) *A Systems Analysis of Political Life.* New York: Wiley.

EDELMAN, Murray (1964) *The Symbolic of Use of Politics.* Urbana: University of Illinois Press.

ETZIONI, Amitai (1968) *The Active Society. A Theory of Societal and Political Processes.* New York: Free Press.

FEYERABEND, Paul (1975) *Against Method. Outline of an Anarchistic Theory of Knowledge.* London: Atlantic Highlands Humanities Press.

GALANTER, Marc (1974) "Why the Haves come out Ahead: Speculations on the Limits of Legal Change," 9 *Law and Society Review* 95.

GLANVILLE, Stephan R. (1975) "The Form of Cybernetics: Whitening the Black Box," in *General Systems Research: A Science, a Methodology, a Technology.* Louisville: University of Kentucky Press.

GOTTHOLD, Jürgen (1983) "Privatisierung oder Entbürokratisierung kommunaler Sozialpolitik," in R. Voigt (ed.), *Abschied vom Recht?.* Frankfurt a. M.: Suhrkamp.

GRIMM, Dieter (1980) "Reformalisierung des Rechtsstaats als Demokratiepostulat," 20 *Juristische Schulung* 704.

HABERMAS, Jürgen (1962) *Strukturwandel der Öffentlichkeit.* Neuwied: Luchterhand.

– (1963) *Theorie und Praxis. Sozialphilosophische Studien.* Neuwied: Luchterhand.

– (1973) "Zum Begriff der politischen Beteiligung," (1958), in J. Habermas, *Kultur und Kritik.* Frankfurt a. M.: Suhrkamp.

– (1975) *Legitimation Crisis.* Boston: Beacon.

– (1976) *Zur Rekonstruktion des Historischen Materialismus.* Frankfurt a. M.: Suhrkamp.

– (1981) *Theorie des kommunikativen Handelns.* Frankfurt a. M.: Suhrkamp.

HART, Dieter (1983) "Contract and Consumer Protection: Organizing Countervailing Power — on the Development of Substantive and Reflexive Elements in Modern Contract Law," in D. Trubek (ed.), *Reflexive Law and the Regulatory Crisis.* Madison.
HAYEK, Friedrich A. v. (1972) "The Theorie of Complex Phenomena," in F. A. v. Hayek, *Studies in Philosophy, Politics and Economics.* Chicago University Press.
— (1973) *Law, Legislation and Liberty* Vol. 1. *Rules and Order.* Chicago: Chicago University Press.
HEJL, Peter M. (1982a) *Sozialwissenschaft als Theorie selbstreferentieller Systeme.* Frankfurt a. M.: Campus.
— (1982b) "Die Theorie autopoietischer Systeme: Perspektiven für die soziologische Systemtheorie," 13 *Rechtstheorie* 45.
HONDRICH, Karl O. (1975) *Menschliche Bedürfnisse und soziale Steuerung.* Reinbek: Rowohlt.
HOPPMANN Erich (1972) *Fusionskontrolle.* Tübingen: Mohr.
IETSWAART, Helen F. P. (1983) "The Conference on Reflexive Law and the Regulatory Crisis," 5 *Zeitschrift für Rechtssoziologie* 349.
INDUSTRIAL DEMOCRACY IN EUROPE (IDE) (1979) *Industrial Research Group: Industrial Democracy in Europe,* Oxford: Oxford University Press.
JOERGES, Christian (1981) *Verbraucherschutz als Rechtsproblem.* Heidelberg: Recht und Wirtschaft.
— (1983) "Regulatory Law, Private Government and Self-Regulation," in D. Trubek (ed.) *Reflexive Law and the Regulatory Crisis.* Madison
KRAUSE, Detlef (1985) "Corporate Social Responsibility: Interests and Goals," in K. J. Hopt and G. Teubner (eds.), *Corporate Governance and Directors' Liabilities.* Berlin, New York: Walter de Gruyter.
LADEUR, Karl-Heinz (1982) "Verrechtlichung oder Ökonomisierung des Rechts?," in V. Gessner and G. Winter (eds.), *Rechtsformen der Verflechtung von Staat und Wirtschaft.* Opladen: Westdeutscher Verlag.
— (1984) *Abwägung — Ein neues Paradigma des Verwaltungsrechts.* Frankfurt a. M.: Campus.
LAMMERS, C. J. (1967) "Power and Participation in Decision-Making in Formal Organizations," 73 *The American Journal of Sociology* 201.
LAWRENCE, Paul R., and Jay W. LORSCH (1967) *Organization and Environment: Managing Differentiation and Integration.* Boston: Harvard University.
LEHNER, Franz (1979) *Grenzen des Regierens.* Königstein: Athenäum.
LINDBLOM, Charles, and David COHEN (1979) *Usable Knowledge. Social Science and Social Problem Solving.* New Haven, London: Yale University Press.
LUHMANN, Niklas (1971) "Die Weltgesellschaft," in N. Luhmann, *Soziologische Aufklärung 2.* Opladen: Westdeutscher Verlag.
— (1981a) *Politische Theorie im Wohlfahrtsstaat.* München: Olzog.
— (1981b) *Ausdifferenzierung des Rechts. Beiträge zur Rechtssoziologie und Rechtstheorie.* Frankfurt a. M.: Suhrkamp.
— (1982) *The Differentiation of Society.* New York: Columbia University Press.
— (1984) *Soziale Systeme. Grundriß einer allgemeinen Theorie.* Frankfurt a. M.: Suhrkamp.
— (1985) "Einige Probleme mit reflexivem Recht," 6 *Zeitschrift für Rechtssoziologie* 1.
LUHMANN, Niklas und Eberhard SCHORR (1979) *Reflexionsprobleme im Erziehungssystem.* Stuttgart: Klett-Cotta.
MACAULAY, Stewart (1983) "Private Government," in D. Trubek (ed.), *Reflexive Law and the Regulatory Crisis.* Madison.
MATURANA, Humberto R. (1970) *Biology of Cognition,* Urbana: University of Illinois Press
— (1975) *Autopoietic Systems. A Characterization of the Living Organization.* Urbana: University of Illinois Press.
— (1982) *Erkennen: Die Organisation und Verkörperung von Wirklichkeit.* Braunschweig: Viehweg.

Maturana, Humberto and Francisco Varela (1980) *Autopoiesis and Cognition*. Dordrecht: Reidel.

Maturana, Humberto R., Francisco E. Varela and R. Uribe (1974) "Autopoiesis: The Organization of Living Systems," 5 *Bio Systems* 187.

Mestmäcker, Ernst-Joachim (1978) *Die sichtbare Hand des Rechts. Über das Verhältnis von Wirtschaftsordnung und Rechtssystem*. Baden-Baden: Nomos.

Mayntz, Renate (1979) "Regulative Politik in der Krise?," in Joachim Matthes (ed.), *Sozialer Wandel in Westeuropa*. Frankfurt a. M.: Campus.

– (1980) "Die Implementation politischer Programme," in R. Mayntz (ed.), *Implementation politischer Programme I*. Königstein: Athenäum.

– (1983a) *Implementation politischer Programme II*. Opladen: Westdeutscher Verlag.

– (1983b) "The Changing Conditions of Effective Public Policy – A New Challenge for Policy Analysis", 11 *Policy and Politics* 123.

Mitnick, Barry (1980) *The Political Economy of Regulation: Creating, Designing and Removing Regulatory Forms*. New York: Columbia University Press.

Nonet, Philippe, and Philip Selznick (1978) *Law and Society in Transition*. London: Harper and Row.

Pitschas, Rainer (1980) "Soziale Sicherung durch fortschreitende Verrechtlichung?," in R. Voigt (ed.), *Verrechtlichung*. Königstein: Athenäum.

Podgorecki, Adam (1974) *Law and Society*. London/Boston: Routledge and Kegan Paul.

Reich, Norbert (1984) "The Regulatory Crisis – Does it Exist and Can it Be Solved," *Government and Policy* 177.

Reidegeld, Eckhart (1980) "Vollzugsdefizite sozialer Leistungen," in R. Voigt (ed.), *Verrechtlichung*. Königstein: Athenäum.

– (1983) "Theorien der Rechtsentwicklung zwischen Empirie und Geschichtsphilosophie". Typescript Berlin.

Rottleuthner, Hubert (1983) *Rechtssoziologische Studien zur Arbeitsgerichtsbarkeit*. Baden-Baden: Nomos.

Scharpf, Fritz (1979) "Die Rolle des Staates im westdeutschen Wirtschaftssystem: Zwischen Krise und Neuorientierung," in: C. C. von Weizsäcker (ed.), *Staat und Wirtschaft*. Berlin: Duncker & Humblot.

Selznick, Philip (1973) "Rejoinder to Donald Black," 78 *American Journal of Sociology* 1266.

Simitis, Spiros, and Gisela Zenz, (1975) *Familie und Familienrecht*. Frankfurt a. M.: Suhrkamp.

Stachowiak, Herbert (1965) "Gedanken zu einer allgemeinen Theorie der Modelle," 18 *Studium Generale* 432.

– (1973) *Allgemeine Modelltheorie*. Wien, New York: Springer.

Stone, Christopher D. (1975) *Where the Law Ends. The Social Control of Corporate Behavior*. New York: Harper.

– (1985) "Public Interest Representation: Economic and Social Policy Inside the Enterprise," in K. J. Hopt, and G. Teubner (eds.), *Corporate Governance and Directors' Liabilities*. Berlin, New York: Walter de Gruyter.

Streeck, Wolfgang, and Philippe C. Schmitter (1985) "Community, Market, State – and Associations? The Prospective Contribution of Interest Governance to Social Order," in W. Streeck and P. Schmitter (eds.), *Private Interest Government and Public Policy*. Beverly Hills: Sage.

Teubner, Gunther (1978) "Generalklauseln als sozio-normative Modelle," in K. Lüderssen et al., *Generalklauseln als Gegenstand der Sozialwissenschaften*. Baden-Baden: Nomos.

– (1983) "Corporate Responsibility als Problem der Unternehmensverfassung," 11 *Zeitschrift für Gesellschafts- und Unternehmensrecht* 34.

– (1983a) "Substantive and Reflexive Elements in Modern Law," 17 *Law & Society Review* 239.

– (1984) "Autopoiesis in Law and Society," 18 *Law & Society Review*, 291.

– (1985) "Corporate Fiduciary Duties and Their Beneficiaries. A Functional Approach to the Legal Institutionalization of Corporate Responsibility," in K. J. Hopt and G. Teubner (eds.), *Corporate Governance and Directors' Liabilities*. Berlin, New York: Walter de Gruyter.

TEUBNER, Gunther, and Helmut WILLKE (1984) "Kontext und Autonomie. Gesellschaftliche Selbststeuerung durch reflexives Recht," 5 *Zeitschrift für Rechtssoziologie*, 4.

UNGER, Roberto M. (1976) *Law in Modern Society. Toward a Criticism of Social Theory*. New York: Free Press.

– (1983) "The Critical Legal Studies Movement," 96 *Harvard Law Review* 563.

VARELA, Francisco J. (1979) *Principles of Biological Autonomy*. New York: Elsevier.

WÄLDE, Thomas (1979) *Juristische Folgenorientierung. "Policy Analysis" und Sozialkybernetik*. Königstein/Ts: Athenäum.

WEDDERBURN, K. W. (1985) "The Legal Development of Corporate Responsibility," in K. J. Hopt and G. Teubner (eds.). *Corporate Governance and Directors' Liabilities*. Berlin, New York: Walter de Gruyter.

WIETHÖLTER, Rudolf (1982) "Entwicklung des Rechtsbegriffs," in V. Gessner and G. Winter (eds.), *Rechtsformen der Verflechtung von Staat und Wirtschaft*. Opladen: Westdeutscher Verlag.

WILLKE, Helmut (1982) "Gesellschaftliche Kriterien ökonomischer Rationalität," Typescript Köln.

– (1983) *Entzauberung des Staates*. Königstein: Athenäum.

WINTER, Gerd (1982) "Literaturbericht zum Thema," in V. Gessner and G. Winter (eds.), *Rechtsformen der Verflechtung von Staat und Wirtschaft*. Opladen: Westdeutscher Verlag.

ZELENY, Milan (ed.) (1981) *Autopoiesis: A Theory of the Living Organization*. Dordrecht: Reidel.

ZIEGERT, Klaus A. (1975) *Zur Effektivität der Rechtssoziologie. Die Rekonstruktion der Gesellschaft durch Recht*. Stuttgart: Enke.

Authors' Biographical Sketches

VILHELM AUBERT, Professor of Sociology, born 1922; Degree in law, University of Oslo 1946; founding member and member of the board, Institute of Social Research, Oslo from 1950; Ph. D. 1954; Fellow, Center for Advanced Study in the Behavioral Sciences, Stanford 1956–57; Professor of Sociology of Law, University of Oslo 1954–71; Professor of Sociology 1971–; Chairman, Department of Sociology 1972–74; Visiting Fellow, Yale Law School, Fall 1973; Member, Norwegian Academy of Science from 1955; Honorary Dr. of Law, University of Edinburgh 1971. Visiting Professor, University of Sydney, June–July 1976; Chairman of the Board, Institute of Social Research, Oslo, 1977–; Distinguished Visitor, La Trobe University, Melbourne, 1984. *Author:* (with T. Eckhoff and K. Sveri) En lov i søkelyset. (A Law in the Searchlight. A Social Psychological Study of the Norwegian Housemaid Law) Oslo 1952; Om straffens sosiale funksjon (On the Social Function of Punishment), 1954; Elements of Sociology, 1966; The Hidden Society, 1965. (Editor): Sociology of Law, 1969; Proeven van rechtssociologie, 1971. Rettens sosiale funksjon (The Social Function of Law) 1976; Den samiske befolkning i Nord-Norge (The Lappish Population in Northern Norway), 1978; Sosiologi: Sosialt samspill (Sociology: Social Interaction), 1979; Rettssosiologi (Sociology of Law), 1982; In Search of Law. Sociological Approaches to Law, 1983.

JAN M. BROEKMAN, Professor of Philosophy, born 1931; studied sociology in Leiden and philosophy in Göttingen; Professor in Philosophy of Law and Contemporary Philosophy at the University of Leuven and Professor in Medical Philosophy at the University of Amsterdam; President of the Belgian section of the International Association for Philosophy of Law and Social Philosophy, 1983–, President of the Netherlands Association for the Philosophy of Law, 1985–, President of the Netherlands Society for the Study of the Foundations of Medicine, 1983–. *Author:* Phänomenologie und Egologie, 1963; Strukturalismus, 1971 (Dutch 1973; Spanish 1973; English 1974; Chinese 1980); Hedendaagse Rechtsfilosofische Literatuur, 1973; Recht en Antropologie, 1979 (German 1979, Dutch second edition); (with van den Bergh) Recht en Taal, 1979. (With A. 't Hart) Justitieel beleid en normverleggend gedrag, 1980. *Editor* (with B. Waldenfels and A. Pazanin) four volumes on Phänomenologie und Marxismus, 1977–1979; the encyclopaedic series "Kolleg Rechtstheorie" (Alber Verlag, Freiburg), in Dutch "Serie Rechtstheorie"(Standaard Wetenschappelijke

Uitgeverij). Various articles on philosophy of law, social philosophy, aesthetics, phenomenology and psychiatry in a great number of European journals.

François Ewald, Chargé de recherche, Centre National de la Recherche Scientifique; born 1946; diplomé en philosophie et en droit, University of Paris; Assistant at Collège de France, Chaire d'Histoire des Systèmes de Pensée (Professor: Michel Foucault) 1977—1984. *Author:* L'accident nous attend au coin de la rue, 1982; L'Etat-providence, 1985. Various articles on social legislation and history of social security in professional journals.

Alberto Febbrajo, Professor of Sociology of Law; born 1944; Dr. jur., University of Pavia, 1968; Professor of Sociology of Law, University of Macerata, 1976—; Director, Institute of Sociology at the University of Macerata, 1978—; Member, Editorial Board of the journal "Sociologia del diritto". 1980; Visiting Professor, University of Freiburg, 1981. *Author:* Funzionalismo strutturale e sociologia del diritto, 1975; Materiali sulla sociologia del diritto di Theodor Geiger, 1980; Theorie e ideologie nella sociologia del diritto (1985); *Co-editor:* Critica del diritto e analisi del linguaggio, 1982. Various articles in professional journals and collective publications.

Lawrence M. Friedman, Professor of Law; born 1930; J. D., M. LL., University of Chicago, 1951, 1953; LL. D. (hon.), University of Puget Sound Law School, 1977; law practice, Chicago, 1955—57; Assistant Professor of Law, St. Louis University, 1957—61; Associate Professor and Professor of Law, University of Wisconsin, 1961—68; Professor of Law, Stanford University, 1968—1975; Marion Rice Kirkwood Professor of Law, Stanford University, 1976—; sometime Fellow, Center for Advanced Study in the Behavioral Sciences; member, American Academy of Arts and Sciences; Fellow, Wissenschaftskolleg zu Berlin; 1985. *Author:* Contract Law in America, 1965; Government and Slum Housing, 1968; A History of American Law, 1973; The Legal System: A Social Science Perspective, 1975; Law and Society: an Introduction, 1977; (with R. V. Percival) The Roots of Justice, 1981; American Law, 1984; Your Time Will Come, 1985; Total Justice, 1985. *Editor:* (with S. Macaulay) Law and the Behavioral Sciences (1969; second edition, 1977); (with H. N. Scheiber) American Law and the Constitutional Order (1978).

Jürgen Habermas, Professor of Philosophy; born 1929; Dr. phil. University of Bonn, 1954; Habilitation, University of Marburg 1961; Professor, University of Heidelberg 1962; Professor of Philosophy and Sociology, University of Frankfurt, 1964; Christian Gauss Lectureship, University of Princeton (U.S.A.) 1971; Director, Max-Planck-Institut, Starnberg 1971;

Honorarprofessor, University of Frankfurt, 1971; Dr. h. c. New School for Social Research New York, 1980; Professor of Philosophy, University of Frankfurt 1983—. *Author:* (with L. v. Friedeburg) Student und Politik, 1961; Strukturwandel der Öffentlichkeit, 1962; Theorie und Praxis, 1963; Erkenntnis und Interesse, 1968; Technik und Wissenschaft als "Ideologie", 1968; Protestbewegung und Hochschulreform, 1969; Zur Logik der Sozialwissenschaften, 1970; (with N. Luhmann) Theorie der Gesellschaft oder Sozialtechnologie, 1971; Philosophisch-politische Profile, 1971; Kultur und Kritik, 1973; Zur Rekonstruktion des Historischen Materialismus, 1976; Kleine politische Schriften I—IV, 1981; Theorie des kommunikativen Handelns, 1981; Moralbewußtsein und kommunikatives Handeln, 1983; Vorstudien und Ergänzungen zur Theorie des kommunikativen Handelns, 1984. *Editor:* Stichworte zur "Geistigen Situation der Zeit", 1980; various articles in professional journals and collective publications.

Thomas Charles Heller, Professor of Law; born 1944; B. A. Princeton 1965; L. L. B., Yale 1968; Attorney: Bogota, Colombia, Santiago, Chile, 1968—72; Professor of Law, Stanford Law School 1978—; Visiting Professor at European University Institute, Florence, University of Barcelona, Free University of Berlin. *Author:* various publications in professional books and journals including "Structuralism and Critique", 1984; "The Legal Economics of American Federalism", 1985.

Niklas Luhmann, Professor of Sociology; born 1927; lawyer; Dr. sc. pol., Habilitation, University of Münster 1966; Professor of Sociology, University of Bielefeld, 1968—; Member, Rheinisch-Westfälische Akademie der Wissenschaften, 1974—; Dr. jur. h. c. University of Gent, 1984. *Author:* (with F. Becker) Verwaltungsfehler und Vertrauensschutz, 1963; Funktionen und Folgen formaler Organisation, 1964; Öffentlich-rechtliche Entschädigung rechtspolitisch bretrachtet, 1965; Grundrechte als Institution, 1965; Recht und Automation in der öffentlichen Verwaltung, 1966; Theorie der Verwaltungswissenschaft, 1966; Vertrauen, 1968; Zweckbegriff und Systemrationalität, 1968; Legitimation durch Verfahren, 1969; Soziologische Aufklärung, 1970; Politische Planung, 1971; (with J. Habermas) Theorie der Gesellschaft oder Sozialtechnologie, 1971; (with W. Dahm and D. Stoodt) Religion — System und Sozialisation, 1972; Rechtssoziologie, 1972; (with R. Mayntz) Personal im öffentlichen Dienst; 1973; Rechtssystem und Rechtsdogmatik, 1974; Macht, 1975; Funktion der Religion, 1977; (with S. Pfürtner) Theorietechnik und Moral, 1978; (with K. E. Schorr) Reflexionsprobleme im Erziehungssystem, 1979; Gesellschaftsstruktur und Semantik I, 1980; II, 1981; Politische Theorien im Wohlfahrtsstaat, 1981; Soziale Systeme, 1984; Articles in various fields of sociological and legal theory.

ANTONIE PETERS, Professor of Sociology of Law; born 1936; studied law at the University of Leiden (LL. M.) 1955—1959; Ph. D. in Law, 1966; Assistant in criminal law and criminology, University of Leiden, 1959—1964; Research Associate and Lecturer, United Nations Asia and Far East Institute for the Prevention of Crime and Treatment of Offenders, in Tokyo, 1964—1967; Associate, Center for the Study of Law and Society, University of California at Berkeley, 1967—1970; Professor of Criminal Law, 1970; Professor of Sociology of Law, University of Utrecht, 1973; Visiting Professor, Wayne State University at Detroit, 1979; Visiting Professor, University of Indonesia at Jakarta. *Author:* Opzet en schuld in het strafrecht, 1966. Comparative Survey of Juvenile Delinquency in Asia and the Far East, 1968. Various articles in professional journals.

ULRICH K. PREUSS, Professor of Public Law; born 1939; Referendar, Free University Berlin 1964; Dr. iur., University of Gießen 1968; Researcher, Max-Planck-Institut für Bildungsforschung, Berlin 1965—1971; Assessor, Berlin 1970; Professor of Public Law, Bremen 1971; Visiting Professor Princeton 1980, University of Calabria (Cosenza) 1982. *Author:* Hochschule in der Demokratie (co-author), 1965; Zum staatsrechtlichen Begriff des Öffentlichen, 1969; Legalität und Pluralismus, 1973; Bildung und Herrschaft, 1975; Die Internalisierung des Subjekts, 1979; (co-author) Kommentar zum Grundgesetz (Reihe Alternativkommentare), 1984; Politische Verantwortung und Bürgerloyalität, 1984; various articles in professional journals and collective publications.

GUNTHER TEUBNER, Professor of Private Law and Legal Sociology; born 1944; Referendar, University of Tübingen, 1967; Dr. iur., University of Tübingen, 1970; Assessor, Stuttgart 1971; M. A., Sociology of Law, Berkeley, 1974; Habilitation in law, University of Tübingen, 1977; Privatdozent, University of Frankfurt, 1977; Professor of Law, University of Bremen, 1977—; Visiting Professor, University of California at Berkeley, 1980—81; Professor of Law, European University Institute, Florence (Italy), 1981—; Head of Law Department, 1984; *Author:* Standards und Direktiven in Generalklauseln, 1971; Public Status of Private Associations, 1974; Gegenseitige Vertragsuntreue, 1975; Organisationsdemokratie und Verbandsverfassung, 1978; (co-author): Alternativ-Kommentar zum BGB, 1979—81. *Editor:* Corporate Governance and Directors' Liabilities, 1984. Various articles in professional journals and collective publications.

RUDOLF WIETHÖLTER, Professor of Private, Commercial and Business Law; born 1929; Referendar, Köln, 1952; College of Europe, Bruges, 1952—53; Dr. iur., University of Köln, 1955; Assessor, Düsseldorf, 1956; Senior Research Associate in Law, University of California at Berkeley, 1958—59; Habilitation, University of Köln, 1960; Professor of Law, University of

Frankfurt, 1963—; Visiting Professor, Louisiana State University, Baton Rouge, 1964. *Author:* Einseitige Kollisionsnormen als Grundlage des Internationalen Privatrechts, 1956; Der Rechtfertigungsgrund des verkehrsrichtigen Verhaltens, 1960; Interessen und Organisation der Aktiengesellschaft im amerikanischen und deutschen Recht, 1961; Rechtswissenschaft, 1968; various articles in professional journals and collective publications.

HELMUT WILLKE, Professor of Sociology; born 1945; Referendar, University of Tübingen, 1972; Dr. jur., University of Tübingen, 1974; Assessor, Stuttgart 1974; M. A. in Sociology, Köln, 1976; Research Fellow University of California at Berkeley, 1979—80; Habilitation in Sociology, University of Köln, 1982; Professor of Sociology (Planning and Decision Theory), University of Bielefeld, 1983—. *Author:* Stand und Kritik der neueren Grundrechtstheorie, 1975; Leitungswissenschaft in der DDR, 1979; Systemtheorie, 1982; Entzauberung des Staates, 1983; various articles in professional journals and collective publications.

Name Index

Subject Index

Bei Fragen zur Produktsicherheit wenden Sie sich bitte an:
If you have any questions regarding product safety,
please contact:

Walter de Gruyter GmbH
Genthiner Straße 13
10785 Berlin
productsafety@degruyterbrill.com